Royal Regulation of Loans and Sales in Medieval England

This book looks at laws prohibiting usury, forestalling and regrating and regulating prices in England during the reigns of the first three Edwards and Richard II (1272–1399). The laws had the potential to affect a vast number of people and their everyday sales and loans, and represent an important aspect of the advancing role of law in the later middle ages; the author takes issue with established opinion, which seems as them as the product of 'monkish superstition and civil tyranny' (in Blackstone's famous phrase), arguing that they are an evolving area of activity, characterised by experiment, compromise and interaction with other rule-making and rule-enforcing bodies.

Dr Gwen Seabourne lectures in the School of Law, University of Bristol.

Royal Regulation of
Loans and Sales
in Medieval England

'Monkish Superstition and Civil Tyranny'

Gwen Seabourne

THE BOYDELL PRESS

First published 2003
The Boydell Press, Woodbridge

ISBN 1 84383 022 1

The Boydell Press is an imprint of Boydell & Brewer Ltd
PO Box 9, Woodbridge, Suffolk IP12 3DF, UK
and of Boydell & Brewer Inc.
PO Box 41026, Rochester, NY 14604–4126, USA
website: www.boydell.co.uk

A catalogue record for this book is available
from the British Library

Library of Congress Cataloging-in-Publication Data
Seabourne, Gwen, 1969–
  Royal regulation of loans and sales in medieval England : monkish
superstition and civil tyranny / Gwen Seabourne.
     p. cm.
Includes bibliographical references and index.
  ISBN 1–84383–022–1 (Hardback : alk. paper)
  1. Usury laws – England – History. 2. Law, Medieval. I. Title.
  KD1740.S43 2003
  346.4207′3′09 – dc21   2003010097

This publication is printed on acid-free paper

Typeset by Joshua Associates Ltd, Oxford
Printed in Great Britain by
St Edmundsbury Press Ltd, Bury St Edmunds, Suffolk

Contents

Acknowledgements

I am grateful for the assistance and supervision of Ian Wei and Brendan Smith of the University of Bristol Department of Historical Studies, and to my Ph.D. examiners, Paul Brand and John Moore. My academic debts stretch back considerably further than this, and I would like to mention those institutions which have helped me along the way: Farringdon Comprehensive School, Houghton Kepier Comprehensive School, Peterhouse, Cambridge, and St Hilda's College, Oxford.

I have received financial assistance from the University of Bristol School of Law, the Maitland Memorial Fund of the University of Cambridge and St John's College, Oxford.

My family have been immensely supportive and interested throughout my academic career, and it is in recognition of this fact that this book is dedicated to them.

Preface

This book began life in the University of Bristol Department of Historical Studies as a Ph.D. thesis , which I researched part-time from 1994 to 2000 whilst carrying on with my 'day job' in the Law Department. The inspiration for the Ph.D. topic grew out of a fascination with the medieval usury laws and the idea of usury, sparked off in my teens by some remarks of a former bishop of Durham, and refuelled by an assignment to investigate a seventeenth-century statutory exception to the usury laws whilst working as a research assistant for the Law Commission.

Unsurprisingly, my ideas have changed somewhat during the process of the work's conversion from Ph.D. to book, the gestation of which has spanned two periods of maternity leave and a fair amount of time for ideas to develop.

The subject matter stands, as I explain in the introduction, at the point of intersection of a number of areas of historical study. This makes it relevant to a fairly large number of scholars. By the same token, however, its position in this 'border country' brings the danger that those whose interests it touches would have taken the subject matter in a different direction, addressing themselves to a different range of issues, looking at a different range of sources. I hope, however, that I have at least highlighted those relevant issues and sources which it has not been possible, within the boundaries of a coherent and reasonably manageable monograph, to address in a comprehensive manner.

Abbreviations

Anonimalle	W.R. Childs and J. Taylor (eds), *The Anonimalle Chronicle 1307 to 1334 from Brotherton Collection MS 29*, Yorkshire Archaeological Society (Leeds, 1991)
Anstey, *MA*	H. Anstey, *Munimenta Academica or Documents Illustrative of Academical Life and Studies at Oxford*, Rolls Series 50.i and 50.ii (London, 1869)
APS	T. Thomson and C. Innes (eds), *The Acts of the Parliaments of Scotland 1124–1707*, 12 vols (London, 1814–75)
B&M, *Sources*	J.H. Baker and S.F.C. Milsom, *Sources of English Legal History: Private Law to 1750* (London, 1986)
BIHR	Bulletin of the Institute of Historical Research
BL	British Library
Bolton, *MEE*	J.L. Bolton, *The Medieval English Economy 1150–1500* (London, 1980)
Bracton	G.E. Woodbine and S.E. Thorne (eds), *Bracton 'On the Laws and Customs of England'*, 4 vols (Cambridge, MA, 1968–77)
Britton	F.M. Nicholls (ed.), *Britton*, 2 vols (Oxford, 1865)
c.	chapter
c.	circa
C.	canon
Cam, *London Eyre 1321*	H.M. Cam, *The Eyre of London 1321*, Selden Society vol. 85 for 1968 and vol. 86 for 1969 (London, 1968 and 1969)
CChR	HMSO, *Calendar of Charter Rolls* (London, 1906–16)
CCR	HMSO, *Calendar of Close Rolls* (London, 1892–1954)
CEH III	M.M. Postan, E.E. Rich and E. Miller (eds), *Cambridge Economic History of Europe*, vol. III (Cambridge, 1965)
CEMCR	A.H. Thomas (ed.), *Calendar of Early Mayor's Court Rolls preserved among the archives of the Corporation of the City of London at the Guildhall A.D. 1298–1307* (Cambridge, 1924)
CIM	HMSO, *Calendars of Inquisitions Miscellaneous (Chancery)* (London, 1916–68)
CIPM	HMSO, *Calendars of Inquisitions Post Mortem* vols 2–17 (London, 1906–1988)
CLB	R.R. Sharpe (ed.), *Calendar of Letter Books preserved among the archives of the Corporation of the City of London: Calendars of Letter Books A–I* (London, 1885–1909)

Court Baron	F.W. Maitland and W. Paley Baildon (eds), *The Court Baron*, Selden Society vol. 4 for 1890 (London, 1891)
CPMR	Thomas, A.H. (ed.), *Calendars of the Plea Rolls and Memoranda Rolls of the City of London* (Cambridge, 1926–61)
CPR	HMSO, *Calendar of Patent Rolls* (London, 1916–68)
de Roover, *JP*	R. de Roover, 'The concept of the just price: theory and economic policy', *Journal of Economic History* 18 (1958), 418–38
Dialogus de Scaccario	C. Johnson (ed.), *Dialogus de Scaccario* (London, 1950)
E.	Easter term
Ec. Hist. Doc.	A.E. Bland, P.A. Brown and R.H. Tawney (eds), *English Economic History: Selected Documents* (London, 1914)
EcHR	Economic History Review
EEJ	A. Musson and W.M. Ormrod, *The Evolution of English Justice: Law, Politics and Society in the Fourteenth Century* (Basingstoke, 1999)
EETS	Early English Text Society
EHR	English Historical Review
Fleta II	H.G. Richardson and G.O. Sayles (eds), *Fleta* vol. II, Selden Society vol. 72 for 1953 (London, 1955)
Foedera	T. Rymer, *Foedera, convenciones, litterae et cujuscunque generis acta publica, inter reges Angliae et alios quosvis imperatores, reges, pontifices, principes, vel communitates, ab ingressu Gulielmi I in Angliam, A.D. 1066, ad nostra usque tempora*, 4 vols in 7 parts (London, 1816–69)
Gilchrist, *CEA*	J. Gilchrist, *The Church and Economic Activity in the Middle Ages* (London, 1969)
Glanvill	G.D.G. Hall (ed.), *The Treatise on the Law and Customs of the Realm of England Commonly Called Glanvill* (London, 1965)
GOT	general oyer and terminer
GOTT	general oyer and terminer and trailbaston
H.	Hilary term
Holdsworth, *HEL*	W.S. Holdsworth, *History of English Law*, 16 vols (London, 1922–66)
Hundred Rolls	W. Illingworth (ed.), *Rotuli Hundredorum temp. Hen. III et Edw. I* (London, 1812–18)
KBIF	King's Bench indictment file
LA	H.T. Riley (ed.), *Munimenta Gildhallae Londoniensis*, vols I and III, *Liber Albus compiled A.D. 1419*, Rolls Series 12.1 and 12.3 (London, 1859 and 1862)
LB	Letter Book (manuscript Letter Book in Corporation of London Record Office)
LC	H.T. Riley (ed.), *Munimenta Gildhallae Londoniensis*, vol. II, parts i and ii, *Liber Custumarum*, Rolls Series 12.2.i and 2.2.ii (London, 1860)
LRB	F.B. Bickley, *The Little Red Book of Bristol*, 2 vols (Bristol, 1900)

M.	Michaelmas term
Maitland, *Eyre of Kent*	F.W. Maitland, W.V. Harcourt and W.C. Bolland (eds), *Year Book of the Eyre of Kent 6 & 7 Edw. II 1313–14*, Selden Society vols 24, 27, 29 (London 1910, 1912, 1913)
Milsom, *HFCL*	S.F.C. Milsom, *Historical Foundations of the Common Law*, 2nd edn (Toronto, 1981)
Mirror	W.J. Whittaker (ed.), *The Mirror of Justices*, Selden Society vol. 7 for 1893 (London, 1895)
MLC	A. Musson, *Medieval Law in Context: The Growth of Legal Consciousness from Magna Carta to the Peasants' Revolt* (Manchester, 2001)
P&C, *Councils*	F.M. Powicke and C.R. Cheney, *Councils and Synods with Other Documents Relating to the English Church* (Oxford, 1964)
P&M	F. Pollock and F.W. Maitland, *The History of English Law before the Time of Edward I*, 2 vols, 2nd edn (Cambridge, 1968)
PQW	W. Illingworth (ed.), *Placita de Quo Warranto Temporibus Edw. I, II & III in Curia Receptae Scaccarii Westm. Asservata* (London, 1818)
PRO	Public Record Office
Putnam, *PJP*	B.H. Putnam, *Proceedings before the Justices of the Peace in the Fourteenth and Fifteenth Centuries* (London, 1938)
Rigg, *Select Starrs*	J.M. Rigg (ed.), *Select Pleas, Starrs and Other Records from the Rolls of the Exchequer of the Jews, A.D. 1220–1284*, Selden Society vol. 15 for 1901 (London, 1902)
Riley, *Memorials*	H.T. Riley, *Memorials of London and London Life in the Thirteenth, Fourteenth and Fifteenth Centuries* (London, 1868)
RP	J. Strachey (ed.), *Rotuli Parliamentorum, ut et Petitiones et Placita in Parliamento*, 6 vols (London, 1767–83)
Salter, *MA*	H.E. Salter, *Medieval Archives of the University of Oxford*, 2 vols, Oxford Historical Society vol. 69 for 1917 and vol. 73 for 1919 (Oxford, 1920 and 1921)
Salter, *MC*	H.E. Salter (ed.), *Munimenta Civitatis Oxonie*, Oxford Historical Society vol. 71 for 1917 (Devizes, 1920)
SR	Record Commissioners, *Statutes of the Realm*, 6 vols (London, 1810)
SS	Selden Society (*annual volumes*, 1887–)
st.	statute
T.	Trinity term
TRHS	*Transactions of the Royal Historical Society*
Vita Edwardi Secundi	N. Denholm-Young (ed.), *The Life of Edward the Second by the so-called Monk of Malmesbury* (London, 1957)
Wakefield *A–H*	A W. Paley Baildon (ed.), *Court Rolls of the Manor of Wakefield vol. I, 1274–1297*, Yorkshire Archaeological Society Record Series vol. 29 for 1900 (Leeds, 1901)

B   W. Paley-Baildon (ed.), *Court Rolls of the Manor of Wakefield vol. II, 1297–1309*, Yorkshire Archaeological Society Record Series vol. 36 for 1906 (Leeds, 1906)

C   J. Lister (ed.), *Court Rolls of the Manor of Wakefield vol. III, 1313–1316 and 1286*, Yorkshire Archaeological Society Record Series vol. 57 for 1917 (Leeds, 1917)

D   J. Lister (ed.), *Court Rolls of the Manor of Wakefield vol. IV, 1316–1317*, Yorkshire Archaeological Society Record Series vol. 78 for 1930 (Leeds, 1930)

E   J. Walker (ed.), *Court Rolls of the Manor of Wakefield vol. V, 1322–1331*, Yorkshire Archaeological Society Record Series vol. 109 for 1944 (Wakefield, 1945)

F   S.S. Walker (ed.), *Court Rolls of the Manor of Wakefield from October 1331 to September 1333*, Wakefield Court Rolls Series of the Yorkshire Archaeological Society vol. 3 for 1982 (Leeds, 1983)

G   H.M. Jewell (ed.), *Court Rolls of the Manor of Wakefield from September 1348 to September 1350*, Wakefield Court Rolls, 2nd ser., vol. II, Yorkshire Archaeological Society (Leeds, 1981)

H   M. Habberjam, M. O'Regan and B. Hale (eds), *Court Rolls of the Manor of Wakefield from October 1350 to September 1352*, Yorkshire Archaeological Society, Wakefield Court Rolls Series vol. VI for 1985 (Leeds, 1987)

Whitelock, *Councils*   D. Whitelock, M. Brett and C.N.L. Brooke (eds), *Councils and Synods with Other Documents Relating to the English Church 1066–1204* (Oxford, 1981)

YB   Year Book

YO   M. Prestwich, *York Civic Ordinances, 1301* Borthwick Papers no.49 (York, 1976)

Introduction

In the rolls for a judicial session in Hertfordshire, held under a royal commission of 1340, one of the many entries records that the jurors of 'divers hundreds' in the county reported a certain Robert le Poleter for 'heightening the market' for corn and for being 'a common usurer, so it is said'.[1] The record raises obvious questions. Was Robert guilty as charged? Was he found guilty? Was he punished? It also raises questions which are less obvious, but of more general historical consequence, concerning the extent and nature of royal interest in the private commercial dealings of a person like Robert who leaves no definite trace outside this roll.

Robert le Poleter's very obscurity is important. His alleged offences involved sales and loans, the most frequent of commercial interactions. The vast majority of the medieval English populace would have participated in numerous sales of goods and a large number would have become involved in loans of money or other fungibles. Laws regulating sales and loans had the potential to affect more people more often than most other laws current in medieval England, and this large potential coverage made the laws under which Robert was accused an aspect of medieval life which is worthy of consideration.

Although early legal treatises suggest that royal authorities had little interest in subjects' sales and loans (the twelfth-century treatise *Glanvill* and the thirteenth-century treatise *Bracton* stating that kings and their courts had no necessary interest in the private bargains of subjects), it is, in fact, clear that, even in the time of *Glanvill*, royal rules went some way towards prescribing both the form and the substance of subjects' bargains, and that the overall pattern was of increased intervention over the course of the thirteenth and fourteenth centuries.[2] Royal regulation of commerce did not, of course, begin or end in this period. There were some trading laws before the Conquest, particularly concerning witnessing and allowed locations for transactions. regulation of the coinage and of weights and measures.[3] Existing rules prescribing the form of bargains dictated that only bargains created in particular ways could be enforced in royal courts or with the aid of royal procedures.[4] There were some early rules to prevent

---

[1] JUST 1/337 m.3. All manuscript sources are in the Public Record Office, Kew (PRO) unless otherwise noted.

[2] *Glanvill* X:18, dealing with 'contracts which are based on the consent of private persons', states that 'it is not the custom of the court of the Lord King to protect private agreements (privatas conuenciones) nor does it even concern itself with such contracts as can be considered to be like private agreements'. See also *Bracton* f.100, cited in S.J. Stoljar, *A History of Contract at Common Law* (Canberra, 1975), 3. For a description of these treatises, see Baker, *Introduction*, 175–7.

[3] Britnell, *Commercialisation*, 24–5 citing II Aethelstan 10, II Aethelstan 12, VI Aethelstan 6.2: F. Liebermann, *Die Gesetze der Angelsachsen*, 3 vols (Halle, 1898–1916), vol. I, 156–7, 176.

[4] Baker, *Introduction*, 319; *Glanvill* X:1–18: W.P. Baildon (ed.), *Select Civil Pleas, Vol. I: A.D. 1200–1203*, Selden Society vol. 3 for 1889 (London, 1890), pl. 89, cited in Stoljar, *History of Contract*, 4; Simpson, *Contract*, 126–32.

fraud.[5] In the thirteenth and fourteenth centuries, royal courts were also in the process of developing rules on procedural fairness in the formation of bargains, such as the requirement of voluntary consent, the effect of minority, and rules against swindling and deceit.[6] As well as these rules and the well-established rules on the weights and measures and the coinage to be used by subjects in their bargains, laws were laid down to govern the substance of bargains.[7,8] Bargains on certain terms were prohibited, on pain of prosecution and punishment. Of particular note, for historians as well as for those such as Robert le Poleter who might be accused of breaking the rules, were the prohibition of usury, price fixing regulations and the laws against forestalling and regrating. It is these laws which form the subject matter of this book.

'Ripping seamless webs': subject matter and period

The usury prohibition, price fixing regulations and laws against forestalling and regrating can properly be regarded as a discrete area of study, making sense without other matters which might seem to be aspects of the same 'topic'. In terms of practical, commercial life, it is difficult to separate them: a sale on credit, for example, might contravene both usury laws and price fixing laws, and a sale outside a market might contravene both pricing laws and laws against forestalling, while a credit sale outside a market could contravene all three sets of rules. The laws also have in common the fact that each was discussed by medieval canon lawyers and theologians as well as being the subject of intervention by medieval English royal authorities.[9] These three areas were, moreover, considered to be inter-connected in literary sources and non-English sources.[10] More recently, all three areas have been the subject of great criticism in accordance with free market doctrines: Blackstone denounced the usury laws as the product of 'monkish superstition and civil tyranny', whilst Adam Smith compared 'the popular fear of engrossing and

---

[5] See Richard I's 'law against false shewing', *Ec. Hist. Doc.* Section 6 no.1 p. 155, cited in D. Wood, *Medieval Economic Thought* (Cambridge, 2002), 114.

[6] Simpson, *Contract*, 537, citing YB 43 Edw. III, H. f.6, pl.15, and Simpson, *Contract*, 133, citing YB 20 Edw. III, 92. Simpson, *Contract*, 540, citing: YB 6 Edw. III M. f.39 pl.14 (1332); YB 13 Edw. III, 304 (1339); YB 18 Edw. III, 410, 500 (1343); YB 18 Edw. III, 378, 380. See, e.g., *Garrick v Heytesbery* (1387) YB 11 Ric. II (1387–8) 4; B & M, *Sources*, 507.

[7] Bolton, *MEE*, 74; Warren, *Governance*, 21–2; M. Prestwich, *Edward I* (London, 1988), 94, 244–8; Britnell, *Commercialization*, 25.

[8] On the distinction between form and substance in private law, see D. Kennedy, 'Form and substance in private law adjudications', *Harvard Law Review* 89 (1976), 1685–778.

[9] R. Morris (ed.), *Dan Michel's Ayenbite of Inwyt or Remorse of Conscience*, Early English Text Society vol. 25 (London, 1895), 44, cited in W. Ashley, *An Introduction to English Economic History and Theory* (New York, 1966), 161, translated from French into English in 1340; G. Le Bras, 'Conceptions of economy and society' in *CEH III*, 554; Gilchrist, *CEA* c.5; R.N. Swanson, *Church and Society in Late Medieval England* (Oxford, 1989), 194–5; Britnell, 'Forstall', 94–5. John Myre's instructions for parish priests of the first half of the fifteenth century mention usury and selling at too high a price together as 'al on': E. Peacock (ed.), *Instructions for Parish Priests by John Myrc* (London, 1868, revised 1902), p. 12, lines 372–83.

[10] See, e.g., R.H. Bowers, 'A Middle-English mnemonic poem on usury', *Medieval Studies* XVII (1955), 236, 227, in which an anonymous author classifies as 'oker' both usury and sales at inflated prices. See the Scots Prices of Food Act 1449, *APS* II, 36 c.11, which 'provided that keepers of victual to a dearth should be punished as ockerers, i.e. usurers': D.M. Walker, *A Legal History of Scotland, volume II* (Edinburgh, 1990), 547. Medieval French law described a sale at an unjust price as usurious: see Fr. Olivier Martin, *Histoire de Droit Français* (Paris, 2nd edn 1995), p. 279 no.211. The late fourteenth-century 'scholastic' Henry of Hesse advocated price fixing to prevent the poor from, *inter alia*, usurers: M. Roche, *Travaile et salaire à travers la scholastique* (Paris, 1933), 30–5, cited in Wood, *Medieval Economic Thought*, 143.

forestalling' to 'the popular terrors and suspicions of witchcraft'.[11] Modern commentators still commonly (although not invariably) deal with usury, forestalling and regrating and price fixing together.[12]

Some explanation must be given for the exclusion of certain areas which may be considered to be connected with the areas to be examined. This book will deal only with sales of goods and loans of money or fungibles, and not (or not directly) with bargains concerning land, such as sales of land or leases. Common lawyers tend to see the distinction between land law (or the 'law of real property') and personal property law as obvious. Although a transfer of land and a transfer of goods or money may seem very similar, the two transactions have always been treated as wholly different in kind by the common law, with different rules on modes of transfer and the passing of property, different legal actions available if a dispute over property rights should arise, and different controls over the right to alienate.[13] Land will be mentioned at some points, as some commercial practice involved using land as security for 'personal property' bargains, but it will not be dealt with in detail.

A matter which is certainly connected with some of the areas covered by this book is the regulation of wages, another area in which royal legislation came to operate in an attempt to control the terms of bargains between subjects. It will be mentioned in connection with price regulation and forestalling and regrating, but it has not been selected as a basic part of the book for two reasons. First, it is rather different from the areas selected in that regulation of wages involves overt ideas of different status between the contracting parties. Secondly, it is a matter which has

---

[11] Blackstone, *Commentaries* Book II, c.30, p. 239a: '[i]n the dark ages of monkish superstition and civil tyranny, when interest was laid under a total interdict, commerce was also at its lowest ebb, . . . but when men's minds began to be more enlarged, when true religion and real liberty revived, commerce grew again into credit; and again introduced with itself its inseparable companion, the doctrine of loans upon interest'. A. Smith, *An Inquiry into the Nature and Causes of the Wealth of Nations*, ed. R.H. Campbell, A.S. Skinner and W.B. Todd, 2 vols (Oxford, 1976), I, 534, cited (with some sympathy) in R.H. Britnell, 'Price setting in English borough markets 1349–1500', *Canadian Journal of History* XXXI (1996), 1–15, at 13–14. Similar comments have been made about wage regulation: B.H. Putnam, 'Chief Justice Shareshull and the economic and legal codes of 1351–1352', *University of Toronto Law Journal* [1943–4], 251–81, at 251; Lord Campbell, *Lives of the Chief Justices*, 2 vols (Philadelphia, 1853), v–vi, stating that the Statute of Labourers '[shows] our ancestors to have then been under the delusion now so fatal to our continental neighbors, that "organisation" of labor' is a fit subject for legislation'.

[12] E.g. P.S. Atiyah, *The Rise and Fall of Freedom of Contract* (Oxford, 1979), 62: 'The notion of a just price . . . and of its opposite – an extortionate price, or usury – was at the centre of medieval economic thought.' J. Le Goff, *Your Money or Your Life* (New York, 1988), 28, described usury as a 'sin against the just price'. See also P. Singer, *How are we to live?* (Oxford, 1997), 67–76. There is also a practical link between price setting and usury: properly fixed prices would mean it would be harder to contract usurious loans disguised as sales: see Britnell, 'Price-setting', 9. The connection between the three areas of action has not, however, always been accepted: H. Pirenne saw the areas to be considered as unconnected, dealing with the prohibition on usury as part of the law influenced by the church, and prohibitions of forestalling and price control as facets of small-scale town regulation: Pirenne, *Economic and Social History of Medieval Europe*, 121–2 and 174–6. Pirenne's model does not, however, fit the facts in England, where all of these areas were the subject of both royal control and, to some extent, of control by local bodies. J.T. Noonan also thought that there were important distinctions between the canonical and theological theories on the just price on the one hand and usury on the other, though this does not necessarily mean that the same distinction applies to royal action in these areas: Noonan, *Usury*, 82. D. Wood has recently stated that the just price and usury are 'completely different' since the 'just price was . . . grounded on justice and equality . . . while usury . . . was grounded on injustice and inequality': Wood, *Medieval Economic Thought*, 159.

[13] Baker, *Introduction*, c.15, p. 246; Simpson, *Land Law*, c.6; Baker, *Introduction*, 231–7, c.22; Simpson, *Land Law*, c.2; Ibbetson, *Obligations*, 20; Powicke, *Thirteenth Century*, 324.

already received detailed consideration elsewhere.[14] Royal regulation of wages does not, therefore, have its own chapter, though it is clearly an important part of the background to the matters which will be considered, and will be referred to as appropriate. Likewise, quality regulation and sumptuary legislation are part of the overall picture of royal control of subjects' sales, but both have other aspects – public health in the case of quality regulations, and a heavy basis in the reinforcement of status in the case of sumptuary legislation – which take them outside the mainstream of the book's subject matter.[15]

Some consideration of the period is also necessary. The main focus is on the years 1272–1399. Although, as has been mentioned, there were certainly legal interventions in subjects' bargains from much earlier times, the reign of Edward I is a sensible starting point for a number of reasons.[16] It has been seen by the greatest of writers on such matters as an important turning point in legal history.[17] Importantly for research, it marks the beginning of a number of different types of record series.[18] In terms of personal attitudes to contracts or agreements, it is attractive to move from one monarch whose epitaph has been held to be 'pactum serva' to one derided for his abuse of 'blank charters'.[19]

It is accepted that there was an overall increase in the level of legal intervention (actual and purported) in everyday life over the thirteenth and fourteenth centuries.[20] Changes included an expansion of the scope of the common law, alterations in court structure and in the nature of judicial personnel and the legal profession.[21] The thirteenth and fourteenth centuries have been described as a crucial period in the increase in 'legal consciousness' in all sections of society.[22] The period includes important statutory developments in the general field of 'contracts'

---

[14] See B.H. Putnam, *The Enforcement of the Statute of Labourers during the First Decade after the Black Death* (New York, 1908); B.H. Putnam, 'Maximum wage laws for priests after the Black Death', *American Historical Review* 21 (1915–16), 12–32; S.A.C. Penn and C. Dyer, 'Wages and earnings in late medieval England: evidence from the enforcement of the labour laws', *EcHR*, 2nd ser., 43 (1990), 356–76; M.J. Hettinger, 'Defining the servant: legal and extra-legal terms of employment in fifteenth-century England' in A.J. Frantzen and D. Moffat (eds), *The Work of Work: Servitude, Slavery and Labour in Medieval England* (Glasgow, 1994), 206–28; E. Clark, 'Medieval labour law in English local courts', *American Journal of Legal History* 27 (1983), 330–3; S.A. Epstein, 'The theory and practice of the just wage', *Journal of Medieval History* 17 (1991), 53–70; L.R. Poos, 'The social context of Statute of Labourers enforcement', *Law and History Review* 1 (1983), 30; S.A. Epstein, *Wage Labour and Guilds in Medieval Europe* (Chapel Hill and London, 1991); J. Bothwell, P.J.P. Goldberg and W.M. Ormrod (eds), *The Problem of Labour in Fourteenth Century England* (York, 2000); A. Musson, 'New labour laws, new remedies? Legal reaction to the Black Death "crisis"' in N. Saul (ed.), *Fourteenth Century England I* (Woodbridge, 2000), 73–88; J.H. Munro, 'Wage-stickiness, monetary changes and real incomes in late medieval England and the Low Countries 1300–1450: did money really matter?' *Research in Economic History* (forthcoming).

[15] Quality laws are mentioned below at pp. 81–2. On sumptuary laws, see, e.g., Bolton, *MEE*, 321; S.H. Rigby, *English Society in the Later Middle Ages: Class, Status and Gender* (Houndmills, 1995), 197, 200.

[16] See, e.g., J. Hudson, *The Formation of the English Common Law: Law and Society in England from the Norman Conquest to Magna Carta* (Harlow, 1996), 135.

[17] *P&M* I, xxviii.

[18] For example, the Rolls of Parliament, the 'statute roll', the continuous stream of *Year Books*: Baker, *Introduction*, 179, 205. A number of series of lower court rolls began under Edward I.

[19] Prestwich, *Edward I*, 566; C.M. Barron, 'Tyranny of Richard II', *BIHR* 41 (1968), 1–18, at 10–14. 'Blank charters' were not literally blank, but were documents leaving subjects open to penalties for treason, used to extort money.

[20] The expansion of the common law between 1272 and the Peasants' Revolt of 1381 is noted in Brown, *Governance*, 100. A. Musson, in *MLC*, 207, notes a growth over a longer period: 1215–1381.

[21] *EEJ*, particularly 1, 115.

[22] *MLC*.

or bargains, such as the institution of the systems of statutes merchant and statutes staple, and some important judicial or administrative developments in the same area, such as the rise of actions for deceit.[23] It ends, however, before the 'law of contract' was transformed by use of the action of *assumpsit*, an action based on the idea of a wrong or *tort*, in the place of the 'old personal actions' and, in particular, the actions of covenant and debt *sur contract*, based on enforcement of a promise.[24] The exclusion of the 'rise of *assumpsit*' was deliberate. Legal historians have often emphasised this development to such an extent that all earlier aspects of the common law relating to bargains or contracts have seemed to be leading up to it.[25] By ending the study before *assumpsit* had begun to be taken seriously as a replacement for covenant and debt, a more balanced picture of the law relating to bargains in medieval England can be seen.[26] The end point of 1399 also cuts out another of the 'rises' popular with legal historians – that of the Chancery's emergence as an important and regular court (or the visible part of this 'rise') with some responsibility for investigating the fairness of subjects' sales and loans.[27]

Not surprisingly, economic and political conditions varied over the century and a quarter to be considered. A summary of these matters risks extreme superficiality, but the major outlines are well known from the detailed work done by many scholars on this period. In economic terms, the period saw 'expansion in most parts of the economy until about 1306' (despite an 'air of malaise' in the last decades of the thirteenth century), rising prices in the 1270s, falling in the 1280s, rising again in the 1290s and 1300s, an economic crisis in the early fourteenth century (1315–25 being a time of famine) and another following upon the Black Death of the late 1340s, with high grain prices in the famine years, falling prices from 1325 until the Black Death, price rises in the 1350s and 1360s, then price decreases and wage rises (and thus an increased standard of living for many people) from the mid-1370s to the end of the century.[28] General trends over a longer period include commercialisation, in the sense of the increasing importance of the sale of produce rather than self-sufficiency.[29] In political terms, we have widely different degrees of royal power, two depositions, squabbles between kings and nobles, kings and church, a number of rebellions, war and the difficulty of its finance and the evolution of Parliament to set against periods of stability.[30]

[23] Baker, *Introduction*, 312, 376–8.

[24] Simpson, *Contract*, generally.

[25] See, e.g., Simpson, *Contract*; Stoljar, *History of Contract*, generally.

[26] Milsom, *HFCL*, 322–55.

[27] See Baker, *Introduction*, c.6. There are few fourteenth-century Chancery records: Baker, *Introduction*, 103; Wood, *Medieval Economic Thought*, 184.

[28] Bolton, *MEE*, 72, 74, 76, 180–1; I. Kershaw, 'The Great Famine and agrarian crisis in England 1315–22' in R.H. Hilton (ed.), *Peasants, Knights and Heretics* (Cambridge, 1976), 85–132. For discussion of the effects of the Black Death, see A.R. Bridbury, *The English Economy from Bede to the Reformation* (Woodbridge, 1992), 200–17; E. Miller and J. Hatcher, *Medieval England: Rural Society and Economic Change 1086–1348* (London, 1978), 64–8.

[29] Britnell, *Commercialisation*.

[30] See, e.g., A. Harding, *England in the Thirteenth Century* (Cambridge, 1993); M. Powicke, *The Thirteenth Century 1216–1307* (Oxford, 1962); McKisack, *Fourteenth Century*; M.H. Keen, *England in the Later Middle Ages: A Political History* (London, 1973); W.M. Ormrod, *Political Life in Medieval England 1300–1450* (Basingstoke, 1995); W.M. Ormrod (ed.), *England in the Fourteenth Century* (Woodbridge, 1986); M. Prestwich, *Edward I* (London, 1988); M. Prestwich, *The Three Edwards: War and State in England, 1272–1377* (London, 1980), cc.4, 5; W.M. Ormrod, *The Reign of Edward III: Crown and Political Society in England 1327–77* (Yale, 1990); F.R.H. Du Boulay and C.M. Barron (eds), *The Reign of Richard II* (London, 1971); N. Saul, *Richard II* (New

Contexts

The rules on the substance of subjects' bargains lie at the point of intersection of political, economic and legal history. The ramifications of royal exercise of jurisdiction over the misconduct of Robert le Poleter and those like him therefore feed into bigger question of the nature and purpose of medieval government. The laws are of relevance to an understanding of the growth of the powers of 'the state' or 'the crown' over new areas of the lives of subjects, of ideas of law and its limits and of royal (and other) conceptions of what amounted to wrongful or unjust conduct.[31]

The late thirteenth and fourteenth centuries saw a number of changes in law enforcement. The subject matter of this book may be useful in furthering understanding of some of these changes. The book must engage with one of the important issues in legal history of recent years, that is to say the thesis of R.C. Palmer in relation to the effect of the mid-fourteenth-century Black Death on legal intervention. Palmer sees the developments of the common law in extending the scope of trespass actions in the late fourteenth century and government regulation of wages as part of a broad, new, pattern of using the law to control 'the lower orders' by making them 'stand to their obligations'.[32] Objections have been raised to his thesis, in particular by A.J. Musson.[33] Musson's view, which is more in line with much of the current historical orthodoxy on other aspects of the effects of the Black Death, such as its economic effects, is that there may have been a change of pace or emphasis after the Black Death, but there was not a complete break from the past: rather than being the impetus for a fresh start, the plague tended to accelerate pre-existing trends.[34]

The laws in question and their enforcement provide some interesting illustrations of the interaction of different authorities and sources of law within the realm. Their study makes some contribution to the debate on relations between 'Church and State' in medieval England, with regard to jurisdiction and the adoption of ideas.[35] It also tells us about the relationship between royal aims and

Haven, 1997); P. Heath, *Church and Realm 1272–1461: Conflict and Collaboration in an Age of Crises* (London, 1988); A. Tuck, *Crown and Nobility 1272–1461* (London, 1985).

[31] On what medieval government was trying to do, see the 'limited ambition' model of medieval government put forward by W.L. Warren, who stated that 'in the Middle Ages, . . . government was more about controlling and managing society than about changing it': Warren, *Governance*, 1. See also Huizinga, *Waning*, 36. On conceptions of wrongful conduct, see Ibbetson, *Obligations*, 15, 17. The question of whether law should focus on guilt, harm or both is a major part of legal philosophy, and much debated. For modern considerations on intention, attempts and accessories in criminal law, see, e.g., A. Ashworth, *Principles of Criminal Law* 3rd edn (Oxford, 1999), 101–7, 124–36, 159–250, 425–59, 460–90. Such questions were also debated by medieval 'scholastics': Evans, *Law and Theology*, 143.

[32] Palmer, *Black Death*, 1, 5, and generally.

[33] Musson, 'New labour', 73–88.

[34] Musson, 'New labour', 78, 86; *EEJ*, 93; A.R. Bridbury, 'The Black Death', *EHR*, 2nd ser., xxvi (1973), 577–92; J. Hatcher, 'England in the aftermath of the Black Death', *Past and Present* cxliv (1994), 3–34.

[35] R.H. Helmholz, 'The writ of prohibition to Court Christian before 1500' in Helmholz, *Canon Law*, c.4; Simpson, *Contract*, 145; G.B. Flahiff, *Medieval Studies* 6 (1944), 261–313, *Medieval Studies* 7 (1945), 229–90. W.R. Jones, 'Bishops, politics and the two laws: the gravamina of the English clergy 1237–1399', *Speculum* XLI (1966), 209–45, 226. For a view of relations as more harmonious in the reign of Edward I, see D. Millon, 'Common Law and Canon Law during the Reign of Edward I' (Cornell Ph.D., 1982); Heath, *Church and Realm*, 352.

jurisdiction and other secular authorities.[36] The latter is a more hazardous question, as there are real problems in distinguishing 'central' or 'royal' action or jurisdiction on the one hand and 'local' action or jurisdiction on the other, coming to conclusions about centralisation or decentralisation of government, contrasting royal and local attitudes, or classifying particular rules as 'royal' or 'local' in origin.[37] It is clear that even defining 'the centre' is by no means straightforward. While some institutions are clearly 'central' on most definitions – the council and Parliament being obvious examples – others are more 'mixed' and may be classified differently, depending on whether one focuses on personnel, geographical location, type of business, source of authority or degree of accountability. To take the example of the justice of the peace: is he properly regarded as a 'local' or a 'central' official? It may be assumed that he and his jurisdiction are 'local' because the typical JP has firm roots in a particular area, but in terms of the source of his authority, he is a royal appointee, subject to a certain degree of royal supervision.[38] In the field of law-making, are we to regard a royal charter to a town as 'royal' or 'local'?[39] According to some plausible theories, all courts were in some sense royal courts – they could be suppressed by the king, actions could be removed by them to royal courts – and all 'local' legislation had a royal aspect – it was either approved or tolerated by the king.[40] It is, however, clear that this theory would not have been acceptable to all – neither to the lord claiming the right to try certain economic offences as a matter of custom nor, perhaps, to the more self-confident urban authorities making and enforcing their own regulations, nor to certain churchmen.[41] The hierarchical relationship (who could legislate on what, who could decide what, whose decisions could be reviewed or overturned) between different authorities was in a state of flux throughout and beyond the medieval period.

A further difficulty with the 'local' v. 'central' opposition when employed in the analysis of a legal system is that it tends to ignore the distinction between law making and law enforcement. In medieval England, it was not at all infrequent for rules to be made 'centrally' and to be enforced – perhaps with some degree of independent interpretation – by officials or courts with tenuous royal links and accountability. Such a situation does not fit easily into discussions of centralisation and devolution of power, and shows that a more sophisticated view must be taken of questions of jurisdiction, separating law-making and law enforcement, and taking into account the ties of authority and accountability between different bodies. A suitable model is provided by S.L. Waugh, who has noted 'the interlocking nature of central and local authority and the crown's dependence on community leaders to enforce its will'.[42]

---

[36] See, e.g., D.M. Palliser, 'Towns and the English state 1066–1500' in J.R. Maddicott and D.M. Palliser (eds), *The Medieval State: Essays presented to James Campbell* (London, 2000), 131, 136 (suggesting conflict in the reign of Henry III and Edward I in particular, with more co-operation under Edward III).

[37] *MLC*, 9–10; Baker, *Introduction*, 12–29, 126–130; G.L. Harriss, 'Political society and the growth of government in late medieval England', *Past and Present* 138 (1993), 46–56; *EEJ*, 5–10.

[38] Putnam, *Enforcement*, 3, 55; Ormrod, *Political Life*, 40.

[39] Palliser, 'Towns and the English state', 127–46, 129, suggests that a process of negotiation leading to charters was common. See also Britnell, *Commercialisation*, 26.

[40] Hudson, *Formation*, 231; Baker, *Introduction*, 22–7; Warren, *Governance*, 47.

[41] *P&M* I, 645; Rigby, *English Society*, 220, citing D.L. Douie, *Archbishop Pecham* (Oxford, 1952), 129–31; *MLC*, 12.

[42] S.L. Waugh, *England in the Reign of Edward III* (Cambridge, 1991), 110; see also Musson, 'New labour', 83.

Regulation of the terms of loans and sales also brings us into the eternally vexed question of the relationship between law and morality or religion. The question of when law should stop and allow morality/religion the field is as old and as new as law itself.[43] Biblical authority might state that breaking the law and sin are co-extensive, but the *Digest* held that there was a point at which law ended and morality carried on.[44] Medieval canonists and theologians debated the question of boundaries and overlaps, though without coming to a clear consensus.[45] Medieval common law sources are not explicit about the matter, although there is certainly much moral or religious content in both *Bracton* and the *Mirror of Justices*.[46] The indications from fifteenth-century English legal theorists is that the place of morality in law was unclear, with some statements suggesting an overlap, and others emphasising the autonomy of law from morality.[47] Given theories of the 'profound spiritual and moral crisis' of medieval Europe with regard to trade, it is extremely interesting to ponder the question of the moral content of secular laws on the terms of loans and sales in medieval England.[48]

---

[43] For an introduction to modern debates, see, e.g., H. McCoubrey and N.D. White, *Textbook on Jurisprudence* 2nd edn (London, 1996), 52–4; M.D.A. Freeman, *Lloyd's Introduction to Jurisprudence*, 6th edn (London, 1994), 56–9, 60–163.

[44] 1 John 3:4: 'Whosoever committeth sin transgresseth also the law: for sin is the transgression of the law' (King James Version); 'Not everything which is "allowed" [or, "legal"] is honest' (*Digest* 50.17, no.144), cited in Evans, *Law and Theology*, 15.

[45] Evans, *Law and Theology*, 12, 15, 24; Doe, *Fundamental Authority*, 49.

[46] *MLC*, 14; D.J. Seipp, 'The Mirror of Justices', in J.A. Bush and A. Wijffels (eds), *Learning the Law: Teaching and the Transmission of Law in England 1150–1900* (London, 1999), 85–112, at 102–4.

[47] Doe, *Fundamental Authority*, especially at 4.

[48] Rigby, *English Society*, 300, citing L.K. Little, *Religious Poverty and the Profit Economy* (London, 1978); Tawney, *Religion* (1972), 43; Gilchrist *CEA*, 64–9.

1

Sources, Opinions and Approaches

Both the available sources and previous opinions present some challenges and shape the approaches which will be adopted in the book.

Sources

Statutes, ordinances, charters and commissions give the most direct evidence of royal action.[1] It must, however, be noted that texts of statutes were neither produced nor approved in a manner recognisable to a modern lawyer, and that a number of documents which started life as more limited measures came over time to be regarded as being definitive, national, legislation.[2] That there is a large amount of fluidity and uncertainty about which documents we should call statutes, particularly in the thirteenth and early fourteenth centuries, is not a new observation. As T.F.T. Plucknett pointed out long ago, 'Those things are statutes which contemporaries themselves describe by that word . . . [T]he description of statute is acquired by reputation.'[3] It is also accepted that the nature and provenance of statutes changed over the period from Edward I to Edward III, with the rise to prominence of the common petition, both at the expense of private petitions and also, as far as some commentators are concerned, at the expense of 'government inspired' measures.[4] Statutes sometimes make statements about the reason for their enactment. It must, however, be borne in mind that one cannot be sure that they give a definitive account of the subjective motivations of those promoting the new rule. All one can hope to learn from these sources is 'the kind of discourse that prevailed and what was acceptable, or calculated to influence people'.[5]

[1] On the nature of statutes, see T.F.T. Plucknett, *Legislation of Edward I* (Oxford, 1949), esp. c.1; T.F.T. Plucknett, *Statutes and their Interpretation in the First Half of the Fourteenth Century* (Cambridge, 1922). It is not possible to see statutes and ordinances as formally separate types of instrument in the period under consideration. G. Barraclough noted a lack of distinction between statutes and ordinances before the time of Richard II: G. Barraclough, 'Law and legislation in medieval England', *Law Quarterly Review* 56 (1940), 75. On statutes in general, see M.S. Arnold, 'Statutes as judgments: the natural law theory of parliamentary activity in medieval England', *University of Pennsylvania Law Review* 26 (1977), 329. On charters and their legal status, see M. Weinbaum (ed.), *British Borough Charters 1307–1660* (Cambridge, 1943), xviii–xxvii.
[2] See, e.g., Baker, *Introduction*, 205–7; Britnell, 'Forstall'.
[3] Plucknett, *Legislation*, 11.
[4] On the changing nature of the legislative process, see *EEJ*, 146–57. On private petitions, see G. Dodd, 'The hidden presence: parliament and the private petition in the fourteenth century' in A Musson (ed.) *Expectations of the Law in the Middle Ages* (Woodbridge, 2001), 135–49.
[5] A. Black, *Political Thought in Europe 1250–1450* (Cambridge, 1992), 4; A.B. Hibbert, 'The economic policies of towns' in *CEH III*, 157.

Legal treatises provide some information about the nature of the rules, though they are a less direct or 'official' source than statutes and other legislative documents. They are also limited in other ways. First, there is nothing like a steady stream of treatises covering the whole period. The main texts, *Glanvill* and *Bracton*, were written in the late twelfth century and mid-thirteenth century respectively, and although there are some examples of general treatises from the reign of Edward I, in the shape of *Britton*, *Fleta* and *The Mirror of Justices*, there is, unfortunately, little information from the fourteenth century. In the late thirteenth century and the fourteenth century, legal treatises seem to have abandoned general theory or attempts at a comprehensive treatment of substantive law and instead concentrated on the minutiae of the writ system used in the royal courts.[6] Secondly, even when treatises are available, it is not always clear that they gave an accurate representation of the law at the time when they were written.[7]

Records of court proceedings will be used to examine actual enforcement of the regulations under consideration, and also to fill in some of the gaps in theoretical discussion by deductions based on practice. Rolls of courts at various different levels in the judicial hierarchy have been examined, from the surviving records of Parliament's judicial proceedings, and crown pleas heard in eyre, King's Bench, *ad hoc* judicial commissions and peace sessions, as well as a small number of the many pipe rolls of the Exchequer, rolls of the Common Bench or Common Pleas and the 'common pleas' sections of eyre and King's Bench rolls.[8] A variety of lower secular courts exercised jurisdiction over the matters under consideration, whether as a result of deliberate delegation or of royal tolerance of their exercise of the jurisdiction. The records of views of frankpledge, hundred, borough and leet courts are numerous, though few sets of records span the entire period 1272–1399 in a complete series.[9] A century and more of careful record scholarship has given us many printed examples of the proceedings of such courts. As a small contribution

---

[6] T.F.T. Plucknett, *Early English Legal Literature* (Cambridge, 1958), 20–41; Baker, *Introduction*, c.11; J.S Beckerman, 'Law writing and law teaching: treatise evidence of the formal teaching of English law in the late thirteenth century' in J.A. Bush and A. Wijffels (eds), *Learning the Law: Teaching and the Transmission of English Law, 1150–1900* (London, 1999), 33–50, at 33. This lack of theoretical discussion in works on the common law of England was noted by an anonymous lawyer from the last years of Edward I or the early years of Edward II, who wrote in a marginal note in a copy of *Bracton* that 'In Anglia minus curatur de iure naturali quam in aliqua regime de mundo' ('In England, less attention is paid to natural law than in any other part of the world'): F.W. Maitland (ed.), *Select Passages from the Works of Bracton and Azo*, Selden Society vol. 8 for 1894 (London, 1895), 123, cited in Arnold, 'Statutes', 342.

[7] See, e.g., F.W. Maitland's introduction to the *Mirror*, especially *Mirror*, xxvi ff, and the partial rehabilitation of the *Mirror* in D.J. Seipp, 'The Mirror of Justices' in Bush and Wijffels, *Learning the Law*, 85–112.

[8] See Bibliography. On the eyres, see H.M. Cam, 'On the material available in the eyre rolls', *BIHR* 3 (1925–6), 152; D. Crook, 'The later eyres', *EHR* 97 (1982), 241; D. Crook, *Records of the General Eyre* (London, 1982). On veredicta, see H.G. Richardson and G.O. Sayles (eds), *Select Cases of Procedure Without Writ under Henry III*, Selden Society vol. 60 for 1941 (London, 1941), cci–ii. For a description of King's Bench files, see Meekings, 'King's Bench files', 97; *EEJ*, 194–205, 'Appendix: the sessions and itinerarires of the court of King's Bench and Parliament 1290–1399'. A number of peace rolls have been printed in Putnam, *PJP*, and also in the volumes produced by local record societies. Manuscript rolls have also been examined. Common pleas may well bring up information of relevance, but the task of locating relevant needles in the haystack of rolls is enormous: see J.H. Baker, 'Why the history of English law has not been finished', *Cambridge Law Journal* 59 (2000), 62–84, at 70–3.

[9] For an idea of the range of available manorial court records, and the incomplete nature of many series, see J. Cripps, R. Hilton and J. Williamson, 'A survey of medieval manorial court rolls in England' in Z. Razi and M. Smith (eds), *Medieval Society and the Manor Court* (Oxford, 1996), 569–637. A number have been printed. I have also looked at a selection of unprinted records: see Bibliography.

to this growing body of work, I have examined the records of the court of (Long) Sutton in Lincolnshire, which survive in an unusually well preserved (though not absolutely complete) run for the fourteenth century.[10] These will be referred to in the following chapters and in Appendix II.

Court sources present problems of uneven survival and discontinuity. The age was one of flux and experimentation in judicial mechanisms, and different bodies, operating at different times, had different jurisdiction and different habits in making and keeping records.[11] It is clear that the roles of the central common law courts, both *inter se* and in relation to other courts, fluctuated over the late thirteenth and fourteenth centuries, and it is far from unusual to see a variety of different courts exercising concurrent jurisdiction over a particular matter.[12] A further problem is posed by the nature of the records. The often terse nature of court records makes it impossible to draw firm conclusions about trends in the number of people convicted of offences against the regulations.[13] As with any system of recording offences, medieval court records are necessarily silent on some of the issues which would be interesting to us. They will never tell us how many people were actually committing offences against the regulations in question, since, obviously, they shed no light on the crimes which were not detected or not reported, nor (generally) on disagreements which went to arbitration rather than court.[14] It is therefore often impossible to make any really satisfactory assessment of the impact which the royal regulations had on subjects' behaviour. Furthermore, statistics, even where they come from what seems to be a good series of records, are, as has recently been noted, 'fundamentally ambiguous: depending on one's position, a peak in the data can be employed either to prove an increase in lawlessness, or, ironically, to demonstrate the greater success of government in bringing its subjects to account for their misdemeanours'.[15] Despite all of the 'health warnings', however, court records can still be good sources of information, as long as they are sensitively handled, and examined in their proper context.

Another set of records which provides some information consists of the reports of arguments on legal points from the royal courts which were collected by common lawyers in the documents known as the Year Books.[16] A number of Year Books have now been printed, in the Rolls Series and by the Selden Society and Ames Foundation, while others are still available only in manuscript.[17] Year Books

---

[10] The rolls run from 1305 to 1306 onwards and have been examined to the end of the fourteenth century. See Bibliogrpahy.

[11] See *EEJ*, 19 and generally; Brown, *Governance*, 116; *EEJ*, 19; Meekings, 'King's Bench files', 97, 99; G.O. Sayles, 'The jurisdiciton of the King's Bench' (1938) 57 SS xxxiv–lxxii (1955) 74 SS xxvi–lxvi; A. Harding, *Law Courts in Medieval England* (London, 1973), 32–123.

[12] Musson, 'New labour', 83–4; B.W. McLane, 'Changes in the Court of King's Bench 1291–1340: the preliminary view from Lincolnshire' in W.M. Ormrod (ed.), *England in the Fourteenth Century* (Woodbridge, 1986), 152–60.

[13] See E. Powell, 'Social research and the use of medieval criminal records', *Michigan Law Review* 79 (1981), 967.

[14] On the problems of gathering quantitative data from medieval court records, see *EEJ*, 76. *MLC*, 16 notes that arbitration was popular at various levels.

[15] *EEJ*, 76.

[16] Baker, *Introduction*, 204–7.

[17] See Baker, 'Why the history of English law has not been finished' at 73–8. As with the rolls of common pleas, I make no claim to have made an exhaustive search of manuscript Year Books. The magnitude of such a task has been noted.

sometimes provide useful detail on the nature of offences or on jurisdiction. Their limitations are that, firstly, because of medieval rules of pleading, often a point which one would like to see discussed is not argued at all, or is not argued through to its conclusion, and, secondly, they only report novel cases or cases of interest to common lawyers, and so are of no use as a guide to the frequency with which particular relevant matters arose.[18]

Opinions

Two major themes from scholarship in areas connected with the substance of subjects' loans and sales require discussion at this point.

1. *Dismissal and revival*

Legal history began in the later twentieth century to move away from its traditional narrow interests, taking in more social history and history of ideas, and modern academic legal studies showed an increasing interest in considerations of fairness and regulatory aspects of 'contract law'.[19] Few twentieth-century legal historians, however, gave the laws concerning usury, price fixing and forestalling and regrating more than a passing mention as curious antiquities.[20] The reason for the dismissal of such matters may be, at least in part, a result of the emphases of legal training. Since 'classical contract law' had few rules on the substance of bargains, the attention of legal historians educated in that tradition or in its shadow has been directed towards formal questions surrounding the enforcement of promises, rather than towards the regulation of the sort of bargains which could be made, and toward 'private law' rather than 'public law', concentrating on the law expounded in the central courts of common law, and regarding legal relations between kings and governments and subjects, and economic aspects of law, as lying outside the scope of legal history.[21] Neglect of the area by legal historians is also a product of the nature of the extant sources, which are much more forthcoming on the subject of formal and procedural rules than on substantive legal rules.

The laws against usury, forestalling and regrating and the price fixing regulations were considered by political and economic historians to some extent in the

---

[18] Baker, *Introduction*, 76–8.

[19] *MLC*, 3; P. Coss (ed.), *The Moral World of the Law* (Cambridge, 2000), 1–3; P.S. Atiyah, *Essays on Contract* (Oxford, 1986), cc.11, 12; H.G. Beale *et al.* (eds) *Chitty on Contracts*, 28th edn (London, 1999), cc.15, 17; J. Beatson, *Anson's Law of Contract*, 28th edn (Oxford, 2002), cc.5–9; P. Birks (ed.), *English Private Law* (Oxford, 2002), 2 vols, vol. 2 c.15.

[20] W.S. Holdsworth is unusual in making any observations about the matters to be considered here: Holdsworth, *HEL*, II, 222, 336, 382, 390; III, 128, 215; IV, 301, 375–8. Legal historians have ignored or dismissed the issue of royal regulation of prices: *P&M* gives it little space; Baker, *Introduction* and Milsom, *HFCL* do not mention the area. Simpson, *Contract*, makes a brief reference to the canonical doctrine of the just price at 446, but has nothing to say about domestic secular law. Palmer, *Black Death*, 18, deals only very briefly with the provisions in the Ordinance of Labourers 1349 concerning control of the price of victuals and other items. The major recent treatment of the law of obligations (which includes the law of contract) pays little regard to regulatory aspects, and states that the law of obligations has 'suffered' a 'tiny amount of legislative intervention': D. Ibbetson, *A Historical Introduction to the Law of Obligations* (Oxford, 1999), 299.

[21] Milsom, *HFCL*; Baker, *Introduction*, cc.18 and 19; Simpson, *Contract*, cc.1–3; M.S. Arnold, 'Fourteenth century promises', *Cambridge Law Journal* 55 (1976), 321; *P&M*, cvi; E. Jenks, *A Short History of English Law from the Earliest Times to the End of the Year 1938*, 3rd edn (London, 1938).

nineteenth century, but then fell out of vogue for much of the twentieth century.[22] In the 1960s, E. Miller wrote that '[t]he nature and the scope of government action in relation to economic affairs are . . . problems of medieval history which still await detailed investigation'.[23] The need for research in the 'border country between economic history and political history' was noted in the 1970s, and in the 1980s; W.L. Warren saw it as an omission which should be remedied.[24] Discussion of royal economic ideas, with the exception of ideas concerning taxation and purveyance, have been few.[25] Discussions of kingship, which might conceivably have mentioned general ideas of the role of the king in the commercial affairs of his subjects, do not generally do so. Some ignore the economic role of kings; others are extremely abstract, discussing the royal role in terms of requirements of 'good lordship' and governance 'with good counsel', with occasional, unhelpfully brief, reference to potentially relevant concepts such as a *'fonction de prospérité'*, or dealing only with particular aspects of kingship, such as the nature of the king's authority, or the relationships between king and nobility, king and church, king and pope, or king and Parliament, or the question of whether the king was above or subject to the law, or on the rules of succession, matters which are not of direct relevance to the royal role in the economic sphere.[26] Economic historians have sometimes deliberately excluded these matters because they are said to involve fairness, rather than commercial policy.[27] In recent years, however, economic historians have again shown an interest in the area, looking particularly at examples of law enforcement at the 'local' level, providing a mass of instances of varying effort and enforcement of the laws, and some consideration of legislation at 'local' (particularly urban) and 'national' levels.[28]

---

[22] W. Ashley, *An Introduction to English Economic History and Theory* (New York, 1888–93, reprinted 1966), cc.3 and 6, discusses the matters under consideration (though almost entirely from the standpoint of canon and civil law rather than royal law). See O. Langholm, *Economics in the Medieval Schools: Wealth, Exchange, Value, Money and Usury according to the Paris Theological Tradition 1200–1350* (Leiden, 1992), 2–5.

[23] E. Miller, 'The economic policies of governments: France and England', *CEH III*, 281, 290.

[24] D.C. Coleman, *What Has Happened to Economic History?* (Cambridge, 1972), 29; Warren, *Governance*, 133. The latter was, however, specifically concerned with an earlier period.

[25] On revenue raising, see, e.g., Prestwich, *The Three Edwards*, c.1; Tuck, *Crown and Nobility*, 25, 34–8, 146, 166, 169–70, 177–8, 201; Warren, *Governance*, 144ff; R.W. Kaeuper, *War, Justice and Public Order: England and France in the Later Middle Ages* (Oxford, 1988), 32–116; Brown, *Governance*, cc.2 and 4; M. Prestwich, *War, Politics and Finance under Edward I* (Aldershot, 1991), cc.7–9; Waugh, *England in the Reign of Edward III*, 184ff. On purveyance, see, e.g., J.R. Maddicott, 'The English peasantry and the demands of the crown 1294–1341', *Past and Present* Supplement 1 (1975); Bolton, *MEE*, 173, 181, 184, 185 192, 298; C. Given-Wilson, 'Purveyance for the royal household 1362–1413', *Historical Research* 56 (1983), 145–63; Ormrod, *Reign of Edward III*, 21, 47, 158.

[26] See, e.g., F. Kern, *Kingship and Law in the Middle Ages*, trans. S. Chrimes (Oxford, 1939); A. Black, *Political Thought in Europe 1250–1450* (Cambridge, 1992), c.5; M. Prestwich, *English Politics in the Thirteenth Century* (Basingstoke, 1990), 3; W.M. Ormrod, *Political Life in Medieval England, 1300–1450* (Basingstoke, 1995), 65; J. Le Goff, 'Le roi dans l'occident médiéval: caractères originaux' in A.J. Duggan (ed.), *Kings and Kingship in Medieval Europe* (London, 1993), 13–14. This might have been a helpful concept for discussions of the royal role in the economic sphere, but its ambit was left vague. Le Goff did not explain the scope of the concept, associating it only with the royal monopoly of minting coin. See, e.g., F.W. Maitland, *The Constitutional History of England* (Cambridge, 1961), 97–105, 195–199; Keen, *England in the Later Middle Ages*, 9; Prestwich, *English Politics*, c.1. Warren, *Governance*, 15ff, is mainly concerned with the authority of kings, but mentions in broad terms their economic role: 21.

[27] W. Cunningham, 'The commercial policy of Edward III', *TRHS*, new ser., 4 (1889), 197, 198.

[28] See in particular the work of R.H. Britnell, particularly: R.H. Britnell, *Growth and Decline in Colchester 1300–1525* (Cambridge, 1986), cc.3, 9, 16; Britnell, 'Forstall'; R.H. Britnell, *The Commercialisation of English Society, 1000–1500* (Manchester, 2nd edn 1996); 'Urban economic regulation and economic morality in

2. *Accentuating the negative*

A general conclusion which might be drawn from reading much of the work which does treat or touch on the laws under consideration would be that they were clumsy, ill-advised and ineffectual, the product of royal government and other authorities laying down rules embodying very high standards of commercial morality which were out of line with contemporary morality, or became so, and which were therefore routinely avoided, evaded and ignored, both by subjects and by agencies of enforcement: to some extent, Blackstone's reaction of 'monkish superstition and civil tyranny' still has support.

The assumption that intervention was foolish and doomed to fail was certainly made in the nineteenth century as was the conclusion (though this may seem to conflict with the assertion of complete lack of effect) that it was damaging, either practically or morally.[29] Some of these themes and assumptions were carried on, with more or less supporting evidence, in works of the twentieth century. The laws have been described as ill conceived, foolish and impractical.[30] Strict regulation of commerce has been described as being 'based on a flagrant misreading of human nature'.[31] Some writers have refused to remain neutral in the face of a lack of information. Raymond de Roover, for example, having admitted that '[t]he history of price regulation remains to be written', still felt able to pronounce that 'we know it to be a tale of woe', that it had been 'haphazard, vexatious, inefficient and arbitrary', and that it 'made matters worse instead of better'.[32] Freedom of contract has been assumed to be an eternal and unchallengeable principle, against which a number of medieval laws offended.[33] It must, however, be remembered that medieval England did not know a general principle of freedom to make bargains. In a world where numerous subjects were still technically 'unfree', one cannot start

---

medieval England', http://www.dur.ac.uk/r.h.britnell/articles/Morality.html (paper at Economic History Society Conference April 2001). See also R.H. Hilton, 'Lords, burgesses and hucksters', *Past and Present* 97 (1982), 3–15; J.M. Bennett, *Women in the Medieval English Countryside: Gender and Household in Brigstock before the Plague* (New York and Oxford, 1987); J.M. Bennett, *Ale, Beer and Brewsters in England: Women's Work in a Changing World 1300–1600* (New York and Oxford, 1996); M. Kowaleski, *Local Markets and Regional Trade in Medieval Exeter* (Cambridge, 1995); J. Davis, 'The Representation, Regulation and Behaviour of Petty Traders in Late Medieval England' (Ph.D., Cambridge, 2001).

[29] For negative views, see: D. Macpherson, *Annals of Commerce*, 4 vols (London and Edinburgh, 1805), I, 557, cited in Miller, 'The economic policies of governments', 281; H.T. Riley, in *LA*, lxii (describing London regulation in a similar area as 'Ordinances of [the] most illiberal and tyrannical complexion'); C. Walford, 'Early laws and customs in Great Britain regarding food', *TRHS*, new ser., 8 (1880), 70, 71; H.R. Fox Bourne, *English Merchants: Memoirs in Illustration of the Progress of British Commerce*, 2 vols (1886, reprinted New York, 1969), 16, 20. On the argument that usury laws were morally wrong, see Lord Brougham, *Hansard* vol. 135 c.583, 24 July 1854.

[30] Pounds, *Economic History*, 431, 436; A.R. Bridbury, 'Markets and freedom in the Middle Ages' in B.L. Anderson and A.J.A. Latham (eds), *The Market in History* (London, 1986), 84, 88, 91; Langholm, *Economics*, 38–9, 64–5; E. Lipson, *The Economic History of England*, 7th edn (London, 1937), 616, 618; H.G. Richardson and G.O. Sayles, *Law and Legislation from Aethelberht to Magna Carta* (Edinburgh, 1966), 85; Baker, *Introduction*, 353; R. Zimmerman, *The Law of Obligations: Roman Foundations of the Civilian Tradition* (Cape Town, 1990), 163; H.G. Richardson, *The English Jewry under Angevin Kings* (London, 1960), 139; A. Steel, *The Receipt of the Exchequer, 1377–1485* (Cambridge, 1954), 121; R.H. Bowers, 'A Middle English Mnemonic Poem on Usury', *Medieval Studies* 17 (1955), 226; F.C. Dietz, *An Economic History of England* (New York, 1942), 71; Gilchrist, *CEA*, 87; A.I. Ogus, 'Regulatory law: some lessons from the past', *Legal Studies* 12 (1992), 1–19, 6–7.

[31] Bridbury, 'Markets and freedom', 63, 87.

[32] de Roover, *JP*, 429–30.

[33] Zimmerman, *Law of Obligations*, 163, describing the prohibition on usury as a 'restraint on contractual freedom'.

an analysis of legal control of commercial bargains with the assumption that freedom to contract on whatever terms one desires, leaving matters of the terms of bargains to 'market forces' is the norm, and control of bargains a derogation from this norm which must be justified.[34]

There are now signs of a welcome reconsideration of some of the views of the past as to medieval economic regulation in theory and practice. A balanced view of the nature of canon law and theological pronouncements on the terms of bargains seems to be emerging, and some authors are prepared to look at economic regulation by medieval governments in a more sympathetic way than was previously the norm.[35]

It should not be *assumed* that the laws *must have been* useless or damaging, but evidence that they were *in fact* a failure must be considered. It cannot be denied that there is some such evidence, and it will be considered in the chapters which follow. In this general discussion, however, it is necessary to give an outline of aspects of opinions of previous writers which will be discussed below, and some of the general questions to which they give rise.

Economic legislation of the late medieval period has been singled out as being 'loosely drafted and of uncertain purpose, [enabling] juries to bring poorly founded charges against individuals or groups held responsible for raising prices'.[36] It has been argued that these laws were clearly ineffectual because there is evidence that some people evaded them.[37] The criticisms are based in truth: no doubt the drafting of regulations and their enforcement were imperfect, but it seems unjust to single out the economic regulations for particular attention when the same criticisms could be made in respect of many other areas of medieval English law. Other laws were badly or imprecisely drafted.[38] 'The nature of offences was often very ill-defined in medieval English law.'[39] General or unspecific charges were brought in relation to other laws: charges of being a 'common thief' or a 'common harlot' were as prevalent and as vague as some of the imprecise accusations relating to the substance of bargains.[40]

Another part of the case against economic regulations having been effective has always been the repetition of such measures.[41] It is, however, wrong to assume that a local – or even a national – measure which looks like legislation carried with it all the theory of a modern statute, in particular with regard to permanence. If a measure is repeated, it may be because it has been ineffective, but it may be because it was not regarded as a perpetual edict in the first place. It should also be noted that, on careful inspection, many instances of 'repetition' actually turn out to be

[34] See, e.g., Ashley, *Introduction*, 381; E.S. Hunt and J.M. Murray, *A History of Business in Medieval Europe 1200–1550* (Cambridge, 1999), 23, 248; M. Bailey, 'The commercialisation of the English economy', 297; K. Polanyi, C.M. Arensberg and H.W. Pearson (eds), *Trade and Markets in the Early Empires: Economics in History and Theory* (Glencoe, 1957), 357, 358; Britnell, *Commercialisation*, xv.

[35] Hunt and Murray, *History of Business*, 242, 247.

[36] Britnell, *Commercialisation*, 174.

[37] M.M. Postan, *The Medieval Economy and Society* (London, 1972), 255; Gilchrist, *CEA*, 87; Ogus, 'Regulatory law', 1; de Roover, *JP*, 429–30; Ross, 'Assize', 332; Bolton, *MEE*, 329.

[38] See, e.g., Baker, *Introduction*, 280–3, on the statute *De Donis* 1285.

[39] Baker, *Introduction*, 594–608.

[40] Baker, *Introduction*, 506; W. Hudson (ed.), *Leet Jurisdiction in the City of Norwich during the Thirteenth and Fourteenth Centuries*, Selden Society vol. 5 for 1891 (London, 1892), 59.

[41] See, e.g., Dyer, *Standards of Living*, 195.

refinements of previously existing law.[42] If a measure is refined to cover new variations on offending behaviour, this could be taken as a sign of ineffectiveness of the initial ordinance, or else as a sign that the original ordinance was successful enough to make people change their practices. Repetition and refinement certainly show some consensus that it is worth bothering – an opinion to which some credence ought to be given.

More generally, a conclusion of failure tends to be based on a combination of instances of breaches of the laws or failure to enforce them to the hilt, and instances of contemporary complaint. Both elements may be challenged, either by producing counter-examples of obedience or satisfaction, or by altering our perspective and viewing a roll of offenders as being as much an indication of the laws working as of them failing, or by questioning the very content of the concept of 'success' in the context of medieval laws. The laws were certainly evaded at times. This should not, however, be surprising. Other laws were evaded and the existence of a gap between prescription and enforcement in medieval law is an accepted fact.[43] Evidence of complaint is equivocal, perhaps saying as much about the concerns and priorities of the complainer as about the actual level of offending behaviour.[44]

One ought also to bear in mind that we may not have the same idea of 'success' of laws as that prevalent in medieval England. Law enforcement might not be seen 'solely in terms of arrests and convictions [under royal law, by "central" agencies]': preventive aspects of law, other forums, other punishments and community exclusion were also important.[45] We should not be too surprised to find a lack of conventional 'success' with regard to enforcement of any medieval regulation, given the general lawlessness which has been said to have prevailed.[46] It is all too easy to set up an opposition between a harsh, absolute law and law-in-practice, calling the law a failure if any breaches or failures to enforce are found. If this is done in relation to only one aspect of law, it has a distorting effect, presenting the aspect being studied as peculiarly inefficient, when, in fact, it may not have been any less effective than the legal system in general.

Connected with this lack of appreciation of the nature of medieval law enforcement is the prevalence of the suggestion that the offences were subject to a licensing procedure rather than being prosecuted vigorously, and that this proves that these laws in particular were not taken seriously by the king and government or by others charged with their enforcement.[47] This view will be considered with reference to the evidence examined, but general arguments against it may also be made here. First, the assumption of a complete opposition between a

---

[42] This point has been made in relation to labour laws: C. Given-Wilson, 'The problem of labour in the context of English government c.1350–1450' in J. Bothwell, P.J.P. Goldberg and W.M. Ormrod (eds), *The Problem of Labour in Fourteenth-Century England* (York, 2000), 85–101, at 86.

[43] Tout, *Edward II*, 138. See Britnell, 'Morals', 29.

[44] R. Horrox, 'Local and national politics in fifteenth century England', *Journal of Medieval History* 18 (1992), 391–403, at 391.

[45] H.R.T. Summerson, 'The structure of law enforcement in thirteenth-century England', *American Journal of Legal History* 23 (1979), 313–27, at 313, 327. Summerson does, however, note the breaking down of community exclusion as a meaningful punishment under Edward I and Edward II, because of population growth and the presence of too many strangers in vills to make it effective: 327.

[46] Harding, *Law Courts*, 95.

[47] See below, chapters 3 and 4.

scheme of licensing and proper prosecution of offenders may be challenged. 'Revenue raising' was part of the motivation for enforcement of all sorts of laws in medieval England, not simply or peculiarly those under consideration here.[48] A very direct link between revenue and judicial income was made under the mid-fourteenth-century labour legislation, with money raised from offending labourers and vendors going in aid of taxation. This was not seen as inappropriate.[49] Modern distaste at such a practice should not be allowed to lead to too great a concentration on it, or an assumption that it must have been exceptional.

Also, one cannot expect medieval enactments to have been enforced to the hilt given the low level of policing in existence and, in medieval English law enforcement, there was nothing unusual about exacting money payments rather than the penalty originally stipulated for an offence, or licensing breaches of what seemed to be a total ban on particular practices.[50] J. Hudson gives a good example from the late twelfth century of the varying use of a commercial regulation – the Assize of Measures – which could be treated and enforced seriously, but could also, at times, be used as the occasion for revenue raising.[51] The two things were not mutually exclusive. To give a few examples from the later thirteenth and fourteenth centuries, the Statute of Mortmain 1279 (which provided that there should be no more alienations of land to religious corporations) was subject to a licensing regime very soon after its promulgation, pardons were issued to those who committed serious felonies, and it was possible, if rare, to buy off an entire eyre.[52] Compromise was endemic in medieval law-enforcement. Edward I called off eyres and other inquiries for political advantage.[53] Individuals could compromise fairly serious 'criminal' cases.[54] Even the church was prepared to countenance departures from important canonical rules such as the prohibited degrees of relationship for marriage.[55] The existence of some degree of licensing of offenders would not, therefore, necessarily mean that the rules against usury, forestalling and regrating and excessive prices were taken less seriously than other rules.

Deciding whether laws have been successful or have failed is difficult at any time, and making such a judgment on the laws of the past is almost impossible. Apart from possible doubt as to what it would have meant to 'succeed' or 'fail', there is so much else which is unknowable. Evidence of obedience and satisfaction is hard to come by. Evidence of the terms of everyday bargains is very rare and what documentary evidence there is is open to allegations that it hides the true terms of

[48] Putnam, *Enforcement*, 98; F.W. Maitland, *Domesday Book and Beyond: Three Essays in the Early History of England* (Cambridge, 1897), 277–8; B.H. Putnam, 'Chief Justice Shareshull and the economic and legal codes of 1351–1352', *University of Toronto Law Journal* [1943–4], 251–81, at 263.

[49] Putnam, *Enforcement*, 99–101; Ormrod, *Reign of Edward III*, 79; Waugh, *England in the Reign of Edward III*, 110.

[50] A.R. Bridbury, 'Thirteenth century prices and the money supply', in A.R. Bridbury, *The English Economy from Bede to the Reformation* (Woodbridge, 1992), 260. He describes medieval society as having been 'in large measure self regulating'.

[51] Hudson, *Formation*, 135.

[52] P.A. Brand, 'The control of mortmain alienation in England 1200–1300', in J.H. Baker (ed.), *Legal Records and the Historian* (Cambridge, 1978), 29, especially 37–40; Baker, *Introduction*, 277, 523–5, 529–30; Ormrod, *Reign of Edward III*, 55; *EEJ*, 81.

[53] Ormrod, *Political Life*, 125.

[54] See, e.g., a stabbing case in London in 1298: *CEMCR*, 11.

[55] Dispensations can be seen in abundance in W.H. Bliss (ed.), *Calendar of Entries in the Papal Registers Relating to Great Britain and Ireland*, vol. I (London, 1893).

bargains.[56] All of this renders pronouncements on success extremely questionable. More fundamentally, there is a real difficulty in judging success in relation to laws when one cannot know what would have happened, had they not been enacted. Generally, a 'control' is not available for comparison. One possibility is to look to other jurisdictions with different levels of legal intervention, but this raises problems as to whether different factors in addition to the legal variation may not have been operating.[57] In the light of these difficulties, this book will not be seeking to come to a grand judgment on the overall effectiveness of the laws being considered, but will comment on what can be known about the setting and enforcement of laws, and the reasons for royal intervention.

The reasons for intervention

An overall question of the book is: why did kings and governments involve themselves in subjects' loans and sales in the ways that they did: why bother with Robert le Poleter?

The primary focus is on the reasons for intervention of kings *and governments*, so some justification for going beyond the monarchs and some explanation of who is meant to be included in discussions of 'governments' are required. It would be extremely artificial to impute to the monarch himself the origination and working out of the detail of regulations and their enforcement, particularly given the fact that between 1272 and 1399 there were a number of periods during which monarchs were absent, minor or not in effective control of the country. Furthermore, one cannot identify statutes or ordinances as the personal will of the king, expressed in his terms.[58] The group whose activity is to be examined must, therefore, be widened.[59] 'The government' will be taken to mean the king's advisers for the time being. Royal justices and 'the legal establishment' (lawyers in royal courts) will not be taken as necessarily falling within 'the government', since, despite the fact that some lawyers and judges were involved in administration and legislation in association with the government, there was no necessary identity of personnel or of purpose. In the case of the courts of common law, there is a problem, or an oversimplification in identifying them and their jurisprudence with royal interests, as it could be argued that there is a gap between the royal will and the common law. The position was ill-defined in medieval England. As one legal historian has noted, 'The common law courts are the king's courts, the justices are the king's justices, although the common law is not the king's law.'[60] Ambiguity concerning the relationship between common law and statute – and thus between

---

[56] Rigby, *English Society*, 151.

[57] Note the innovative work in relation to wage legislation and its effect, using a comparison between regulated England and unregulated parts of the Low Countries, by J.H. Munro: Munro, 'Wage-stickiness'.

[58] G. Unwin, *Finance and Trade under Edward III* (Manchester, 1918), xviii.

[59] The term 'governments' is convenient, though it was not used in medieval England to denote particular ministers or officials. On the difficulty of defining medieval governmental bodies, see Ormrod, *Political Life*, 18–30. G. Barraclough, 'Law and legislation in medieval England', *Law Quarterly Review* 56 (1940), 75, 79, cautions against 'too early and too abrupt a differentiation of the judiciary and the legislature'. I will not generally be differentiating between the king in his role as *dominus*, or feudal suzerain, the personal *princeps* or *rex* role and the impersonal crown role, since such distinctions are not made in the documents consulted. For such distinctions in use, see, e.g., Harriss, *King, Parliament and Public Finance*, 17, 45.

[60] Barraclough, 'Law and legislation', 86.

'judicial' and 'executive' 'branches of government' – persisted into the fourteenth century.[61]

An examination of reasons for intervention could operate at a number of different levels. One might look at the immediate political and economic motivations for a particular measure, and much careful work has been done on some of the measures which will be discussed here. This is not, however, the approach to be adopted by this book, which will instead be attempting to create a broader picture of royal involvement.

An understanding of the immediate spur for the passing of a particular law is, of course, important, but there is a danger of ignoring deeper patterns if we think of laws having just one 'cause'. Playing down the immediate political or economic circumstances avoids the risk of too ready, exclusive, attribution of causation to short-term external factors, political or economic, and facilitates the investigation of deeper, underlying perceptions of the royal role in medieval England.[62] As has been pointed out in relation to the legislation on wages of the post-Black Death period, even when a measure has as an important cause a particular economic crisis, it is apt to take on a 'life of its own' and become accepted as a part of royal activity even when that cause no longer persists.[63] Royal activity in particular instances may have been 'reactive', but it was a reaction within some sort of framework rather than a random response.[64] It is the framework, the idea of the royal role, which is of concern here.

The obvious way of beginning to examine the issue of why kings and governments involved themselves in regulating subjects' commercial bargains would seem to be by looking at what they said about their role in general and their reasons for intervention in this area in particular. There are some comments in legislation about reasons for acting in a particular instance, and these will be considered in the individual subject-specific chapters, but not a great deal of information can be gleaned from them, as they are brief and rare. Explicit justifications of their more general actions or policy by kings and governments were also rare, as were analyses by others of the royal role in subjects' lives, and even English legal theorists did not have explicit, worked out theories of crown, state or royal powers and duties before the fifteenth century.[65]

---

[61] Plucknett, *Statutes*, 70–1.

[62] 'The desire to discover economic causes is to some degree a craze with us, and sometimes leads us to forget a much simpler psychological explanation of the facts': J. Huizinga, trans. F. Hopman, *The Waning of the Middle Ages* (London, 1924, reprinted 2001), 20.

[63] Musson, 'New labour', 88, makes the point that 'another thirty pieces of legislation were drafted, issued or adopted as law in the century after . . . 1349' but that 'While these initiatives were obviously influenced to an extent by successive outbreaks of plague occurring (for instance) in the years 1361–2, 1368–9, 1371, 1375, the numerous statutes show how the desire to legislate nationally on economic and labour-related issues had gained impetus during the late fourteenth and early fifteenth centuries.'

[64] See *EEJ*, 91.

[65] J.E.A. Jolliffe, *Angevin Kingship* (London, 1955), 16; Brown, *Governance*, 5; *P&M*, I, 209; *MLC*, 218–19; McKisack, *Fourteenth Century*, 7. N. Doe, *Fundamental Authority in Late Medieval England* (Cambridge, 1990), 3, notes the lack of theoretical writing about secular law (and particularly issues of authority) before the fifteenth-century works of Fortescue and Pecock. E. Powell, *Kingship, Law and Society: Criminal Justice in the Reign of Henry V* (Oxford, 1989), c.1 on concepts of justice and kingship in the age of Henry V, is obliged to turn to the considerably later Fortescue to make comments on kingship ideas of the early fifteenth century. On the lack of consideration of, or conclusions on, the limits of the royal role, see A. Musson, *Public Order and Law Enforcement: The Local Administration of Criminal Justice 1290–1350* (Woodbridge, 1996), 226.

Some very broad pronouncements as to the duties of a king can be found in coronation oaths, legal treatises and treatises on kingship.[66] Examples are the king's duty to do justice, which is always included in coronation oaths of the period; *Fleta*'s suggestion that 'Kingly power should be equipped . . . with laws for the meet governance of his peaceful subjects and peoples'; Edward III's 1330 statement that he would govern his people 'according to right and reason'; and the idea of serving the common profit or common good.[67] These duties are so broad as to be capable of justifying diametrically opposed action by kings, and do not take us very much further forward, raising, as they do, further questions as to when kings were supposed to make laws, and what was meant by 'doing justice': was this a question of the active promotion of fairness (whatever that might mean) or simply of remaining neutral rather than being biased? Elements of both 'active' and 'passive' duties with regard to justice can be found in contemporary or later medieval sources.[68]

More useful are the 'lower level', or more specific, justifications for action in this area which have been suggested either in contemporary sources or in the interpretations of historians. These are desires to establish or preserve public order, to suppress vice or immoral conduct, to ensure economic well-being for subjects and the realm, to protect the poor, to increase revenue and to increase or maintain political power.[69] In each case, action might have been calculated either to improve matters or else to prevent them from deteriorating.

A royal duty to keep public order is indisputable, and was clearly accepted as a force properly motivating royal action.[70] Most obviously connected with royal intervention against violent conduct, it is less likely to have been a motivating force behind action concerning subjects' bargains, though it might have played a part in situations where unscrupulous lenders or sellers took advantage of a shortage and caused particular resentment amongst the people.

A royal desire or perceived duty to suppress vice or immoral conduct may have arisen either from the church and its teachings, or from 'secular' ideas of morality. Medieval English kings were keen to express conventional piety and orthodoxy, and may have seen it as part of their role to act as 'the executive arm of the church's

---

[66] H.G. Richardson, 'The English coronation oath', *Speculum* 24 (1949), 44; R.S. Hoyt, 'The coronation oath of 1308', *Traditio* 11 (1955), 255; Powicke, *Thirteenth Century*, 7; Brown, *Governance*, 17; Ormrod, *Political Life*, c.4.

[67] *Glanvill*, prologue; *Bracton*, Introduction (vol. II, p. 19), *quae sunt regi necessaria. Bracton* f.107 mentions mercy as well as justice. The meaning of 'justice' is ambiguous. Generally, however, the duty to do justice seems to imply a rather static or negative concept of abstaining from partiality rather than a dynamic concept of ensuring distributive or commutative justice: Doe, *Fundamental Authority*, 84–92. Justice as giving to each his due: *Bracton*, Introduction (vol. II, p. 23) *Quid sit iustitia; Fleta II*, 1, Prologue. This follows the prologue to *Glanvill*, and its Roman roots, very closely. Waugh, *England in the Reign of Edward III*, 5. (Common profit or common good); Doe, *Fundamental Authority*, 47.

[68] See *MLC*, 164, 218–23; Black, *Political Thought 1250–1450*, 24, 47; G.R. Evans, *Law and Theology in the Middle Ages* (London, 2002), 12. For active conceptions of the royal role with relation to justice, see, e.g., the 1284 Statutes of Wales, 'all those which are subject unto our power should be governed with due order, to the honour and praise of God and of Holy Church, and the advancement of justice': Heath, *Church and Realm*, 22 (*SR* I:55).

[69] Clearly, there is a potential connection between protection or promotion of the interests of the poor and preservation of public order. It is, however, possible to see a separate factor of protecting the poor on grounds of charity, rather than as a method of preserving the peace.

[70] Baker, *Introduction*, 9, 14. The concept of 'peace' could be extensive, see *P&M*, I, 44–6; II, 463–4.

teaching on morals and religion'.[71] Kings were clearly regarded as deriving their authority, wholly or partly, from God.[72] The view that, as well as legitimating royal authority, the role of the king as Vicar of God required action to suppress vice was put forward in literary and legal sources of the twelfth and thirteenth centuries. The 'Laws of Edward the Confessor' described the king as 'the vicar of the highest king' and stated that he had a duty to 'destroy and eradicate evildoers'.[73] According to the *Song of Lewes* (1264), one of the king's duties was to 'work for the salvation of the realm'.[74] This implies a duty to act against vicious conduct. *Bracton* linked law to the enforcement of virtue and avoidance of vice.[75] *Fleta* also laid upon kings a duty to suppress vice and promote virtue.[76] An anonymous tract from the late fourteenth century or early fifteenth century, *Tractatus de regibus*, held that a king ought to enforce God's law so that his realm would be 'purgid by tho lawe of God'.[77] A royal function of the 'advancement of virtue' has been identified in the fifteenth-century treatises of Pecock and Fortescue.[78] A connected, though less dynamic, idea was that expressed in coronation oaths, of upholding the rights of the church, which might include upholding its law, or at least its right to intervene in particular areas of subjects' conduct.[79]

Of particular relevance to this book, it has been argued that kings and governments followed the ideas of 'the scholastics' in some economic matters.[80] The idea that there was a clear link between 'ecclesiastical doctrines as to usury and prices' and royal action in prohibiting usury, forestalling and regrating and in regulating prices has been favoured by some historians.[81] W.M. Ormrod considered that it was an 'inevitable result' of the teachings of the canonists and theologians on 'what was sinful and what was not in the economic sphere' that kings and governments should 'attempt . . . to correct particular evils'.[82] R.H. Britnell also emphasises the links between urban economic regulations and 'medieval philosophy and canon law'.[83]

---

[71] See, e.g., Ormrod, *Reign of Edward III*, 44; Black, *Political Thought*, 27.

[72] Brown, *Governance*, 5. See also the anonymous thirteenth-century tract 'What should be the office of a king', in B. Wilkinson, *Constitutional History of Medieval England 1216–1399 with Select Documents*, 3 vols (London, 1948–58), III, 100–1.

[73] O'Brien, *God's Peace*, 174–5, c.17.

[74] *Song of Lewes*, T. Wright (ed.), *The Political Songs of England* (London, 1839), 72, cited in M. Prestwich, *English Politics in the Thirteenth Century*, 12.

[75] *Bracton*, Introduction (vol. II, p. 25) cited by Doe, *Fundamental Authority*, 49, with civilian precedents: W. Ullman, 'Baldus' conception of law', *Law Quarterly Review* 58 (1942), 386.

[76] The author wrote with approbation that, in the days of Edward I, 'the passions of vice are rooted out, the springs of virtue everywhere burst forth': *Fleta II*, Prologue. This passage draws upon the prologue of the late twelfth-century treatise *Glanvill*, which, in turn has roots in the Roman law of the reign of Justinian: J. Dunbabin, 'Government' in J.H. Burns (ed.), *The Cambridge History of Political Thought c.350–c.1450* (Cambridge, 1988), 477, 486.

[77] *Tractatus de regibus* in J.P. Genet (ed.), *Four English Political Tracts of the Later Middle Ages*, Camden Society, 4th ser., 18 (1977), 9.

[78] Doe, *Fundamental Authority*, 47.

[79] Powicke, *Thirteenth Century*, 7; see also S. Walker, 'Richard II's views on kingship' in R.E. Archer and S. Walker (eds), *Rulers and Ruled in Late Medieval England: Essays presented to Gerald Harriss* (London, 1995), 49, 51.

[80] Harriss, *King, Parliament and Public Finance*, 60.

[81] Ashley, *Introduction*, 385; Tawney, *Religion and the Rise of Capitalism*, 49; Evans, *Law and Theology*, preface.

[82] W.M. Ormrod, 'The crown and the English economy 1290–1348', in Campbell, *Before the Black Death*, 140, 147.

[83] Britnell, 'Price-setting', 15.

Alternatively, medieval kings and governments might have been attempting to put into practice a commercial morality not wholly dependent upon the teachings of the church and canon lawyers. It would, of course, be ahistorical to argue for wholly 'secular' in the sense of 'humanist' morality in medieval England, but it is possible that moral ideas not springing directly from the church may have been influential.[84] A. Harding referred to 'general ideas of commercial morality' as being present in a late thirteenth-century court leet.[85] Perhaps similar ideas can be identified at a higher level, informing the actions of kings and governments in intervening in the substance of subjects' bargains.

It may also be plausible to argue that kings and governments intervened pursuant to a perceived duty to ensure economic well-being for subjects and the realm, acting against bargains which caused economic damage to subjects, in terms, for example, either of a reduction in the supply of goods or of a rise in prices. A problem with attempting to discern 'economic' policies or motivations of medieval governments is that they never described what they were doing in terms of 'economics'.[86] Some commentators have accepted that kings and governments did pursue certain apparently relevant economic objectives, such as a 'policy of plenty', or '[the promotion of] economic well-being', though more ambitious and specific claims of a consistent economic strategy such as 'mercantilism' seem improbable.[87] The idea that medieval kings and governments might perceive themselves to have a role in the area now regarded as the province of economics is, however, rather different to the claim that they had specific economic theories: it amounts simply to saying that they perceived, and took it as their duty to act against, harm to their subjects which we would call economic damage.

Royal action may have been prompted by a desire to protect the poor, on grounds of charity.[88] Kings certainly made *ex gratia* payments to the poor.[89] A less discretionary *duty* to act in the interests of the poor was ascribed to the king in a number of medieval texts, such as the twelfth-century *Leges Henrici Primi* and the late thirteenth-century treatise *Mirror of Justices*.[90] A special link between the poor and the king was suggested by the disgruntled 'peasants' in their appeals to Richard II in 1381.[91] Modern historians have also seen such a

---

[84] For such a concept, see S. Reynolds, *Kingdoms and Communities in Western Europe 900–1300*, 2nd edn (Oxford, 1997), lv.

[85] Harding, *England in the Thirteenth Century*, 135, discussing the Norwich court leet.

[86] Gilchrist, *CEA*, 4. See also Wood, *Medieval Economic Thought*, 1; Langholm, *Economics*, 1, 22–4; A.S. McGrade and J. Kilcullen (eds), *William of Ockham: A Letter to the Friars Minor and Other Writings* (Cambridge, 1995), 136.

[87] Pounds, *Economic History*, 435–7; Prestwich, *The Three Edwards*, 234; H. Pirenne, trans. I.E. Clegg, *Economic and Social History of Medieval Europe*, 6th edn (London, 1958), 220, 92.

[88] On charity, see, e.g., Rubin, *Charity*, c.3.

[89] See, e.g., W.L. Warren, *King John*, 2nd edn (Yale, 1997), 141; Prestwich, *Edward I*, 4, 112–13, 161–2; Dyer, *Standards of Living*, 248.

[90] The role of the king as 'kinsman and protector to all . . . strangers, poor people and those who have been cast out, if they have no one else at all to take care of them': L.J. Downer (ed.), *Leges Henrici Primi* (Oxford, 1972), 108–9. The *Mirror* in its fictitious 'original constitutions', supposedly laid down by Alfred the Great, noted that it had been ordained 'that the poor should be sustained by parsons, rectors of the church and parishioners', thus suggesting that the king had some sort of duty to ensure the well-being of his poorest subjects, at least by ordering others to do something for them: *Mirror*, 14. For comment on the fictitious use of Anglo-Saxon 'laws' see Seipp, 'The Mirror of Justices', 104–112.

[91] C. Dyer, 'The economy and society' in N. Saul (ed.), *The Oxford Illustrated History of Medieval England* (Oxford, 1997), 140, 185.

duty.[92] This duty to protect the poor might lead English kings and governments to intervene in subjects' bargains where those bargains were to the detriment of the poor, who would, characteristically, be borrowers and consumers, and might give another reason for them to become involved in this area. The picture is somewhat complicated by the fact that the moral status of the poor and of poverty were fiercely debated in medieval Europe.[93] It should also be noted that action to help the poor might be based on fears that if the poor were treated too badly, they would pose a threat to public order.[94]

Finally, kings and governments may have taken action on the substance of subjects' bargains based on pragmatic self-interest, wishing to increase their own revenue and political power. They might have acted from financial self-interest, either seeking to prevent conduct which damaged royal financial interests, or else seeking to profit from the imposition of penalties for offences.[95] They might have been motivated by a desire to increase or bolster their political power, acceding to the requests of powerful groups in return for their political support, or to appease those in the lower orders who might otherwise rebel.[96]

That self-interest or sectional interest played some part in this area as in all areas of royal activity is completely uncontroversial. Participation in the formation of policy and law was limited to a small section of better-off male subjects, and it would be surprising if those involved in government did not take some account of their own interests when making decisions. Moral/religious and altruistic arguments should not, however, simply be dismissed out of hand as being a hypocritical subterfuge for action calculated to fill royal coffers.[97]

The possible factors prompting royal action are not mutually exclusive: it would be somewhat naive to assume that we can speak of motivation for legal action in simple, one-dimensional terms. The attempt to find a single 'reason' or 'motive' for any action is, of course, open to challenge.[98] The real task is to identify the combination of factors which played a prominent role.

It should be noted that, although its major concern is with the royal role in this area, this book will mention action not only by 'the centre' but also by other authorities, whose own reasons for action may have been somewhat different to those of the king and government. Prominent amongst reasons suggested for

---

[92] A. Black, discussing Western European rather than specifically English political theory, noted that '[i]t was commonly said that rulers [had] a special duty to care for those in need . . .': Black, *Political Thought*, 27. G.L. Harriss saw a 'consistent regard to spare the poor' in medieval taxation: Harriss, *King, Parliament and Public Finance*, 61.

[93] *MLC*, 170; Wood, *Medieval Economic Thought*, 45, 61.

[94] Bridbury, 'Markets and freedom', 82.

[95] Harriss, *King, Parliament and Public Finance*, 404–5, suggests the latter as a motivation for some royal drives for enforcement of the regulations under consideration in the late 1340s and 1350s. E. Miller saw the increased role of governments in 'economic affairs' in and after the thirteenth century as having been driven by a desire to increase royal revenue: E. Miller, *CEH III*, 306. J.L. Bolton also assumed that medieval governments were motivated by self-interest in this area: 'There [is not] much evidence that when [the government] did intervene, it was motivated by anything other than self interest': Bolton, *MEE*, 329.

[96] Dyer, *Standards of Living in the Later Middle Ages*, 251; R.H. Hilton, 'Lords, burgesses and hucksters', *Past and Present* 97 (1982), 3, 8; Harriss, *King, Parliament and Public Finance*, 73.

[97] It is, as C. Dyer has noted in a different context, often inappropriate to ridicule or dismiss as hypocritical, pointless and unworthy of discussion the ideals and principles expressed in historical documents: Dyer, *Standards of Living*, 89.

[98] Compare the view on causation in *EEJ*, 6–7.

urban action are varying proportions of protection of consumers, poor and not so poor, public order and protection of the interests of 'insiders' at the expense of 'outsiders'.[99] Recent work has frequently suggested that measures which came to be enacted or accepted as royal, national statutes or laws, often had an origin either in 'local' (particularly urban) models, or else that they were generalised from measures connected to the verge and the royal household.[100] Clearly, this is an important observation, but it does not detract from the importance of such measures as part of 'royal intervention in subjects' bargains'. In each case, positive royal action was required to adopt the measure as a general one, and reasons for doing this may well not have been the same as those for the original, limited measures.

---

[99] A.B. Hibbert, 'The economic policies of towns', *CEH III*, c.4; Dyer, *Standards of Living*, 195, 199; Britnell, 'Price setting', especially 11–14. See, e.g., Britnell, 'Morals'; Britnell, *Colchester*, 35, 37, 80; C. Gross, *The Gild Merchant*, 2 vols (Oxford, 1890), 184–5, 228, 291. In some urban areas, a simple model of 'the insiders' making rules in their own favour against 'outsiders' and others in the area does not suffice, as there were disputes between different interest groups within the rule-making 'oligarchy', as was clearly the case in London in the 1380s: L.C. Hector and B.F. Harvey (eds), *The Westminster Chronicle 1381–94* (Oxford, 1982), 58–63.

[100] R.H. Britnell's picture of regulation of food trades (in all aspects, including quality, not simply price controls) is of original 'local' regulation, with later royal intervention: Britnell, *Commercialisation*, 25–7. Britnell, 'Forstall', shows royal regulation moving into an area already occupied to some extent by local regulation which differed from it in some respects. In the context of labour laws, similar observations were made long ago by B.H. Putnam (*Enforcement*, 156), and have recently been expanded on by A.J. Musson in his important article, 'New labour', at 75.

Part I: Loans

The loan is one of the basic transactions in any society which does not exist entirely on a self-sufficiency basis. Medieval England was increasingly 'commercialised', and we can thus assume that loans formed part of everyday life for many medieval Englishmen and women, as well as in government, merchandise and the great industries.[1] Lending went on at almost all levels of society.[2] Evidence as to actual credit transactions is, however, patchy. Although there is a 'wealth of material on credit and indebtedness', and a growing body of scholarship on credit-debt relationships, it is naturally skewed towards formal debt and what was recorded of it, leaving out many lower level and informal transactions, and often leaving historians uncertain as to the actual terms of a loan.[3]

Royal intervention in subjects' loans increased over the thirteenth and fourteenth centuries. Methods of using royal mechanisms to enforce one's loans had existed since well before the reign of Edward I, in the form of recognizances.[4] In the thirteenth and fourteenth centuries, these were joined by new methods: the statute merchant and statute staple.[5] The law relating to debt was also developing in terms of rules as to jurisdiction, creation of enforceable debts, defences, forms of security, transmissibility of benefit and liability of debts, arguably moving in favour of creditors.[6]

---

[1] See, e.g., P.R. Schofield, 'Introduction' in P.R. Schofield and N.J. Mayhew (eds), *Credit and Debt in Medieval England* (Oxford, 2002), 1–18, at 2–3; P. Nightingale, 'Monetary contraction and mercantile credit in later medieval England', *EcHR*, 2nd ser., 43 (1990), 560–75.

[2] Schofield, 'Introduction', 9, citing J.A. Raftis, *Peasant Economic Development within the English Manorial System* (Stroud, 1997).

[3] Schofield, 'Introduction', 3. See, e.g., M.M. Postan, 'Credit in medieval trade' in Postan, *Medieval trade and finance*, 3–4; E. Clark, 'Debt litigation in a late medieval English vill' in J.A. Raftis (ed.), *Pathways to Medieval Peasants* (Toronto, 1981); S.J. O'Connor (ed.), *Calendar of the Cartularies of John Pyel and Adam Fraunceys*, Camden Society, fifth series, vol. 2 (Oxford, 1993); C Muldrew, *The Economy of Obligation* (Basingstoke, 1998); R.R. Mundill, 'Christian and Jewish moneylending patterns and financial dealings during the twelfth and thirteenth centuries' in Schofield and Mayhew, *Credit and Debt*, 42–67; P.R. Schofield, 'Access to credit in the early fourteenth century English countryside' in *ibid.*, 106–26; P. Nightingale, 'The English parochial clergy as investors and creditors in the first half of the fourteenth century' in *ibid.*, 89–105; C. Briggs, 'Creditors and debtors and their relations at Oakington, Cottenham and Dry Drayton (Cambridgeshire) 1291–1350', in *ibid.*, 127–48.

[4] *P&M*, II, 203.

[5] See C. McNall, 'The business of statutory debt registries 1283–1307' in Schofield and Mayhew (eds), *Credit and Debt*, 68–88; C. McNall, 'The Recognition and Enforcement of Debts under the Statutes of Acton Burnel (1283) and Merchants (1285) 1283–1307' (D. Phil., Oxford, 2000).

[6] See, e.g., P. Brand, 'Aspects of the law of debt 1189–1307' in Schofield and Mayhew, *Credit and Debt*, 19–41; Palmer, *Black Death*, 59–76.

2

The Prohibition of Usury

Three rolls of the eyre of Worcestershire 1275 note presentments by the hundred of Oswaldslow concerning a dead man, Milo of Evesham, said by the jurors to have been a Christian usurer, accustomed to sell his grain at an over-value 'on account of the loan' (i.e. because he was selling it on credit).

> De usurar[iis] christianis dicunt quod Milo de Evesham carius solebat vendere blad[um] suu[m]causa mutui quam valebat die quo vendidit et est mortuus. Et habuit bona in villa de Evesham. I[de]o ibi inquir[atu]r.[7]

(Of Christian usurers, they say that Milo of Evesham was accustomed to sell his grain at a higher price than it was worth on the day of the sale, on account of the loan, and he is dead. And he had goods in the vill of Evesham. So let it be inquired of there.)

> De usur[ariis] christianis dicunt quod Milo de Evesham carius vendere solebat bladum suum causa mutui quam valebat die quo vendidit. Et est mortuus.[8]

(Of Christian usurers, they say that Milo of Evesham was accustomed to sell his grain more dearly than it was worth on the day when it was sold, on account of the loan. And he is dead.)

The case demonstrates the existence of a royal proscription of usury, the involvement of central royal justice in investigating those who had perpetrated it and some co-operation from those charged with bringing such matters to the attention of the authorities. It also gives some information as to the nature of conduct which might be regarded as usurious. This chapter will investigate why royal action might be taken with regard to somebody like Milo in 1275, and the shifts and fluctuations in royal interest in usury in medieval England over the next century and a quarter.

It is well known that medieval theology and canon law prohibited usury, although there were debates as to exactly what fell within the prohibition other than the receipt of profit on a loan.[9] Much has been written on the subject of canonical theory and ecclesiastical practice on usury.[10] The involvement of English

---

[7] JUST 1/1028 m.16; JUST 1/1026 m.35 (virtually identical).

[8] JUST 1/1025 m.4.

[9] A common definition is that usury is any profit over and above the principal in loan transactions: 'Quicquid ultra sortem exigitur usura est': Gratian, Decretum, C.14 q.3 c.4; G. Le Bras, 'Conceptions of economy and society' in CEH III, 364; Noonan, Usury, 19. Wider definitions were, however, also used, as will be discussed below.

[10] See in particular: T.P. McLaughlin, 'The teaching of the canonists on usury', Medieval Studies 1 (1939), 82–107, and Medieval Studies 2 (1940), 1–22; B. Nelson, The Idea of Usury: From Tribal Brotherhood to Universal

secular authorities in this area, as exemplified by the case of Milo of Evesham, has, however, been neglected, perhaps due to the vehement criticism by eighteenth- and nineteenth-century commentators unsympathetic to the medieval usury laws, deeming them the product of narrow minded superstition.[11] There is, however, much of interest in this area.

Jews and Christians: the shadow of Shylock

A preliminary point which should be made is that, for most people, medieval royal action against usury means action against Jewish usury. Shakespeare's Shylock and other fictional characters loom large.[12] In medieval England, Jews were regarded as usurers, but it was clear that not all usurers were Jews.[13] Foreigners or Italians were also seen as typical usurers, and, as will be seen, native Christians were accused of usury.[14]

Whilst royal action against the usury of Jews in the reigns of Edward I and his predecessors has already received a great deal of attention from historians, royal action against Christian usurers, predating and surviving the 1290 expulsion of the Jews from the realm, has been the subject of much less attention.[15] Royal action

---

Otherhood (Chicago, 1969); Noonan, *Usury*; O. Langholm, *The Aristotelian Analysis of Usury* (Bergen, 1984); R.H. Helmholz, 'Usury in the medieval English church courts', *Speculum* 61 (1986), 364; O. Langholm, *Economics in the Medieval Schools: Wealth, Exchange, Value, Money and Usury according to the Paris Theological Tradition 1200–1350* (Leiden, 1992). Helmholz, 'Usury', 364, notes that attention has not been given to the practical aspects of the usury laws, but deals almost exclusively with the ecclesiastical rather than secular royal jurisdiction.

[11] Blackstone suggested that they were the product of narrow-mindedness, stating that they came to be relaxed 'when men's minds began to be more enlarged': Blackstone, *Commentaries*, Book II, c.30, 455. A similar attitude was displayed in the House of Commons in 1854, during the debate on the final repeal of the remaining usury laws. Gladstone, then Chancellor of the Exchequer, was disdainful of 'the superstition which formerly prevailed on the subject [of usury, which] was partly Judaical and partly Mahomedan': *Hansard (HC)*, 29 June 1854, col. 930.

[12] See, e.g., J. Gross, *Shylock: A Legend and its Legacy* (New York, 1992).

[13] The 1275 royal document *Breve contra contractus usurarios factos per Christianos* instructs royal justices to make enquiries about Christians in Norfolk acting like Jews (*judaizantes*) in lending money and other goods to poor Christians, taking money above the principal sum lent: BL, MS Harley 409, f.40r–v; C 66/95 m.36d (I am grateful to Dr P. Brand for this reference). On the association of usury and Judaism: defamation case of *Burgeys v Nedham* in Ipswich borough court, Suffolk Record Office, C 5/3; Roll of 17–18 Edw I Friday before Ascension (13 May 1289) 'ipsum vocavit iudeum et usurarium': R.H. Helmholz (ed.), *Select Cases on Defamation to 1600*, Selden Society 101 (London, 1985), liii–liv. Even at the end of the fourteenth century, long after the Expulsion, Chaucer, echoing older models, still expected the audience for his Canterbury Tales to make the connection: see 'The Prioress's Tale', in A.C. Cawley (ed.), *Chaucer, Canterbury Tales* (London, 1958, reprinted 1992), 375. A later example of an association between Jews and usury in a case can be seen in *Warren's Case* (1605) in W.P. Baildon (ed.), *Les Reports del Cases in Camera Stellata 1293–1609* (London, 1894), 236–7. I am grateful to John Lock for this reference.

[14] See, e.g., H. Chew and M. Weinbaum (eds), *Eyre of London 1244* (London, 1970), no.231 (foreigners or those abroad accused of usury) and no.327 (merchants of Siena and Rome accused of usury). Note also that Dante's usurious sufferers in the seventh circle of Hell, for example, were Christians: J. Schenk Koffler, 'Capital in Hell: Dante's Lesson on Usury', *Rutgers Law Review* 32 (1979), 609.

[15] See, e.g., G.H. Leonard, 'The expulsion of the Jews by Edward I: an essay in explanation of the Exodus, A.D. 1290', *TRHS*, new ser., 5 (1891), 103; I. Abrahams, *Jewish Life in the Middle Ages* (New York, 1896) c.XI; J.M. Rigg, *Calendar of the Plea Rolls of the Exchequer of the Jews, vol. II, 1273–1275*, Jewish Historical Society of England (London, 1910), xx–xxxiii; H. Loewe, 'On usury' in H. Loewe (ed.), *Starrs and Charters preserved in the British Museum, vol. II* (London, 1932), xcv; C. Roth, 'The European age in Jewish history (to 1648)' in L. Finkelstein (ed.), *The Jews: Their History, Culture and Religion, vol. I* (Philadelphia, 1949), 216, 229–33; S. Dubnov, *History of the Jews, vol. III: From the Later Middle Ages to the Renaissance*, 4th edn (South Brunswick, 1969), 66–70; S. Menache, 'The King, the Church and the Jews: some considerations on the

against Christian usurers is my principal concern, and it must always be borne in mind that the relationship between a king and 'his' Jews was, in medieval Europe, very different to that between a king and the Christian majority, but it would be perverse and impossible to consider Christian usury in complete isolation from Jewish usury.[16] There is an area of overlap in terms of definition of usury, and materials on Jewish usury may serve to illuminate some of the darkened corners of justification for and detail of royal action against Christian usury. Also, it should be noted that even 'Jewish usury' generally involves the participation of Christians, as borrowers, and sometimes as transferees of lands or fee rents used as security, so that regulation of Jewish usury also affected Christian subjects.[17]

The prohibition

Evidence of presentments such as that against Milo of Evesham show that there was, at the beginning of Edward I's reign an established royal prohibition on Christian usury. It is, however, far from easy to trace its origin.

There is some sign of a royal prohibition from at least the early twelfth century, as Bricstan of Chatteris is said to have been convicted of offences including usury in a trial of 1116 in Huntingdon county court before the justiciar Ralph Basset.[18] The earliest surviving statement of a general royal prohibition of usury for Christians is in the 'Laws of Edward the Confessor', dating from the reign of Henry I or of Stephen.[19] It is suggested that Henry II 'took active measures to suppress usury by Christians', from 1163, when usury was condemned at a conference in his realm.[20] Whether this can be called legislation is, however,

---

[16] expulsions from England and France', *Journal of Medieval History* 13 (1987), 223–36; J. Richards, *Sex, Dissidence and Damnation: Minority Groups in the Middle Ages* (London, 1991), c.5; K.R. Stow, *Alienated Minority: The Jews of Medieval Latin Europe* (Cambridge, Mass., 1992), cc.10 and 12; R. Mundill, 'Lumbard and son, the business and dealings of two Jewish moneylenders in late thirteenth-century England', *Jewish Quarterly Review* 82 (1991); R.C. Stacey, 'Parliamentary negotiations and the expulsion of the Jews from England' in M. Prestwich, R.H. Britnell and R. Frame (eds), *Thirteenth Century England VI: Proceedings of the Durham Conference 1995* (Woodbridge, 1997), 77–102; P. Brand, 'Jews and the law in England 1275–90', *EHR* 115 (2000), 1138–58; R.R. Mundill, 'Christian and Jewish moneylending patterns and financial dealings during the twelfth and thirteenth centuries' in Schofield and Mayhew, *Credit and Debt*, 42–67.

[16] Brand, 'Jews and the law', 1142, notes the idea of Jews as the 'king's serfs'.

[17] Stacey, 'Parliamentary negotiations', 93; Dyer, *Standards of living*, 38; Richardson, *English Jewry*, 83–108; J. Melland Hall, 'Pynchecumb – abstracts of original document in the register of St Peter's Gloucester', *Transactions of the Bristol and Gloucestershire Archaeological Society* 14 (1889–90), 141–62.

[18] E.S. Kealey, *Roger of Salisbury, Viceroy of England* (California, 1972), 63, citing C. Johnson and H. Cronne (eds), *Regesta Regum Anglo-Normannorum*, vol. II (Oxford, 1956), no.1129; A. le Prevost (ed.), *Orderic Vitalis* (Paris, 1838–55), III, 123–4; M. Chibnall (ed.), *The Ecclesiastical History of Orderic Vitalis*, vol. 3 (Oxford, 1972), pp. 346–58. See also Hudson, *Formation*, 53–6, 58, 68, 77, citing the above authorities, and, in addition, R.C. Van Caenegem (ed.), *English Lawsuits from William I to Richard I*, 2 vols, Selden Society 106, 107 (1990–1), no.204B. There is some disagreement in the authorities as to whether Bricstan was a usurer or not.

[19] B.R. O'Brien, *God's Peace and King's Peace: The Laws of Edward the Confessor* (Philadelphia, 1999), 200; B. Thorpe (ed.), *Ancient Laws and Institutes of England*, 2 vols (London, 1840), I, 199, s.37. These anonymous 'laws' do not seem to have any definite connection with Edward the Confessor and, according to Richardson and Sayles, date from the time of Henry I: H.G. Richardson and G.O. Sayles, *Law and Legislation from Aethelberht to Magna Carta* (Edinburgh, 1966), 47–9, 57. Wormald puts their date somewhat later, at about 1140: P. Wormald, *The Making of English Law: King Alfred to the Twelfth Century, vol. I: Legislation and its Limitation* (Oxford, 1999), 128, 409–11. O'Brien favours a date for composition of the 'Laws' late in the reign of Henry I or in Stephen's reign, with c.37 being a late addition to the original 34 chapter code, perhaps following the legatine council at Westminster in 1138: O'Brien, *God's Peace*, 38, 39, 45.

[20] O'Brien, *God's Peace*, 277.

open to question. There is some evidence of royal rules on usury in the twelfth-century treatises *Dialogus de Scaccario* and *Glanvill*. The provenance and date of enactment of these rules, if, indeed, they were the subject of formal enactment, is, however, mysterious.[21]

Edward I made proclamations and statutes dealing with usury in 1274, 1275 and 1290 and possibly in 1284–6.[22] A King's Bench case of 1286 refers to an unidentified 'provision' against usury, which may be one of those mentioned, or may be an additional measure.[23] No new measures seem to have been passed under Edward II, but there was some legislation under Edward III. A pronouncement on jurisdiction over usurers was made in 1341, royal approval of arrangements for the trial of usurers in London was given in 1363, and a pronouncement on usury (in response to a request for action) was made in 1377.[24] Under Richard II, there were pronouncements on jurisdiction in 1382 and 1390.[25] There is, therefore, evidence of an assumption that this was an appropriate area for royal intervention at a number of points during the late thirteenth and fourteenth centuries. There are extant laws concerning Jewish usury – either banning it or regulating it – from at least 1215 until the 1290 expulsion.[26]

Nature of prohibited conduct

There were, therefore, laws against usury, but what was understood to be usury, and which usury was prohibited? Logically, these are distinct questions, but in view of the lack of detailed treatments of the legal theory, and the great reliance which must be placed on distillations of principle from instances of prosecution, it will be impossible to separate them. One must, therefore, be content to ask what was prohibited as usury.

Unfortunately, there are problems in giving an answer to this question as well. There is no definitive statement of the conduct which amounted to prohibited usury for the purposes of the royal regulations. *Glanvill* states that when something was lent, if more was received in return, that was usury.[27] A 1244 prohibition of usury by merchants shows that the prohibition covered penalties for late payment on bonds as well as the more straightforward case of a definite arrangement that usury would be paid in all events.[28] A definition of prohibited usury may also be extracted from the commissions issued to royal justices by Edward I from 1275 onwards. In 1275, a document entitled *Breve contra contractus usurarios factos per Christianos* instructed the justices to make enquiries about Christians in Norfolk acting like Jews (*judaizantes*) in lending money and other goods to poor Christians, taking money above the principal sum

---

[21] *Dialogus de Scaccario*, 98–100; *Glanvill* VII:16.
[22] See further below.
[23] G.O. Sayles (ed.), *Select Cases in King's Bench Edward I vol. 1*, Selden Society vol. 55 for 1936 (London, 1939), xiii, 163, *Thomas de Berevile v Master Nicholas of Ellerker*, Coram Rege Roll no.101, m.4. It refers to 'provisionem nostram de usuriis in regno nostro cessandis'.
[24] See further below in App. III.
[25] See further below at pp. 65–6.
[26] *SR* I:10. Brand, 'Jews and the law'.
[27] *Glanvill* X:3.
[28] *CCR, 1242–7*, 242. I am grateful to Dr P. Brand for this reference. It is ordered that 'nullus mercator decetero mutuo det pecuniam pro aliquo lucro vel super penam'.

lent.[29] This tells us that profit on loans of money or goods would be seen as usurious, and prohibited, but leaves a number of other issues unclear.

Examination of the entries relating to usury which have been found in records of prosecutions in courts serves to expand the detail of the rules against usury in medieval England to some extent. Although the entries are rather terse, some give information which can be used to make statements about the sort of conduct which was investigated and penalised as usury, and about the assignment of culpability in cases of usury.

All profit or excessive profit?

One question of principle is whether or not there was a *de minimis* rule, i.e. whether the exaction of *any* profit above and beyond the principal sum lent was regarded as usury (or prohibited usury), or whether only *excessive* profiteering (however defined) was prohibited. There may be different answers to this question for Jewish and Christian lenders.

Before the reign of Edward I, and at points in the years of his reign before 1290, Jewish usury was tolerated if it remained within certain limits. A charter of Richard I of 1190, referring to an earlier charter of Henry II, suggests tacit acceptance of Jewish profits on loans.[30] The tenth clause of John's Magna Carta of 1215 banned the running of usury on Jewish debts against minor heirs after the death of the debtor, though this provision was left out of subsequent issues of the Charter.[31] A 1235 Close Roll entry and the fifth clause of the Statute of Merton 1235–6 show a revived ban on the running of usury against minor heirs.[32] Both of these statutes assumed that Jews would generally be allowed to take usury without hindrance from the king and government, except in the circumstances discussed. A measure of 1233 allowed Jews to take a set amount of usury.[33] A charter of Henry III to the University of Oxford also demonstrated tolerance of limited Jewish usury, allowing the Jews of Oxford to take up to two pence (2d) per pound ($\pounds$) per week from scholars of the university.[34] The royal regulatory framework for Jewish usury also forbade exaction of compound interest.[35] This policy of regulating rather than banning Jewish usury was consistent with canon law, which had, from the Fourth Lateran Council of 1215 onwards, prohibited Jews from taking 'oppressive and excessive interest' from Christians.[36] Both canon law and royal law, therefore, tacitly accepted that moderate Jewish usury would be allowed.

---

[29] *CPR 1272–81*, 172; BL, MS Harley 409, f.40r–v; C 66/95 m.36d. I am grateful to Dr P. Brand for the last reference.

[30] *Foedera*, I, i, 51.

[31] *SR* I:10.

[32] The 1235 concession is at *CCR 1234–7*, 214, referring specifically to Jewish usury. The statute of Merton provision is at *CCR 1234–7*, 338, and *SR* I:3. This statute did not specify that the debts were to Jews, though it is likely that this provision was understood to apply to Jewish usury, since Christians were not allowed to take any usury. It was seen to refer to Jewish usury in fifteenth-century legal readings: S.E. Thorne (ed.), *Readings and Moots at the Inns of Court* vol. I, Selden Society vol. 71 for 1952 (London, 1954), cv, Reading at Gray's Inn *c*.1433.

[33] Richardson, *English Jewry*, 294.

[34] Salter, *MA*, vol. I, 777 (1248), described in JUST 1/705 m.26.

[35] The Statute of the Jewry 1233: Richardson, *English Jewry*, 293; *Law Quarterly Review* 54 (1938), 392–4: 'nichil ponatur in sortem nisi primum mutuum'. Repeated 1239: *Liber de Antiquis Legibus*, 237–8, which suggests that the provision pre-dates Henry III.

[36] Rigby, *English Society*, 290.

Before 1275, no change was made to the policy of regulating the practice of Jewish usury.[37] In 1275, however, Edward I made 'an attempt at radical social engineering' and changed the rules, completely prohibiting the Jews in the kingdom from lending their money at usury.[38] They were instructed to live by legitimate merchandise instead.[39] A degree of retreat (or planned retreat) from this absolute prohibition of Jewish usury can be seen in the Draft Statute of the Jewry of *c.*1284–6.[40] Its provisions set limits for the usury which Jews could charge Christians. They were to take no more than half a mark for a loan of 20 shillings (20s), or 8 shillings and 8 pence (8s 8d) a year, and for 40s, one mark, or 17s 4d, 'and for more, more, and for less, less'.[41] Usury was only to run for a limited period (three or four years) from the date of the contract.[42] Repeating a measure of 1269, it was also provided that no Jew was to grant or sell his debt to anyone, Christian or Jew, without the special licence of the king.[43] The level of Jewish usury was thus to be regulated, and the number of people who might become involved in collecting debts tainted by usury was to be controlled by the licensing procedure. The whole measure suggests royal acceptance of some level of Jewish usury, although there is no real indication that it was ever enacted, and it survives only in an obviously unfinished form.[44] Even if it was brought into force, in 1290, Edward I reverted to the idea of a total prohibition on usury, expelling the Jews from the realm, citing as a justification for this expulsion the fact that they had carried on making usurious loans after the statute of 1275.[45]

For Christians, the theoretical position seems to have been that all profit above the principal was banned. It should be noted that there was never a royal licensing system for public Christian usurers in England as there was in other realms, for example in the Low Countries, or public (or church-run) lending institutions as in parts of Italy, which suggests that all Christian usury, however minor, was covered by the prohibition: formally at least, there was no exception for moderate profits.[46] The 1275 commissions' definition shows concern with the exaction of all sums over and above the principal, rather than banning only 'excessive', or 'exorbitant' profit.[47] Treatises are generally silent on this issue. The example of usury given in

---

[37] Richardson, *English Jewry*, 293. Edward I was, of course, out of the country until 1274.

[38] Brand, 'Jews and the law', 1153.

[39] Statutes of the Jewry: *SR* I:221. A similar provision had been made by Louis IX of France in 1254: Richards, *Sex, Dissidence and Damnation*, 113.

[40] Rigg, *Select Starrs*, lvi.

[41] Rigg, *Select Starrs*, lvi. A piece of evidence which may suggest a narrower range of dates (1285–6) is the clerical complaint of 1285 which brought up the issue of royal (or court) tolerance of Jewish usury, 'Item, quod iudeorum fraudibus et malitiis salubriter obvietur': P&C, *Councils*, 959, 962–3. Although usury is not specifically mentioned in this *gravamen*, there can be little doubt that it was in fact the main focus of the grievance, since the clerical rejoinder to the king's answers to these complaints noted the prelates' amazement that the royal courts did not hinder, and even helped, the Jews in their usurious contracts.

[42] Rigg, *Select Starrs*, lvi–lvii. The alternative legitimate rates of interest and periods for which it would run are due to the draft nature of this document: Brand, 'Jews and the law', 1155.

[43] *CPR 1266–72*, 376; Rigg, *Select Starrs*, lix. I am grateful to Dr P. Brand for the former reference.

[44] Brand, 'Jews and the law', 1155.

[45] Richardson, *English Jewry*, 229, citing Rigg, *Select Starrs*, xl–xli; Rigby, *English Society in the Later Middle Ages*, 290.

[46] Gilchrist, *CEA*, 65, citing Noonan, *Usury*, 34; Zimmerman, *Law of Obligations*, 171; Hunt and Murray, *History of Business*, 215.

[47] *CPR 1272–81*, 172; BL, MS Harley 409, f.40r–v; C 66/95 m.36d. Gilchrist, *CEA*, 64.

the late thirteenth-century *Mirror of Justices* is of a large profit on a money loan, where ten times the sum loaned is demanded, but it is not suggested that the profit needs to be of this order to be usurious.[48]

Court roll entries concerning usury were not generally particularly careful to set out the length of the loan period. Their primary focus was on the fact that more had been received than was lent, again suggesting an absolute rule. The cases of Milo of Evesham and Robert le Poleter are good examples of unspecific allegations. Some details may be given, but still not enough to work out the rate of usury. In the 1285 Macclesfield eyre case of Jordan the servant of John the Comber, for example, the defendant's alleged usury consisted of lending 9s for 3s 6d to Emma the sewer of Gut; that of Thomas son of Robert Crampe consisted of lending the same woman 3s, taking 18d in usury.[49] No idea of the loan period is given. Sometimes the period of the loan is specified, or can be worked out, as in the case of Robert Marescall who was said to have lent 6s to Robert Buran at 3d a week, 10s and 3d in all, and to have taken for 2s lent to Alice del Nol half a bushel of flour for one week.[50] More often, however, there is no clue to the period. A Wakefield case gives information about the fact that a certain amount of money was taken each week rather than about the sum taken in excess over and above the principal. In the report of the tourn at Wakefield on 16 November 1316, it is noted that William, son of Richard of the Haghe, was amerced 40d because he lent 20s to Alice the Stinter, taking 10d in usury every week.[51] I have only found four cases from the records of courts before royal justices in which the rate of usury could possibly be calculated: the 1341 accusations that John Sale loaned Richard atte Welle 13s 4d for four weeks, taking a quarter of wheat as usury, and that John de Botyngham loaned Thomas Orvyntyn 60s for three years, requiring 20s of usury *per annum*, with the principal to be returned at the end of the three year term, the 1343 conviction of Henry de Rudyng for lending John Whitsyde 20s for a week, requiring 2s in usury, and the 1352 indictment in which Thomas Judde of Bradewell was said to have lent 20s to a woman (term unspecified) at 4s a year in usury.[52] This lack of detail about the term of the loan suggests that royal courts made no formal distinction between moderate and excessive usury: taking anything beyond the principal was usury, and it was not formally necessary to show that the usury was excessive. It is not clear whether or not a distinction between moderate and excessive usury was made in practice, because cases in which a rate can be calculated are so scarce. It may be that, as Helmholz has observed as a possibility in English ecclesiastical court practice, a *de minimis* rule did operate to keep out cases where the rate of usury was very low, but it is not apparent from the sources consulted.[53]

An advantage of an outright ban without any *de minimis* exception or gauge of moderation would have been its simplicity. The early attempts to regulate usury, and set an allowed rate, were problematic in that the arithmetical ability of at least

---

[48] *Mirror*, Book II, c.27.
[49] R. Stewart-Brown (ed.), *Calendar of County Court, City Court and Eyre Rolls of Chester 1259–97*, Chetham Society 84 (Aberdeen, 1925), 208.
[50] Stewart-Brown, *Calendar of Chester Court Rolls*, 209, Macclesfield eyre 1285.
[51] Wakefield *D*, 156.
[52] JUST 1/258 m.7; JUST 1/430 m.25; JUST 1/268 m.7.
[53] Helmholz, 'Usury', 375; Gilchrist, *CEA*, 64.

one statutory draftsman seems to have been inadequate for the task. In the 'Draft Statute of Jewry' of *c.*1284–6, there was some uncertainty as to the allowed rate of usury. On a loan of 20s, a Jew was allowed to take either 6s 8d or else 8s 8d, and on a loan of 40s, he could take a mark (13s 4d) or 16s 4d.[54] It could be that the uncertainty would have been ironed out at a later stage, had the draft statute been enacted, but it suggests that there might well have been practical problems in a regulatory scheme, rather than a simple ban. A lack of understanding in medieval England of the basis of calculating interest has been suggested.[55] Had there been some official licit rate of interest for Christians in the late thirteenth and fourteenth centuries, we might expect to find detailed workings out of the sums which could be charged for loans of particular sizes, in documents similar to the London *Liber de Assisa Panis* and its counterparts, but no such tables have been found.[56] Taken together, the evidence suggests that the ban on Christian usury was, in theory, absolute.

Subject matter

The next matter to consider is what can be known about the 'reach' of the usury prohibition in terms of subject matter: which deals offended against it? The most familiar type of bargain which would be covered by the prohibition was the loan of money with repayment of the principal plus an additional sum. Canon law, however, had rules against fraudulent transactions which fell outside a simple definition of making money profit on a money loan.[57] Some canonical and theological conceptions of usury were very wide, taking in 'profiteering in general as well as the specific practice of charging interest on consumption loans'.[58] In its widest contemporary constructions, usury could encompass profit on any commercial bargain which, in substance, amounted to a loan, not simply money taken or demanded on money loans. Pecuniary or non-pecuniary profits on loans or credit sales of fungibles would also be convered, as would profit on loans secured on land.[59] Secular English sources seem to point in a similar direction: (prohibited) usury went beyond money loans, though perhaps secular law did not go quite as far as canon law.

As noted above, both *Glanvill* and the 1275 royal commissions suggest that the royal conception of (prohibited) usury encompassed profits on both money loans and loans of other fungibles. The *Glanvill* definition is unspecific, noting that when something (not necessarily money) was lent, if more was received in return, that was usury.[60] The 1275 *Breve contra contractus usurarios factos per Christianos* is clearer, instructing royal justices to make enquiries about Christians in Norfolk lending money and other goods to poor Christians, taking money above the principal sum

[54] BL, MS Add. 32085, ff.120r–121r; Rigg, *Select Starrs*, liv–lx. Dated by P. Brand: Brand, 'Jews and the law', 1154.

[55] H.G. Richardson, *The English Jewry under Angevin Kings* (London, 1960), 81.

[56] *Liber de Assisa Panis*, Corporation of London Record Office MS. See chapter 3 below.

[57] Helmholz, 'Usury', 366.

[58] R.H. Bowers, 'A Middle English mnemonic poem on usury', *Medieval Studies* 17 (1955), 226, 227; Langholm, *Economics in the Medieval Schools*, especially at 50, 83, 85–6, 296–7, 318–19, 547–9 (credit sales), and 61, 272–5, 292–4, 587, 591 (rent contracts).

[59] Noonan, *Usury*, 18.

[60] *Glanvill* X:3.

lent.[61] The Milo of Evesham case, among others, shows that money profits made on loans of items other than money, and non-money profits on loans of money, were caught in the definition of usury in practice as well as in theory.[62]

There is little difference between an outright loan of a fungible item such as wheat and its sale on credit, and both transactions were caught by canonical and theological prohibitions on usury, if a profit was made. The *Mirror of Justices* referred to usury on credit sales.[63] No royal statement mentions credit sales, but these would seem to have fallen within the prohibition in practice. Milo of Evesham may have been selling on credit, but there are clearer examples, as can be seen in the presentments relating to the misdeeds of Roger de Burton in the Eyre of Westmorland 1292.[64] Roger was said to lend money and to sell on credit 'goods of all kinds, such as wool, cattle, sheep . . . which he sells on credit for future payment, taking on account of the term more than the proper value, sometimes doubling the sale price'. Similar accusations were made against two more men in the same eyre.[65]

These sales may well have been genuine. A more dubious transaction caught by the laws of the church was the fraudulent or at least collusive attempt to evade the usury laws by an artificial sale at an inflated price and resale at a lower price, masking an underlying loan. From at least 1363, there were rules in London against this offence, which was known as *chevisance*. The offence did not find its way into a national statute until 1487.[66]

Profit which might be considered usurious could also be made in 'security' cases, if a lender took land or a chattel as security for a loan and, rather than taking a lump sum as profit when the loan was paid off, or receiving a weekly or monthly sum from the borrower, he took the profits which arose from the security and did not set it off against the money owed. It is clear that medieval English kings and governments were aware of these species of usury, since the Statute of the Jewry 1275 stipulated that usury would not run on deals involving '[security of] land or rent or anything else'.[67] As far as loans secured on land are concerned, *Glanvill* states that, although the mortgage (which was 'unjust, dishonest and usurious') was not prohibited by the king's court during the life of the usurer, if a lender could be proved to have died during the existence of a mortgage arrangement, his property

---

[61] BL, MS Harley 409, f.40 r–v; C 66/95 m.36d. It was alleged that the lenders were not merely lending at usury but were also detaining the pledges given as security for repayment of the sums lent, and engaging in other unfair practices.

[62] See cases of Alan de Sutton (Common Pleas debt case, BL, MS Add. 31826, f.102, grain profit claimed on grain loan: App. III below); William the beadle (Eyre of Devon 1281, JUST 1/1025 m.4, loans of grain, grain profit); William Goatchild (Eyre of Gloucestershire 1287, JUST 1/278 m.4, grain profit on money loan); Thomas son of William Kenemerford (Eyre of Gloucestershire 1287, JUST 1/278 m.51d, grain profit on grain loan); William de Luda (Eyre of Cambridgeshire 1299, JUST 1/96 mm.73, 75r, loans/credit sales of grain, profit in money); John Sale of Colchester (presentments under commission of 1340, Essex, JUST 1/258 m.7, loan of money, profit in wheat); John Hagezerd (Norfolk peace roll 1378, KB 9/80 m.4, loan of gold and silver, profit in money) (App. I below).

[63] *Mirror*, Book III, c.30.

[64] JUST 1/986 m.7. See App. I below.

[65] William de Goldington, Thomas, son of Master William de Goldington: JUST 1/986 mm.7d and 9. See App. I below.

[66] See G. Seabourne, 'Controlling commercial morality: the London usury trials of 1421', *Journal of Legal History* 19 (1998), 116–42.

[67] Statutes of the Jewry clause 1: *SR* I:221.

would be treated as the property of a usurer.[68] This shows recognition of the usurious nature of such dealings, and some royal rules against it. The limitation on action against living participants in such deals may be explained by a jurisdictional division between royal and ecclesiastical authorities in this area, with royal authority holding sway over the dead usurer and ecclesiastical authority over the living usurer.[69] The apparent limitation, to the effect that only those who died during the currency of the mortgage (as opposed to limiting royal jurisdiction to those who died unrepentant) would be treated as usurers by royal law, cannot be so explained. It may stem from a desire not to upset titles to land gained by (possibly) innocent third parties after a moneylender had 'foreclosed' on the land of a defaulting borrower.

The (limited) evidence of court practice concerning mortgages which has been consulted does not demonstrate that the rule in *Glanvill* held sway in the thirteenth and fourteenth centuries. First, there are, in fact, apparent cases of amercement of a (living) creditor for the usurious nature of his mortgage arrangement in records from 1220 and 1293.[70] Secondly, a fragment of evidence from the 1390s suggests that even those dying during the existence of a possibly usurious security arrangement did not merit particular royal interest. The inquest into the lands of Thomas Earl of Warwick in the Welsh marches near Hereford, which were forfeited to the king in 1397 for reasons unconnected to usury, mentions without particular interest the fact that he was in possession of a piece of land which Llewelyn ap Mo. . . had put in pledge [morgagio] to him for a debt of 2 quarters of wheat worth 20s, 'until he should finally be satisfied of that sum'.[71] This was not necessarily a usurious arrangement, but the matter was not pursued to see whether it was or was not usurious. It has been suggested that medieval conveyancers or those dealing with land seem to have ignored the possibility of mortgages being usurious, drawing up arrangments in ways blatantly showing profit on the loan, when this could easily have been avoided.[72]

Although it has been made tolerably clear that lending on the security of land continued to be important at all levels of society in medieval England, a great deal more research into land transactions needs to be done before much can be said about their nature in terms of usury.[73] It has been suggested that the transparently usurious mortgage described in *Glanvill* had given way to different forms of land security, which could include usury in a less obvious way, before the beginning of the period under consideration, though Dr Brand notes that the decline in arrangements in which the creditor took possession of the land was not complete

---

[68] *Glanvill* X:8. *Dialogus de Scaccario*, 98, deals with mortgage arrangements, classing them as 'covert usury' despite the fact that some people are reported not to consider them as reprehensible as other forms of usury. The thirteenth-century law books, *Bracton, Fleta* and *Britton*, do not mention mortgages in connection with usury.

[69] See further below at pp. 44–9.

[70] Brand, 'Aspects', 30, citing *Hamon Brand v John Pim* in *Curia Regis Rolls* ix, 76–7, and *Thomas Chamberlain v John son of John fitzJuliana*, CP 40/101 m.70d; YB 21 and 22 Edw I 17–19. None of the cases from 'crown pleas' sections of eyre rolls or King's Bench rolls from 1272–1399, however, indicate that they involve land.

[71] *Calendar of Inquisitions Miscellaneous (Chancery) vol. 12 (1392–99)* (1963), no.228.

[72] J.L. Barton, 'The common law mortgage' *Law Quarterly Review* 83 (1967), 229–39, 238–9.

[73] See, e.g., P. Hyams, 'The origins of a peasant land market in England', *EcHR* 23 (1970), 18–31, 28–31; Schofield, 'Introduction' in Schofield and Mayhew, *Credit and Debt in Medieval England*, 14; R. Hilton, *The English Peasantry in the Later Middle Ages* (Oxford, 1975), 46–7; B.F. Harvey, *Westminster Abbey and its Estates in the Middle Ages* (Oxford, 1977), 317, 318; Dyer, *Standards of Living*, 180.

by the end of the thirteenth century.[74] Plea roll research by Dr Brand has shown the existence of a variety of different forms of land security transactions in the thirteenth century, both mortgages and the definitely non-usurious vifgages.[75] Hilton gives a 1398 example of a 'peasant' land security arrangement involving a transfer of possession to the lender.[76] The arrangement whereby a piece of land designated as security for a debt would become the creditor's at the end of a period if the principal was not paid off might or might not be regarded as usurious, depending on one's view of penalties. As can be seen in Appendix III, there was uncertainty and a shift of opinion on this question amongst common lawyers in the fourteenth century. There is some evidence that in the reign of Edward I it was possible to recover at common law lands which had been mortgaged and lost, in a case from Norfolk in the King's Bench rolls for 1290, but it is not yet clear whether this would have been possible following the apparent change of view on penalties and usury in the mid-fourteenth century.[77]

Church courts may have taken action against mortgages as being usurious. R.H. Helmholz mentions a fifteenth-century case in which an accusation of usury was made with regard to a mortgage. It is illuminating to note that the usurious nature of a mortgage was considered to turn on the intent with which the deal was struck – was it meant to compensate the lender, or to profit him?[78] Intention may have been a matter not particularly suited to the methods and proofs of the secular courts.

Canon law and theological texts show that the borderline between acceptable commercial practice and prohibited usury could give rise to conflict and complexity. Sadly, the lack of theoretical discussion and the nature of court records mean that it is impossible to know how some knotty borderline issues would have been untangled in the royal jurisdiction. The cases from royal courts and lower secular courts almost all concern simple loans or credit sales with what seem to have been transparent requirements of usury. Complex economic and moral problems do not seem to have been discussed. There is no evidence of consideration of the effects of devaluation, and little on price fluctuations, despite the well known inflationary problems of the period.[79] What we have from royal and secular sources, therefore,

---

[74] See, e.g., Simpson, *Land Law*, 142. Brand, 'Aspects', 30, citing *Thomas son of Master William of Goldington and wife Avice v William of Hastings* (1292), JUST 1/987 m.3; *Anon.* (1293) YB 20 & 21 Edw. I 423; *Katherine dau. of Alexander Osewold v Nichs s.o. Hugh de la Chambre* (1300), CP 40/132 m.213d, reported in BL, MS Add. 31826, f.164r.

[75] Brand, 'Aspects', 30, citing CP 40/151 m.199 (1288), pleading in the 1279–81 Yorkshire eyre case *Emma daughter of William White & others v John son of William of Beningborough*, JUST 1/1065 m.47; enrolled deed in *BNB* pl.458 (1230); *Hugh Peverel v William de la Forde and Richard of Anstey* (1260), KB 26/169 m.24; *Bartholomew de Castello v Adam de Creting and his wife Nicholaa and others* (1281), CP 40/38 m.78d. A 'penalty mortgage' example can be seen in YB 21 and 22 Edw. I 224 (1293) – a mortgagee gained both principal and the land pledged as security, as agreed; no mention was made of usury.

[76] Hilton, *English Peasantry*, 47.

[77] KB 27/123 m.27; KB 27/124 m.10d; KB 27/125 m.7r. See App. III below.

[78] R.H. Helmholz, *Canon Law and the Law of England* (London, 1987), c.17, 'Usury and the medieval English church courts', 323–39, 331, for an example of 1447 (Rochester) which turned on the question of intent to evade the usury prohibition.

[79] Canonists debated this subject: see G. Le Bras, 'Conceptions of economy and society', in *CEH* III, 554–75, 564; Langholm, *Economics*, 522–3; Bolton, *MEE*, 73, 77. A case from the reign of Henry III did deal with usury and varying prices of corn according to the season: *Anon. v Parson of Glen*, in

suggests that the body of rules on the bargains which could be usurious being applied in secular courts followed the broad pattern of canon law, but was less worked out, and possibly narrower, than those of the canon law.[80] The fact that it was considered necessary to institute a separate usury jurisdiction in London from the 1360s, which did deal with more 'sophisticated' usurious deals, is also some evidence of the relatively narrow scope of royal rules on usury, which apparently did not suffice for the London business community of the late fourteenth and early fifteenth centuries.[81]

Attempts and completed actions

Another aspect of the scope of the usury prohibition which must be considered is whether attempts as well as the completed action were covered by the prohibition. Whereas canonists and theologians regarded attempts as potentially culpable regardless of success, and in some circumstances regarded even the intention to exact usurious profit as potentially culpable, there is no sign (with the possible exception of a passage from the *Mirror of Justices*) that the 'secular' law went beyond prohibiting the successful exaction of usury.[82] This discrepancy is not surprising, given that the common law had not generally begun to cover attempts to commit offences, or worked out a theory of intention, in the thirteenth and fourteenth centuries.[83] It also lends some support to the contention that royal rules may have been somewhat narrower in scope than canon law rules, though perhaps neither English church court nor secular courts actually punished attempts: Helmholz's study of usury in English church court practice gives no examples of attempts, and implies that a completed action was necessary for an instance case at least.[84]

'Aiding and abetting usury'

The question as to whether only 'principals' or also 'accessories' were guilty of usury must now be considered. Canon law had rules against the aiding and abetting of usurers, for example banning property owners from letting houses to usurers, but there seem to have been no comparable royal rules.[85] Records of cases show very little discussion of the guilt of those associated with usurers. One Nicholas le Convers was, however, accused of 'communication with usurers' in 1274.[86] Action

H.G. Richardson and G.O. Sayles (eds), *Select Cases of Procedure Without Writ under Henry III*, Selden Society 60 (London, 1941), 104 no.95.

[80] It must, however, be noted that a painstaking search of common pleas rolls may produce instances of discussion of trickier issues and of usury in relation to land securities which will refute this tentative conclusion.

[81] See Seabourne, 'Controlling commercial morality'.

[82] Evans, *Law and Theology*, 143; Wood, *Medieval Economic Thought*, 159. There is some evidence of attempts being treated as culpable in later ecclesiastical court records: R.H. Helmholz, *Canon Law and the Law of England* (London, 1987), 129 (fifteenth-century homicide and theft attempts).

[83] Baker, *Introduction*, 523–6. A. Kiralfy, 'Taking the will for the deed: the medieval criminal attempt', *Journal of Legal History* 13 (1992), 95–100, notes an exception in the case of treason and some fourteenth-century cases in which, in practice, attempts were punished with the same severity as completed actions, but concludes at 97 that 'The seeds planted in the fourteenth-century common law were not destined to sprout and the doctrine that the will should be taken for the deed seems soon to have died out.' See also D.J. Seipp, 'Crime in the Year Books' in C. Stebbings (ed.), *Law Reporting in Britain* (London, 1995), 15–34, 26.

[84] Helmholz, 'Usury', 336, 'the courts required proof that usury had been paid for a loan'.

[85] See Helmholz, 'Usury', 366.

[86] M. Weinbaum, *London Eyre 1276* London Record Society Publications (London, 1976), 85 no.306.

was proposed against Jews acting as frontmen for Christian usurers in the Draft Statute of 1284–6.[87] Being a broker of usury came to be an offence in London in the 1360s, and rules were being worked out there with relation to the culpability of maters for servants involved in usurious transactions and there was a request in Parliament in 1377 to enforce such laws across the whole realm, though the official response was not favourable to change.[88] This suggests that royal law on usury was not keeping pace with commercial developments or understanding of the extent of usury. It has, however, also been noted that English church courts did not put into practice canon law rules on indirect participation in usury.[89]

Another way of participating in an offence is as a third party who profits from it or receives the proceeds of the offence. According to canon law and theology, usury tainted not just the original usurer, but also those into whose hands the usurious profit came.[90] In a sense, the royal instruction to enquire into the chattels of deceased usurers gave effect to this idea, but, since there is actually little evidence of the recovery of the chattels of dead usurers after the twelfth century, it seems that this was not a doctrine which kings and governments were particularly concerned to put into effect.[91] It may, however, have been the reason that, in 1376, Edward the Black Prince refused a barrel of gold from the financier Richard Lyons, accused of usury in the Good Parliament. The prince seems to have been more incensed at the 'ill-gotten' nature of the gold than at the fact that it was a bribe, which is an interesting illustration of courtly mores.[92]

One person who, logically, may be considered to aid and abet usury is the borrower. The question of the potential culpability of the 'other participant' in a prohibited transaction (the borrower in usury, the buyer in a sale of goods at an excessive price and the original seller or eventual buyer in a forestalling arrangement) is an interesting one, as it may contribute to an understanding of contemporary views of the nature of such bargains: were they viewed as bilateral, mutual agreements into which people entered voluntarily, but which should be prohibited because they caused harm, or as deals which, whilst expressed in terms of agreement, were actually forced by one side on the other? It certainly came to be possible for both parties to a damaging or unfair transaction to be penalised by the mid-fourteenth century, as can be seen in the case of labour contracts which broke the rules laid down in the Ordinance of Labourers.[93] Canon lawyers and theologians had begun to consider the issue of the borrower's culpability and there was certainly an idea in theological sources that one ought to avoid 'leading into temptation' novice usurers.[94] A number of canonists and theologians did not

---

[87] Brand, 'Jews and the law', 1155.

[88] Seabourne, 'Controlling commercial morality'; *RP* II:350b.

[89] Helmholz, 'Usury', 329.

[90] John Pecham, in a letter to Eleanor of Castille, wrote: 'usury is a mortal sin to those who take the usury and those who support it, and those who have a share in it': Parsons, *Eleanor of Castille*, 120–1. See also Langholm, *Economics*, 49, 86–7, 97, 244–5, 287.

[91] See further below at pp. 42–3, 50–1.

[92] N. Saul, *Richard II* (New Haven, 1997), 17, citing E.M. Thompson (ed.), *Chronicon Anglie 1328–88* Rolls Series (London, 1874), 79–80.

[93] *SR* I:307, Ordinance of Labourers 1349, c.3.

[94] Mundill, 'Christian and Jewish moneylending', 49, citing the view of Archbishop Langton that 'it was a greater sin to seek credit from a novice usurer rather than an established one, just as it was more wicked to frequent a young rather than seasoned prostitute'. See Helmholz, 'Usury', 369 n.31; Baldwin,

consider needy borrowers who paid usury to be sinful.[95] The maverick trreatise *Mirror of Justices* suggests that the borrower at usury sins, even if he does not commit a 'secular' offence.[96] London borrowers of the later fourteenth century and fifteenth century who proceeded against those who had made them usurious loans showed a definite wish to justify their involvement in transactions on grounds of necessity.[97] Royal rules on usury, however, never entertained the possibility that some guilt might lie with the borrower. This apparent failure to consider the potential guilt of the borrower might be taken to suggest that the focus of the English usury laws was the wrongdoing and unjust enrichment of the usurer rather than the damaging effect of usurious transactions, either on the borrower or more generally, and/or that it was assumed that a borrower was not culpable because he or she had no choice but to accept the terms offered by the lender. The fact that kings themselves sometimes borrowed on usurious terms may have had some bearing on this failure to stigmatise borrowers as culpable participants in usurious transactions.[98] From a practical point of view, there might also be some difficulties caused by penalising borrowers, as this would be likely to mean that the main source of information on usury would not be inclined to be forthcoming.

The statements which may be made about the nature of the conduct proscribed as usurious are limited. Partly, this is a result of our dependence on the matters which presenting juries or individuals wished to raise, but there are some signs that royal courts had not developed a sophisticated body of jurisprudence on usury, and, in particular, that they were not trying to ensure that every potentially usurious arrangement was covered. It should also be noted that, although usury may have been regarded in theological or literary sources (and in the *Mirror of Justices*) as morally equivalent to theft, there is no sign that secular law regarded or punished it as such.[99]

Consequences: treatment of offenders and the question of restitution

Royal sources mentioned two main approaches to dealing with those found to have committed usury: banishment (generally for Jews and foreigners only) and forfeiture of property (for all usurers). The 'Laws of Edward the Confessor' also

---

Masters, Princes and Merchants: The Social Views of Peter the Chanter and his Circle, 2 vols (Princeton, 1970), 272, 273; Langholm, *Economics*, 60, 81, 162, 195, 369, 426, 481.

[95] Langholm, *Economics*, 107, 163, 195, 369, 481. This view was not shared by all 'scholastic' theorists: see Langholm, *Economics*, 426. Helmholz, 'Usury', 328, notes that canon law left open the possibility of the guilt of the borrower at usury, making culpability depend on, *inter alia*, the need of the borrower. Theories of free will were developing in medieval scholastic circles, using Aristotle's concept of 'mixed voluntariness' for borrowers at usury (i.e. neither wholly voluntary nor wholly involuntary, as where a sea captain in a storm jettisons his cargo to save his ship): Wood, *Medieval Economic Thought*, 165–6.

[96] *Mirror*, Book 5, c.1 no.81, 'It is an abuse that law should suffer vicious contracts and such as are forbidden and those in which sin interferes. Is not usury a sin? . . . How then can a man oblige himself to usury . . . without sin?'

[97] Seabourne, 'Controlling commercial morality'.

[98] See further below at pp. 62–3.

[99] Wood, *Medieval Economic Thought*, 107, citing Langholm, *Economics*, 69 and 164, citing P. Heath Barnum (ed.), *Dives and Pauper* (Oxford, 1976–80), part 2 Commd. VII, xxiv, p. 195, lines 1–2, in which Pauper describes usury as 'wol gret thefte'. *Mirror*, Book 1, c.10.

mentioned a subsidiary punishment not found in later sources, that of outlawry.[100] Banishment, not a 'judicial punishment' in the sense of coming only after 'due process', but a response to offending or suspected offending nonetheless, was proposed as the way to deal with usurers in 1274, when Edward I ordered the mayor and sheriffs of London to make it known in the city that all merchant usurers must leave the realm within twenty days from 9 November, under pain of forfeiture of their bodies and goods. If found in the city after that date, they were to be arrested and kept safely until further orders, 'as the king wills that merchant-usurers shall not stay in the city or elsewhere in the realm'.[101] Another example of banishment connected with usury was the expulsion of the Jews in 1290, an act which was justified by Edward I partly on the ground of their practice of usury.

It is not clear how strenuously Edward I's 1274 orders that merchant usurers should leave the realm were enforced. It is uncertain whether any merchant usurers did leave the realm. The only evidence which exists is evidence of those who do not seem to have been expelled. The pipe rolls for the reign of Edward I show evidence of usury convictions of a number of Italians in the judicial sessions ordered in 1274. The entry for London on the pipe roll for 1276–7 shows that Francis Puienelli and associates still owed £100 as a fine for their usury, and Jacobus Cus and his associates owed a similar sum for the same reason.[102] These entries also appear in the pipe rolls for Michaelmas 1280–1.[103] The implication is that the merchants in question broke the prohibition and yet were allowed to stay. The patent rolls for May and June 1275, January 1276 and July 1281 contain grants to various merchants of Pistoia, Florence and Siena that they should be allowed to stay in the realm and to recover debts due to them in England, but prohibiting them from lending money at usury or taking usury in any way in future, on pain of forfeiture of their merchandise and goods, showing even more clearly that those who acted contrary to the specific royal prohibition were not necessarily expelled.[104]

In contrast, the banishment of the Jews was carried out rigorously, with the whole colony leaving England in October 1290.[105] This was not, however, a 'judicial' punishment, as there is no evidence that there were any court proceedings against the Jews before the Expulsion.[106]

No doubt financial motives played their part in Edward I's expulsion of the Jews, and attempted or threatened expulsion of the Italians, but it should also be noted that there was canon law or theological authority for treating the usury of Jews and Christians differently, and also for treating foreigners and natives differently.[107] The Council of Lyons 1274 had said that foreign usurers must be

---

[100] B. Thorpe (ed.), *Ancient Laws and Institutes of England*, 2 vols (London, 1840), I, 199, c.37.

[101] *CCR 1272–9*, 108, 144.

[102] E 372/121 1276 M. – 1277 M.

[103] E 372/125 1280 M. – 1281 M.

[104] *CPR 1272–81*, 91, 92, 95, 128, 448.

[105] *CCR 1272–9*, 108. Recent estimates prefer a figure of around 2,000 Jews, whilst earlier estimates varied from 4,000 to 16,000. R.R. Mundill, *England's Jewish Solution: Experiment and Expulsion, 1262–1290* (Cambridge, 1998), 26; S. Dubrov, *History of the Jews, vol. III: From the Later Middle Ages to the Renaissance*, 4th edn (South Brunswick, 1969), 69; C. Roth, 'The European age in Jewish history' in L. Finkelstein (ed.), *The Jews: Their History, Culture and Religion*, vol. I (Philadelphia, 1949), 216, 231.

[106] Brand, 'Jews and the law', 1157.

[107] Rigby, *English Society*, 90.

expelled, though expulsion of native Christian usurers was not suggested.[108] In 1295, Godfrey of Fontaines also noted the different requirements of royal conduct towards native and foreign usurers: foreign usurers must be expelled and native usurers must be punished but not expelled.[109] Edward I's actions reflected suggestions made as long before as the 1180s, and were not without precedent in England, where, for example, Simon de Montfort had in 1231–2 'expelled the Jewish community from his town of Leicester, on the grounds that Christians suffered from their usurious activities', and Edward himself had expelled Jews from Gascony in 1287.[110] Foreign rulers had banned Jewish usurers from their lands, or were to do so thereafter.[111] It also seems that both in ordering banishment and in allowing foreign merchants to stay after initially ordering banishment, Edward I was repeating a policy of his father, since an entry on the Patent Roll for 1240 mentions a royal order 'that merchants practising usury in the realm should not stay in England beyond a fixed time', but grants certain merchants of Siena permission to stay in England.[112]

Banishment still seems to have been seen as an appropriate response to usury by foreigners in the late fourteenth century, since in 1376, the commons in Parliament asked that Lombards who had no other trade but that of broker should be banished, because of their usury.[113] It should, however, be noted that there is no sign of a positive royal response to this request.

Glanvill made no mention of banishment of usurers but did mention forfeiture of possessions, asserting that when a usurer died, all his chattels went to the king.[114] The slightly earlier treatise *Dialogus de Scaccario* also stated that the chattels of a dead usurer were to go to the king.[115] There is, however, a disagreement between these two texts as to what was to happen to the lands of the deceased usurer. The *Dialogus* held that the usurer's heir took his father's estate and immoveable property, whereas *Glanvill* stated that the usurer's heirs would be disinherited, and the usurer's rights in land would escheat to his lord.[116] There is slender evidence that it was the rule in *Glanvill* which was accepted in the thirteenth centuriy, at least in London.[117] The *Mirror of Justices* also shows the opinion that the

[108] *Sexti decretali*, lib. V, tit. V De Usuris; Friedberg, *Corpus Iuris Canonici*, vol. II c.1081; Langholm, *Economics*, 295.

[109] Godfrey of Fontaines, *Quodlibet* XII.9, J. Hoffmans (ed.), *Les quodlibets onze-quatorze de Godefroid de Fontaines*, Les philosophes belges 5 (Louvain, 1932), 114–18. I am grateful to Ian Wei for this reference. See also Langholm, *Economics*, 295.

[110] Prestwich, *English Politics*, 91; J.R. Maddicott, *Simon de Montfort* (Cambridge, 1994), 15; Stacey, 'Parliamentary negotiations', 100, citing J.S. Brewer (ed.), *Giraldi Cambrensis Opera*, Rolls Series (1861–91), viii, 183–6; SC 1/49/125, 179.

[111] Pirenne, *Economic and Social History of Medieval Europe*, 134, notes that in 1261 Duke Henry of Brabant ordered the expulsion of usurers from Brabant, and that Philip the Fair expelled usurers from France in 1306. Charles of Anjou expelled Jewish and other foreign usurers from Anjou and Maine in 1289: Mundill, *England's Jewish Solution*, 299–301.

[112] *CPR 1232–47*, 239. Orders of Henry III suggest very strongly that his motive was financial: see *CCR 1242–7*, 314–15, 317–18. The entry on p. 314 is headed 'De pecunia a mercatoribus de partibus transmarinis extorquenda' and that on p. 317 'De pecunia ab usurariis extorquenda'.

[113] *RP* II:332a. It was alleged that many of the 'Lombards' were in fact Jews and Saracens and private spies, and that, as well as practising usury, they had brought into the land a vice 'too horrible to name'.

[114] *Glanvill* VII:16. On escheat, see Baker, *Introduction*, 274–5.

[115] *Dialogus de Scaccario*, 98–100.

[116] *Dialogus de Scaccario*, 98; *Glanvill* VII:16.

[117] Case of 1309–10, Coram rege roll H. 3 Edw. II rot. 90; cited in *Placitorum Abbreviatio*, 310. H. 3 Edw. II London. Rot. 90 and *Borough Customs, vol. II*, 162.

land of usurers ought to escheat to lords (though complians that it did not do so in practice).[118] As will be discussed below, there is no conclusive proof that kings in the period under consideration made efforts to confiscate the land of deceased usurers.

Though not mentioned in royal pronouncements or legal treatises, the punishment actually imposed on convicted usurers by royal justices was generally a money payment to the king. Eyre records and the records of other royal sessions suggest that amercement or fine was the norm for convicted living usurers, at least between the late thirteenth century and the mid-fourteenth century.[119] One case of a confiscation of the chattels of a living usurer has been found.[120] Reports of usury in lower secular courts also show financial penalties.[121]

In contrast to the apparently usual royal and secular response of financial penalties for Christian usurers, canon law and theology laid great stress on restitution. It was an important element in canon law treatment of usurers that they were to be required to make restitution to borrowers.[122] There is, however, little reference to restitution in royal usury prosecution records. A fascinating mid-thirteenth-century record, the case of Goda la Gablere from the Eyre of London 1244, does mention restitution having been made, though it shows that this was a matter dealt with by the church not the royal courts.[123] Restitution of usurious profit to the borrower is not mentioned in other records of offences of usury, either from royal or from lower courts, with the exception of the London usury tribunal of the later fourteenth century onwards.[124] It is, however, possible that restitution was made following a conviction, but was not recorded on the royal courts' rolls, as it was of no interest to the king. For the present, based on 'criminal' cases, it may be concluded that restitution was not a matter pursued by secular courts. This would be in line with the general under-development of restitutionary actions at common law.[125] In one 'common pleas' case from the 1290 King's Bench

---

[118] *Mirror*, Book 5, c.1 no.132.

[119] See cases of Thomas Hert *et al.* (Lincolnshire 1281, JUST 1/497 m.38); William Goatchild (Gloucestershire, 1287, JUST 1/278 m.41, though this is contradicted by JUST 1/284, m.15); Jominus son of Elias (Channel Islands 1331, JUST 1/1166 m.8); Richard of Keynsham (Somerset 1341, JUST 1/770 m.12d); Henry de Rudyng (Lancashire 1343, JUST 1/430 m.25); Adam son of Robert de Blakeborye (Lancashire 1343, JUST 1/430 m.25), all in App. I below. There are some cases in which usurers were imprisoned, although this seems to have been a temporary measure, designed to encourage the offender to make fine with the king, rather than an appropriate punishment: e.g. JUST 1/430 m.25.

[120] *CPR 1272–81*, 73 (Nicholas le Convers, 1274; his chattels were returned when he was pardoned).

[121] See, e.g., the 1296 Chester case of Robert the Murager: Robert was said to be a usurer of corn, and made fine for this offence with half a mark: Stewart-Brown, *Calendar of County Court, City Court and Eyre Rolls of Chester*, 203, Chester Plea Roll no.6 (1288–97) Chester 29/6 m.15. A man is mentioned as having been amerced for usury in the tourn at Wakefield on 16 November 1316: Wakefield *D*, 156. Another made fine for usury with one mark in the court at Wakefield on 26 November 1316: Wakefield *D*, 159. Also in the Wakefield records, a man indicted for usury is recorded as having made fine with the lord 'for this trespass and for all the other counts of trespass in any wise to be charged against him up to this moment' with the large sum of £10 in silver, at the sheriff's tourn at Birton, on Tuesday after the feast of St Andrew, 1330: Wakefield *E*, 160. It was further stipulated in this case that if the same man should be convicted again of committing 'the crime of usury against any specified person for any specified sum' he was to pay the lord another £10. In the tourn of Wakefield on 27 May 1349, Henry Attecrosse was amerced 2s for being a 'common usurer of grain': Wakefield *G*115.

[122] Noonan, *Usury*, 16, 17, 19, 75.

[123] H.M. Chew and M. Weinbaum (eds), *Eyre of London 1244* (London, 1970), pp. 126–7, no.314.

[124] *CLB, G*, 161, ff.117–18; Seabourne, 'Controlling commercial morality'.

[125] Baker, *Introduction*, 390–1; Ibbetson, *Obligations*, 265–8.

rolls, a piece of land which had been held as security for a loan, and which had been taken as a means of enforcing the security, was recovered, though this is not necessarily an instance of full restitution, as no mention is made of the issues of the land during the time in which it was out of the hands of the owner.[126] The lack of emphasis on restitution suggests that royal and other secular justices were not primarily concerned with direct enforcement of the law of the church on usury, and that the process of investigating and convicting usurers was seen as having a purpose and a value independent of the desire to enforce the law of the church. The fact that secular reports do not usually replicate the language or concepts used in ecclesiastical usury cases, such as manifest usury or exorbitant usury, tends to reinforce this conclusion.[127]

Finally, convicted usurers, like any other offenders, might be pardoned by the king. The case of Italian usurers under Edward I and Henry III have been mentioned. The London usurer Nicholas le Convers also proferred a royal pardon when reporterd under the article 'Of Christian usurers alive and dead . . .' at the eyre of London 1276.[128]

Jurisdiction: judging the quick and the dead

Given the interest of the church in this matter, jurisdiction over offenders against the usury prohibition was an area both of overlap and of potential dispute between the king and the church. One should not assume jurisdictional dispute just because there is jurisdictional overlap, but there does seem to have been a degree of argument over usury jurisdiction at some points.[129] The division of jurisdiction over usury is a relatively complex matter, and one which has not been well understood. It has been claimed that 'until 1485, the royal courts declined to exercise any jurisdiction at all over usury except at the usurer's death'.[130] This is not entirely accurate. The 'Laws of Edward the Confessor' might be read as suggesting that kings should involve themselves in punishing living usurers by banishment, and they certainly assume royal action against those proved to have been usurers during their lifetime, as, in addition to their chattels being confiscated (possibly, though not certainly, after death) they are to be held as outlaws (which must indicate sanctions against them during life).[131] This does not necessarily assume royal

---

[126] KB 27/123 m.27; KB 27/124 m.10d; KB 27/125 m.7r; App. III below. Restoration of the land alone might not be sufficient to amount to restitution if the lender had taken profits from the land whilst he held it.

[127] There are exceptions: JUST 1/986 m.7 (also in JUST 1/988 m.7d) and JUST 1/986 m.7d (also in JUST 1/988 m.8d) do mention 'manifest usury'. For the canonical and theological distinction between manifest and covert usury, see, e.g., Gilchrist, *CEA*, 66.

[128] M. Weinbaum, *London Eyre 1276* (London, 1976), 85, no.306. The charter of pardon is in *CPR 1272–81*, p. 73, dated 3 December 1274, and mentioning usurious extortion and communication with usurers. Nicholas's goods had 'lately' been seized by the mayor and sheriffs of London by the king's order and were to be released. Nicholas and Hugh had been imprisoned in the Tower of London pending trial for the offences: *CCR 1272–9*, p. 107. Nicholas and Hugh seem to have been close: both appeared as pledges for a witness: *CLB, B*, 266 (1277), f.123.

[129] Fr. Olivier Martin, *Histoire de Droit Français* (Paris, 2nd edn 1995), no.139, p. 190, suggests that, in medieval France, either royal or ecclesiastical courts could have jurisdiction over usury.

[130] Helmholz, 'Usury', 365.

[131] 'Usurarios eciam defendit Edwardus, ne esset aliquis in regno suo . . . [S]i aliquis inde probatus esset, omnes possessiones perderet, et pro exlege haberetur': Thorpe, *Ancient Laws*, I, 199.

jurisdiction to decide whether somebody was, in fact, a usurer, but certainly envisages royal intervention in connection with living usurers. The *Dialogus de Scaccario* notes that 'those learned in the law' believed that 'the king has no ground of action against a Christian usurer . . . so long as he is alive' and sets out exclusive jurisdictions for the king and ecclesiastical courts.[132] In *Glanvill*, the only royal jurisdiction over usurers which is mentioned is that over dead usurers who had died unrepentant, which suggests exclusive jurisdiction for the church courts over living usurers and exclusive jurisdiction for the royal courts over deceased usurers and their goods.[133] If this was the situation at the end of Henry II's reign, however, it had not always been so, and was not so in the thirteenth and fourteenth centuries. The case of Bricstan of Chatteris shows that living usurers might be tried by royal justice in the early twelfth century.[134] H.G. Richardson has demonstrated that the royal jurisdiction over living usurers existed in the early years of Henry II's reign, but that the jurisdiction over dead usurers probably arose only around 1170, perhaps as a compromise with the church.[135]

'Royalist' sources of the thirteenth century seem to limit some aspects of church jurisdiction which might concern usury, saying that lay debts were for royal courts and not for Courts Christian.[136] English churchmen complained in 1239 that 'laymen had proclaimed in London that Church courts were not to hear cases of perjury, breach of faith, usury, simony or defamation'.[137]

Some evidence from the London eyre of 1244 tends to support the idea of a division of jurisdiction. The London jurors, when asked about dead Christian usurers, initially replied that they knew of none. When pressed, however (apparently by the king) they told the tale of Goda la Gablere, mentioned above. She had been a usurer, but had repented, done public penance, and made restitution to many people, then lived as a nun for twenty years before dying a 'good death'.[138] The story is interesting in many ways (the gender of the usurer, the very public nature of her turning away from usury, the king's particular inquiry) and it seems to show a high degree of respect by the royal judges for the ecclesiastical jurisdiction.

There is, however, good evidence against the idea of exclusive jurisdictional competence in this area in the thirteenth century. It is clear that kings set rules for

---

[132] *Dialogus de Scaccario*, 99.

[133] *Glanvill* VII:16.

[134] E.S. Kealey, *Roger of Salisbury, Viceroy of England* (California, 1972), 63, citing C. Johnson and H. Cronne (eds), *Regesta Regum Anglo-Normannorum*, vol. II (Oxford, 1956), no.1129; A le Prevost (ed.), *Orderic Vitalis* (Paris, 1838–55), III, 123–4; M. Chibnall (ed.), *The Ecclesiastical History of Orderic Vitalis*, vol. 3 (Oxford, 1972), pp. 346–58. See also Hudson, *Formation*, 53–6, 58, 68, 77, citing the above authorities, and, in addition, R.C. Van Caenegem (ed.), *English Lawsuits from William I to Richard I*, 2 vols, Selden Society 106, 107 (1990–1), no.204B.

[135] H.G. Richardson, 'Richard Fitz Neal and the *Dialogus de Scaccario*', *EHR* 63 (1928), 333, 335.

[136] E.B. Graves 'Circumspecte Agatis' *EHR* 43 (1928), 1–20; *Britton* 1.5.4, *Bracton* f.107, ff.400–12. Note, however, the muddy waters concerning breach of faith doctrine: R.H. Helmholz, 'Assumpsit and fidei laesio'. *Law Quarterly Review* 91 (1975), 406.

[137] Millon, 'Common Law and Canon Law', 224. He considered that it was 'almost certainly a reference to royal policy against pecuniary exactions by the Church, whether as penance or as compensation in civil cases'.

[138] H. Chew and M. Weinbaum (eds), *The London Eyre of 1244*, London Record Society Publications 6 (London, 1970), no.314. It is not clear when Goda lived and died, but it was at least twenty years before 1244, and she received her penance from 'the lord Richard, bishop of London', who is identified by the editors as Richard fitz Neal (bishop 1189–98).

living usurers after *Glanvill.* They certainly did so for Jewish usury until the Expulsion.[139] That kings should deal with living Jewish usurers is unsurprising, and not contrary to any presumed jurisdictional deal with the church. More obviously contrary to such a deal are the articles in certain eyres from at least 1244 which ask about living Christian usurers and the judicial commissions from 1274–6 which instructed the royal justices to investigate and do justice upon living Christian usurers.[140] Aside from an isolated possible instance in 1290, there are no signs of reluctance by secular authorities to prosecute usurers because of possible encroachment on the jurisdiction of the church.[141]

Royal justice seems, therefore, to have been moving into the area of judging living Christian usurers from the mid-thirteenth century. We should not assume that this necessarily meant that there would have to be a conflict with the ecclesiastical jurisdiction. The fact that Edward I used a cleric, Brother Stephen of Fuleburne, to hear a high-profile usury case in 1274. suggests continued co-operation.[142] There is, however, some evidence of conflicting claims of jurisdiction over Christian usury in the reign of Edward I. There was a complaint about interference with the ecclesiastical jurisdiction in 1285. A clerical complaint from Canterbury province stated that sheriffs were inhibiting church courts from hearing matters within the church's jurisdiction, including usury, and that the crimes were going unpunished.[143] In Lent 1300 and Hilary 1301, the English clergy complained to Parliament that ecclesiastical judges were being brought before secular courts to justify their jurisdiction over matters including usury.[144]

There is little evidence of royal use of the writ of prohibition to interfere with the hearing of usury cases by Courts Christian during the reign of Edward I (though it is conceivable that some of the instances in which ecclesiastical courts were alleged to be hearing cases concerning lay debts or chattels which were not testamentary could have involved usury).[145] One case appears in the roll of complaints of the Norfolk inquisition of 1286 which is associated with the *Circumspecte Agatis* row, though this seems to be a case which alleges extortion through false allegations of usury rather than a straightforward claim that the ecclesiastical court was not the

---

[139] There are statutory pronouncements from the reigns of John and Henry III dealing with the running of usury on a debt after the death of the debtor (John's Magna Carta 1215 cl.10, *SR* I:10; Statute of Merton 1235–6, c.5; *SR* I:3), which presumably concern Jewish usury (this was presumed in a fifteenth-century reading on the statute: S.E. Thorne (ed.), *Readings and Moots at the Inns of Court in the Fifteenth Century, vol. I,* Selden Society vol. 71 for 1952 (London, 1954), cv) and there was a royal regulatory regime for Jewish usury which existed in the reign of Henry III and in the early years of the reign of Edward I.

[140] See, e.g., Chew and Weinbaum, *The London Eyre of 1244,* 7, 8, 130; *CCR 1272–9,* 108.

[141] In 1290, William de Clervaus petitioned the king in Parliament for a remedy against the usurious conduct of Peter de Appleby, bailiff of York: *RP* I:46b. The original petition is in the PRO: SC 8/263 no.13138 (reference from Dr P. Brand). The reluctance to proceed may have been because the matter was already before the ecclesiastical jurisdiction, rather than because it was not thought to be an appropriate matter for secular authority.

[142] M. Weinbaum (ed.), *The London Eyre of 1276,* London Record Society Publications 12 (London, 1976), 85–6, no.306.

[143] P&C, *Councils,* 970.

[144] P&C, *Councils,* 1205, 1208.

[145] On prohibitions, see R.H. Helmholz, *Canon Law and the Law of England* (London, 1987), c.4 'The writ of prohibition to Courts Christian before 1500', 59–76, and c.5 'Writs of prohibition and ecclesiastical sanctions in the English Courts Christian', 77–99. At p. 82, Helmholz mentions one case of a usury prohibition being received by a Court Christian and noted in its records, but does not give details.

right place to try usury.[146] It was alleged that Master Gregory of Pontefract had had Lucy, who was the wife of Adam Silvistre, cited in his court as a usurer, that she was not a usurer, and that she had been so vexed by these frequent citations that she made fine with him for 5s, 'by extortion'.[147]

An accommodation appears to have been reached by the later years of Edward II's reign. In a case from the manor court of Boxley from 1322, a man was prosecuted for bringing his case in the ecclesiastical court rather than the correct secular forum, but when he explained that the case involved usury, he was acquitted.[148] In 1341, however, the clergy were once again complaining that royal justices were encroaching on their jurisdiction over usury, contrary to the common law.[149] In late 1340, royal commissions for matters including usury had been issued and in early 1341 a similar article on usury was included in the planned eyre of London.[150] In 1341, Edward III enacted a provision which set out exclusive jurisdictions for church and royal authorities:

> Item, it is accorded and assented that the King and his heirs shall have the conisance of the usurers dead, and that the ordinaries of holy church have the conisance of usurers in life, as to them appertaineth, to make compulsion by censures of holy church for the sin, to make restitution of the usuries taken, against the laws of holy church.[151]

It has been assumed that the 1341 statute settled the jurisdictional question.[152] In fact, it is unclear how long this rule remained in force. The statute in which it was contained, which was also concerned with various other matters, was found in 1343 to be contrary to the laws of the realm, since the king had not agreed to the provisions of his own free will, and it was repealed, though those articles which were reasonable were to be re-enacted.[153] The proposed re-enactment of some clauses was, however, never carried out.[154] It is clear that royal justices in 1341–3 did entertain suits against usurers.[155] There is evidence of possible jurisdictional dispute in the obtaining of a prohibition against an ecclesiastical court hearing a case concerning a living usurer in 1348.[156] Signs of dispute can also be seen in an

---

[146] See, e.g., Graves, 'Circumspecte Agatis'.

[147] It was adjudged that Lucy should recover her 5s from Master Gregory, plus damages assessed at 4s, and that Master Gregory should be placed in custody: JUST 1/575 m.107. Note that the associated roll of complaints from Suffolk, JUST 1/829 m.58, contains no cases relating to usury.

[148] Helmholz, *Canon Law*, 65, citing SC 2/180/9 m.10.

[149] '[I]ls acrochent a eux jurisdiction & conussance, contre la Lei de Seinte Esglise & de la terre de usures': *RP* II:129b.

[150] *CPR 1340–3*, 111; C.66/199 m.2d. G.J. Aungier (ed.), *Croniques de London depuis l'an 44 H. 3 jusqu'à l'an 17 Edw. III* (London, 1844), 88–9, includes 'De ceux qe chaunge fount de monee ou des autre biens ou ascun autre manere colour de usure'.

[151] *SR* I:296, st.15 Edw. III c.5. See also: *RP* II:130b, 133a; T. Scott Holmes (ed.), *Register of Ralph of Shrewsbury, Bishop of Bath and Wells 1329–1363* (Taunton, 1896), 398–9. The *RP* version adds to the text given above that 'Ministers of holy church shall have writs in the chancery to the justices and other ministers at all times.'

[152] Tawney, *Religion*, 63.

[153] *RP* II:139b; McKisack, *Fourteenth Century*, 174–7.

[154] Harriss, *King, Parliament and Public Finance*, 309; G. Lapsley, 'Archbishop Stratford and the parliamentary crisis of 1341', *EHR* 30 (1915), 6–18, 193–215, at 202–4.

[155] See further below at pp. 54–5.

[156] *Elcock v Springman* (1348) in C. Johnson (ed.), *Registrum Hamonis Hethe*, Canterbury and York Society (Canterbury, 1948), pp. 996, 1001, 1005, 1009, 1017, 1023, 1028–9, 1034, 1041 (mention of prohibition).

odd incident in 1364 in which 'a writ was issued from the chancery ordering the observance of a clause of the statute of 1341 relating to usury, but it had to be cancelled for having surreptitiously emanated from the chancery without the knowledge of the chancellor and others of the council'.[157] This episode suggests that the 1341 jurisdictional split was no longer regarded as official policy, but that this was controversial. The fact that a tribunal was set up in London in 1363–4 to deal with living usurers, with the approval of Edward III, supports the contention that the rule in the 1341 statute did not hold sway at that period, and that the government was not particularly respectful of the jurisdictional rights of the Church as it saw them.[158] The 1340s may have seen particular friction over jurisdictional rights in general, as can be deduced from commissions and a statute of 1344 concerning secular interference in testamentary jurisdiction.[159] There may, however, be seen to have been a change in royal attitude in the last year of Edward III's life and under Richard II. In 1377, when the commons in Parliament proposed that all cities, boroughs and vills of the realm be given the same right to try usury as London, this request did not receive a favourable response.[160] When, in 1382, there was an effort to increase the powers of the London usury tribunal, the government of Richard II was not prepared to diminish the powers of the ecclesiastical jurisdiction with respect to living usurers, and it was ordained that the church would keep its jurisdiction over usury as of old.[161] In 1390, Richard II, in response to a parliamentary petition urging punishment of usurers, and against 'meddling' by the church, ordered that the statute of 1341 and the 1363 ordinance allowing London's tribunal should be examined and, if found to be good ('bones et honestes'), that they should be confirmed, but there is no record of whether that was done.[162] It seems that Richard II did not go back on his predecessor's permission to London to try usury, since the London tribunal continued to function during his reign, but he was not prepared to make greater incursions into the area which the church perceived to be its exclusive jurisdiction.[163] The high-points of royal encroachment on what might have been considered the jurisdiction of the church over living usurers can, therefore, be seen to have come in the reigns of Edward I and Edward III, with some accommodation between the jurisdictions in the 1320s, and a conservative policy at the end of Edward III's reign and under Richard II. This is broadly in line with accepted views of church-state relations in general.[164] Richard II's government in particular

---

[157] Ormrod, *The Reign of Edward III*, 91, citing *CLB, G,* 162–3.

[158] *CLB, G,* p. 160, f.117; p. 196, f.161; *CPMR,* 97.

[159] *SR* I:303, 18 Edw. III (1344), st.2 cc.5 and 6.

[160] *RP* II:350b.

[161] 'come ele soloit avoir d'ancientee': *RP* III:142b, 143a. *CLB, H,* p. 206, f.159b.

[162] *RP* III:280b. The two documents seem, in any case, to be contradictory.

[163] See further below at pp. 55–6. Henry IV also took a conservative line on the questions of the jurisdictional spheres of church and royal courts. In 1403–4, a parliamentary petition requested action against brokers of usury, during life. The royal response was that this matter should be governed by the law of Holy Church during the life of the usurers: *RP* III:541a.

[164] See, e.g., Heath, *Church and Realm;* W.A. Pantin, *The English Church in the Fourteenth Century* (Notre Dame, 1962). A picture of gradual royal erosion of ecclesiastical jurisdiction is presented in J. Robert Wright, *The Church and the English Crown 1305–54* (Toronto, 1980), 176, and R.N. Swanson, *Church and Society in Late Medieval England* (Oxford, 1989), 141; W.R. Jones, 'Bishops, politics and the two laws: the gravamina of the English clergy 1237–1399', *Speculum* 41 (1966), 209–45, 226. For a view of relations as more harmonious in

seems to have preferred to maintain the jurisdictional status quo on a number of issues.[165]

It seems tolerably clear that there were genuine disagreements about jurisdiction, and the ecclesiastical jurisdiction lacked the power to enforce its apparent view of exclusive jurisdictional spheres for church and secular courts. Ecclesiastical authorities were not squeezed out, however, and certainly still claimed jurisdiction over usury at the end of the fourteenth century and beyond.[166]

Enforcement: mechanisms and practice

Medieval kings and governments ordered the use of existing (secular) tribunals at different levels and also special commissions to royal judges to investigate, try and punish usurers. They also supported or tolerated the exercise of jurisdiction by lower secular courts.

It is clear that royal courts were given and exercised jurisdiction over dead and living Christian usurers. There is an article on usury (specifically on dead usurers) in the earliest surviving set of eyre articles, from 1194.[167] Early sets of eyre articles do not always have a usury article, but a question on usury was generally asked in eyres throughout the thirteenth century and into the fourteenth century.[168] *Bracton*'s version of the usury article was: 'Of Christian usurers: who they were, what chattels they had and who has the chattels now'.[169] Understanding of what was being asked in this article changed, with jurors presenting living usurers on some occasions. An article specifically asking about living usurers can also be seen in the rolls of the London eyre of 1244 in the following forms: 'Of living Christian usurers, who they are and what chattels they have, and into whose hands they have come' and the alternative, more logical, 'Of living Christian usurers, who they are and what chattels they have, and what they are worth'. A separate article in the older form 'Of dead Christian usurers, who they were and what chattels they had' was also put to the jurors.[170] Separate questions also appear to have been asked in the eyre of Devon 1281.[171] Sometimes it is not clear from surviving records whether dead or living Christian usurers were being investigated, as in the version of the article from the Channel Islands eyre of

the reign of Edward I, see D. Millon, 'Common Law and Canon Law during the Reign of Edward I' (Ph.D., Cornell, 1982).

[165] Heath, *Church and Realm*, 212, 1377 commons petition to ensure that penances should not be commuted to fines by the church authorities answered with an order to all bishops and ordinaries to give penalties according to the law of the church and not otherwise: *RP* III:25; see also *RP* III:43; similarly on disputes about tithes: *RP* III:27, 43, 65, 116, 201, 281, 295, 307, 318.

[166] Helmholz, 'Usury', cites numerous later cases. Chaucer's 'Friar's Tale' describes an archdeacon who exercised jurisdiciton over usury, amongst other matters: A.C. Cawley (ed.), *Chaucer: Canterbury Tales* (London, 1958, reprinted 1992), 193.

[167] W. Stubbs (ed.), *Chronica Rogeri de Houedene*, vol. IV (London, 1868–71), 61.

[168] *Bracton*, f.118; H. Cam, 'Studies in the Hundred Rolls: some aspects of thirteenth century administration', in P. Vinogradoff (ed.), *Oxford Studies in Social and Legal History, vol. VI* (Oxford, 1921), 7, 9–71.

[169] 'De usurariis christianis mortuis, qui fuerunt, et quae catalla habuerunt et quis ea habuerit': *Bracton*, f.117.

[170] 'De usurariis christianis vivis: qui sint et que catalla habuerunt, et ad quorum manus devenerunt'; 'De usurariis christianis vivis, qui sint et que catalla habeant et quantum valeant'; 'De usurariis christianis mortuis qui fuerunt et que catalla habuerunt': Chew and Weinbaum, *London Eyre of 1244*, 7, 8, 130. Dr Brand suggests that the inclusion of the article on living usurers may have been connected to a proclamation against usury in the same year: *CCR 1242–7*, 242.

[171] The veredictum of North Tawton Hundred lists two separate usury articles, 'Of usurers' and 'Of dead Christian usurers': JUST 1/1569.

1331: 'Item de usurariis et eorum catal[lis]', though the fact that the article mentions chattels suggests that it refers to dead usurers, whose chattels were at the mercy of the king.[172] In fact, both living and dead usurers were presented at eyres in the time of Edward I, and living usurers were presented in eyres after his reign.

Although the pipe rolls of Henry II and Richard I show examples of royal collection of the forfeited chattels of usurers, and eyre rolls from the reigns of John and Henry III provide some examples of presentments of dead usurers, evidence of action involving the seizure of Christian usurers' assets after death is scarce in the records of royal courts and other royal records of the thirteenth and fourteenth centuries.[173] There are presentments of dead usurers in the crown pleas sections of rolls from the eyre of Worcestershire in 1275, as we have seen, and from the eyre of Cambridgeshire in 1299, but it is not clear whether the chattels of either of these alleged usurers found their way to the king.[174] There is no record of the outcome of Milo of Evesham's case in Worcestershire. William de Luda, accused of usury by two juries in the Cambridgeshire eyre of 1299, was buried in a lavish tomb in Ely Cathedral, so it seems somewhat unlikely that he was considered to be a usurer (or to have died an unrepentant usurer) either by royal or church authorities.[175] The existence of these eyre presentments does show that royal rights over the chattels of deceased usurers were not wholly forgotten in the reign of Edward I. After 1299, however, there are no presentments of dead usurers in the rolls of the eyre or of the King's Bench, or of any other secular tribunal examined, which suggests either that investigations of dead usurers were made using another mechanism, of which there is no sign, or that royal concern with the goods of usurers fell into abeyance in the fourteenth century. The pipe rolls offer no information as to whether royal rights over the chattels of deceased usurers continued to be exercised in the period under consideration. Their silence does not necessarily show that the exchequer did not receive the chattels of deceased usurers during the period under consideration, because, unlike the twelfth-century pipe rolls, those from the later thirteenth and fourteenth centuries do not identify with any precision the reason for payments into the exchequer by royal officials, so that it is possible that chattels of usurers might have been possessed by royal officers without appearing in such records. Some evidence against continued collection of the goods and debts of deceased Christian usurers in the thirteenth and fourteenth centuries can be seen in the fact that escheators were not asked to investigate such matters, and whilst statute set out the procedure for confiscation of the possessions of deceased felons, nothing similar survives with respect to dead usurers.[176] It is impossible to draw from this

---

[172] JUST 1/1166 m.1.

[173] J.H. Round (ed.), *Pipe Roll 33 Henry II*, Pipe Roll Society 37 (London, 1915), 126; D.M. Stenton (ed.), *Pipe Roll 3 & 4 Ric. I*, Pipe Roll Society 40 (London, 1926), 273; F.W. Maitland (ed.), *Select Pleas of the Crown, vol. 1: 1200–1225*, Selden Society vol. 1 for 1887 (London, 1888); Chew and Weinbaum, *London Eyre of 1244*, no.208, no.212.

[174] JUST 1/1025 m.4; JUST 1/1028 m.16r; JUST 1/1026 m.35; JUST 1/96 m.73r; JUST 1/95 m.65; JUST 1/96 m.75r; JUST 1/95 m.70r. The version of these presentments from JUST 1/95 is mentioned in E. Miller, *The Abbey and Archbishopric of Ely* (Cambridge 1951), 265 n.3.

[175] P.G. Lindley, 'The tomb of Bishop William de Luda: an architectural model at Ely Cathedral', *Proceedings of the Cambridge Antiquarian Society* 73 (Cambridge, 1984), 1–14.

[176] S.L. Waugh, 'The origins and early development of the articles of the escheator' in P.R. Coss and S.D. Lloyd (eds), *The Thirteenth Century V: Proceedings of the Newcastle upon Tyne Conference 1993* (Woodbridge, 1995), 89–114, 112–13; *SR* I:230, *De Catallis Felonium* (temp. incert.)

evidence firm conclusions as to whether or not the right of seizure of the chattels of dead usurers was moribund in the late thirteenth and fourteenth centuries, but there is no evidence that it was being exercised.

There is, however, far more evidence of action in royal courts against living usurers. There are records of presentments of living usurers in the eyres of London in 1276, Devon in 1281, Lincolnshire in 1281, Gloucestershire in 1287, Westmorland 1292 and the Channel Islands in 1331.[177] There are also some presentments of living usurers in the rolls and files of the King's Bench from 1342 and 1352.[178] Moreover, in the rolls of the *ad hoc* judicial commissions involving usury issued by Edward III in 1340, there are presentments from Somerset, Essex and Hertfordshire in 1341–2 and from the related session in Lancashire held in 1343.[179]

Usury cases might be aired before tribunals even closer to the king, or the king himself. The usurious transactions of two particular Jews were the subject of a petition for the king's grace on an occasion early in the reign of Edward III, the exact date of which is uncertain.[180] There were, in addition, parliamentary accusations in 1376 against two important (Christian) figures at court and in the London financial world respectively, for matters including usury, and there is a single example, from 1393, of a man being impeached before the King's Council for usury.[181] The London vintner and financier Richard Lyons and William Latimer, court chamberlain, were impeached in Parliament in 1376, for offences including usury, specifically getting the king involved in usurious loans from which, secretly, they profited.[182] The Close Rolls for 1393 contain procedural matters for the impeachment and trial of Walter Dautre for usury before the Council. The case broke down because Dautre was certified to be dead, which certainly suggests a lack of interest in dead usurers.[183]

Reports of living usurers are far more common than reports of dead usurers at all levels of secular jurisdiction in late thirteenth- and fourteenth-century England. It seems that the king and government transferred their attention from discovery of deceased usurers to the prosecution of living usurers in the reign of Edward I. No indication is given as to why this should be so, but it seems to be some indication

---

[177] JUST 1/497 m.3; JUST 1/491 m.2d; JUST 1/486 m.2d; JUST 1/497 m.3; JUST 1/491 m.2d; JUST 1/486 m.2d; JUST 1/497 m.38; JUST 1/486 m.28; Weinbaum, *London Eyre of 1276*, 85, no.306; JUST 1/181 m.38d; JUST 1/278 m.41; JUST 1/284 m.15; JUST 1/278 m.51d; JUST 1/986 m.7; JUST 1/988 m.7d; JUST 1/986 m.7d. Also in JUST 1/988 m.8d; JUST 1/986 m.9; JUST 1/1166 m.8.

[178] G.O. Sayles (ed.), *Select Cases in King's Bench Edward III, vol. VI*, Selden Society vol. 82 for 1965 (London, 1965), 18–19, *coram rege* roll no.327 m.28 for Hilary term 1342, presentment from Norfolk. JUST 1/268 m.7.

[179] JUST 1/770 m.12d; JUST 1/258 m.4d and m.7; JUST 1/337 m.3; JUST 1/430 m.25.

[180] *RP* II:402a. The petition was unsuccessful.

[181] *RP* II:323b–325a. See also: Brown, *Governance*, 81; McKisack, *Fourteenth Century*, 390; *CCR 1392–6*, 131, App. I.

[182] N. Saul, *Richard II* (New Haven, 1997), 19. Latimer was imprisoned and Lyons was sentenced to forfeiture and imprisonment, though John of Gaunt managed to reverse the effects of the Parliamentary proceedings shortly thereafter. See also A.R. Myers, 'The wealth of Richard Lyons' in T.A. Sandquist and M.R. Powicke (eds), *Essays in Medieval History presented to Bertie Wilkinson* (Toronto, 1969), 300–29. The latter claims (at 302) that some of the Good Parliament extortionate gain allegations were exaggerated, and notes (at 307) that Lyons' goods were confiscated but, when he was pardoned, they were restored (20/3/1377) and (at 305) that he was buried in some splendour, which may suggest that he was regarded as innocent or truly penitent by the church and government.

[183] *CCR 1392–6*, 131, App. I.

of a desire to act to punish usurers or to discourage further usury by offenders, rather than merely taking a windfall profit when usurers died.

Views of frankpledge seem to have had some jurisdiction over usury from at least the reign of Edward I, though no royal order dealing with this jurisdiction can be found. The articles of view of frankpledge in *Statutes of the Realm*, said to date from 1323x1325, do not contain an article on usury, but *Fleta*'s list of articles does include usurers; an article on usury appears in the articles of inquiry of the Stoneleigh frankpledge; the *Mirror of Justices* lists 'Of Christian usurers and all their goods' as an article of the view of frankpledge; there is an article 'Enquire of the chattels of any dead Christian usurer' in a set of articles from a view of frankpledge from a manuscript of *c.*1307; an early fourteenth-century list of lawday chapters includes an article on Christian usurers; and a tract from the mid-fourteenth century reporting as an example of the articles of a view of frankpledge the articles used by the court held at Weston on an unknown date in 1340 included 'Whether there be amongst you any usurer: present the facts'.[184] This version of the article clearly seems to have been aimed at living usurers, and the Stoneleigh article may also be taken to suggest an investigation of living usurers There is no evidence of royal action against views of frankpledge which tried usurers, so it may be concluded that kings and governments probably tolerated the exercise of jurisdiction over usurers by views of frankpledge. London wardmoots were required to inquire as to usurers from at least the reign of Edward II.[185] London aleconners were also required to make enquiries as to certain types of usury (chevisance by brokers) from 1380.[186] Usury was occasionally prosecuted in views of frankpledge, hundred courts, manor courts and courts leet. Although the rolls of the court and view of frankpledge of Sutton in Lincolnshire contain no examples of presentments for usury, there are presentments for usury in the Norwich leet records of 1290, the view of frankpledge in Tamworth in 1311, in the Court of Clun in 1328–9, 1337 and 1401, and the court of the hundred of Appletree in 1389.[187] The records of tourns at Wakefield show a small number of usury presentments, from 1277, 1316 (2), 1330 and 1350.[188] Usury presentments can be seen in civic jurisdictions in Chester in the late thirteenth century, and in London in the

---

[184] *SR* I:246; *Fleta II*, 175–6, Book II, c.52; Hilton, *English Peasantry*, 47; *Mirror*, Book 1, c.12; F.J.C. Hearnshaw, *Leet Jurisdiction in England* (Southampton, 1908), 373, citing Cambridge University Library, MS Dd.7.6, f.60 col.2; BL, MS Arundel 310, f.116v (I am grateful to Dr P. Brand for this reference); *Court Baron*, 95.

[185] *LA*, 293, f.213: 'If any bargain of usury has been made within the ward since the last wardmote'. Duty retained in 1363 ordinance: *CLB, G*, 161, ff.117–18.

[186] *CLB H* 157, f.127.

[187] Hudson, 'Leet Jurisdiction in Norwich', 33, 37; G.E.A. Raspin, 'Transcript and Descriptive List of the Medieval Court Rolls of the Marcher Lordship of Clun deposited in Salop Record Office by the Earl of Powis' (unpublished, 1963), 30, 33, 91, 175. DL 30/45/523 m.8.

[188] Usury is mentioned tangentially in a slander case in *A*, 1, court at Halifax, 16 October 1274; in a debt case in *A*, 90, court at Wakefield, 22 November 1274; in a debt or slander case in *A*, 281, court at Rastrick, Monday after the Feast of St John of Beverley 1297. There is a presentment of usury in the tourn at Halifax, Tuesday after the Translation of St Thomas Martyr 1274: *A*, 172. A man is mentioned as having been amerced for usury in the tourn at Wakefield 16 November 1316: *D*, 156. A man made fine for usury in the court at Wakefield, 26 November 1316: *D*, 159. A usury indictment is found in the sheriff's tourn at Birton, Tuesday after the Feast of St Andrew 1330: *E*, 160. A usury presentment is found in the tourn of Wakefield 27 May 1349: *G*, 115.

second half of the fourteenth century.[189] The liberty of Chester appears to have been planning to prosecute a living usurer in 1358.[190]

According to *Britton*, a law book from the early 1290s, sheriffs were given the right to deal with usury in their tourns. The article 'Of usurers' appears in *Britton*'s list of the articles of the sheriff's tourn.[191] Sheriffs and bailiffs seem to have been able to take action, as can be seen from an entry in the Hundred Rolls for Kent in which the hundred of Oxeneye complained in 1275 that a bailiff appointed by a former sheriff of Kent had extorted 20s from a man by threatening to make an accusation of usury against him.[192] After the conquest of Wales, sheriffs' tourns in Wales were also given an article on usurers.[193]

The overall number of usury cases in the records of secular courts is small, but it is clear that the possibility of prosecuting usurers remained into the fourteenth century, and was used by those responsible for presenting offenders in many different areas of England. No doubt the steady endeavour of many historians working on local archives will unearth further examples. Helmholz's assessment of the usury jurisdiction of the medieval English ecclesiastical courts also fits the situation in secular courts. He found that usury cases were 'regular but infrequent', 'a distinctly minor part of the business of an ordinary English ecclesiastical court': it is not a surprise to find them and it is not a surprise not to find them.[194]

As well as using settled institutions to enforce the usury laws, a number of occasional expedients were tried. Under Henry III, there is evidence of the issue of a special commission for a judge to investigate whether or not one particular individual had died a usurer, and, if so, to find out about his assets.[195] With one possible exception in the 1274 case of Nicholas le Convers and Hugh de Gyzors, which might have been the only case Brother Stephen de Fuleburne was appointed to hear in 1274, no similar single-case commissions have been found for the period under examination, but there were limited campaigns against usury in the reigns of Edward I and Edward III.[196]

A campaign against usury was instigated from 1274 onwards. As mentioned above, in 1274, Edward I ordered the mayor and sheriffs of London to make it known in the city that all merchant usurers must leave within twenty days from 9

---

[189] R. Stewart-Brown (ed.), *Calendar of County Court, City Court and Eyre Rolls of Chester 1259–1297*, Chetham Society 84 (Manchester, 1925), 61, 203, 208, 242: Chester Plea Roll no.3, Chester 29/3 m.7. no.52; Chester Plea Roll no.6 [1288–97], Chester 29/6 m.15; Macclesfield eyre roll 1285, Chester 17/12 m.12; Macclesfield eyre roll 1290, Chester 17/12 m.10. London: *John atte Ram v Peter de Mildenhale* (1364) *CPMR 1323–64*, 280; *Richard Cornewaylle v Walter Southous* (1376) *CLB, H*, p. 24 f.31b and p. 27 f.35b; *John Edward v Walter Southous* (1376), *CLB H*, p. 26 f.36b; *Henry Cauntebrigge v Geoffrey Puppe and William Brampton* (1382), *CPMR 1381–1412*, 25.

[190] HMSO, *Register of Edward the Black Prince*, 4 vols (London, 1930–3), *Part III, 1351–1365*, f.173d (Black Prince ordered Chester officials not to 'impeach' John Furneys, servant of Master Humphrey de Chorleton, in respect of his indictment as a 'common usurer' and offered a charter of pardon).

[191] 'De usurers': *Britton*, Book 1, c.30.

[192] *Hundred Rolls*, I, 225–6.

[193] Statute of Wales 1284, st.12 Edw. I, c.4; *SR* I:57.

[194] Helmholz, 'Usury', 328.

[195] *CPR 1266–72*, 675 (1272). Note that the assets to be investigated were debts and goods, there being no mention of land.

[196] Weinbaum, *London Eyre of 1276*, pp. 85–6, no.306.

November, under pain of forfeiture of their bodies and goods. If found in the city after that date, they were to be arrested and kept safely until further orders.[197] This order was followed up in January 1275 by an order to Joseph de Chancy, the Treasurer, John de Lovetot and Geoffrey de Neubaud, to 'enquire cautiously whether any merchant-usurers are found in the city of London or elsewhere in the realm, and to cause the bodies and goods and chattels of any such to be arrested and kept safely until otherwise ordered, conducting themselves so circumspectly and diligently in this matter that the king may commend their diligence'. This was necessary because the king had found that 'some [merchant usurers] dwell in the city and elsewhere in the realm contrary to the inhibition'.[198] Lovetot was also sent to do a similar job in Norfolk in November of the same year.[199] In December 1276, he and Gregory de Rokesley were commissioned to enquire as to Christians in Surrey and London who committed usury and other offences, some involving Jews.[200] On the same day, a similar commission was issued to Walter de Stirkely and Henry de Tibetot for Nottingham and Nottinghamshire.[201] In April 1276, Lovetot was ordered to enquire into usurious moneylending by Christians in Essex.[202] Edward I also ordered particular action against Jewish usury. An inquiry into a number of offences by Jews, including usury contrary to the Statutes of Jewry, was commissioned in or around 1276.[203] There is, however, no trace of indictments for usury at the special sessions of the Jews in which offences against other articles in the same set were investigated (particularly coin offences and receiving stolen goods), though it has been suggested that there was a connection between coin clipping and disguised usury.[204]

No new campaigns against usury seem to have been instigated after the first decade of Edward I's reign, or under Edward II, despite the facts that the issue of usury was highlighted at the Council of Vienne in 1311, and that a commons legislative programme of 1322x1326 suggested an inquiry by certain magnates and judges into usury.[205] Edward III did order the investigation of usury by *ad hoc* commissions, though in this case, usury was not by any means the only matter being investigated. Several commissions were issued in 1340, when the king returned from his military campaign on the continent in order to raise money and put the administration of the country in order.[206] Royal justices were instructed to go out to the counties and hear and determine various matters. The main thrust

---

[197] *CCR 1272–9*, 108.

[198] *CCR 1272–9*, 144 (January 1275). Pardons purchased by Italians: *CPR 1272–81*, 92–5 (June 1275), 128 (January 1276), 448 (July 1281).

[199] *CPR 1272–81*, 172.

[200] *CPR 1272–81*, 236.

[201] *ibid.*

[202] *CPR 1272–81*, 176.

[203] Rigg, *Select Starrs*, liv; BL, MS Add. 38821, f.82r–v; Lincoln's Inn MS Hale 140, f.49r. I am grateful to Dr P. Brand for these references.

[204] Brand, 'Jews and the law', 1140, 1145; Stacey, 'Parliamentary negotiations', 97, citing a Plea Roll of the Exchequer of the Jews: S. Cohen (ed.), revised P. Brand, *Plea Rolls of the Exchequer of the Jews, vol. V: 1277–1299* (London, 1992), nos 681, 889; Z.E. Rokeah, 'Money and the hangman in late thirteenth-century England', Part I, *Jewish History Studies* 31 (1988–90), 83–109; Part II, *Jewish History Studies* 32 (1990–2), 159–218.

[205] N.P. Tanner (ed.), *Decrees of the Ecumenical Councils* (London, 1990), 384, no.29; C 49/5; W.M. Ormrod, 'Agenda for legislation, 1322–c.1340', *EHR* 105 (1990), 1–33. See App. IV below.

[206] McKisack, *Fourteenth Century*, 168ff; Ormrod, *Reign of Edward III*, 14–15.

of the commissions was the detection and punishment of officials' misconduct, but there was also a requirement to inquire into usury, though the description in the *Calendar of Patent Rolls* does not mention this aspect. The list of matters to be investigated includes 'Of the names of all, who, either by lending money or by lending other things, or in any other way, have been accustomed to take wicked usury on the pretext of honest gain'.[207]

The position of the clause concerning usury makes its purpose a little ambiguous. It is at the end of a series of clauses which clearly concern the misdeeds of officials, and before a series of clauses concerning all the king's subjects. It is not clear, therefore, whether the king and government wished only the usury of officials to be investigated, or whether all usury was to be examined. Whatever was intended, however, the presentments for usury in sessions held under this commission do not seem to be confined to royal ministers. Only one accused person is identified as holding an office.[208]

There is no evidence of further *ad hoc* investigations concerning usury being ordered. When the justices of the peace became a regular part of the judicial landscape, from the 1360s onwards, it seems that they did not have jurisdiction over usury, although some of them tried unsuccessfully to assume this jurisdiction in Norwich in 1378 when jurors presented a man as a usurer before them.[209] These facts suggest quite strongly that kings ceased to innovate in enforcement of the usury prohibition after the early 1340s, preferring to take action through existing institutions, or to leave it to other tribunals well outside the central royal law-enforcement hierarchy. In 1377, there was governmental disapproval of a proposal to extend the London scheme to other parts of the country, with the very undynamic response 'Y courge la loy ancienement usee'.[210] The fact that innovation and effort seems to have decreased from the latter part of Edward III's reign will be seen to be in contrast to the level of royal concern with the terms of subjects' sales of goods.

'Contractual' aspects

As well as, or instead of, penalising the participants in a dubious bargain, another way of dealing with such arrangements is to render them void or unenforceable. There is evidence of this strategy being used by medieval English law, though certain detailed issues remain uncertain.

The 'contractual' rules concerning Christian usury are not set out in any positive legislation, though they may be illuminated by examination of the records of 'private' cases brought by one subject against another in the common pleas

---

[207] 'De nominibus omnium & singulorum qui per mutuacionem pecunie seu aliarum rem vel quocumque colore quesito usi fuerunt usuraria pravitate': commission relating to Somerset: JUST 1/770 m.1. The same commission, directed to different men, heads: JUST 1/521 (Lincoln), JUST 1/858 (Suffolk), JUST 1/638/1 (Northamptonshire), JUST 1/258 (Essex), JUST 1/715 (Oxfordshire), and JUST 1/337 (Hertfordshire). The version of the commission given on the patent roll is in very poor condition: *CPR 1340–3*, 111; C 66/199 m.2d, the version to Robert Burgcher *et al.* for London. The marginal note says 'Inquirendo de extorsionibus etc.'

[208] John de Botyngham of Colchester 'used his official position' to imprison a debtor under a usurious loan: JUST 1/2587 m.7.

[209] Baker, *Introduction*, 29–30; Putnam, *PJP*, 111, no.40.

[210] *RP* II:350b.

jurisdiction of the central royal courts. Those legal historians who lay the traditional emphasis on private law or 'common pleas' will find this the most important aspect of a discussion of usury. As has been mentioned, however, 'indirect' royal action in the sense of entertaining pleas brought by one private individual against another, is not the principal focus of this book. As a consequence, a limited amount of primary material relevant to common pleas has been examined, so that only very tentative remarks may be made concerning them. I will confine myself to three points in the main body of this chapter, and then present the remainder of the material which has been discovered on usury in common pleas in Appendix III. The first point to note is that a small number of common pleas in which usury is pleaded have been discovered. These are discussed in Appendix III. The second point is that, in debt cases, which form the most obvious class of cases in which one would expect to see some usury pleas, such pleading seems to be rare, a fact which may be interpreted in a number of different ways. Thirdly, the cases discovered so far do not really illuminate the question of whether the whole of a usury-tainted debt was unenforceable, or whether only the usury was unenforceable.

The possibility that intervention might take the form of a refusal to enforce bargains tainted by usury (i.e. the whole bargain, and not just the usury, might be considered unenforceable) was certainly mooted. The *Mirror of Justices* stated that obligations tainted by sin would not be enforceable if a borrower made this objection when the lender took him to court to secure payment.[211] More concrete evidence of this strategy is visible in the Jewish regulations. The 1275 Statute of the Jewry allowed existing loans to be enforced, but provided for the practical unenforceability of those future loans made by Jews to Christians which were tainted by usury, in that if a Jew should lend at usury contrary to the statute, the king would not 'lend his aid for the recovery of the loan'.[212] The situation with regard to Christian usury is less clear.

The possibility of challenging bargains on grounds of usury was undermined by the formal methods of recording debts, and enforcing them without investigation, which had existed long before the reign of Edward I in the form of recognisances, and which were expanded in his reign and in the fourteenth century in the form of statutes merchant and statutes staple. Once such an agreement had been entered into, serious government machinery was put at the disposal of a creditor, with little or no prospect for the debtor to challenge the basis of the bargain and raise questions of usury.[213]

Efficacy

It is impossible to say much about the overall effect of the laws, the number of people who got away with usury, and I make no attempt to do so. Documentation

---

[211] *Mirror*, Book II, c.27; Book III, c.32.

[212] Statutes of the Jewry, clause 1: *SR* I:221. The Statutes of the Jewry 1275 did not render void the existing contracts made by Jews: only the usury clause would be unenforceable, in so far as usury accruing after St Edward's day 1275 could not be collected (although usury which had accrued before that date could be collected). If, however, a Jew made a usurious contract from the date specified, the whole deal would be unenforceable and the Jew would be punished at the king's discretion. No negative consequences would accrue to the Christian.

[213] McNall, 'Recognition', especially 41–6.

of many medieval loans is opaque, and although it does not show usury being demanded, we cannot be sure that it was not taken. It is, however, necessary to enter into this area, if only to discuss the opinions put forward by others, which are generally negative.[214]

The opinion has been expressed (with occasional dissent) that the ban on Jewish usury under the 1275 Statutes of the Jewry was not hard to evade.[215] There is support for such propositions in clerical complaints of Jewish usury and in the fact that the 1284x1286 Draft Statute of the Jewry mentions that there has been evasion of the prohibition.[216] There is also evidence of the existence of a writ concerning breaches of the 1275 statute, suggesting a degree of evasion.[217] As far as Christian usury is concerned, effort and effectiveness of ecclesiastical courts are also criticised, and the prevalence of usury bewailed in an English confessor's manual of the first half of the fourteenth century.[218] The commons legislative programme of 1322x1326 noted the existence of Christian usurers, operating 'in various ways, some secret and some open', causing 'great suffering to the people'.[219]

A number of ways of evading and avoiding the usury laws have been suggested. Usury might be disguised by stating that a higher sum had been lent than had in fact been lent, the sum recorded representing the principal plus usury, as was noted in the early thirteenth century.[220] J.L. Bolton assumes this to have been the case in

---

[214] H.G. Richardson and G.O. Sayles described the prohibition on usury as 'remote from the practical conduct of affairs, . . . maintained in principle [but] in practice largely ignored': H.G. Richardson and G.O. Sayles, *Law and Legislation from Aethelberht to Magna Carta* (Edinburgh, 1966), 85. J.H. Baker has implied that the prohibition of usury was 'unworldly': Baker, *Introduction*, 353, a view shared by Langholm (Langholm, *Economics*, 38–9), and R. Zimmerman described the usury prohibition as an 'idealistic but impractical canonical restraint on contractual freedom, and on business life in general': Zimmerman, *Law of Obligations*, 163. There are unsupported statements that the usury laws did not work: H.G. Richardson's statement that 'neither ecclesiastical courts nor royal courts afforded effective control [over usury] . . . [V]ery little was effected except gradually to disguise the open taking of interest' (Richardson, *English Jewry*, 139); A. Steel made the similarly unsupported statement that usury was, in fourteenth- and fifteenth-century England, 'an everyday affair', and R.H. Bowers asserted that '[a]s is well known, the practice of usury was ubiquitous and persistent during the later Middle Ages' (A. Steel, *The Receipt of the Exchequer, 1377–1485* (Cambridge, 1954), 121; R.H. Bowers, 'A Middle English Mnemonic Poem on Usury', *Medieval Studies* 17 (1955), 226). E. Lipson made a similar claim: although he recognised the fact that the evidence was 'scanty', he felt able to state that, 'on the whole, [it] appears to point to the conclusion that the economic development of the Middle Ages was retarded by the prohibition' (Lipson, *Economic History of England*, 616). He did not specify the evidence to which he referred. The supposed causal link between the usury prohibition and adverse economic conditions was repeated, again without substantiation, by F.C. Dietz, *An Economic History of England* (New York, 1942), 71, and Gilchrist, *CEA*, 87. Lack of efficacy assumed merely because instances of breaches of the rules found, in connection with usury: Gilchrist, *CEA*, 87.

[215] Mundill, 'Christian and Jewish moneylending', 48; Rigg, *Select Starrs*, xxxvii; V. Lipman, *The Jews of Medieval Norwich* (London, 1967), 165–8; Stacey, 'Parliamentary negotiations', 97 (all see 'the great majority of Jewish bonds from the 1275–90 period as disguised moneylending transactions' (Stacey, 96)). Contrary views are expressed in: R. Mundill, 'Anglo-Jewry under Edward I: credit agents and their clients', *Jewish Historical Studies* 31 (1988–90), 1–21; R. Mundill, 'Lumbard and son: the business and debtors of two Jewish moneylenders', *Jewish Quarterly Review* 82 (1991), 131–70. Brand, 'Jews and the law', 1153, accepts Mundill's argument that the statute changed the contractual behaviour of at least some Jews, but finds that the post-1275 commodity contracts which Mundill describes could still have been regarded as usurious.

[216] Rigg, *Select Starrs*, lvi. The issue of royal tolerance of Jewish usury was brought up in a clerical complaint of 1285: P&C, *Councils*, 959–63.

[217] Brand, 'Jews and the law', 1156, citing BL, MS Harley 748. f.30r–v; Philadelphia Free Library, MS LC 14.16, f.174r; Library of Congress, MS 131, f.27r–v.

[218] *Memoriale Presbiterorum*, in Harding, *Law Courts*, document 17, p. 159; Wood, *Medieval Economic Thought*, 173.

[219] C 49/5; Ormrod, 'Agenda for legislation'; App. IV below.

[220] Mundill, 'Christian and Jewish moneylending', 49.

large-scale thirteenth-century loans by Italian merchants, to be repaid in wool.[221] R.R. Mundill assumes that there was a lot of disguised profit on recognizances and statutes merchant, and that the availabiliy of the new types of formally and definitively recorded debt from the 1280s (statutes merchant and staple) increased opportunities for doing this, though, as McNall notes, there is no definite evidence of this before the fifteenth century, with the exception of a statute merchant apparently being used in an unsuccessful attempt to avoid detection of usury in the roll of the Westmorland eyre of 1292.[222] Usury might also be disguised by cloaking a loan as a sale of goods or a land transaction or an exchange of currencies.[223] It is also suggested that prominent citizens might make mortgages with impunity in the fourteenth century.[224] Coin clipping is mentioned as an apparently successful method of disguising usury by 'Coveitise' in *Piers Plowman*.[225] A transaction which might look like a loan of 20s without usury might actually be usurious if the loan was made in clipped coin and the repayment was to be made in unclipped coin.[226] Cases connecting coin clipping and disguised usury have been found in Jewish cases, but no such connection has been found in cases involving Christian usurers.[227]

Although historians very frequently assume that much lending must have been usurious, there is a lot less evidence of this than one might imagine from the level of certainty displayed. There are indications that loans might be made for rewards which were intangible or not readily quanitifiable (and therefore not amenable to the usury laws) in terms of personal or social credit.[228] There is the usual point

[221] Bolton, *MEE*, 176.

[222] Mundill, 'Christian and Jewish moneylending', 52; McNall, 'Business', 77, suggests that it is 'not possible to rule out the possibility of chevisance' from Statute of Merchants 1285 London recognizances, though he notes that there is no definite evidence that it was happening, at least before the fifteenth century. He cites E. Zwanzig Bennett, 'Debt and Credit in the Urban Economy, London 1380–1460' (Ph.D. thesis, Yale, 1989), *Stirkeland v Goldington*, JUST 1/987 m.34; JUST 1/988 m.8d, is cited and discussed.

[223] Postan, 'Credit in medieval trade' in *Medieval Trade and Finance*, 1–27; F. Jouon des Longrais took the view that 'early' leases were designed to evade the ecclesiastical prohibition of usury: Simpson, *Land Law*, 72, citing Jouon des Longrais, *La Conception anglaise de la saisine* (Paris, 1925); T.F.T. Plucknett, review, *Harvard Law Review* 40 (1926) 921–4, at 924; Schofield, 'Introduction', 7, citing fifteenth-century evidence: G.A. Holmes, 'The libel of English policy', *EHR* (76) (1961), 201; E.E. Power, 'The wool trade in the fifteenth century' in E.E. Power and M.M. Postan (eds), *Studies in English Trade in the Fifteenth Century* (London, 1933), 65. There were restrictions on currency exchange: *CLB, C*, p. xii; *RP* I:29.

[224] Wood, *Medieval Economic Thought*, 189, citing the 1,000 mark loan of Archbishop Melton of York to the earl of Atholl in 1332, which brought him fruits of the manor of Gainsborough for nearly two years: L.H. Butler, 'Archbishop Melton and his neighbours and his kinsmen, 1317–1340', *Journal of Ecclesiastical History* 2 (1951), 54–67. In fact, as Butler noted at p. 61, the loan was paid off early, so Melton did not make as much on the arrangement as he might have done. His record seems generally not to have been terribly usurious: though he used penalties for late payment, in a number of cases these were not exacted, and usury does not seem to have been intended in a number of instances of loans. Melton made interest-free loans to Edward III, and, despite being a fairly regular moneylender, did not have a usual interest rate: Butler, 'Archbishop Melton', 56, 57, 59, 61.

[225] W. Langland, *The Vision of Piers the Plowman by William Langland, done into modern English by Walter W. Skeat* (London, 1905) I, p. 150, B Text Passus V II.241–6; Goodridge (trans.), *Piers the Plowman*, p. 106, cited in Mundill, 'Christian and Jewish moneylending', 48.

[226] Stacey, 'Parliamentary negotiations', 97.

[227] Stacey, 'Parliamentary negotiations', 97, citing S. Cohen (ed.), rev. P. Brand, *Plea Rolls of the Exchequer of Jews, vol. V: 1277–1299* (London, 1992) nos 681, 889; Z.E. Rokeah, 'Money and the hangman in late thirteenth century England', Part I, *Jewish History Studies* 31 (1988–90), 83–109; Part II, *Jewish History Studies* 32 (1990–2), 159–218.

[228] This has been suggested at both high and low levels of society. See, e.g., C. Briggs, 'Creditors and debtors and their relations at Oakington, Cottenham and Dry Drayton (Cambridgeshire) 1291–1350', 127–148, 130; and G.L. Harriss, 'Cardinal Beaufort: patriot or usurer?' *TRHS* 20 (1970), 129–48.

which must be made whenever one is considering the 'success' or 'efficacy' of laws, which is that we cannot know how things would have developed, had there been no legal inhibitions. There is no unregulated 'control' with which to compare the evidence which we have. There is evidence that secular tribunals investigated Christian usury, as noted above, and there is evidence of requests for action which assume that it would not be useless to try to do something about usury.

Rationales

Based on the existence of ecclesiastical writing and rules against usury and the work of previous commentators, one might have assumed that this was an area in which the influence of the church and ideas of acting to prevent immoral conduct was the predominant influence. The medieval Western church condemned usury on many occasions and campaigned against it with some energy in the thirteenth and fourteenth centuries.[229] Usury was an extremely popular subject for medieval theologians and canon lawyers, who discussed at length the definition of usury and appropriate responses to such sin, and for medieval preachers.[230] Action and pronouncements by English prelates were in accordance with the teaching of the Western church.[231] General excommunication of usurers was routinely pronounced.[232] Evidence of ecclesiastical prosecution of usurers exists from different English dioceses from dates throughout the period under consideration, and R.H. Helmholz has demonstrated that 'the canon law of usury was by no means the dead letter in England that critics have sometimes assumed'.[233] It is true that there is no sign of popes giving kings of England direct instructions or encouragement to act against usury, but it is not implausible that it might have been considered part of the royal role to support and give effect to the teachings of the church on usury.[234]

---

[229] N.P. Tanner (ed.), *Decrees of the Ecumenical Councils* (London, 1990), p. 200, no.13; p. 293, no.2; p. 328, no.26; p. 384, no.29; J. Brundage, *Medieval Canon Law* (London, 1995), 77; J. Le Goff, *Your Money or Your Life: Economy and Religion in the Middle Ages* (New York, 1986), 26; Gilchrist, *CEA*, 109–10; R.M. Fraher, 'Preventing crime in the High Middle Ages: the medieval lawyers' search for deterrence' in J.R. Sweeney and S. Chodorow (eds), *Popes, Teachers and Canon Law in the Middle Ages* (Cornell, 1989), 212, 218, 228; J.D. Mansi (ed.), *Sacrorum Conciliorum Nova et Amplisimus Collectio* (Graz, 1960–2), vol. 25, 411.

[230] O. Langholm noted that '[n]o single subject fills more pages of medieval economic writing than usury does': O. Langholm, *The Aristotelian Analysis of Usury* (Bergen, 1984), 9.

[231] Whitelock, *Councils*, I, 741; P&C, *Councils*, vol. II, part 1, 55, 74, 144, 178, 318, 652. Archbishop John Pecham condemned usury by a fellow ecclesiastic, the abbot of Bristol, though he was later accused of usury himself: Wood, *Medieval Economic Thought*, 172; Helmholz, 'Usury', 336.

[232] P&C, *Councils*, vol. II, part 1, 167, 192, 333, 356, 466.

[233] See, e.g., R.M.T. Hill (ed.), *The Rolls and Register of Bishop Oliver Sutton, 1286–1299, vol. IV*, Publications of the Lincolnshire Record Society 52 for 1957 (Hereford, 1958), 10; W. Brown, *Register of John le Romeyn, Lord Archbishop of York 1286–1296, part I*, Surtees Society 123 (Durham, 1913), 312, no.892; W. Brown, *The Register of Thomas of Corbridge, Lord Archbishop of York 1300–1304, part I*, Surtees Society 138 (Durham, 1925), 187; W. Brown and A.H. Thompson (eds), *Register of William Greenfield, Archbishop of York 1306–1315*, Surtees Society 152 (Durham, 1938), 7, no.1687; J.W. Willis Bund, *Worcester Registrum Sede Vacante 1301–1435* (Oxford, 1897), 180, f.99d; A.T. Bannister (ed.), *Registrum Ade de Orleton* (London, 1908), 370; C. Johnson (ed.), *Registrum Hamonis Hethe* (Canterbury, 1915–48), 996, 1001, 1009, 1005, 1017, 1023, 1028–9, 1034, 1041. Helmholz, 'Usury', 367. See also L.R. Poos (ed.) *Lower Level Jurisdiction in Late-Medieval England: The Courts of the Dean and Chapter of Lincoln 1336–49 and Deanery of Wisbech 1458–1484* (Oxford, 2001), 102 (Lincoln Chapter case of 1339).

[234] The calendar of original papal letters in England for 1305–1415 (P.N.R. Zutshi (ed.), *Original Papal Letters in England 1305–1415* (Vatican, 1990)), contains nothing on usury, though since many papal letters were destroyed after the Reformation this does not rule out the possibility that there may be lost missives

Canon lawyers and theologians regarded suppression of usury as part of the duty of civil as well as ecclesiastical authorities, although they sometimes accepted that kings would not be able to impose a complete ban on usury in their realms.[235] The Council of Vienne 1311 made it clear that princes should at least not protect usurers, and no authority should tolerate laws licensing usury (though there is no indication that these provisions were directed against practice in England, or that this council prompted action against usury in England).[236] The inclusion of an anti-usury clause in the twelfth-century pseudo-royal 'Laws of Edward the Confessor' seems to have been calculated to portray the saintly (but not yet canonised) king as having been prescient enough to legislate in accordance with what would be decided by the legatine council at Westminster in 1138.[237] Reference to the influence of the teachings of the church can be seen in the 'Draft Statute of Jewry' of *c*.1284–6, which notes that Edward I (or somebody speaking in his voice) has been led to action by love of God and devotion to the Church.[238]

There are some instances of the use by kings and governments of language emphasising the sinful nature of usury as the reason for intervention, or of the attribution to them of such language. The pseudo-royal 'Laws of Edward the Confessor' call usury the root of evil.[239] Turning to documents which are definitely royal in provenance, the 1275 Statute of the Jewry condemned Jewish usury as a source of evil.[240] In Edward I's justification of his expulsion of the Jews from England in 1290, the Jews were accused of having 'wickedly conspired and conceived a new species of usury more pernicious than the old'.[241] Edward's descriptions are, however, far less condemnatory and pious than those of Charles of Anjou in his Edict of Expulsion in 1289.[242] This mentions the Jews' 'devious deceits' and wickedness, and his own 'zeal for the life-giving cross'. The adjective 'depraved' is used to describe usury in commissions of 1275 and 1340.[243] The 1275 commission also described usury as a 'scandal upon the name of Christians', and mentioned the 'illicit greed' of the usurers. In 1341, Edward III (or his spokesman) used the image of the 'abyss' of usury, which can be seen in the decrees of the Councils of Lyons 1243 and 1274.[244] Condemnation of Christian usury as vicious

---

concerning usury. There is evidence of papal intervention in January 1273, when two papal nuncios, Raymond de Nogenis and Peter d'Aussone, were asked to enquire into various matters, including 'de prelatis aliisque clericis usurariis': P&C, *Councils*, 806. This, however, was a matter of internal regulation of church personnel rather than a call for royal action.

[235] Langholm, *Economics*, 84–5, 387, 477.

[236] N.P. Tanner (ed.), *Decrees of the Ecumenical Councils* (London, 1990), p. 384, no.29. Elsewhere, for example in Marseilles, this did produce legislative action, with legislative measures tolerating a degree of usury being abrogated following the Council: Pernoud, *Les Statuts Municipaux de Marseille* (Marseilles, 1949), xlvi. Of course, England had no such measures to cancel, so it may be that England did not feel the need to do anything more.

[237] O'Brien, *God's Peace*, 200; B. Thorpe (ed.), *Ancient Laws and Institutes of England* (London, 1840), I, 199, s.37.

[238] BL, MS Add. 32085, ff.120r–121r; Rigg, *Select Pleas*, liv–lx.

[239] 'usura enim summa radix viciorum interpretatur': O'Brien, *God's Peace*, 200; Thorpe, *Ancient Laws*, I, 199.

[240] *SR* I:221.

[241] Rigby, *English Society*, 290; Powicke, *Thirteenth Century*, 283; Richardson, *English Jewry*, 225–33; *Ec. Hist. Doc.*, 50–1.

[242] Mundill, *England's Jewish Solution*, 299–301.

[243] *CPR 1272–81*, 172; App. IV below.

[244] M. Packe, *King Edward III* (London, 1983–5), 101; Waugh, *England in the Reign of Edward III*, 215, 217; McKisack, *Fourteenth Century*, 170; *Foedera*, II, ii, 1152–3; Tanner, *Decrees*, p. 293, no.2; p. 328, no.26.

can be found in a writ of Edward III of 1363, in which it was referred to as a 'fraud' and a 'horrible vice'.[245]

There is, however, some evidence which goes against the idea of English kings and governments seeing it as their duty to extirpate usury as a sinful or wrongful practice. It has been suggested that Edward I's court was 'awash in' money-lending.[246] There is clear evidence that kings were not averse to enforcing usury when it was in their own financial interest to do so. Before the expulsion of the Jews, Edward I clearly profited by enforcing the debts owed to Jews by Christians, sometimes in a very strict manner, and took a third of the value of the possessions of Jews, including the profits of usury, on the Jew's death.[247] Such profiting from Jewish usury had been condemned by Thomas of Chobham and Bishop Robert Grosseteste.[248] Despite the fact that he decreed that Christian debtors need only pay the principal sum due to Jews, not the interest, Edward I may have participated in the profits of Jewish usury even after the Expulsion, as it has been said that he was reluctant to remit usury on Jewish bonds.[249]

Some further evidence of the willingness of kings and governments to profit from usury may be seen in a petition by John de Oldebury de la Legh of Wiltshire, of uncertain date but ascribed to the reign of Edward III. The petition stated that in the time of King Edward [I], John's father had borrowed 40s in silver from Bonefay and Bonefaz de Crekelade, two Jews, to be paid at a fixed date, with usury at one penny per shilling per week if the date set passed without repayment. The date did pass without repayment and so usury began to run, mounting up to £40 or £43 16s 1d. When the Jews were banished, the king took over the debt, including the usury due. John paid £9 3s 4d into the Exchequer, but asked to be relieved of the rest because of poverty, 'for the love of God', and because the debt was tainted by usury. He claimed that the king had previously granted him a pardon for the debt, but, due to his failure adequately to prove this pardon, the debt was still being demanded by the Exchequer.[250] The debt is mentuoned in the Pipe Roll Wiltshire section for 1330–1.[251] The entries do not specifically mention usury and suggest that John was really concerned about the fact that he had already paid part of the debt, and was being charged more than the remaining sum agreed at the time of

---

[245] *CLB, G*, p. 160, f.117. Writ of Edward III to the mayor, aldermen, sheriffs and commonalty of London. Usury is described as 'lorible vice & fausure de usure', which the London authorities are to extirpate (destruire).

[246] Stacey, 'Parliamentary negotiations', 81. The examples which Stacey gives do not exactly justify the claim that the court was 'awash' with moneylending or usury, as they mention only two members of the court, the queen and Edmund of Lancaster, as being involved with Jewish moneylenders.

[247] Parsons, *Eleanor of Castille*, 127–8; Richardson, *English Jewry*, 293. Stacey, 'Parliamentary negotiations', 97, citing *Exchequer of the Jews, V*, nos 141, 169, 429, 436, 611 (examples of enforcement of old debts, sometimes against heirs, assigns or tenants). There is an admission that Edward I and his predecessors have profited from Jewish usury in the Statute of Jewry 1275: *SR* I:221, and in the Draft Statute of Jewry 1284x1286.

[248] Wood, *Medieval Economic Thought*, 167–8, citing Thomas of Chobham, *Summa confessorum*, art. 7, dist. 6, q.11, c.4, p. 510; J.A. Watt, 'Jewish serfdom' in D. Wood (ed.), *The Church and Sovereignty: Essays in honour of Michael Wilks*, Studies in Church History Subsidia 10 (Oxford, 1991), p. 170, nn.61–2.

[249] Wijffels and Bush (eds), *Learning the Law*, 19, citing Richardson, *English Jewry*, 229, and *CCR 1288–96*, pp. 109, 148. Stacey, 'Parliamentary negotiations', 89; J. Carmi Parsons, *Eleanor of Castille: Queen and Society in Thirteenth Century England* (Basingstoke, 1995), 120–1; Richardson, *The English Jewry under Angevin Kings*, 229, citing Rigg, *Select Starrs*, xl–xli.

[250] *RP* II:402.

[251] E 372/176, membranes for Wiltshire (unnumbered).

that payment.[252] It is made clear that John (or his father, Robert) had made a bond with the king recognising his debt in the tenth year of Edward I, well before the expulsion of the Jews, and the Exchequer under Edward I and II and in the early part of the reign of Edward III (a writ of 25 January 1328 is mentioned) had been trying to enforce the debt due on this bond. The pipe roll entry makes it clear that John or Robert was excused from paying the debt, and the *fieri facias* issued to recover the sum due was cancelled. The fact that there had been attempts to enforce it before the petition does, however, show that Edward I and II and their governments and the government during the minority of Edward III did not dissociate themselves from usury (or Jewish usury at least) when they could profit from it.

Kings and governments also participated in usury as borrowers. They borrowed large sums of money from foreign and native lenders. In at least some cases, they seem to have paid usury.[253] This fact might be used to argue that there was no strong conviction in the minds of medieval English kings and governments that they ought to be attempting to eradicate the vicious practice of usury from England. The better view, however, seems to be that usury was conceived as an offence in which the lender alone was guilty. Royal borrowing at usury was not a free choice: it was due to a lack of alternative sources of credit rather than being due to indifference to usury. Edward III certainly saw himself as a victim. In 1341, when he was quarrelling with Archbishop Stratford, and accusing him of mismanagement of government and its finance, he commented that Stratford had, amongst other things, 'compelled Us to plunge Ourselves into the Devouring Gulf of Usury'.[254] He was portrayed by others as a victim at the end of his reign when he was again thrown into the 'Devouring Gulf', by William Latimer, who, with his confederates, 'had negotiated loans for the king and charged him up to 50% interest for their pains'.[255] Both instances demonstrate that the king might well be aware, through personal experience, of the adverse effects of usury, and the 'Devouring Gulf' image is an interesting one, conveying as it does the idea of

---

[252] i.e. £20 10s.

[253] On royal borrowing, see: E.B. and N.M. Fryde, *CEH III*, c.7; J.F. Willard, 'The crown and its creditors 1327–33', *EHR* 42 (1927); G.L. Harriss, 'Aids, loans and benevolences', *Historical Journal* 6 (1963); *KPPF*, cc. 3, 4; E.B. Fryde, 'Materials for the study of Edward III's credit operation', *BIHR* 22 (1949), 105–138; M. Prestwich (ed.), *Documents Illustrating the Crisis of 1297–8 in England*, Camden Society, fourth series, 24 (1980), 35; R.W. Kaeuper, *Bankers to the Crown* (Princeton, NJ, 1973); Butler, 'Archbishop Melton', 61; E. Russell, 'The societies of the Bardi and the Peruzzi and their dealings with Edward III 1327–45', in G. Unwin (ed.), *Finance and Trade under Edward III* (Manchester, 1918), 93–135; A. Beardwood, *Alien Merchants in England 1350 to 1377* (Cambridge, MA, 1931); N. Fryde, 'Antonio Pessagno of Genoa, king's merchant of Edward II of England', in *Studia in memoria di Frederigo Melis*, ii (1978); E.B. Fryde, *William de la Pole, Merchant and King's Banker* (London, 1988); E.B. Fryde, 'Loans to the English Crown 1328–31', *EHR* 70 (1955), 198–211; T.H. Lloyd, *Alien Merchants in the High Middle Ages* (Brighton, 1982); S.L. Waugh, *England in the Reign of Edward III* (Cambridge, 1991), 183; Ormrod, *Reign of Edward III*, 183; C.M. Barron, 'Tyranny of Richard II', *BIHR* 41 (1968), 1–18, at 5, suggests that 'There is no hint either of force or of usury in the [loans to the crown which she has examined, from 1397 onwards]'; Prestwich, *The Three Edwards*, 287; C. Given-Wilson, 'Wealth and credit, public and private: the earls of Arundel 1306–97', *EHR* 106 (1991), 1, 11; G.L. Harriss, 'Aids, loans and benevolences', *Historical Journal* 6 (1963), 1–19.

[254] M. Packe, *Edward III* (London, 1983–5), 101; Waugh, *England in the Reign of Edward III*, 215, 217; *Foedera*, II, ii, 1152–3.

[255] Packe, *Edward III*, 290. Latimer, however, claimed that he had only borrowed at usury on grounds of dire necessity: McKisack, *Fourteenth Century*, 391.

something monstrous and powerful, which can imprison and destroy even a king of England.[256]

There are some apparent differences between the nature of royal and canonical usury laws which suggest that, even if the ecclesiastical ban on usury played a part in motivating kings of England to act in this area, royal authorities were not simply giving effect to ecclesiastical law or doctrine. The conception of usury which can be seen in the sources consulted may be less broad than that of the canon lawyers and theologians, and does not seem to have dealt with some of the more complex questions concerning usury which the canon lawyers and theologians treated. The punishments inflicted upon usurers at the behest of royal authority were not necessarily inconsistent with the rules of the church, but they made no reference to or provision for restitution of usury, which was a major focus of canonical and theological treatment of usury.[257] The information about royal pronouncements on the jurisdiction of royal, secular and ecclesiastical tribunals also shows some divergence from church views. There is evidence of kings and governments acting contrary to the perceived or claimed exclusive jurisdiction of church courts (though a change in attitude may be detected from the late 1370s). The discrepancies between canon law rules and theological views on usury on the one hand and royal rules concerning usury on the other hand suggest that medieval kings and governments were not acting merely as enforcers of the law of the church in this area, but that they had their own reasons for action, and, perhaps, their own conception of the type of conduct which ought to be penalised as usury. It is now necessary to consider what, apart from a consciousness of the vicious nature of usury, these might have been.

It has occasionally been suggested that royal proscription of and action against usury may have been prompted by a desire to manipulate the macro-economy or to redistribute wealth. Academics of the 'law and economics school' have called usury laws 'a primitive means of social insurance'.[258] Not surprisingly, no such general statements were made by medieval English kings or their governments. Certain adverse economic consequences of usury were, however, mentioned in royal pronouncements on Jewish usury. The 1275 Statute of the Jewry claimed to have been prompted by various evils caused by usury, including the 'disinheritance of the good men of [the] land'.[259] The adverse effects of Jewish usury were mentioned once again in the Draft Statute of the Jewry of 1284–6, which stated that Jewish usury led to the 'confusion and destruction of many people' and to the 'disherison of many'.[260] These descriptions of adverse effects are somewhat vague, but suggest a concern with the problems which usury caused to borrowers who were unable to keep up repayments, and, perhaps, particularly to those borrowing at usury on the

---

[256] The abyss image also features in Charles of Anjou's Edict of Expulsion 1289: Mundill, *England's Jewish Solution*, 299–301.

[257] Whitelock, *Councils*, I, 741; Langholm, *Economics*, 114, 140, 166, 239, 272, 306, 337–9, 343, 354, 367, 397, 410, 417, 488, 513, 522.

[258] E.L. Glaeser and J. Scheinkman, 'Neither a borrower nor a lender be: an economic analysis of interest restrictions and usury laws', *Journal of Law and Economics* 61 (1998), 1, citing R. Posner, 'A theory of primitive society with special reference to law', *Journal of Law and Economics* 23 (1980), 1.

[259] *SR* I:221.

[260] Rigg, *Select Starrs*, lvi; BL, MS Add. 32085, ff.120r–121r.

security of land.[261] Edward III's personal experience of the adverse effects of usury in the early 1340s could be seen as a spur for his inclusion of usury in the 1340 commissions.

Both a concern with sin and a concern with the adverse economic effects of usury can be seen in the 1275 commission to royal judges to investigate and hear cases of Christian usury in Norfolk. Consciousness of the sinful and wrongful nature of usury can be seen in the observations that usury was not allowed to Christians, and that its practice brought scandal upon them, and in the description of usurers 'acting like Jews' (presumably not a compliment) and acting 'because of illicit greed'. Royal concern with adverse (presumably economic) effects is evident in the statement that usury caused grave damage to subjects, 'which the king did not wish to sustain, nor ought he to do so'.[262]

It has been suggested that royal intervention against usury reflected a desire to protect the poor. J. Gilchrist saw 'consumer protection', which he treated as synonymous with protection of the poor, as the reason for action against usury, and R.H. Tawney stated that the main purpose of the (canonical) usury laws was to protect the poor.[263] Usurers were denounced by medieval canonists and theologians as 'devourers of the poor'.[264] Although, as noted above, some English royal statements mention the reduction to poverty or the disherison of borrowers at usury, they do not evince a special concern for those who were already poor. No royal pronouncements mention protection of the poor in particular as a reason for action against usury. An argument may, however, be constructed in relation to the cases, to the effect that most cases in royal and secular courts (with the exception of the impeachments of Lyons and Latimer in 1376 and those cases in the London usury tribunal in the late fourteenth and early fifteenth centuries) concentrated on the type of usury most likely to affect the poor and comparatively humble (unsecured loans of money or fungibles rather than loans secured on land, no examples of very big loans to individuals).[265]

Financial self-interest could have been served by raising money from transgressors, or by making royal borrowing less expensive, or by securing a grant of taxes in return for action against usury. Edward I's conduct with regard to Italian usurers seems to be an example of revenue raising, but there is no evidence that kings manged to reduce interest rates on their own borrowing. R. Stacey suggests that the 1275 statute of Jewry was part of the price which Edward I had to pay for the consent of knights of the shire to taxation, and he and others portray the 1290 expulsion of the Jews, justified by Edward I on the grounds of their usury, as the price which he had to pay in order to secure a grant of taxes or assent from

---

[261] There is, however, little trace of another adverse economic consequence elsewhere attributed to usury, which is that the ease of profit in usury caused people who ought to have been engaged in other, useful, occupations to abandon them in order to pursue usurious profit. The Third Lateran Council of 1179 stated that 'too many men were abandoning their social station or their trade in order to become usurers', cited in J. Le Goff, *Your Money or Your Life* (New York, 1988), 25. This concern may be seen to be reflected in Edward I's instruction to the Jews that they should live by legitimate merchandise, in the Statutes of the Jewry 1275: *SR* I:221.

[262] BL, MS Harley 409, f.40r–v; C 66/95 m.36d. I am grateful to Dr P. Brand for the former reference.

[263] Gilchrist, *CEA*, 63–4; R.H. Tawney, *Religion and the Rise of Capitalism* (London, 1922, reprinted 1961), 57.

[264] M. Mollat, trans. A. Goldhammer, *The Poor in the Middle Ages: An Essay in Social History* (Yale, 1986), 66; Wood, *Medieval Economic Thought*, 164.

[265] See Seabourne, 'Controlling commercial morality', 116.

Parliament to royal statutes.[266] The imposition of financial penalties upon living usurers, which was the usual form in recorded cases, would have contributed to royal coffers, but, given the relatively small number of presentments and convictions which have been found, only in a modest way. Also, with the exception of William de Luda, none of the usurers convicted in 'normal' royal courts (i.e. outside Parliament and the Council) seem to have been operating on a very large scale. Obscure people like Milo of Evesham and Robert le Poleter seem more common than high financiers like Richard Lyons. It should also be noted that the jurisdiction on usury was not used in England as a revenue raising device to anything like the same extent as it apparently was in the first half of the fourteenth century in France.[267]

Royal action or pronouncement could be used to reward or appease powerful interest groups. J. Gilchrist stated, for example, that Edward I expelled the Jews from England partly because of pressure on him from 'Christian merchants and moneylenders', who wished to be rid of Jewish competition.[268] During the period under consideration, several requests and proposals for royal action against usury were made, suggesting that the section of the community which had a voice in Parliament wanted the king and government to take action against usury. A document which W.M. Ormrod interprets as a legislative proposal from the reign of Edward II, dated 1322x1326, initiated by the commons in Parliament, contains a complaint about the prevalence of Christian usury.[269] There is evidence of other requests to the king and government to take action against usury. Edward III referred to the complaints of many, great and small, of damage caused by usurious transactions as a reason for ordering the London civic authorities to take action against usury in 1363.[270] The commons in Parliament requested action against Lombard usurers in 1376 and, in 1377, asked that the London civic ordinance against usury should be enacted across the whole realm.[271] The commons were concerned that the prevalence of 'the horrible vice of usury' in the realm was diminishing the virtue of charity, and that many gentlemen had been ruined because of usury.[272] In 1382, the civic authorities in London brought a petition to

---

[266] Prestwich, *English Politics*, 90. A similar view is put forward in Stacey, 'Parliamentary negotiations'. See also: S. Dubrov, *History of the Jews, vol. III: From the Later Middle Ages to the Renaissance*, 4th edn (South Brunswick, 1969), 69; K.R. Stow, *Alienated Minority: The Jews of Medieval Latin Europe* (Cambridge, MA, 1992), 293. It is suggested elsewhere that the expulsion itself did not bring the king 'a great financial gain' (Stow, *Alienated Minority*, 282), though this opinion is controversial. R.R. Mundill has recently argued that 'Edward [I] himself did not make much financial gain from the Expulsion [of the Jews in 1290]', even though their land and debts passed to him: Mundill, *England's Jewish Solution*, 259, 63.

[267] J.B. Henneman, 'Enquêteurs-réformateurs and fiscal officers in fourteenth century France', *Traditio* 24 (1968), 309–49.

[268] Gilchrist, *CEA*, 72. Stacey suggests that by the late 1260s the most likely borrowers from Jews were knights and townsmen rather than great lords, who had other sources of credit (Stacey, 'Parliamentary negotiations', 94), so that opposition to Jewish usury might have been a concern of 'the middling sort' rather than the very great or very poor.

[269] Ormrod, 'Agenda for legislation', 1; C 49/5. See App. IV below. Note that petitions by the commons in Parliament cannot necessarily be taken as demonstrations of widespread, popular feeling. G.L. Harriss noted that '[t]he commons' represented only a small section of England's subjects, and that they were, in the early fourteenth century, 'heavily influenced by, if not wholly dependent on, the magnates': Harriss, *King, Parliament and Public Finance*, 118.

[270] Letter under privy seal from the king to the mayor and sheriffs of London, *CLB, G*, 196, f.161.

[271] *RP* II:332a; *RP* II:350b.

[272] The royal response was not favourable: the existing law was to stand: *ibid.*

Parliament, asking that the city's ordinances 'for the remedy of usury, usurers and brokers' be confirmed, ratified and strengthened in Parliament.[273] The royal response was a little unclear, but seems to have been negative, showing that kings did not always comply with the requests for action of influential subjects.[274] In 1390, the commons asked that the London usury ordinance of 1363–4 be put into effect and reinforced, since they stated that usury led to the displeasure of God, and the impoverishment of the king's subjects, and that it was a cause of vengeance being visited on the realm.[275] The usurer was a stock character in medieval instructional and other literature, which is also some evidence of antipathy to his activities.[276] Action against usury by the king and government would also have been welcomed by the English clergy and the wider hierarchy of the Western church. Although, as was mentioned above, there is no sign of there having been papal calls for royal action on usury, the English clergy did ask for such action, at least against the Jews. There had been pressure on kings to act against Jewish usury in 1215 and 1258, and the clergy put pressure on the king to act against Jewish usury until the eventual expulsion of the Jews from England.[277] Concern with usury was shown in appeals made in 1283 and 1286 by Archbishop John Pecham to the Queen, Eleanor of Castille, not to associate herself with Jewish usury.[278] The issue of royal tolerance of Jewish usury was brought up in a clerical complaint of 1285.[279]

There seems, therefore, to be some scope for arguing that political self-interest was influential in prompting royal action against usury, since a number of different groups desired it, but it should be noted that kings and governments did not always grant their requests, and there is, perhaps, evidence that other elements in the medieval polity were keener on royal action against usury than were the kings and governments themselves.

Conclusion

In terms of explaining how kings and governments acted against usury, this chapter has shown that, not surprisingly, action was not consistent over the long period under consideration. Particular concern seems to have existed in the first half of the

---

[273] *RP* III:142b.

[274] The response was that the king wished the church to have its jurisdiction *come ele soloit avoir d'ancientee*, and advanced the opinion that the common law and the good customs and usages of the city would provide sufficient remedy for those aggrieved by usury: *RP* III:142b, confirmed in *CPR 1381–5*, 204, 6 Ric. II m.34.

[275] *RP* III:280b.

[276] M.M. Banks (ed.), *An Alphabet of Tales*, EETS (London, 1904), 181, Tale CCLX; H.O. Coxe (ed.), *Chronicle of Roger de Wendover*, English Historical Society 4 (London, 1841–4), 206; G.R. Owst, *Literature and Pulpit in Medieval England* (Oxford, 1961), 259, 553–4; G.R. Owst, *Preaching in Late Medieval England* (Cambridge, 1927), 68; J. Le Goff, *Time, Work and Culture in the Middle Ages* (Chicago, 1980), 119; Chaucer, *The Romaunt of the Rose*, Fragment A, in W. Skeat (ed.), *The Poetical Works of Geoffrey Chaucer* (London, 1878), 3, line 181; Wood, *Medieval Economic Thought*, 160; G.C. Macauley (ed.), *The English Works of John Gower*, EETS 81–2 (Oxford, 1900–1), bk 5, p. 67, lines 4408–9.

[277] Prestwich, *English Politics*, 91.

[278] Parsons, *Eleanor of Castille*, 120–1, citing H. Rothwell (ed.), *The Chronicle of Walter of Guisborough*, Camden Society, third series, 89 (1957), 216; H.R. Luard (ed.), *Annales Monastici*, Rolls Series 36.iii (London, 1866), *Annales Prioratus de Dunstaplia*, 363; C.T. Martin (ed.), *Registrum epistolarum Fratris Johannis Peckham Archiepiscopi Cantuarensis*, Rolls Series 77 (London, 1882–5), ii 619–20, iii 937–8.

[279] P&C, *Councils*, 959, 962–3.

reign of Edward I. Various modes of investigating and punishing usury were employed at that time, from special commissions and general eyres to the regulation and expulsion of the Jews. Interest in the matter seems to have died away to a great extent by the end of the thirteenth century, and usury is not mentioned at all in the York Ordinances of 1301, which, as will be discussed in the next two chapters, set out a fairly comprehensive regime for commercial dealings in York whilst the royal administration was there.[280] There was less concern, or at least less action, in the reign of Edward II, when jurisdictional disputes with the church seem to have eased, though the fragment of a legislative proposal from the 1320s shows that usury was still on the agenda as a matter which needed to be looked at even after the expulsion of the Jews. Edward III instigated special investigations which included a usury article, but there was not much action in the first years of his reign. Usury was not specifically dealt with in the post-Black Death legislation which provided a wide regime for fair wages and fair or reasonable prices.[281] A desire to see something done about usury prompted the royal approval of the special usury tribunal in London in 1363–4, but there was resistance to extension of the usury laws in the last year of Edward III's reign and there was no new action under Richard II who resisted requests for royal approval of the extension of local secular jurisdiction over usury. There was, perhaps, a growing gulf between what the government was prepared to do and what certain other elements in the country – and particularly the London business community – wanted to be done about usury. 'The centre' seemed to be losing the desire to get involved in detailed rules or active pursuit of usury just as the London civic jurisdiction was increasing its role, though causal connections must remain obscure.[282]

When action was taken, various different methods were used. Sometimes, kings and governments acted directly, by statute or by executive action, and sometimes indirectly, by delegation or by providing a forum in which usury could be presented or pleaded. Such variation is not surprising in a time of flux and experimentation in institutions. The overall pattern, however, seems to be a (tolerated) move away from royal control of enforcement from the mid-fourteenth century onwards.

Conclusions on the details of the law must be more tentative, but it can be said that the definition of usury used was perhaps narrower than that in use in other systems. It seems that there was no detailed statute explaining the rules on what amounted to usury. A degree of reliance was placed on there being a general understanding of what amounted to usury – presumably deriving from general knowledge of basic canon law – or on tribunals working out more detailed rules for themselves.[283]

An important part of the picture of royal action was the way in which the church jurisdiction and rules were treated by successive kings and governments. The church and its teachings were referred to more often in royal action against usury

---

[280] *YO.*

[281] See further below in chapters 3 and 4.

[282] Seabourne, 'Controlling commercial morality'. It can be argued that the London authorities and the 'central' government had slightly different reasons for pursuing usury. The 1363 London usury ordinance mentioned damage to London's commercial reputation as well as moral disapproval: *CLB, G*, 161–2, ff.117–19.

[283] *Glanvill* VII:16 implies a large degree of co-operation between royal and ecclesiastical authorities, as the judgment of priests would be required in ascertaining whether or not the usurer had died impenitent.

than in price regulation or other matters to be considered in this book, but the church and the king were not always in agreement about the extent of their jurisdiction, and the canonical rules on usury were by no means simply adopted in the practice of royal courts. Despite the idea which can be seen in the *Dialogus de Scaccario* and possibly also in *Glanvill* that there was a strict split of jurisdiction between church and royal courts as regards the living and the dead, an eyre article asking about living usurers was in existence in the 1240s and there are a number of instances of prosecution of living usurers in eyres, the King's Bench, *ad hoc* commissions and lower level tribunals. This suggests a genuine desire to enforce the usury laws, since living usurers might easily have been left to the church. The evidence shows that there were some serious efforts on the part of kings to punish those guilty of usury, even if not all potential defendants ran the risk of royal sanctions. The jurisdiction of the church was not generally treated as exclusive, and was encroached upon at some periods. This is in keeping with the view that the jurisdiction of the church was, on the whole, suffering at the expense of royal and secular jurisdiction in the thirteenth and fourteenth centuries, though it should not be exaggerated, given the small number of usury cases actually found in royal sources.

With regard to the question of why kings and governments acted in the area of usury, traces of several different reasons for action emerge from words and conduct. In royal pronouncements, there are allusions to canonical rules, and also expressions of concern with the effect of usurers' actions, with the latter seeming to be regarded as justifications for royal intervention which are independent of religious precept and canon law. There are also signs of financial motivation in some royal action, such as that taken against the Jews and Italian merchant usurers in the time of Edward I, both of which resulted in financial gain to the Crown, and the inclusion of a usury article in the 1341–3 investigations at a time when Edward III was desperate for money to finance his French wars. There is, therefore, a temptation to see the primary reason for taking action as a desire for financial gain. It should, however, be noted that governments did not use the usury prohibition to raise as much money as they might have done, since there is little evidence of widespread confiscation of the goods of deceased persons on the ground that they were unrepentant usurers, and the opportunity to punish usurers involved in common pleas in royal courts often seems to have been ignored. There is, moreover, no sign that the prohibition on usury was to the financial advantage of kings and governments in the sense of enabling them to borrow money without usury themselves. Self-interest is not the whole story. It seems arguable that, in prohibiting Christian usury, thirteenth- and fourteenth-century kings and governments were taking the royal role beyond their own interests, proposing to act, and sometimes acting, against vicious or wrongful conduct, and to avoid adverse economic consequences for the realm or for their subjects. They were not, however, particularly ambitious in this extension of royal activity. They did not aim to deal with all conduct which could potentially be classed as usury, and, while they may have been concerned with economic damage, this was not particularly a concern with damage to the actual borrower, since he or she was not given a right to restitution, and, in some cases, he or she was not even mentioned in the presentment, the accused simply being said to be a usurer or 'common usurer' as in the case of Robert le Poleter seen in the introduction.

Usury was particularly associated with unpopular foreigners and Jews in a way in which the other offences to be considered were not (although, as we will see, there was an element of differentiation between 'insiders' and 'outsiders' in many urban rules concerning pricing).[284] The unpopularity of the Jew and the foreigner is clear and has been much discussed.[285] Although the stereotypical usurer may have been (and may be) the Jew, or, to a lesser extent, the Italian, lending money on a large scale, or to large numbers of people, the court rolls appear to show that the laws were actually used on a different target, the native Christian usurer who might not be lending on a large scale at all. Although the influence of Jewish unpopularity on action against usury was important, this chapter has demonstrated that action was taken against Christian usurers such as Milo of Evesham, and that it continued to be taken against usury after 1290, from which point the concern could only have been with Christian usury. Though concern was less intense, the royal jurisdiction clearly persisted, showing a continued acceptance of the appropriateness of kings and governments intervening in this area.

---

[284] Usury might be used as a xenophobic insult: see, e.g., the bald statement in P. Hamelius (ed.), *Mandeville's Travels* EETS, original series, 153 (1919), p. 12, line 19, describing Constantinople and the Greek faith, 'and they say also that usure is no dedly synne'. 'Covetousness' in *Piers Plowman* associates usury with Jews and Lombards: Mundill, 'Christian and Jewish moneylending', 42–67.

[285] See, e.g., Richards, *Sex, Dissidence and Damnation*, 88–115; R.H. Hilton, *Bond Men Made Free: Medieval Peasant Movements and the English Rising of 1381* (London, 1973), 195–8; T.H. Lloyd, *Alien Merchants in the High Middle Ages* (Brighton, 1982), 3–4, c.2.

Part II: Sales

As well as regulating their subjects' lending and borrowing, medieval English kings and governments involved themselves in regulating the terms of subjects' sales and purchases. Such legal intervention would certainly impinge on the lives of virtually all English men, women and children.[1] Further, sales of goods became increasingly important over the medieval period as more people came to be occupied outside agriculture and so the proportion of goods sold increased.[2] Facilities for sales in the shape of markets and fairs grew between the eleventh and fourteenth centuries, without necessary royal creation or intervention, and in advance of the royal claim to exclusive rights to license markets, a product of the thirteenth century.[3] Much work has been done on the movement of prices of goods in medieval England.[4] The legal concept of sale, in terms of requisite formalities and the theory of property and contract, has received some attention from legal historians.[5]

Chapters 3 and 4 will be concerned with the rules about the substance of sales, Chapter 3 examining direct royal action in setting price limits for various commodities, and Chapter 4 considering less direct forms of price control. These matters are clearly related, and connections between direct and indirect action will be noted.

[1] For example, regulation of the ale trade could potentially concern a large proportion of the population because so many of them were involved in it as producers as well as consumers: see Bennett, 'The village ale-wife: women and brewing in fourteenth century England' in B. Hanawalt (ed.), *Women and Work in Pre-Industrial Europe* (Bloomington, 1986), 23; H. Swanson, *Medieval Artisans: An Urban Class in Medieval England* (Oxford, 1989), 21; R.H. Britnell, 'Morals, Laws and Ale in Medieval England' in U. Mueller, F. Hundsnurcher and C. Sommer (eds), *Le Droit et sa Perception dans la Littérature et les Mentalités Médiévales* (Göppingen, 1993), 21–9, 22.

[2] R.H. Hilton, *Bond Men Made Free – medieval peasant movements and the English rising of 1381* (London, 1977) 15; Britnell, *Commercialisation*, esp. 104. See also Davis, *Regulation*, 33.

[3] Britnell, *Commercialisation*, 10, 11, 19–20, 81, 84; B. Harvey, 'The aristocratic consumer in England in the long thirteenth century' in M. Prestwich, R.H. Britnell and R. Frame (eds), *Thirteenth Century England VI* (Woodbridge, 1995), 17–38, at 17–18. On urban shops, see D. Keene, 'Shops and shopping in medieval London' in L. Grant (ed.), *Medieval Art, Architecture and Archaeology in London* (London, 1990), 29–46.

[4] See, e.g., J.E. Thorold Rogers, *A History of Agriculture and Prices in England*, 7 vols (Oxford, 1866–1902); H.E. Hallam, 'Prices and wages' in H.E. Hallam (ed.), *The Agrarian History of England and Wales* (Cambridge, 1988), 787–91; N.J. Mayhew, 'Money and prices in England from Henry II to Edward III', *Agricultural History Review* 35 (1987), 121–32.

[5] See, e.g., D. Ibbetson, 'From property to contract: the transformation of sale in the middle ages', *Journal of Legal History* 13 (1992), 1–22; Baker, *Introduction*, 384–6; D. Ibbetson, 'Sale of goods in the fourteenth century', *Law Quarterly Review* 107 (1991), 480–99; S.F.C. Milsom, 'Sale of goods in the fifteenth century', *Law Quarterly Review* 77 (1961), 257–84; Ibbetson, *Obligations*.

3

Price Regulation

To take one example from amongst the many in the rolls of courts at different levels in the medieval hierarchy, in an entry in rolls concerning proceedings before justices of the peace in Norfolk in 1378, we see the accusation that

> Marion, wife of Stephen Bulwere of Boketon brewed and sold against the assize, making two shillings above the assize price that year.[6]

Marion's alleged offence was in selling her produce at too high a price, measured against the price fixed under the assize of ale. This chapter will examine the assize and other laws which placed a set price on particular goods, or else set up a scheme or mechanism to set such prices.

The scope of the laws

The ale price regulations were an important part of the regulatory system, but ale was by no means the only product, the price of which was regulated.

The first point to note is that two different strategies seem to have existed: ambitious claims of general regulation of prices in all sales of goods on the one hand, and, on the other, measures regulating the sale of small numbers of types of goods. The idea of general coverage appears to be indicated in commissions of 1307 and 1308 from Edward II to his keepers of the peace, which included an instruction to proclaim and enforce the rule that all goods ('bona venalia') were to be sold at their true price, as they were accustomed to be sold in the reign of Edward I.[7] The only antecedent which can be found in royal sources for such a broad idea is in a set of ordinances of 1301 for the city of York, which stated that all things for sale and hire in York were to be at the same price as before the advent of the king's court in that city. On closer inspection, however, it is clear that both this and the 1307–8 peace commissions were linked to particular problems with substandard coins and an attempt to stabilise the currency.[8] They cannot, therefore, be taken as indications of a decided and expansive line of policy. Similarly vague is Edward III's 1331 writ to the London civic authorities, bidding them see that 'all kinds of victuals are sold at a reasonable price'.[9]

There is little evidence that the idea of a wide and general royal duty or right to

---

[6] Putnam, *PJP*, 120, no.184; KB 9/80 m.21.
[7] Palgrave, *Parliamentary Writs*, vol. 2, division II, 2, Appendix, 8, 9; 11; *CPR 1307–13*, 29.
[8] *YO*, 4, 14–15; *Liber Cistumarum*, 191–2, f.97–97b; Prestwich, *Edward I*, 531; *CEMCR*, 59–64.
[9] *CLB, E*, 219, f.175b.

set prices was prevalent, either in legislation or in the thirteenth- and fourteenth-century common law.[10] Not until the rise of the equitable jurisdiction of the Chancellor in the fifteenth century was there an idea of a general jurisdiction to enter into the fairness of prices in sales of goods.[11] No examples of the fairness of a price in a sale of goods being raised in a case at common law in the period under consideration have been found. Actions on the case for deceit, which can be seen in the fourteenth century, were based not on a sale at too high a price, but on a deliberate misrepresentation as to the quality of goods.[12] There are examples of cases concerning excessive profit before justices of the peace in the latter part of the fourteenth century, but these were based on specific statutory provisions, not on general doctrines.[13] There is certainly no evidence of anything like the civil and canon law concept of *lesion*, which allowed courts to adjudicate on the fairness of exchanges, in the common law of the thirteenth and fourteenth centuries.[14] The fact that specific goods continued to be dealt with in price fixing legislation in the fourteenth century may also be taken to show that there was no assumption of a right or duty to regulate the prices of goods in general.[15] It is certainly the case, however, that the reigns of Edward I and Edward II saw the beginning of an expansion of the subject matter covered by individual royal price fixing measures.

The main pieces of legislation dealing with specific rather than general price regulation which existed in 1272 concerned bread, ale and wine. By the end of the fourteenth century, several new statutes had been added to that already-existing body of price regulations.

The idea of a measure which regulated the amount and quality of bread and ale which could be sold for a certain price, the assize of bread and ale, was already old by the late-thirteenth century. The idea has antecedents in both 'local' and 'royal private' spheres. R.H. Britnell cites the examples of a charter of Henry I's time, concerning tenure by the bishop of Ely's baker of certain land, stating that 'he and his assistants should make the number and size of loaves from each *summa* of grain "according to the assize of our household"', and of royal regulations about the size of loaves to be made for the royal household from at least *c.*1136, and notes that a measure concerning bread called an assize 'proved by the bakers of the lord king Henry II' was 'copied into a large compendium of English laws compiled for the Guildhall of London . . . between 1206 and 1216'.[16] He has suggested that this text 'probably concerned only the verge of the

---

[10] In the chapter in *Fleta* on buying and selling in general, there is no mention of the need to set a fair price: *Fleta II*, Book 2, c.58. There is no mention of fair prices in *Britton*.

[11] On the Chancery's jurisdiction, see Baker, *Introduction*, c.6.

[12] See, e.g., *Ferrers v John, Vicar of Dodford* (1307) and *Garrok v Heytesbury* in G.O. Sayles (ed.), *Select Cases in the Court of King's Bench under Edward I, vol. III*, Selden Society 58 (London, 1939), 179; B&M, *Sources*, 506.

[13] See further below at p. 77.

[14] Olivier Martin, *Histoire du droit français*, no.211.

[15] In the London civic jurisdiction, there are a small number of examples of what seem to be attempts to regulate sales of goods, or at least sales of victuals, in general. A general jurisdiction over victual prices seems to be implied by ordinances of 1371 and an uncertain date?: Riley, *Memorials*, 347. *CLB, G*, 242, f.224b: 'All other victuals in the city to be sold at a reasonable price . . .' On the whole, however, the London civic authorities adopted the strategy of regulating the price of specific goods.

[16] Britnell, *Commercialisation*, 26, citing E. Miller, *The Abbey and Bishopric of Ely: The Social History of an Ecclesiastical Estate from the Tenth Century to the Early Fourteenth Century* (Cambridge, 1950), 130; *Constitutio Domini Regis* of *c.*1136 *Dialogus de Scaccario*, 130; BL, Add. MS 14252, f.85v; F. Liebermann, *Über die Leges Anglorum saeculo XIII ineunte Londoniis collectae* (Halle, 1894), 79, 101.

court'.[17] It should, of course, be noted that this would still, potentially, apply all over the kingdom, as the 'verge' was a movable entity. It has been suggested that the assize of ale was also a 'local' phenomenon in origin, with antecedents possibly going back to the eleventh century.[18]

Royal, national legislation creating an assize of bread and ale was created in the 1190s. R.H. Britnell mentions that 'sometime between 1193 and 1199' an assize of bread and ale was made 'in the presence of Hubert Walter, archbishop of Canterbury, by King Richard', implicitly for the whole kingdom, and using a mechanism for fixing the price/weight of bread which would remain the basis of later legislation.[19] Punishment for breach (the pillory) was specified in an apparently national assize of 1202.[20] Both bread and ale are dealt with in royal assizes dating from after 1202, but during John's reign, and general enforcement of the assizes has been seen to date from *c.*1202.[21] Variations in the 'royal assizes' during the reign of Henry III have been noted.[22] There was also geographical variation, or a degree of independence for certain urban authorities in terms of the setting of rules, though they generally followed a similar model to that of the central measures (or *vice versa*).[23]

As far as the legislation in force in the later thirteenth century and the fourteenth century is concerned, 1266–7 is the 'traditional date' for the 'quasi statute', the *Assisa Panis et Cervisie*, which was regarded as the seminal legislation.[24] Evidence from manorial court records shows that it is likely that there was some central enactment or order at about this time, as J.M. Bennett notes that manor court rolls show that at about 1266–7, manorial and civic court officers began to keep more detailed records, and, to some extent, standardised their practice.[25] The *Assisa*

---

[17] Britnell, *Commercialisation*, 26, citing Richardson and Sayles, *Law and Legislation*, 102–3.

[18] Bennett mentions signs of early versions or precursors of the assize of bread and ale in charters of the twelfth century to Tewkesbury, Walsall and Egremont, and gives evidence of an aletaster at work in the early thirteenth century (although it is not clear whether he was checking quality, price or both): J.M. Bennett, *Ale, Beer and Brewsters in England: Women's Work in a Changing World 1300–1600* (New York, 1996), 99–100, citing A. Ballard (ed.), *British Borough Charters 1042–1216* (Cambridge, 1913), 157–9. See also A. Clark (ed.), *The English Register of Godstow Nunnery near Oxford, vol. I*, EETS 142 (1911), 101; Britnell, 'Morals', 26.

[19] Britnell, *Commercialisation*, 94; H. Hall (ed.), *Red Book of the Exchequer*, 3 vols (London, 1896), II, 750.

[20] Britnell, *Commercialisation*, 94, citing H.R. Luard (ed.), *Matthew Paris. Chronica Maiora*, 7 vols (London, 1872–83), II, 480–1. See also Ross, 'Assize', 335.

[21] Britnell, *Commercialisation*, 95, citing N. Neilson (ed.), *A Terrier of Fleet Lincolnshire* (London, 1920), 106. See also Ballard, *British Borough Charters 1042–1216*, 159; R.H.C. Davis (ed.), *Kalendar of Abbot Samson of Bury St Edmunds and Related Documents* (London, 1954), charter 105, pp. 135–6; H. Hall (ed.), *Pipe Roll of the Bishopric of Winchester 1208–91* (London, 1903), 45, 47, 49, 65.

[22] L. Zylbergeld, 'Les regulations du marche du pain au XIIIe siècle en occident et l'"assize of bread" de 1266–1267 pour l'Angleterre' in J.-M. Duvosquel and A. Dierkers (eds), *Villes et campagnes au Moyen Age* (Liège, 1991), 791–814, at 794; Britnell, *Commercialisation*, 95; *CCR 1234–7*, 519; *CCR 1237–42*, 180, 221, 242, 274, 276; BL, Add. MS 35179, f.90v; BL, Egerton MS 2733, ff.175v–176v; BL, Add. MS 35179, f.89r.

[23] Britnell, *Commercialisation*, 95, citing P.R. Coss, *The Early Records of Medieval Coventry* (London, 1986), 41–2; BL, Lansdowne MS 564, f.109. This is a set of trading regulations including an assize of bread which resembles the *Assisa Panis et Cervisie*, and assize of ale, which has small variations from that document (though an important one is the notion of different grades of ale), and various other matters concerning timing of trading, public health regulations and forestalling. It was made at Coventry, 8 October 1278. It seems to show 'local' adoption of royal rules into the body of trading regulations in force in the vill, but no real conflict with royal rules.

[24] Bennett, *Ale*, 100.

[25] Bennett, *Ale*, 100.

provided for the trial and punishment of offenders against its price regulations, and was supplemented by the *Judicium Pillorie*, another statute of uncertain date probably from the later years of the reign of Henry III, which includes clauses on the price of wine as well as the prices of bread and ale.[26] Versions of the assizes can be found throughout the period, varying little from this model. The *'Statutum de Pistoribus'* or *Composicio*, parts of the contents of which have been dated to 1274–5, assumes the continued existence of assizes on the same model, and similar punishments for breach, with some matters slightly refined.[27] *Fleta* shows that the *Assisa Panis et Cervisie* and the *Judicium Pillorie* were still the seminal legislation governing regulation of prices and weight of bread, ale and wine in the reign of Edward I.[28] The York Ordinances of 1301 ordered the Assize of Bread and Ale to be kept.[29] An ordinance reproduced in *Statutes of the Realm* from the early fourteenth-century London collection *Liber Horn* shows that the provisions of *Judicium Pillorie* also continued to apply in the period under consideration.[30] A copy is found in the records of Oxford, dated *c.*1356.[31] The *Little Red Book of Bristol* contains fourteenth-century tables working out the assize of bread and ale on the same model.[32] The rules on the assize of ale were updated in 1317.[33] A statute of 1389–90 shows government concern to affirm the assizes of bread and ale up to the end of the fourteenth century.[34]

The price of wine had also been regulated by English kings and governments from the late-twelfth century onwards and continued to be regulated throughout the thirteenth and fourteenth centuries and beyond.[35] Wine price regulation was mentioned in the *Judicium Pillorie*, which also includes a check on the quality of wine, and also in the *Composicio*, which fixed a price for wine (12d a sester).[36] There were legislative refinements in procedural and enforcement matters for London in the Statute of Gloucester 1278.[37] The York Ordinances 1301 regulated wine prices.[38]

---

[26] *SR* I:201 (uncertain date, suggested 51 Hen. III); Britnell, 'Forstall', 94.

[27] *SR* I:202–4; Britnell, 'Morals', 26; Britnell, 'Forstall', 94–6. The *Composicio ad puniendem infringentes assisam panis et cervisie, forestallarios, cocs, etc.* has a statement of the assize of bread 'according to what is contained in a writing delivered to them from the . . . Marshalsea'. A similar document is the *Statutum Mareschaucie*, a set of instructions sent by Robert de Belvero and John de Swyneford 'assigned to the pleas of the Marshalsea' to mayors and bailiffs of Suffolk in 1275: BL, MS Stowe 386, ff.50r–51r.

[28] *Fleta II*, Book 2, c.9, virtually reproduces the *Assisa Panis et Cervisie* as it appears in *Statutes of the Realm*. *Fleta II*, c.12, reproduces the *Judicium Pillorie* with variations and additions.

[29] *YO*, 10.

[30] *SR* I:202, from London, *Liber Horn*, f.121b. *LA*, xvi; N. Ker, *Medieval Manuscripts in British Libraries* (Oxford, 1969), vol. I, 17–34.

[31] Anstey, *MA*, I, 180–5, 'De Assisa Panis, Vini et Cerevisie, quae observanda est per totam Angliam circa A.D. 1356'.

[32] *LRB*, p. 217, ff.187b–191b, pp. 236–7, f.206b, inside back cover (late fourteenth century or early fifteenth century); ale: p. 217, f.191b (fourteenth-century hand).

[33] *CCR 1313–18*, 449.

[34] *SR* II:63, 13 Ric. II, st.1 c.8.

[35] Warren, *Governance*, 133; Britnell, *Commercialisation*, 94, places the introduction of an assize of wine during the reign of Henry II. Early adjustment upwards of price of wine for places remote from ports (1223): H. Summerson, *Medieval Carlisle*, 2 vols (Kendal, 1993), 102. On the wine trade and its regulation, see F. Sargeant, 'The wine trade with Gascony' in G. Unwin (ed.), *Finance and Trade under Edward III* (Manchester, 1918), 257.

[36] *SR* I:202; *SR* I:203; Britnell, *Commercialisation*, 94; *LRB*, 218, f.191b, Assisa vini (fourteenth-century hand).

[37] *SR* I:50.

[38] *YO*, 12.

Wine prices were regulated again in 1315.[39] In 1330, a statute was passed dealing with the method of enforcing the wine price regulations.[40] This provision was restated in 1331, beginning a series of royal price fixing measures.[41] Further adjustments to the legal price of wine were made in 1342, 1353, 1381, and 1387.[42] The adjustments and restatements of legislative rules suggest that the assizes of bread and ale and the provisions regulating the price of wine were in force and important throughout the period (though it was clearly recognised that a degree of flexibility and local variation was appropriate or at least tolerable).

In the reign of Edward II, new items began to be covered by royal price control regulations. A short-lived 1315 measure of Edward II attempted to set the price for various foods, in particular meat and poultry.[43] This has been described as a 'remarkable step'.[44] There had, however, also been price regulation with regard to a fairly long list of items in the limited case of the York Ordinances of 1301, dealt with below, and general if temporary assumption of control over the price of all goods in the commissions of 1307–8 mentioned above, so that it was not wholly unprecedented. In any case, the 1315 measure did not last long, never making it to the statute roll and being repealed or withdrawn in 1316.[45] There was more lasting expansion in the reign of Edward III. A measure which, unusually, set minimum rather than maximum prices was passed in respect of wool in 1337.[46] The Ordinance of Labourers 1349 included a wide provision that victuals should be sold at reasonable prices.[47] Other trade items made by small-scale craftsmen were regulated in the 1351 Statute of Labourers.[48] Iron was ordered not to be sold at an excessive price in 1354.[49] In 1357, a statute primarily concerned with the sale of fish in Great Yarmouth, but which also covered sales of fish in other ports and markets, was passed.[50] A statute of 1363 provided maximum prices for poultry and another of 1389–90 regulated the price of horse bread and hay sold by hostelers.[51]

On occasion, royal authorities enacted price control regulations in particular geographical areas, rather than in respect of certain items. In the last decade of his reign, Edward I made elaborate provision for the city of York, which served as

[39] *Foedera*, II, part I, 268; *CCR 1313–18*, 182, 187; *Vita Edwardi Secundi*, 59. The measure was soon withdrawn, in October 1315: Y. Rennuard and R. Faukner (eds), *Gascon Rolls Preserved in the Public Record Office 1307–17* (London, 1962), 425, nos 1479, 1480.

[40] *SR* I:264, 4 Edw. III, c.12.

[41] *CCR 1330–3*, 410.

[42] Sargeant, 'Wine trade with Gascony', 257, 298, citing *CLB, F*, 83; *CLB, G*, 4, 41; *SR* II:19, 5 Ric. II, st.1 c.4. A King's Bench indictment file of 1387 refers to a 'general proclamation' by Robert Tresilian C.J. and the bailiffs of the vill of Gloucester, concerning wine prices: KB 9/32 m.18.

[43] *RP* I:295a.

[44] *EEJ*, 91.

[45] *EEJ*, 91; *Foedera*, II, part 1, 286. The act was repealed in favour of the rule that 'they should buy and sell as cheaply as they could': *Anonimalle*, 88–91, or 'at reasonable prices'; *RP* I:351a; *Vita Edwardi Secundi*, 59; *Foedera*, II, part 1, 286. The alternative formulations could be taken to show different degrees of abandonment of royal interest, with the 'reasonable price' formulation possibly suggesting some continued government interest, whilst the 'as cheaply as they could' formulation suggested abdication to 'the market'.

[46] Ormrod, *Reign of Edward III*, 102.

[47] *SR* I:307, st. 23 Edw. III. A statute of Richard II from 1389–90 sought to ensure that the section of the 1349 Ordinance of Labourers on sellers of victuals was upheld: *SR* II:63, 13 Ric. II st.1 c.8.

[48] *SR* I:312, 25 Edw. III, c.4.

[49] *SR* I:345, st. 28 Edw. III, c.5; *RP* II:260a (petition); Putnam, *Enforcement*, 15.

[50] *SR* I:353, 31 Edw. III, st.2 c.2.

[51] *SR* I:378, st. 37 Edw. III, c.3. This statute also ordered that prices should be lower in rural areas. It remained in force throughout the period: *RP* II:277; *SR* II:63, 13 Ric. II, st.1 c.8.

administrative capital during the Scottish wars.[52] His ordinances for the city set out in great detail various provisions for commercial practice in York, *inter alia* setting prices for food and other items.[53] Short-term regulations were promulgated when circumstances made it likely that prices would rise. In 1306, Edward I had to act to stop people putting up prices when a papal delegation came to their town.[54] Edward III took action in an attempt to prevent armourers putting up their prices because those going to war needed their wares quickly.[55] In the 1360s, Edward III felt obliged to forbid tilers and makers of roofing materials in the south-east of England from overcharging in the aftermath of great storms.[56] Specific regulation for fish sales at Blakeney fair were made in 1357, revised in 1360–1.[57] During the years in which the eyre was perambulating the country, it brought with it a temporary increase in the level of regulation of prices. The royal justices in eyre had the power to set a special tariff for food prices for the period of the eyre, at which time sellers might be tempted to take advantage of the increased demand to put up their prices. There was regulation of wine and at least some foodstuffs in connection with the eyre from the 1290s.[58] The records of the eyre of Kent of 1313–14 show that one of the first things which was done when the justices in eyre arrived in the county was to fix the 'assize of food', i.e. the price of all victuals.[59] Wine quality was also regulated.[60] By 1329–30, a warning was given against raiising all prices (including those of accommodation), and prices were fixed for food wine and ale whilst the eyre was present.[61] Another temporary difficulty causing the possibility of price rises and drawing a royal response in terms of price regulation was the matter of the 'pollards and crockards' in the late 1290s. Edward I ordered that the price of victuals should not be enhanced as a consequence of the revaluation of pollards and crockards.[62] This currency problem was referred to, and explicitly connected with regulation of prices, in the York Ordinances of 1301.[63] Concerns with the value of currency at the changing of regime from Edward I to Edward II were also part of the reason for the pricing provisions in Edward II's commissions to the keepers of the peace in 1307–8.[64]

A general view of European royal price regulation in the middle ages is that of Raymond de Roover, who maintained that royal authorities only wished to

[52] Prestwich, *Edward I*, 530. *YO*.

[53] Exchequer Plea Roll E 13/26 mm.75–6, translated in *YO*.

[54] *CPR 1301–07*, 487; C 66/128 m.42.

[55] *Foedera*, III, part 1, 303.

[56] Riley, *Memorials*, 308; LB, G, f.99.

[57] *SR* I:355, 31 Edw. III, st.3; *SR* I:369–70, st. 35 Edw. III.

[58] Eyre of Northumberland 1293 fines for offenders against an assize of the justices as well as that of the king: JUST 1/650 m.25; offence of selling a hen at a price double that in 'the proclamation': JUST 1/650 m.57. I am grateful to Dr P. Brand for these references. See also Cam, *London Eyre 1321*, I, 21, 25.

[59] F.W. Maitland, W. Vernon Harcourt and W.C. Bolland (eds), *The Eyre of Kent 6 & 7 Edward II A.D. 1313–1314*, vol. I, Selden Society vol. 24 for 1909 (London, 1909), 10. See also the account in Cam, *London Eyre 1321*, xxv and 21–30.

[60] Maitland, *Eyre of Kent 1313–14*, 8, 15, 22.

[61] D.W. Sutherland (ed.), *The Eyre of Northamptonshire 1329–30*, Selden Society vol. 97 for 1981 (London, 1983), 9, 14, 24, 29, 32–4.

[62] *CLB, C*, 56, f.39b, writ to mayor and sheriffs of London, 28 January 1299–1300; arrest of offenders ordered in royal writ *CLB, C*, 61, f.43, 10 February 1299–1300. See also n.8 on p. 73 above.

[63] *YO*, 14–15.

[64] F. Palgrave (ed.), *The Parliamentary Writs and Writs of Military Summons*, 2 vols (London, 1830), vol. 2, division II, 2, Appendix, 8, 9, 11; *CPR 1307–13*, 29.

intervene to set prices in cases of emergency or collusion, and that 'medieval price regulation usually embraced only a few basic necessities'.[65] In the case of thirteenth- and fourteenth-century England, two of the items subject to early royal price regulation, bread and ale, had in common the fact that they were basic goods necessary to all subjects, which most subjects had to buy, rather than producing for themselves. Bread, obviously a staple, was bought by many, but not all subjects.[66] Ale was a staple product for all classes, which virtually all, including those one might have thought capable of producing it for themselves, had to purchase at some times, particularly before the technological breakthrough of the introduction of hops into the brewing process in the later fourteenth century, which allowed a longer-lasting beverage – beer – to be produced.[67] Wine, however, was not a staple product for most of the population, and control of the price of wine cannot have been undertaken in the interests of the poor, or of the majority of ordinary subjects.[68] The wine trade was rather different from the sale of bread and ale in that a small number of traders controlled the supply of wine, which made it relatively easy for them to demand high prices, and it is likely to have been the ease for wine sellers of extracting large profits which prompted kings to set prices in this area.[69] Of the items which came to be covered by royal price control regulations in the fourteenth century, most were victuals, though not such staples as bread and ale. The York Ordinances of 1301 regulate the prices of some items which should be classed as luxuries such as mustard and ginger.[70] After the Black Death, regulation also seems to have been aimed at non-food items produced by small-scale craftsmen. Regulations in the latter area are linked to the policy of controlling the economic power of the 'lower orders', which also produced wage regulation in the Ordinance and Statute of Labourers.[71] They have a dual nature, being part of the labour clampdown and also fitting into the earlier established pattern of royal regulation of the price of subjects' sales.

Some sale transactions, even those concerning vitally important commodities, were never subject to royal price legislation. There is no evidence of royal control of or provision for the price of raw materials like grain (except in connection with the eyre and with purveyance), though this was controlled at local level and an assessment of its current price had to be made for the assizes of bread and ale.[72] A writ of 1376 to the mayor of London shows that 'the centre' expected at least this 'local' authority to take action to prevent the enhancement of grain prices, without giving instructions as to how this was to be done.[73] There was virtually no regulation in respect of land sales. There was some action in connection with

[65] de Roover, *JP*, 421, 425, 429.
[66] Dyer notes that aristocratic households typically produced enough bread for their own needs: Dyer, *Standards of Living*, 57.
[67] J.M. Bennett, *Women in the Medieval English Countryside: Gender and Household in Brigstock before the Plague* (Oxford, 1987), 120; Bennett, *Ale*, 8; Dyer, *Standards of Living*, 57. See also Britnell, 'Morals', 21.
[68] McKisack, *Fourteenth Century*, 360, 361.
[69] Dyer, *Standards of Living*, 62; Britnell, *Colchester*, 90–1.
[70] *YO*, 15.
[71] Palmer, *Black Death*.
[72] Prestwich, *War, Politics and Finance under Edward I* (London, 1972), 128–30; Maitland, *Eyre of Kent 1313–14*, 51; Ashley, *Introduction*, 187–8; Thrupp, *Short History*, 12; Ross, 'Assize', 332; Britnell, 'Price setting', 3.
[73] *CLB, H*, 48, f.50.

agreements to rent, as opposed to buying, land in particular areas, which demonstrated that kings had the power to intervene here, but it was not carried through to a national statute.[74] The idea that rent levels should be regulated nationally was put forward by the rebels of 1381, who demanded that free rents should be set at 4d per acre.[75] There is, however, no suggestion that it was perceived to be part of the role of the king and government to regulate the price of land in general. As noted in the introduction, transactions concerning land were regarded as being fundamentally different to transactions in chattels or goods (in that there was not, and could not be, a fresh bargain struck each time land was transferred: services were attached to the land, and were not renegotiated on each transfer).[76] The only comparable measures with regard to land fixed 'feudal incidents' or else emphasised that they must be 'reasonable'.[77] Much land was, of course, definitely outside royal control in any case as it was 'unfree' and thus for the lord of the manor to decide the rules (although he was increasingly considered to be bound in some sense by custom of the manor).[78]

As was noted above with respect to bread and ale, royal regulations were not the only rules operating to set prices of other goods. 'Local' (particularly urban) authorities and guilds also set prices of goods.[79] London was particularly regulated, with proclamations made on prices of a variety of goods, including bread and ale, but also a somewhat wider collection of things, including corn and oats, armour, lime, charcoal, faggots and coal.[80] In some cases, regulations were extended to particular sales significantly earlier than were national regulations, and London regulations were updated more frequently. Lasting regulation of meat and poultry prices, for example, came earlier in London than in national statutes.[81]

---

[74] Domestic and commercial leases were to be controlled under the York Ordinances, 1301: *YO*, 16. The prices of lodgings during an eyre were controlled: see material on the eyre of Northamptonshire 1329–30: Sutherland, *Eyre of Northamptonshire 1329–30*, 9, 14, 24, 29, 32–4.

[75] Bolton, *MEE*, 215.

[76] Baker, *Introduction*, 227.

[77] P. Brand, *The Making of the Common Law* (London, 1992), 306; *P&M*, I, 289–90, 331; Baker, *Introduction*, 238; *Magna Carta* (1215) clauses 12 and 15; *Statute of Westminster I* (1275), c.36.

[78] Rigby, *English Society*, 76, 10, 109; Britnell, *Commercialisation*, 33–4, 60, 111. See, e.g., Simpson, *Land Law*, 158–60; Baker, *Introduction*, 230–1, 307.

[79] London: see 1363 civic proclamation concerning wine and victuals: Riley *Memorials*, 312; 1371 prices of ale: Riley, *Memorials*, 348; cited in Wood, *Medieval Economic Thought*, 144. Evidence has been found of regulation of the price of grain and fish in borough markets in the second half of the fourteenth century and thereafter: Britnell, 'Price setting', 6, suggests that this price setting went back at least to 1347 in London; Rigby, *English Society* 160, citing Lipson, *Economic History, vol. I*, 329, 337; Hereford: CUL Dd.7.14, assize of 1 Edw. II fixing prices in the city of Hereford of articles in common consumption, and use 'long and curious' according to the editor of *YB* 20 & 21 Edw. I.

[80] For an outline of the history of the assize of bread in London, see Thrupp, *Short History*, 12–39, and, e.g., *CLB, G*, 174, f.135; *CLB, H*, 106, f.96b; *CLB, G*, 225 f.261b. Wine: e.g. *CLB, I*, 151, f.166; Riley, *Memorials*, 180; LB, E, f.221; *CLB, G*, 4; *CLB, G*, 5, f.3b; *CLB, G*, 129, f.92b; *CLB,G*, 148, f.107; *CLB,G*, 255, f.238b; *CLB, G*, 311, f.306b; *CLB, G*, 318, f.312b; *CLB, G*, 311, f.306b; *CLB, H*, 27, f.35; *CLB, H*, 214 , f.164; *CLB, H*, 323, f.224b; *CLB, H*, 365, f.260; *CLB, I*, 35, f.33b; *CLB, K*, 16, f.10b; *CLB, I*, 71, f.76b; *CLB, G*, 145, f.103b; *CLB, G*, 260, f.244b; *CLB, G*, 318, f.312b; *CLB, H*, 108, f.97; *CLB, I*, 151, f.166. Ale: *CLB, A*, 215, ff.129b–130 (1276–8); LB, D, ff.155b–159b (1312?) printed in *LC*, 280–2, again recorded in *LA*, 260–80; *CLB, F*, 189, f.161b (1337); *CLB, G*, 4 (1352–3); *CLB, G*, 52, f.41b; *CLB, G*, 148, f.107 (1362–3); *CLB, G*, 197, f.164b (1364); *CLB, G*, 255, f.238b (1369); *CLB, G*, 260, f.244b (1369–70); *CLB, G*, 270–1, ff.259b–260 (1370); *CLB, G*, 311, f.306b (1373); *CLB, H*, 3, ff.14–16 (1375); *CLB, H*, 121, f.107b (1379); *CLB, L*, 178, f.160b (1481); *CLB, H*, 3, ff.14–16 (1375); *CLB, G*, 242, f.224b (no date); *CLB, H*, 69, f.68b (1377); *CLB, H*, 108, f.97 (1378); *CLB, I*, 44, f.47 (1405). Lime: (1329) *CLB, E*, 241, ff.117–117b.

[81] Meat prices: *CLB, G*, 139, f.100b (1360–1); *CLB, H*, 61, f.59 (1377); *CLB, H*, 257, f.187 (1384–5). London

Cordwainery, meat and fish were regulated from at least 1299–1300.[82] London also made specific regulations for sales by hostelers before the appearance of national regulation on this subject.[83] London was by no means the only area with its own set of regulations.[84] Local price setting was tolerated, and relied upon. In 1331, Edward III explicitly commended the London civic authorities for having set an assize of bread, ale and wine, in the light of a recent economic upturn, and told them to ensure that it was kept.[85] Local regulation certainly continued into the fifteenth century and there is no sense of the 'state' taking over this function completely, or trying to become exclusively competent.[86] A particularly interesting example of the 'cross-fertilisation' or hybridisation of 'local' and 'national' in terms of law making can be seen in the York Ordinances of 1301. They were made by the King's Council 'with the assent of the citizens', and their content shows links with 'royal' measures and with 'local measures' (particularly those of London).[87]

Quality and openness
Regulations as to the quality of goods, particularly food, are connected with pricing laws (although they are clearly also connected with 'public health').[88] Elements of quality judgment can be seen in royal regulations such as those on cloth, but it is more characteristic of 'local' rather than royal/national rules.[89] The *Composicio* has

had laws regulating the price of poultry from at least 1345: *CLB, F*, 123, f.101b; *CLB, G*, 148, f.107. Some laws had some royal inspiration, such as an ordinance made 'on the king's behalf', regulating the price of poultry, rabbits and eggs: *CLB, G*, 273, f.262. Municipal proclamations and ordinances on poultry and meat prices: (1378) *CLB, H*, 110, ff.98–9 (1403–4); *CLB, I*, 35, ff.33b, 42 (also lamb prices), 43; *CLB, I*, 151, f.166; (1370) *CLB, G*, 270–1, ff.259b–260; *CLB, I*, 35, f.33b. There are examples of these laws being enforced in *CLB, H*, 326, f.226b (1388).

[82] *CEMCR*, 60, 61.

[83] *CLB, G*, 300, f.295 (1372); *CLB, H*, 27, f.35 (1376); *CLB, G*, 300, f.295 (1371). Examples of laws being enforced: *CLB, H*, 257, f.187 (1384–5).

[84] See, e.g., *LRB*; Anstey, *MA*; M. Bateson (ed.), *Borough Customs*, 2 vols, Selden Society vol. 18 for 1904 and vol. 21 for 1906 (London, 1904 and 1906); P. Coss (ed.), *The Early Records of Medieval Coventry*, British Academy Records of Social and Economic History, new ser., 11 (Oxford, 1986); C.A. Markham (ed.), *Records of the Borough of Northampton*, vol. 1 (Northampton, 1898); Salter, *MA*; Salter, *MC*; P. Studer (ed.), *The Oak Book of Southampton, vol. I: The Anglo-French Ordinances of the Ancient Guild Merchant of Southampton* (Southampton, 1910); W. Hudson and J.C. Tingey, *Records of the City of Norwich*, 2 vols (Norwich, 1906, 1910).

[85] *CLB, E*, 219, f.175b.

[86] See, e.g., the examples in Britnell, 'Price setting', 6.

[87] *YO.*

[88] 'Public health' was regulated both locally and nationally. See, e.g., the measures on disposal of meat waste, filth and garbage in the Statute of 1388, *SR* II:57, 12 Ric. II, c.4. See T.M. Theilmann, 'The regulation of public health in late medieval England', in J.L. Gillespie (ed.), *The Age of Richard II* (Stroud, 1997), 205–24.

[89] Assize of Cloth: see, e.g., Bolton, *MEE*, 327; *RP* II:28; *RP* III:159, 271. Differentiation of grades of ale can be seen in Coventry rules of the 1270s, and similar differentiated rules were adopted nationally in 1317 legislation, *CCR 1313–18*, 449, citing an example from London. Different grades of ale can also be seen in the price regulations associated with the eyre: Maitland, *Eyre of Kent 1313–14*, 49, 51, 55. *Judicium Pillorie* deals with quality of wine and meat products. *Composicio* (butchers) *SR* I:202. The jury of twelve assisting the royal 'officer of measures' in *Britton*'s scheme were also to inquire about salesmen and cooks who make a practice of selling to passers-by bad meat, 'tainted or diseased or otherwise dangerous to the health of man', *Britton*, p. 192, f.76b.

Early local regulation of the quality of ale, with punishment, are noted in Chester in 1086: Blackstone, *Commentaries*, Book IV, c.12, p. 159, also mentioned in Britnell, *Commercialisation*, 25–6; Wood, *Medieval Economic Thought*, 115. On London quality regulations, see, e.g., *CEMCR*, 4 (cordwainers and cobblers), 56 (meat). On fifteenth-century local quality regulations for food and manufactured goods: Britnell, *Commercialisation*, 175–6.

provisions on the quality of meat products.[90] The York Ordinances 1301 have quality criteria in regulations on ale and wine and 'public health'/swindling and anti-adulteration regulations of quality for bread, butter, cheese, wine, vinegar, meat and fish.[91] Quality control rules were enforced actively in urban jurisdictions in the fourteenth century, and were also dealt with by justices of the peace.[92] The difficulty of stipulating national quality standards, and the perishability of victuals both militated against national standards in this area and made it something more appropriately left to lower level officials.

'Local' regulations were very specific about sales being conducted in particular places, and openly not secretly, part of the reason being that this would prevent breach of pricing laws (though they also show a concern with avoiding fraud and protection of 'insiders' against 'outsiders').[93] Again, this was a matter generally left to lower level authorities.[94] This made sense in practical terms, since 'national' legislation could not hope to be specific enough to cover all variations in local conditions and institutions.

Nature of the pricing laws

The prices which were to apply to sales of goods were sometimes set exactly, and sometimes a more flexible formula was laid down.

Prices for some goods were stipulated exactly in the York Ordinances of 1301, and in national measures in 1274–5, 1311, 1315, 1342, 1353, 1354, 1357, 1363 and 1383.[95] Some of these allowed for variation in prices between cities and market towns on the one hand and remote upland areas on the other. The Assize of Ale

---

[90] *SR* I:203.

[91] *YO*, 10–16.

[92] Musson, 'New labour', 81, and examples cited therein, of a London cook (1355), London baker (1375), in London courts. *CPMR 1324–64*, 251; *CPMR 1364–81*, 187. Gloucester butcher 1385: E.G Kimball (ed.), *Rolls of the Gloucestershire Sessions of the Peace 1361–1378*, Transactions of the Bristol and Gloucestershire Archaeological Society vol. 62 for 1940 (Kendal, 1942) 108. Warwickshire shoemaker 1384: E.G. Kimball (ed.), *Rolls of the Warwickshire and Coventry Sessions of the Peace 1377–97*, Dugdale Society 16 (London, 1939), 166. Oxfordshire sellers of defective tiles 1395: E.G. Kimball (ed.), *Oxfordshire Sessions of the Peace in the Reign of Richard II*, Oxfordshire Record Society vol. 53 for 1979 and 1980 (Banbury, 1983), 76. See also *CLB, G*, 1, 33, 126, 141, 143.

[93] Local rules about certain nuisance trades being confined to certain places: *MLC*, 90. London: LB, F, f.102; *CLB, G*, 271, f.259b; P. Nightingale, *A Medieval Mercantile Community: The Grocers' Company and the Politics and Trade of London 1000–1485* (Yale, 1995), 102; M. Kowaleski, *Local Markets and Regional Trade in Medieval Exeter* (Cambridge, 1995), 190; Britnell, *Commercialisation*, 176 (fifteenth-century examples). Local rules about sales not being in private places: *MLC*, 90; W. Hudson, *Leet Jurisdiction in the City of Norwich during the Thirteenth and Fourteenth Centuries*, Selden Society vol. 5 for 1891 (London, 1892), 80–2; Kowaleski, *Local Markets*, 181, 188; S. Rees Jones, 'York's civic administration 1354–1484' in S. Rees Jones (ed.), *The Government of Medieval York: Essays in commemoration of the 1396 Royal Charter*, Borthwick Studies in History 3 (York, 1997), 123, 126–7.

[94] A partial exception (because there was local 'input') is in the York Ordinances of 1301 regulations for locations of fish sales: *YO*, 13. There are also occasional prosecutions for secret sales in central records of the later fourteenth century. See, e.g., Putnam, *Enforcement*, 401.

[95] *YO*, 12, 15, 16: prices of wine, poultry, rabbits, hares, herrings, eggs, Paris candles, onions, mustard, ginger or galantine sauce, verjuice, shoes, turf and robes and the rates for stalling a horse and for a guest's bed and room were set. The maximum price of cooked chicken and goose was set. *Composicio* (wine) fixed a price of 12d a sester: *SR* 1:203; Britnell, *Commercialisation*, 94; (poultry and other victuals) *RP* I:295a; (wine) *CLB, G*, 4, 41; (fish) *SR* I:353, 31 Edw. III, st. 2 c.2; (poultry) *SR* I:378, 37 Edw. III, c.3; (wine) *SR* II:19, 5 Ric. II, st.1 c.4. The measures of 1342, 1353 and 1354 concerning wine prices seem to have been made under the Ale 1330 legislation.

differentiated brewers in and out of urban areas, taking some account of different conditions and expenses which would be incurred in different areas, with brewers in cities ordered to sell two gallons of beer or ale for a penny, and those outside ordered to sell three gallons for a penny. When three gallons were sold in a town for a penny, out of a town they are to sell four gallons for the same price.[96] The 1315 victual price statute had variations for London, with higher prices being allowed there than elsewhere in the country.[97] The poultry price statute of 1363 also included regional variation.[98]

Other statutes did not set exact prices but left them to be ascertained by reference to a small number of variables. The *Assisa Panis et Cervisie* set the prices of bread and ale by basing calculation on the price of the raw materials used in their manufacture.[99] The assize of bread started from the position which would exist when a quarter of wheat was sold for 12d. It then fixed the size of loaves of various types which could be sold for a particular price. Raymond de Roover described the idea of varying the size of loaves in such bread price regulations as 'crude'.[100] Though his judgment seems unfair as far as the idea of varying the size of loaves is concerned, the assize of bread as enacted in England has been seen to have lacked sophistication in its conception of price ratios, because on one possible construction of the scheme, the relative value of different types of loaf would fluctuate as the price of wheat increased.[101] Problems with the ambiguity of statutory provisions concerning the fixing of prices of bread under the assize when the price of wheat changed became a real issue in London in the sixteenth century, though they may have been noticed earlier, prompting London's authorities to devise and, perhaps, use a system based on experimtental bakings rather than paper calculations in the late thirteenth and fourteenth centuries.[102]

As well as setting the size of bread according to the price of the raw materials, the assize laid down the amount which a baker could charge for various expenses and for profit. The assize does not explain how the price of the raw materials was to be assessed, but this is clarified by the *Judicium Pillorie*, which provided that twelve law-worthy men were to be used for this purpose. They were to ascertain the price of the raw materials, i.e. 'how a quarter of the best wheat was sold the last market day, and how the second wheat, and how the third, and how a quarter of

---

[96] *SR* I:199. J.M. Bennett notes that 'the *Assisa* allowed urban brewers to sell ale at much higher prices than their counterparts in the countryside – perhaps because brewers in towns were more essential to their localities, perhaps because they faced more expenses, perhaps because they brewed stronger drink': Bennett, *Ale*, 21. The legislation of 1317 also differentiated between prices in cities, boroughs and market towns on one hand and villages on the other: *CCR 1313–18*, 449.

[97] *RP* I:295; *CLB, E*, 44; *CCR 1313–18*, 160–1; *Foedera*, II, part i, 263.

[98] *SR* I:378, 37 Edw. III, c.3.

[99] *SR* I:199.

[100] de Roover, *JP*, 429.

[101] For ideas of proportion and their familiarity at least to the elite amongst contemporary mathematicians, see M.S. Mahoney, 'Mathematics', in D.C. Lindberg (ed.), *Science in the Middle Ages* (Chicago, 1978), 145, 159. For problems with proportion in the assize of bread, see L. Zylbergeld, 'Les regulations du marche du pain au XIIIe siècle en occident et l' "assize of bread" de 1266–1267 pour l'Angleterre' in J.-M. Duvosquel and A. Dierkers (eds), *Villes et campagnes au Moyen Age* (Liège, 1991), 791–814; F. Nicholas, 'The assize of bread in London during the sixteenth century', *Economic History* 2 (1932), 323–47, at 326. A different interpretation of the idea behind the assize scheme can be found in Davis, *Representation*, 189.

[102] S.L. Thrupp, *A Short History of the Worshipful Company of Bakers* (London, 1933), 15; Corporation of London Record Office, *Liber de Assisa Panis*, f.1b; Nicholas, 'Assize of bread', 329.

barley and oats'.[103] Then they were to state how much of an increase or decrease in the price of wheat was needed before a baker ought to change the weight of his bread, and how much various loaves ought to weigh, according to the price of a quarter of wheat. A version of the assize from the patent roll of 1389–90 explains that the assize of bread is to be calculated 'by the middle price of wheat', which suggests a mean average.[104] It also makes explicit the idea in the early assizes that only a fairly large increase in the price of wheat, a 6d increase, would be enough to move up or down to the next set of prices and specifications.

There is direct evidence from the 1270s to the 1370s of the London civic authorities setting the price of bread, and evidence of enforcement of the laws extending well beyond the end of the fourteenth century.[105] S.L. Thrupp regarded the London system of bread price regulation as working 'smoothly enough' during the middle ages.[106] Although the London records are unparalleled in length, there is evidence of the schemes set out for York in the Ordinances of 1301, and used in Oxford between 1309 and 1338, with local assessments of the price of grain used to gauge appropriate prices of bread (although the bread prices are not set out) and, similarly, in much smaller jurisdictions, such as that of the bishop of Ely at Littleport, where, in 1325, the chief pledges, on oath, reported the value of wheat (three grades) last market day, and the difference from the last assessment of the assize.[107]

The assize of ale was drawn up in a broadly similar, if simpler, fashion to the assize of bread. There are differing scales in the *Assisa Cervisie* and the *Judicium Pillorie*.[108] Ale price regulations did not take specific account of the labour and expenses of the brewer, in contrast to the assize of bread.[109]

The mechanics of setting and enforcing the assize of ale in practice, in the rural and urban contexts, have been analysed by J.M. Bennett, who has examined a very large number of manorial and urban records relating to the assize of ale.[110] She finds that the price was commonly set by a jury, in relation to the cost of grain and malt, at least once a year.[111] She notes, however, that the scale of the *Assisa Cervisie* 'was not strictly observed' and suggests a reluctance amongst those charged with

---

[103] Thus, we have some idea of the mechanism for assessing the price of wheat and other grains, which prices were required to be known before the assizes could be calculated. This question suggests that there was a rigid division of grades of wheat, which would be apparent to the jurors. This in itself raises questions as to who graded wheat, and how they did so.

[104] *SR* II:63, 13 Ric. II, c.8.

[105] Most is contained in the *Liber de Assisa Panis*, with a few relevant entries in LB A, B and D. *Liber de Assisa Panis* includes reports of assays from 1283 to 1375, with mention being made of assizes set in 1264–5 (f.2a), and records of offenders from 1293 to 1438. The nature of the reports in the *Liber de Assisa Panis* changes in the 1370s, with no more recording of the setting of the assize, and individual 'case reports' rather than complete records of the investigation of loaves. See also *CLB, A*, 207, 215, 216; LB, A, ff.110–29 (assize for 5–20 Edw. I); LB, B, ff.85–9 (26–9 Edw. I); *CLB, D*, 311, ff.170–90 (3–10 Edw. II). *Liber de Assisa Panis* also mentions assays going back to the end of Henry III's reign, though it does not set them out. The London authorities claimed in 1351–2 to have had jurisdiction over the assize since time immemorial: *CLB, F*, 239, ff.206b, 209, although this does not necessarily mean that they claimed to have been setting the weight/price of bread since that point.

[106] Thrupp, *Short History*, 13.

[107] *YO*, 10; Salter, *MA*, vol. II, 142–82; *Court Baron*, 145.

[108] *SR* I:199–202; Bennett, *Ale*, 192.

[109] Bennett, *Ale*, 192.

[110] Bennett, *Ale*, 171.

[111] Bennett, *Ale*, 112.

setting prices to change the price of ale too dramatically.[112] The price of ale was set in London in the Assizes of the City of London 1276–8, a royal order of 1305, and in civic regulations or proclamations in 1337, 1352–3, 1362–3, 1369, 1373, 1354, 1364, 1369–70, 1376, 1386, 1387, 1387–8 and 1391.[113] There is, however, no equivalent to the *Liber de Assisa Panis* for ale prices, and the fact that the maximum prices stated in the ordinances vary very little over the fourteenth century suggests that this was not as sensitive a mechanism as the assize of bread as practised in London. In the Oxford records, only one example of the setting of the assize of ale survives, from 1311, showing a valuation of different grains.[114]

A consideration of the mechanism used to fix the price of bread and ale in the assizes suggests that there was no desire on the part of the king and government to seek and enforce the absolutely correct price, or indeed the same price everywhere in the realm. As long as the price of bread or ale was not wildly out of line with the price of wheat or other raw materials, that seems to have been sufficient. A degree of local control was also built into the system.

Prices of some commodities were set with reference to prices in other locations, or to the price which had prevailed in the past. This was the case with wine from at least 1331, when a price for wine in Oxford was set in relation to the price of wine in London. The wine in Oxford was to be no more than 2d per gallon more expensive.[115] Wine price legislation of 1381 also set prices in relation to those prevailing in other locations.[116] In the 1390s in York, wine prices were set with relation to the price of wine imported through Kingston-upon-Hull, as assessed by eleven men before the mayor and bailiffs, and in Winchester, they were set with reference to the price in Southamptom.[117] The York Ordinances of 1301 appealed to an earlier price as the appropriate price for a number of types of victual, as did the 1351 Statute of Labourers in respect of craft goods (though not victuals).[118] 'Labour-related' pricing presentments of the 1350s mentioned not only that a person had broken the current price for selling goods, but drew the contrast with the price at which he had formerly sold the same goods, as in the following case from the King's Bench session at Chelmsford 1352 M.

> *Item dicunt quod Willelmus le Hare de Thundresle solebat vend[ere] par[iam] rotarum car[ectae] pro iv.s vi.d & modo non vult vend[ere] nisi pro x.s contra statut[um] ordinac[ionemque] etc.*

---

[112] Bennett, *Ale*, 192, 21, citing W.F. Lloyd, *Prices of Corn in Oxford* (Oxford 1830), table IX and app., as evidence for the relative stability of ale and beer prices compared to grain prices.

[113] *CLB, D*, 298, ff.155b–159b; *LC*, I, 280–2, ff.201–206b; *LA*, I, 260–80; Riley, *Memorials*, 56; LB, C, f.86; *CLB, F*, 189, f.161b; *CLB, F*, 27, f.18b; LB, E, f.57; *LA*, I, 358–60; *CLB, G*, 4; *CLB, G*, 148, f.107; *CLB, G*, 255, f.238b; *CLB, G*, 52, f.41b; *CLB, G*, 33, f.29; *CLB, G*, 260, f.244b; *CLB, G*, 311, f.306b; *CLB, H*, 3, ff.14–16; Riley, *Memorials*, 388–90; *CLB, H*, 293, f.208; *CLB, H*, 311, f.218; *CLB, H*, 323, f.224b; *CLB, H*, 365, f.260.

[114] Salter, *MA*, vol. 2, 156.

[115] *CPR 1330–34*, 186; Salter, *MA*, vol. 1. 118; *CCR 1330–33*, 410. Prices set in London may have been taken as a benchmark in other areas: Britnell, *Commercialisation*, 94, citing Essex Record Office Colchester Muniments, *Red Paper Book* f.124r.

[116] *SR* II:19, 5 Ric. II, st.1 c.4 (ports).

[117] M. Sellers (ed.), *York Memoranda Book*, Surtees Society 120 (1911), 172, f.68; Keene, *Survey of Winchester*, 271 (it was 'city practice to send a man to Southampton to investigate the wine there').

[118] *YO*, 14–15. The 1330 statute regulating fares of passage from ports also used a price from former years as the standard: *SR* II:263, st. 4 Edw. III, c.8; *RP* II:233–5.

(They say that William le Hare of Thundersley used to sell a pair of cart wheels for 4s 6d and now will only sell them at 10s, contrary to the statute and ordinance etc.)[119]

Another method of legislating on prices was to state simply that the price was to be a reasonable one. The York Ordinances of 1301 left some items, such as cloaks and tents, to be sold at reasonable prices.[120] On the repeal of the 1315 poultry statute, poulterers were ordered to sell their wares at reasonable prices, but it was not explained how these should be calculated.[121] Generally, however, some matters were mentioned in statutes as being relevant to this evaluation. In the York Ordinances of 1301, the reasonable price of meat was to equal the price at which the carcass had originally been bought plus a sum for the labour involved in preparing it for sale, as assessed by two neighbours.[122] In the 1330 wine statute, the price prevailing at the port of entry and the cost of carriage to the place of sale were to be taken into account.[123] In the material dealing with adjustment of the prices set in the statute, the cost of wine in Gascony, the 'freight, stipends, carriage, ullage etc.', the price at which wines were being sold in neighbouring ports, the wages of servants and hire of storehouses were to be taken into account.[124] A different way of arriving at a reasonable price was to base the calculation on an assessment of a reasonable *profit* for the seller. A close roll entry, from 1332 orders the mayor and bailiffs of Oxford to enquire at what price wines were being sold in London, and to cause wines to be sold in Oxford according to the statutes and ordinances, so that the merchant vintners bringing wine there should not make a loss.[125] In the Ordinance of Labourers 1349, the reasonable price for victuals was to be calculated having regard to the price at which a particular commodity was sold in neighbouring places, so that the seller took a moderate but not excessive profit, which depended on the distance which the goods had been transported.[126] The 'reasonable gain' of the seller was also to be calculated under the statute of 1389–90.[127] It is, however, unclear exactly what was meant by 'profit' or 'gain' in this context: was it understood as 'expenses', or compensation for loss, or pure *lucrum*?

Sometimes the price was to be fixed with regard to the price at which an item was commonly sold, as in the Ordinance of Labourers 1349 and in the statute of 1389–90 which ordered that hostelers were to sell hay and oats at a reasonable price, taking no more than a halfpenny per bushel above the common price in the market place.[128] There is, however, no reference to scarcity as a criterion for

---

[119] JUST 1/267 m.18.
[120] *YO*, 15.
[121] *Vita Edwardi Secundi*, 59; *RP* I:351a; *Anonimalle*, 88–91.
[122] *YO*, 12.
[123] *SR* II:263, st. 4 Edw. III, c.8.
[124] Letter on the close roll for 1332 to the mayor and sheriffs of London: *CCR 1330–33*, 545.
[125] *CCR 1330–33*, 557. Similar provisions for Northampton, Colchester, York, Nottingham, Lincoln, Worcester, Hereford and Meresleye are at 557–8.
[126] *SR* I:308. Victuals were ordered to be sold 'pro precio racionabili . . . ita quod habeant hujusmodi venditores moderatum lucrum, non excessivum'.
[127] 'resonable gaigne': *SR* II:63, 13 Ric. II, st.1 c.8.
[128] 'le commune pris en marche', *SR* II:63, 13 Ric. II, st.1 c.8. 'Market' is here to be understood in the sense of geographical/juridical entity rather than economic abstraction. The use of the current price of goods in a particular place as a criterion for fixing fair prices was also used by some medieval canonists and theologians: Langholm, *Economics*, 44–5, 55, 92–5, 179–80, 257, 304.

price setting, in contrast to a provision of 1390 concerning the setting of wages.[129]

Other statutes ordered prices to be set by a particular official or specially appointed group, again with varying guidelines as to what should be taken into account in setting it. Such a mechanism can be seen in the 'assize of food' set in conjunction with the sessions of the eyres, where selected men were to fix 'suitable' or 'appropriate' (*convenables*) prices for all victuals. The assessment was to be carried out either by two knights and two 'serjeants', or by six men of good repute who were not members of the victualling trades.[130] Similarly, in the York Ordinances of 1301, as mentioned, the price at which butchers were to be allowed to sell meat was include an element of assessment by two neighbouring butchers.[131] Some discretion in fixing profits of those selling victuals was given to urban authorities in the Ordinance of 1349.[132] Justices of Labourers or other specially assigned justices were ordered to inquire of those who sold iron at too dear a price ('a trop cher pris'). In the reign of Richard II, the justices of the peace came to have an important role in determining the price of goods. An Act of 1389 which regulated victual prices ordered the justices of the peace in every county, in their sessions between Easter and Michaelmas, to fix the profits which victuallers should make on sales, according to their discretion based on a 'reasonable gain' for the seller.[133] Justices of the peace seem to have acted to set the price of goods.[134]

Local price laws show the use of experts and those involved in the trade to set prices. A London mechanism for ensuring that wine was sold at a reasonable price was set up in 1367–8, making use of trade 'insiders' or experts.[135] Likewise, the official price of fish in London may have been arrived at by negotiation with those involved in the fish trade from the 1380s. There is evidence that in 1382, the civic authorities took some trouble to negotiate a reduction in the price charged for herrings by a particular fishmonger.[136] This practice was generalised and embodied in legislation by at least 1416.[137] Similarly, in connection with regulation of the price of grain and fish in borough markets in the second half of the fourteenth century and thereafter, R.H. Britnell suggests that prices were set by declaration of borough officials, 'perhaps after negotiation with dealers, or with certain principal dealers' and cites evidence of the mechanisms set up in various places for enforcement of these rules.[138] In towns, some regulation of prices was also in the hands of trade bodies, power having been delegated by municipal authorities, who retained varying degrees of theoretical and actual supervisory

---

[129] *EEJ*, 95; 13 Ric. II, st.1 c.8; *SR* II:63; Putnam, *PJP*, cviii–cx.

[130] Maitland, *Eyre of Kent*, 10; Cam, *London Eyre 1321*, 21, 26, 28–9.

[131] *YO*, 12.

[132] *SR* I:307. It does, however, seem to be going too far to say that they were given the power to set profits 'according to their whim': Britnell, *Commercialisation*, 172.

[133] *SR* II:63, 13 Ric. II, st.1 c.81.

[134] See, e.g., R. Sillem (ed.), *Some Sessions of the Peace in Lincolnshire 1360–1375*, Publications of the Lincolnshire Record Society vol. 30 for 1937 (Hereford, 1936), no.373; JUST 1/530 (1373).

[135] *CLB, G*, 221, f.201b. Eleven vintners undertook that wines of Gascony should be sold at a reasonable price, 'so that no complaint should come before the Mayor'.

[136] Riley, *Memorials*, 467; LB, H, f.154.

[137] *CLB, I*, 168, f.185.

[138] Britnell, 'Price setting', expanding on statements by Ashley, *Introduction*, 187–8. Britnell suggests that this price setting went back at least to 1347 in London: Britnell, 'Price setting', 5–6; *CLB, E*, 56; *CLB, F*, 83; *CPMR 1323–64*, 115; *CLB, C*, 58; *LA*, I, 692.

jurisdiction.[139] This delegation or negotiation suggests increasing consciousness that economic fluctuations would be likely to occur in the future, as well, perhaps, as a lack of confidence in the legislator's ability to devise a pricing formula to cover future eventualities.

Roman law antecedents have been suggested for the use of 'wise men' to set prices of goods, particularly foodstuffs, though there less distant precedents in the schemes set up to appraise foodstuffs purveyed by the king.[140] A 1330 scheme was for constables and good men of the towns where purveyance was made to appraise at the true value, without threats or duress by officials.[141] This was slightly refined in 1331 – prises were to be made by constables and four discreet men of the towns, sworn to this duty, without menace.[142] In a 1362 statute, prices were to be reached by agreement, and, failing that, by 'view, testimony and appraisement of lords or their bailiffs, constables and four good men of every town'.[143] Another precedent for 'local' regulations using 'wise men' might be the special tribunal of citizens set up to enforce the assizes of bread and ale in York by the York Ordinances of 1301, which also made use of representatives of trades to control prices of the wares of their own trade.[144] More generally, a variety of common law and statutory procedures required an official or a group to come to a view on the value of goods or land.[145]

In some cases, there seems to have been doubt as to whether setting exact prices was the right strategy for kings and governments to adopt. The 1315 victual statute and its swift repeal have been mentioned above. The Great Yarmouth Herring Statute of 1357, which fixed prices of fish, was replaced in 1360–1 by provisions which instead provided rules requiring sales to be conducted openly and not in secret, but, with that limitation, regarded as legitimate any bargain agreed between buyer and seller.[146] There was not, however, a general move against the very idea of fixing prices.

Royal schemes were not inflexible. In the York Ordinances of 1301, for example, although exact prices were laid down for ale and wine, it was conceded that if the price of grain went up or down, or 'if there is a great scarcity of wine, or an improvement in trade'; the prices could be adjusted in a new assize.[147]

---

[139] For London bakery, see, e.g., Thrupp, *Short History*.

[140] Britnell, 'Price setting', 4, citing J.W. Baldwin, 'Medieval theories of the just price: romanists, canonists and theologians in the twelfth and thirteenth centuries', *Transactions of the American Philosophical Society*, new ser., 49 part 4 (Philadelphia, 1959), 79. At p. 20, Baldwin discusses Roman law use of the *index* and *arbitrium boni viri* to set prices.

[141] *SR* I:262–3, st. 4 Edw. III (1330), c.3; *SR* I:265, st. 5 Edw. III (1331), c.3.

[142] *SR* I:265, st. 5 Edw. III (1330), c.2. This also made provision for receipts (tallies) to be given to sellers. Similar scheme in statute of 1351–2: *SR* I:319, 25 Edw. III, st.5 c.1.

[143] *SR* I:371, st. 36 Edw. III (1362), c.2.

[144] *YO*, 12, 14.

[145] Examples include the process of *elegit* and the sale by view of 'honest men' under the statute of Acton Burnel (1383), and extents of moveables under the Statute of Merchants (1285): McNall, 'Recognition', 144–52, 228. It appears to have been possible to challenge these valuations, at least for procedural impropriety.

[146] 1357 statute: *SR* I:353, 31 Edw. III, st.2 c.2; replacement: *SR* I:369. An act of 1389 regulating victual prices may also be read as containing some disillusion with precise royal price fixing. According to the translation in *Statutes of the Realm*, the preamble states that 'one cannot [ever hope to] ['pur ce qe home ne purra mye'] put the price of corn and other victuals in certain', but it may be better to interpret the passage as meaning 'one cannot be sure of the price of corn and other victuals [at the moment]': *SR* II:63, 13 Ric. II, st.1 c.81.

[147] *YO*, 11, 12.

This examination of the methods of regulation shows that it is not possible to trace a progression of methods of fixing prices: a number of different methods continued to be used throughout the period. The statutes and ordinances do not give an entirely clear picture of the idea of a reasonable price which kings and governments were attempting to reflect in their price fixing regulations.[148] When the basis for assessing a reasonable price can be glimpsed, there are elements of giving appropriate reward for labour and recompense for cost of production or transport, and of ensuring conformity with the usual price of the commodity in that area: both 'cost theory' or 'labour theory' and 'market theory' of prices. This may be seen as a difference from medieval canon law and theological rules of fair dealing and theories of the just price, if the view that the 'market theory' prevailed, is accepted.[149] The contrast is not, however, so sharp if one accepts the view that elements of both 'market price' and 'cost or labour price' were included in the just price theory of 'the scholastics'.[150]

Overall, the only conclusion which seems to fit is that these regulations were attempting in various ways to ensure that no one charged or was charged very unreasonable prices for regulated goods, not that the one absolutely correct price was calculated for every sale. Perhaps the attitude is best summed up in the instructions to those setting prices for the duration of an eyres in the early fourteenth century, where matters were to be arranged so that 'the sellers may make a fair profit and the buyers pay no more than a fair price' ('Les vendours bonement puissent en mesme les choses gaigner en resoun, et les achatours nient trop oiutrageousement acheter ne paier').[151] This would, presumably, leave a fairly large margin for disagreementt. This has implications for the way in which we approach the evidence of enforcement (or non-enforcement), since, if the system is not universal, monolithic, absolute, we should not be surprised to see gaps, undercurrents and inconsistencies in the ways in which it is enforced.

Jurisdiction

Sometimes instructions about jurisdiction are included in legislative sources, but often, we are dependent upon records of practice. It is, however, clear that royal jurisdiction was sometimes exercised directly, by using royal tribunals and officials to punish offenders, and sometimes indirectly, by supervision of those with jurisdictional franchises. Direct royal enforcement took place in a number of different ways, using a number of different officials. At the highest judicial level, jurisdiction over certain price fixing provisions was given to the royal justices. An article on the sale price of wine is included amongst the articles of the eyre reproduced in *Statutes of the Realm*, ordering the jurors to report 'Of wines sold contrary to the assize in cities, boroughs, market towns and other towns, wherever

---

[148] A variety of methods of setting values can also be seen in the wages legislation of the mid-fourteenth century. Whilst the 1349 Ordinance of Labourers did not specify exact wages, but apparently left them to local regulation, the 1351 statute did set exact wages: Musson, 'New labour', 77.

[149] de Roover, *JP*, 418.

[150] Langholm, *Economics*, 179, 180, 232, 304, 574–5.

[151] D.W. Sutherland (ed.), *Eyre of Northamptonshire 3–4 Edw. III, 1329–1330*, 2 vols, Selden Society vol. 97 for 1981 and vol. 98 for 1982 (London, 1983), I, 24. A similar test can be seen in Maitland, *Eyre of Kent 1313–14*, 55–6.

wines are sold, who sold them, how may casks a year, and for how many years'.[152] An article on the assize of wine is also to be found in the articles used in the eyre of Northampton of 1329–30.[153] There is no article requiring presentment of offenders against the assizes of bread and ale except in the articles used in the eyres of the Channel Islands.[154] *Britton* suggests that justices in eyre were limited in their jurisdiction over assize breaches to the area around the site of the eyre.[155] Exchequer barons were to amerce offenders against the assize of wine in London under c.15 of the *Statute of Gloucester* 1278.[156] Other officials had a role too. *Britton* and *Fleta* note that sheriffs were instructed to make inquiries concerning the assizes of bread, ale and wine.[157] The 1315 poultry and victual statute ordered all sheriffs to ensure that it was kept throughout the country.[158] Sheriffs were used to enforce the wine regulation of 1330.[159] Under the Ordinance of Labourers 1349, mayors and bailiffs were given power to inquire after and punish offenders against the price fixing chapter as well as the labour regulation chapters, and were to be accountable to 'justices to be assigend' for negligence if they failed to obey the statute.[160] Special justices of labourers and justices of the peace were given jurisdicition over this msatter.[161] It was, therefore, an area in which both 'central' and 'local' involvement was expected. The 1351 statute envisaged a system of 'local' officials reporting on those selling contrary to the statute.[162] Special commissions were ordered to be appointed under the poultry price provision of 1363.[163] The justices of the peace were ordered to enforce the victual statute of 1389–90.[164]

In certain cases, breach of the assizes of bread and ale came under the jurisdiction of the royal official called the king's coroner or serjeant, later clerk, of the market. The duties of the clerk of the market were explained in an ordinance of 1318 as being to go before the king on his journeys and see that bread and ale were made ready for the coming of the household, and to proclaim the assize of bread, wine, ale and oats in each market town within the verge.[165] Although this may seem like a limited role, the concept of the verge, or the jurisdiction of the clerk of the market, could be extensive. In a commission of 1257, it seems to be regarded as comprising an entire county which the king has 'passed through'.[166]

---

[152] *SR* I:233. This seems to demand a high level of publicity or local knowledge about transactions. An article on the assize of wine had been included in the eyre articles since 1194: C.A.F. Meekings, *Crown Pleas of the Wiltshire Eyre 1249* (Devizes, 1963), 29.

[153] Sutherland, *Eyre of Northamptonshire 1329–30*, II, 775.

[154] JUST 1/1166, e.g. m.8d, and JUST 1/1165, Channel Islands eyre 1323.

[155] Britnell, *Commercialisation*, 96; *Britton*, I, 84.

[156] *SR* I:50.

[157] *Britton*, Book 1, c.30, paragraph 3; *Fleta II*, 176. When Edward I introduced English law to Wales, he provided that sheriffs' tourns should enquire into 'non-observance of the assize of bread and beer, and of breakers thereof': *SR* I:57, Statute of Wales 1284.

[158] *Anonimalle*, 88–91.

[159] *CCR 1330–33*, 410.

[160] *SR* I:307, st. 23 Edw. III.

[161] Putnam, *Enforcement*, 10–40.

[162] *RP* II:233–5; Putnam, *Enforcement*, App., 15.

[163] *SR* I:378, 37 Edw. III, c.3.

[164] *SR* II:63, 13 Ric. II, st.1 c.8.

[165] Ordinance of York, 1318, in Tout, *Edward II*, 252. See also H.G. Richardson, *The Medieval Fairs and Markets of York* (York, 1961), 5.

[166] *CPR 1247–58*, 569 (Berkshire).

In an interesting parallel with the campaign against usury of the 1270s seen in the previous chapter, there was also a wider campaign into 'trading offences', primarily concerning standard weights and measures, but also including the assizes of bread, wine and ale and their administration in the early part of the reign of Edward I, from 1273 to 1276, following a pattern set in the reign of Henry III.[167] Clerks of the market were dispatched to a large part of the country.[168] Commissions including price offences were sometimes issued in the fourteenth century, as can be seen in a commission to Geoffrey de Staunton and others to look into forestalling and also taverners selling wine at excessive, unreasonable, prices in Nottinghamshire in 1347 and a commission of oyer and terminer concerning, amongst other matters; the sale of victuals in Cornwall in 1367.[169]

As an alternative to exercising jurisdiction over the assizes themselves, either by means of royal courts or royal officials, successive kings granted to favoured subjects the right or franchise of jurisdiction over the assizes of bread and ale, and, occasionally, over other price control regulations.[170] The franchising-out of these jurisdictions is an important part of the picture of price regulation. The law relating to jurisdictional franchises in general developed greatly as a result of the litigation in the *Quo Warranto* campaign of Edward I, but some matters remained unsettled.[171] The rules on acquisition of franchises such as the right to try breaches of the assizes were not entirely clear.[172] Another matter which remained unsettled was the exact nature of the franchise of emendation of the assizes of bread and ale. Opinions can be found which saw it as appurtenant to the franchise of view of frankpledge, whereas others saw it as a right appurtenant to the right to hold a market or even, unlikely as it seems, to the right of *infangtheof* or summary punishment of thieves.[173]

Whatever the theoretical nature of the right, it had been granted to many people before 1272 and it continued to be granted out during the late-thirteenth and

---

[167] *CPR 1247–58*, 427, 488, 502, 569; *CPR 1258–72*, 454; *CPR 1272–81*, 16, 31, 73, 136. (Instructions to sheriffs and urban officials to prepare for a visit by the king's clerks.) Britnell, 'Forstall', 95.

[168] *CPR 1272–81*, 73 (1274); *CPR 1292–1301*, 99 (1294).

[169] *CPR 1345–8*, 387; *CPR 1364–7*, 444.

[170] Oxford University had the right to try assizes of wine: *CChR*, vol. 5, *1341–1417*, 143–6 (1355); C 53/140 m.2.

[171] D.W. Sutherland, *Quo Warranto Proceedings in the Reign of Edward I 1278–1294* (Oxford, 1963); P. Brand, '*Quo Warranto* Law in the reign of Edward I: a hitherto undiscovered opinion of Chief Justice Hengham' in Brand, *Making of the Common Law*, 393–443.

[172] The records of the *Quo Warranto* enquiries of the reign of Edward I show a number of claims of a right to hold the assizes of bread and ale based on prescription, long user or custom rather than royal grant, e.g. *PQW*, 37. See Sutherland, *Quo Warranto*, 78–110, on prescription of franchises generally. Lords in Northumberland, Cumberland, Yorkshire and Lincolnshire claimed that they held the right to try the assize of ale by the common custom of their counties: *PQW*, 125–6, 189, 191–3, 196, 220, 226, 417, 599, cited in *P&M*, I, 582. Dr Brand notes a difference of opinion amongst lawyers as to the question of acquisition by long seisin: Brand, '*Quo Warranto* Law', 435–6. See also *P&M*, I, 569.

[173] The 'Articles of the View of Frankpledge', in *SR* I:246 from BL, MS Cott. Claudius D II, f.236 (probably from 1323x1326), include 'of the assize of bread and ale broken'. The abbot of Keynsham attempted to argue that he had a right to try breaches of the assizes because that right was appurtenant to the royal grant of a market which he had undoubtedly been given. William Inge, on behalf of the king, maintained that the right to try breaches of the assizes had to be granted specifically, but the case ended inconclusively: Gloucester eyre 1287, *PQW*, 690–1. R.H. Britnell has stated that 'We have no reason to suppose that twelfth century market charters carried with them any rights of jurisdiction': Britnell, *Commercialisation*, 19. Hereford eyre of 1292, *YB (RS)*, 20 & 21 Edw. I, 158–9, 'Note that amends of bread and ale and pillory and tumbril are appendant to *infangtheof* and the right of the grantee to compel the attendance of his men twice a year to keep the peace of our lord the king. Note that the amends of bread and ale are appendant to the view of frankpledge.'

fourteenth centuries, either to individuals or to cities and boroughs. Cities and boroughs aspired to exemption from the jurisdiction of the king's clerk of the market, who inquired into the assizes and their enforcement as well as a number of other matters. London was exempt, and, during the period under consideration, Lincoln, York, Hedon in Holderness, Northampton and Bristol all gained their freedom.[174]

Jurisdiction over the assize of wine was not granted out as a franchise to the same extent as was jurisdiction over the assizes of bread and ale, although a small number of franchise holders had the right to try offenders against the wine price regulations.[175] There is evidence of franchising out of other price control jurisdictions in the reign of Richard II. A grant of 1391 to the prior and canons of Bridlington, for example, gave them not only amends of the assizes of bread and ale, but also jurisdiction over all victuallers, butchers, buyers and sellers of victuals, forestallers and regraters in Bridlington.[176] Similarly wide powers were given to the bishop, dean and chapter of Hereford in 1394.[177] A charter of confirmation in favour of the duke of Lancaster of 1396 granted him franchise jurisdiction over the assize of bread, wine and ale, and of all other victuals, and over other things pertaining to the office of the clerk of the market, but only for the life of the current duke.[178]

The fact that kings granted franchises of jurisdiction over offences against the price control regulations should not be seen as an abdication of power or interest in this area. When a franchise was granted in the late thirteenth and fourteenth centuries, a right for the king to intervene if there were complaints of failure to enforce the regulations was often specifically reserved. In the grant of 1316 to Lincoln, for example, although the citizens were generally to be free from the intervention of the clerk of the market, there was a saving in the grant which provided that if anyone should complain that the mayor, bailiffs or keepers of the city had been negligent in these matters, the king's chancellor was, at the suit of the complainant, to look into the complaint. If negligence were to be found, he was to correct the matter and punish the mayor, bailiffs and keeper.[179] Such a complaint was investigated in 1331.[180] In the case of jurisdiction over regulations other than the assize of bread and ale, in the York Ordinances of 1301, the mayor, bailiffs and keepers of the ordinances were warned to take care to keep the ordinances well, or

---

[174] Lincoln (1316: *CChR*, vol. III *1300–26*, 312–13); York (1316: *CChR*, vol. III, *1300–26*, 329); Hedon (1348: *CChR*, vol. V, *1341–1417*, 87); Northampton (1385: C.A. Markham, *Records of the Borough of Northampton*, vol. I (Northampton, 1898), 68); Bristol (1396: *CChR*, vol. V, *1341–1417*, 353).

[175] e.g. Oxford in 1332: *CCR 1330–33*, 557. Colchester: Britnell, *Colchester*, Appendix, table 2; Britnell, *Commercialisation*, 94. Essex Record Office, Colchester Muniments CR 2.2d, 6d, 10r; CR 3/1d. 3d. Winchester: D. Keene, *Survey of Medieval Winchester*, 2 vols (Oxford, 1985), 271. Norwich: W. Hudson and J.C. Tingey, *Records of the City of Norwich*, 2 vols (Norwich, 1906, 1910), I, 176. Northampton from 1385: C.A. Markham (ed.), *Records of the Borough of Northampton, vol. I* (London, 1898), 68.

[176] 1391: *CChR*, vol. V, *1341–1417*, 332.

[177] 1394: *CChR*, vol. V, *1341–1417*, 349.

[178] *CChR*, vol. V, *1341–1417*, 361. A great deal of discretion was left to the duke as to how he enforced the regulations: assizes and punishment were to be held 'whenever and so often as it shall be necessary and expedient'.

[179] Lincoln (1316: *CChR*. vol. III, *1300–26*, 312–13). A similar provision can be found in the grant to the citizens of York of freedom from the clerk of the market in 1316: *CChR*, vol. III, *1300–26*, 329.

[180] Britnell, 'Morals', 27, citing J.W.F. Hill, *Medieval Lincoln* (Cambridge, 1948), 246; *CIM*, vol. II, no.1201; *CCR 1330–33*, 235.

else the king would punish the city for electing a mayor and keepers who did not do so, and complaints about official negligence in this respect were certainly entertained.[181] In the 1330 wine statute, the chancellor, treasurer and justices were given a supervisory jurisdiction to enquire whether the mayors, bailiffs and ministers of towns were following the statute, and to punish them if they were not doing so.[182] The Ordinance of Labourers 1349 provided that if mayors and bailiffs were to be convicted before royal justices of negligence in following their instructions under that ordinance, they would have to pay treble the value of the thing sold, either to the injured party, or to another prosecutor, and would also be punished grievously by the king.[183]

The king was regarded as having an interest after granting jurisdiction to others, even if a supervisory jurisdiction was not specifically reserved. In the passage in *Fleta* concerning the clerk of the market's functions, there is evidence of a residual supervisory jurisdiction retained by the king over the assizes of bread and ale even where a franchise had been granted. An apparently high level of conduct was required in order to keep the jurisdiction. The jury articles specifically mention questions to be asked if the lord of the place being visited had the franchise of view of frankpledge, the jurors were to say whether he had instruments of punishment. If he did not, the franchise would immediately be taken into the King's hand, 'since it is to be assumed that the lord of the franchise has not rightly judged those who have broken an assize'. The jurors were also to look at the lord's actual exercise of his jurisdiction in specific cases, in terms of whether the correct punishments were being administered. If the lord had erred in his enforcement, the franchise would be taken into the king's hands, if it seemed that the lord had erred through ignorance of the proper law, he would be amerced. The king could act directly to amerce the offenders himself, even if not removing the franchise from the lord.[184] *Britton* also gives duties to examine loaves in each town to the royal 'officer of the measures', assisted in his inquiries by a jury of twelve 'of the most lawful householders'. They were to inquire, *inter alia*, about lords with franchises, whether they had the correction of the breach of assize of bread and ale, whether they had pillory and tumbrel. Unwarranted franchises were to be seized as were those where no appropriate (or unsafe) instruments of punishment existed. They were to inquire about breaches of the assizes of bread and ale and the way in which offenders wee punished, whether by amercement or pillory, and for what offences each punishment was used. If judgments were 'illegal' ('desleal'), the franchise was to be seized. They were also to inquire of taverners, who had sold wine contrary to the assize since the last eyre in the county, and how much profit ('gayng') above the right assise they had made. If living, they were to be pilloried and fined in double the value of their gain. Bakers and brewers convicted of breaking the assise were to be punished in proportion to their offence either by amercements or pillory.[185]

Edward I inquired in his *Quo Warranto* investigations into the rights of those who claimed an entitlement to try offenders against the assizes of bread and ale and, if

---

[181] *YO*, 10, 18–22.
[182] *SR* I:263, st. 4 Edw. III, c.8.
[183] *SR* I:307, st. 23 Edw. III.
[184] *Fleta II*, Book II, c.12.
[185] *Britton*, 189, f.76.

there was any challenge to their right, the way in which offenders were punished.[186] Edward II also envisaged an inquiry into whether lords having the right to hear cases of offences against the assizes of bread and ale had been neglecting their duty.[187] Edward III's government during his minority also made some *Quo Warranto* inquiries into holding and exercise of this jurisdiction.[188] All four of the kings reigning between 1272 and 1399 were involved in some supervision of those exercising delegated powers over offences against the price control regulations.

Successive kings were asked to intervene in enforcement of the assizes of bread and ale in Oxford and Cambridge. Although jurisdiction to try offenders against the assizes in Oxford had long since been granted away from the crown, there were frequent disputes between the civic and university authorities over their respective rights to jurisdiction which went to the king for a solution.[189] Disputes were referred to the king in the reigns of Edward I, Edward II, Edward III and Richard II.[190] In Cambridge, too, kings were called upon to balance the jurisdictional interests of town and university authorities.[191] Individual lords who had the right to try offenders against the price regulations might also ask for the king's help, as happened in 1330, when Thomas de Berkeley complained that his court in the suburb of Bristol, in which he had for a long time had the right to try offences against the assizes of bread and ale, had been disrupted by the mayor and bailiffs of Bristol.[192] In 1283, the municipal authorities in Bristol apparently feared royal punishment unless the assize of ale was 'strictly observed' in the city.[193] There are instances of franchises being taken into the king's hand for failure to punish offenders against the assizes of bread and ale, as in Gloucestershire in 1287, and in Cornwall in 1284, when an eyre jury reported that the prior of Bodmin had in his court of Bodmin the right to hear and determine offences against the assizes of bread and ale, but always took amercements from the offenders, rather than executing corporal punishment. The liberties were taken into the king's hand because of his misconduct.[194] Liberties were also taken into the king's hand in Gloucestershire in 1287, when a jury claimed that the assizes of bread and ale had not been observed for twenty years in Winchecombe, where they were the responsibility of the abbot of Hayles.[195] On one occasion, a royal justice confiscated

---

[186] The records can be found in *PQW*.

[187] *CCR 1313–18*, 449; H.T. Riley (ed.), *Joh. De Trokelowe et Anon. Chronica et Annales*, Rolls Series 28.iii (London, 1866), 95, writ to the sheriff of Hertfordshire and Essex (1317).

[188] See *PQW*.

[189] Oxford University was granted a charter in 1248 which set up a system allowing participation of the university in the setting and enforcement of the assizes: Salter, *MA*, 18–19; Anstey, *MA*, 777–9. This charter was brought to the eyre by the university authorities in the Oxfordshire eyre of 1285: JUST 1/705 m.26.

[190] Salter, *MC*, 6 (1305), *MA*, 100–1 (1321); *CCR 1327–30*, 17 (1327); Salter, *MC*, 53 (1327), 82 (1330); 86 (1332); *CChR*, vol. V, *1341–1417*, 143–6 (1355); Salter, *MA*, 187 (1360); *RP* III:109b (1381).

[191] Petition of 1320: *RP* I:381a; charter of 1327: *CChR*, vol. IV, *1327–41*, 58.

[192] *CPR 1327–30*, 571. This was part of a general jurisdictional dispute. It was also possible to sue in the royal courts in trespass for such an alleged offence: E. de Haas and G.D.G. Hall (eds), *Early Registers of Writs*, Selden Society vol. 87 for 1970 (London, 1970), 79 no.152.

[193] *LRB*, II, 222, f.192b.

[194] Gloucestershire, case of Bogo de Knovill: *PQW*, 241, 249; Cornwall: JUST 1/111 m.28.

[195] *PQW*, 250. Henry III had been able to cite a failure to enforce the assizes of bread and ale as his reason to take the city of London into his hands: H.T. Riley, *Chronicles of the City of London* (London, 1863), 11, 15, 18, 22.

the market charter of a man who had no tumbrel, on the ground that 'a market cannot be held unless the assize of bread and ale is daily enforced'.[196] Failure to exercise jurisdiction properly or at all did not, however, always result in the right to try offences against the price regulations remaining for long in the king's hand, as can be seen from the government's dealings with the prior of Llanthony and the earl of Hertford and Essex in 1330–1 in respect of some of their manors in Bedfordshire and Huntingdonshire. Both were found to have used inappropriate punishments for offenders against the assizes of bread and ale (i.e. always to have amerced and never to have used corporal punishment, despite the requirement to do so). Their franchises were taken into the king's hand but were swiftly returned on payment of a fine of a mark.[197]

Looking at evidence from royal sources, of royal supervision of jurisdiction delegated to private citizens or boroughs, it is easy to form the impression that there were a lot of problems with local enforcement of price regulations. It should be borne in mind, however, that these jurisdictions would only be likely to be mentioned in royal records if problems occurred. The many other jurisdictions which aroused no concern or complaint are ignored by royal records. Also, complaints about enforcement may bear a number of meanings. They may be a sign of a system which is in terminal decline, or which has never worked properly. They may, on the other hand, indicate that somebody thinks that the particular instance is exceptional, and/or that it is possible to rectify the situation. A good example of potentially contrasting interpretations may be found in the 1331 complaint concerning enforcement of the assizes in Lincoln.[198] Taken by itself, this could be used as an indictment of the effectiveness of the price regulations.[199] If, however, its provenance is considered (it is a presentment/report from a royal inquest) and it is taken in conjunction with the instrument granting jurisdiction to the Lincoln authorities, and specifically setting up a procedure for complaint, it may be seen as the product of a successful exercise in royal supervision of a local jurisdiction.

Unlike the case with usury jurisdiction, there is no trace of jurisdictional conflict with ecclesiastical courts over price offences or unfair prices. Although divine law according to scholastic theologians indicated that accepting a price over the just price was sinful, and there are faint indications of ecclesiastical censure of those guilty of such conduct, in other times, in other places, no such trace has come to light either in the pronouncements of English prelates or in the practice of English church courts.[200]

There are large numbers of presentments of offenders against the assize of wine and some cases of presentments of offenders against the assize of bread in the

---

[196] C.J. Scrope in the 1329–30 Northamptonshire eyre, cited in D.L. Farmer, 'Marketing the produce of the countryside' in H.E. Hallam (ed.), *The Agrarian History of England and Wales, vol. II: 1042–1350* (Cambridge, 1988), 427, 429.

[197] J.B. Post, 'Manorial amercements and peasant poverty', *EcHR* 28 (1975), 304–11, at 308. *PQW*, 21.

[198] See above, p. 92 and *CChR*, vol. III, *1300–26*, 312–3; *CCR 1330–33*, 235; *CIM*, vol. II, no.1201.

[199] Britnell, 'Morals', 27.

[200] Wood, *Medieval Economic Thought*, 149, citing Baldwin, *Peter the Chanter* I, p. 268: 2, p. 180 n.61. L.R. Poos (ed.), *Lower Level Jurisdiction in Late Medieval England: The Courts of the Dean and Chapter of Lincoln 1336–49 and Deanery of Wisbech 1458–1484* (Oxford, 2001), has no examples.

crown pleas sections of eyre rolls.[201] No records of presentments against the assize of ale have been found in the eyre rolls, except in those of the eyres of the Channel Islands, which had their own sets of articles including one on breaches of the assize of ale.[202] The fact that there were many presentments in eyres of offences against the assizes of wine in comparison to offences against the assizes of bread and ale is unsurprising, given that the right to try offences against the assize of wine was not granted away by kings to their subjects in the same way as was the right to try offences against the assizes of bread and ale. Offences against the assizes of bread and ale were commonly dealt with by lower level or 'local' courts, making it surprising that bread presentments ever appear in eyre records.

After the demise of the eyres in the fourteenth century, the court of King's Bench exercised jurisdiction over offences against the price fixing legislation. The indictment files of the King's Bench which were compiled for its sessions outside London in the fourteenth century show numerous examples of presentments for economic offences including breaches of the assizes and breaches of all of the other measures set out in this chapter.[203] All of the files seen contain indictments for breaches of the assize of wine. Examples of various other offences can be found in indictments. The file for the session at St Albans in Michaelmas 1354, for example, mentions offences against regulations on wine and victuals, and the file for the session at Middlesex in 1349 shows indictments of offenders against the assizes of bread and ale, and indictments of carpenters taking excessive prices for wheels.[204] The file for the session at Chelmsford in Michaelmas term 1352 shows the range of items the prices of which were controlled by Edward III's legislation: breaches of regulations on meat, ale, cart wheels, tiles and salt were all reported to the court.[205] Indictment files from the reign of Edward III also contain a large number of presentments of officials for selling contrary to the Statute of York 1318, which was a measure tightening up enforcement of earlier price regulations.[206] In the King's Bench session held in 1363 at Gloucester, people were successfully prosecuted for the following offences (some of which are clearly similar to each other, but formulated slightly differently):[207]

(i) selling wine and ale at retail contrary to the assize whilst in office as mayor or as an official prohibited from so doing;[208]

(ii) selling wine and victuals contrary to the assize and contrary to the proclamation of the king;

---

[201] A roll from the Devon eyre of 1281–2, for example, contains reports of eighty-five persons in mercy for offences against the assize of wine and three persons in mercy for offences against the assize of bread: JUST 1/184. In the 1286 eyre of Norfolk, the jurors of Great Yarmouth were amerced for concealing (i.e. not reporting) the defaults of five bakers: JUST 1/573 m.81d.

[202] JUST 1/1166, e.g. m.8d, and JUST 1/1165: Channel Islands eyre 1323.

[203] For a list of King's Bench indictment files examined, see Bibliography below.

[204] KB 9/38. Reports concerning breaches of the wine regulations show the application of the prescribed scheme for determining the price of wine with reference to the distance from London, m.15 containing a presentment of three taverners for selling wine in Barnet at a penny above the London price when Barnet was only ten leagues from London: KB 9/66.

[205] JUST 1/267.

[206] e.g. JUST 1/528 for sessions at Lincoln 1333 M. and 1334 H.

[207] KB 27/411 at m.30ff.

[208] This conduct would be contrary to the Statute of York 1318, *SR* I:177–9, 12 Edw. II, c.6, which provided that no officer keeping the assize of wine and victual should deal in those things during his time in office.

(iii) selling wine contrary to the assize;

(iv) selling wine contrary to the assize and contrary to the king's statute;

(v) selling wine after the statute of pardon;[209]

(vi) selling wine after the statute of pardon and contrary to the assize;

(vii) selling ale contrary to the assize;

(viii) taking excess lucre in the sale of fish and meat;

(ix) selling fish in Bristol after the statute of pardon by regrating, taking excess lucre;

(x) divers regratings and forestallings;

(xi) forestalling and regrating;

(xii) forestalling fish and other victuals;

(xiii) forestalling and regrating fish and other victuals;

(xiv) forestalling and excess;

(xv) selling fish in Bristol after the statute by forestalling and taking excess;

(xvi) acting as both tanner and shoemaker contrary to the statute and ordinance of the king and after the statute of pardon, taking excess lucre.[210]

The main thrust of prosecutions seems to have been directed against transgressors against the more recent measures such as the labour regulations, but the assize of wine, an 'old' law, was not ignored. It is interesting to note the relatively frequent combination of 'old' and 'new' royal initiatives in the charges against particular individuals The majority of prosecutions for victual price offences concerned wine and fish, not bread and ale, still widely regulated at a lower level.

Royal justices did, therefore, play their part in dealing with price offences when called upon, but people could not use the eyre or the King's Bench as their normal recourse to complain about breaches of price control regulation, since they came too infrequently to any particular place. At a less exalted level, sheriffs exercised the royal jurisdiction over the assizes in their regular tourns. Few records of sheriffs' tourns survive, so it is almost impossible to make any claims about the way in which sheriffs exercised their jurisdiction.[211]

Justices of the peace and justices of labourers often tried offences against price regulations, both the old assizes and the newer regulations on the prices of other goods, in the second half of the foruteenth century in the first case, and in the 1350s in the second case.[212] Peace rolls of the later fourteenth century contain some examples of presentments for excessive pricing in sales of bread, using the concepts of the Labourers legislation rather than the old assizes of bread and ale. This can be seen in a case from the peace roll of Norfolk 1378:

[209] Reference to a 'statute of pardon' from the king is made in many entries. This statute seems to have been recent, and seems to have covered prices offences and forestalling and regrating.

[210] The statute referred to here is 37 Edw. III c.6 (1363), *SR* I:379.

[211] Examination of a small sample (E 389/88 and 90, E 389/149, E 389/96 and E 389/104) suggests that the records in class E 389 at the PRO, sheriffs' accounts, are at too general a level to provide conclusions on their activities. There is evidence of amercement of offenders against the assize of ale: e.g. the four tourn rolls in SC 2/161/75, Hundreds and Tourns in Cornwall 35–9 Edw. III.

[212] e.g. R. Sillem (ed.), *Some Sessions of the Peace in Lincolnshire 1360–1375*, Publications of the Lincolnshire Record Society vol. 30 for 1937 (Hereford, 1936), no.373: JUST 1/530 (1373).

Iohannes Baxstere de Dounham Hythe vendidit panes nimis excessive in Dounham anno predicto, unde in excessu ii.s.[213]

(They say that John Baxter of Dounham Hythe sold bread very excessively in Dounham in 1378, in excess 2s.)

Examples of local enforcement of the assize of wine or of other price control regulations are rarer than examples of local enforcement of the assizes of bread and ale, since this jurisdiction was not as frequently granted out as a franchise, though there are some signs that the jurisdiction was being exercised by local non-royal courts in the later fourteenth century.[214] There are few examples of local non-royal jurisdictions acting to enforce other price control regulations. The Sutton rolls, for example, show almost no presentments of offenders against price control regulations other than the assizes of bread and ale. The sole exception is a report in a court of 1374 of over-pricing of shoes.[215] The infrequency of local action based on these other price control regulations is likely to have been because these were specifically ordered in the statutes to be enforced by the justices of the peace, and jurisdiction does not seem to have been franchised out to lords of manors or to most boroughs.

Detection and prevention

A number of different approaches were taken to the prescription of methods of detecting and trying offences against the regulations. Sometimes prosecutions of offenders were ordered to be brought by presenting juries, as with the assizes of bread and ale. The *Judicium Pillorie* stipulated that twelve lawful men were to be sworn to answer a number of questions asked of them on the king's behalf. They were to provide information on the enforcement of the assizes of bread and ale in their local court, and to give the names of brewers who had sold contrary to the assize.[216] A broadly similar procedure is described in *Fleta*.[217] At other times, individual initiative was invited: reliance was placed upon information being provided by individuals, and incentives could be provided for them to come forward. The York Ordinances of 1301 proposed to reward those reporting people selling victuals for illegal prices by letting them have the goods free.[218] Those who felt aggrieved by having been charged high prices for lodgings were also invited to bring a bill of complaint in the Eyre of Northamptonshire, 1329–30.[219] The 1349–51 Labourers legislation also envisaged individuals coming forward to complain about over-pricing, and being 'rewarded'. Under the Ordinance of Labourers 1349, if an 'injured party' sued the offender, the offender was to pay

[213] Putnam, *PJP*, 120, no.183.

[214] They ordered that no wine should be sold before it should be sampled and valued by the bailiffs, under pain of half a mark: M.K. Dale, *Court Rolls of Tamworth* (Tamworth, 1959), 125; Keene, *Survey*, 271; Britnell, *Colchester*, Appendix, table 2. A local jurisdiction over offences against the wine price regulations was exercised in London in the 1380s, since a Londoner was imprisoned in 1383 for selling wine at 8d per gallon: *CPMR 1381–1412*, 41.

[215] DL 30/88/1196 m.10, court Wednesday Invention of the Holy Cross 1374.

[216] *SR* I:201.

[217] *Fleta II*, 121–2. It is also specified here that if a person was found guilty, the jurors were to be asked if he had offended previously.

[218] *YO*, 15.

[219] Sutherland, *Eyre of Northamptonshire 1329–30*, I, 33, 34.

double the sum received to the injured party. If the injured party did not pursue the matter, anyone else who would do so would be awarded the same sum.[220]

A high degree of local supervision and inspection seems to have been assumed. The eyre article on wine mentioned in *Statutes of the Realm* is a good example of this. It orders the jurors to report 'Of wines sold contrary to the assize in cities, boroughs, market towns and other towns, wherever wines are sold, who sold them, how may casks a year, and for how many years'.[221] This suggests either a high degree of transparency in business transactions, or a great deal of 'neighbour supervision'. A thorough investigation process is suggested by some of the detailed reports of offences in the King's Bench records. In the King's Bench plea roll for the session held in 1363 at Gloucester, for example, the presentments of the jurors of Gloucester are extremely detailed, setting out the number or amount of items sold by particular offenders contrary to the regulations.[222] The system of gathering information seems to have been particularly effective, with minute details of the infractions of many offenders being reported and recorded. An example can be seen in the report that Walter Canynges, bailiff of Bristol, whilst he was bailiff, sold thirty tuns of wine in gross at ten marks per tun, contrary to the statute and two tuns of wine by regrating contrary to the statute.[223] However it was obtained, the fact that such information found its way into the records suggests both that there was co-operation with the investigation of these offences, and also that the clerks and judges involved in these sessions were actually investigating and discussing offences, rather than merely accepting the word of presenting juries or local officials that a list of people had broken the price regulations.

Detection of offenders against the assize of bread was to be aided, according to the *Composicio*, by requiring all bread to be sealed with the seal of its baker.[224] This had been the rule in a royal order relating to Winchester in 1203 and a charter to Oxford of 1255.[225] Such a requirement can also be seen in the York Ordinances 1301 and in 'local' rules.[226] The York Ordinances also have an apparently unique provision for the bread of a baker who has previously been found to have committed serious defaults in weight is to be marked twice with his seal, presumably to warn customers to be on their guard.[227]

The use of inspecting officials, often known in the case of the assize of ale as aletasters or aleconners, was a common method of detection of offenders against the assizes of bread and ale.[228] Regular inspections of loaves of bread

[220] *SR* I:307, st. 23 Edw. III. For trespass actions based on the assizes, see *Court Baron*, 23–5.
[221] *SR* I:233.
[222] KB 27/411. at m.30ff.
[223] m.30.
[224] *SR* I:202.
[225] A. Ballard (ed.), *British Borough Charters 1042–1216* (Cambridge, 1913), 159; A. Ballard and J. Tait (eds), *British Borough Charters 1216–1307* (Cambridge, 1923), 293.
[226] *YO*, 10. London: *CLB, A*, 215, f.129b.
[227] *YO*, 10.
[228] An account of the tasks of an aletaster in London can be found in *LA*, 274, f.209b. The role of taster could be onerous, since it was common for tasters to incur amercements for failure to fulfil their office, or to refuse to do it at all: *Robert Rawland v Abbot of Rufford et al.*, KB 27/324 m.106d, in M.S. Arnold (ed.), *Select Cases of Trespass from the King's Courts 1307–1399*, Selden Society vol. 103 for 1987 (London, 1987), 241.

were held in London and Oxford at least.[229] In Oxford, ale offences were dealt with at courts held twice a year in the early fourteenth century.[230]

A London civic case of 1382 sees the civic authorities engaged in some mild detective work. Thomas de Welford, a fishmonger, alleged that he could not sell fish at a lower rate than five herrings for a penny, which the mayor and aldermen regarded as too high a price. He was caught out when it was discovered that he had sold 600 herrings to William Botild, a stranger, at ten herrings a penny. The evidence was obtained from the acknowledgment of the purchaser.[231] London officials (constables of wards) had in the fourteenth century powers of 'search and seizure' to prevent secret sales of victuals and 'to prevent ale being sold for more than the regulation price'.[232]

At least some jurisdictions experimented with a scheme of presumptions of guilt of pricing offences for certain groups.[233] This would make matters somewhat simpler for a court, which would have somewhere to begin, rather than no evidence at all. Although such schemes might sound harsh, it should be borne in mind that presumptions of innocence are an extremely modern idea. Furthermore, they did allow a person presumed guilty to rebut the presumption by successful wager of law with a small number of oath-helpers.[234]

Another weapon intended to prevent offences was the requirement of an oath to observe the rules. This can be seen in the York Ordinances of 1301.[235] Oath-swearing was shown to be part of the scheme to enforce pricing regulations in an entry in the King's Bench indictment file for Chelmsford, 1352 H.:

> *Johannes Baneyt et Johannes Dynmur bracatores de Upland vend[ideru]nt servic[iam] pro ii.d ubi deberent vend[ere] pro i.d . . . et jur[ati] fuerunt cor[am] . . . Johanne de Sutton & soc[iis] suis & per fals[as] mensur[as] etc. ad magn[am] oppression[em] populi.*[236]
>
> (John Baneyt and John Dynmur, brewers of Upland (or upland brewers) sold ale for 2d, when they should have sold it for one penny, and they had been sworn [not to do this] before John de Sutton and his associates, and they sold using false measures etc., to the great oppression of the people.)

London butchers were obliged to swear to observe civic meat price regulations in 1377.[237] The Sutton rolls also show oath-swearing as a method of attempting to ensure compliance with the assizes, at least in the 1390s.[238]

Consequences: responses to offending behaviour

The next matter to consider is the punishment which was set out for those who broke the rules. Amercement of the offender was commonly prescribed in royal

---

[229] Salter, *MA*, II, 129.
[230] Salter, *MA*, II, 129.
[231] Riley, *Memorials*, 467; LB, H, f.154.
[232] *CLB, G,* 197–8, ff.164–5.
[233] See, e.g., *LRB*, II, 222–3, cited in Davis, *Representation*, 211.
[234] Baker, *Introduction*, 5–6, 74, 507.
[235] *YO*, 18.
[236] JUST 1/268 m.1. A number of entries in the file show oath swearing as a 'back up' to the rules of the assize of ale.
[237] *CLB, H*, 61, f.59.
[238] DL 30/89/1209 m.12d, view of frankpledge Thursday in Pentecost week 1392.

regulations, and there are also some examples of the prescription of corporal punishment.

The pre-Edwardian statutes provided for amercement for lesser offences, and corporal punishment for repeated offending.[239] In the *Assisa Panis et Cervisie*, it was provided that, if a baker or brewer breached the assizes, he was to be amerced for the first three breaches, in proportion to the offence, provided they were not serious breaches. If a baker committed a serious breach, making farthing loaves short in weight by more than 2s, he was to be put in the pillory.[240] Recidivists were also to suffer corporal punishment. The *Composicio* altered the boundary slightly, with bread less than a farthing weight underweight per 2s 6d resulting in amercement, and if the deficit was greater, then the pillory (without remission).[241] The 1275 *Statutum Mareschaucie*, which includes provisions on the assizes of bread, ale and wine, also suggests imprisonment for those breaching its rules, as 'contemner[s] of the mandates of the lord King', not to be released without royal instructions.[242] In a London civic ordinance of 1337, three days' imprisonment as well as a 40d fine were stipulated for a first offender.[243] Prison was also contemplated for certain sellers at excessive prices under the 1351 Statute of Labourers.[244] The York Ordinances of 1301 prescribed penalties increasing with seriousness of offence and recidivism for bakers breaking the pricing rules (financial penalties, pillory, destruction of oven, forfeiture of bread and perpetual abjuration of calling), brewers doing likewise (financial penalty, tumbrel, destruction of brew house, perpetual abjuration of calling), taverners, sellers of victuals or clothes at prices above the regulations doing likewise (financial penalty, beating or larger financial penalty and perpetual abjuration of calling), and butchers doing likewise (financial penalties, perpetual abjuration of calling).[245]

Corporal punishment for breach of the assize of bread might also take the form of being drawn on the hurdle. This was the punishment used in London from at least 1281–2, was confirmed by the King and Council in 1327, and permission to do likewise was granted to the Bristol municipal authorities in a 1347 charter.[246]

The place of corporal punishment in the prescribed punishment of offenders against the price regulations was re-emphasised in the reign of Richard II. A statute of 1389–90 provided that no one entrusted with keeping the assizes of bread and ale was to take an amercement or fine on occasions when the correct punishment was corporal punishment.[247] Corporal punishment continued as the theoretical punishment of serious or recidivist offenders against the assizes of bread and ale

[239] There were 'local' precedents for such a scheme. Britnell, 'Morals', 26, citing J. Tait, *Medieval Manchester and the Beginnings of Lancashire* (Manchester, 1904), 89–90.
[240] It was stipulated that there was to be no possibility of substituting a money payment for this punishment.
[241] *SR* I:202.
[242] Britnell, 'Forstall', 95, citing BL, MS Stowe 386, ff.50r–51r.
[243] Britnell, 'Morals', 27, citing *CLB, F*, 27–8.
[244] *RP* II:233b–235a.
[245] *YO*, 10–15.
[246] *CLB, A*, 120–1, f.52b ff (1282); *LC*, 219a (with the extra humiliation of defective bread being hung around the neck: scheme of penalties rising from hurdle to hurdle and pillory, to forfeiture and abjuration of mistery for ever in the city); *CPR 1327–30*, 61; N. Dermot Harding (ed.), *Bristol's Charters 1155–1373*, Bristol Record Society 1 (Bristol, 1930), 109.
[247] *SR* II:63, 13 Ric. II, st.1 c.8. See also *CIM*, vol. V, 172–3, no.300 (1390 inquisition concerning prior and convent of Christchurch, Hampshire, reveals that they have been taking money penalties rather than inflicting corporal punishment, and are to answer for it).

throughout the period, but it was not always adopted in later regulations. The Ordinance of Labourers, 1349, for example, provided for a double financial penalty for victual pricing offenders, and no corporal punishment.[248] Punishment was left to the discretion of the justices in a statute of 1389 which regulated victual prices. Where no penalty had previously been set, those who took prices above those stipulated were to be punished 'grievously' at the discretion of the justices.[249]

Occasionally, offenders were ordered to be put out of business. The *Composicio* provided that taverners breaching the assize of wine would have their doors shut up until they obtained the king's licence to sell wine again.[250] The York Ordinances of 1301 provided that those who broke the ordinances might be have their premises destroyed and they might be made to abjure particular callings for ever, and those who refused to swear to keep the ordinances could be imprisoned.[251] A different response to those who would not sell at set prices can be seen in a statute of 1383. Rather than acting after sales at high prices had been made, a wine statute of this year envisaged intervention where wine sellers refused to sell at the prices set in the statute by forcing them to do so.[252] This is reminiscent of forced sales under purveyance rights, and the two areas may well be linked, given the royal household's importance as a purchaser of wine.

There was never any mention of posthumous confiscation of the assets of those who made excessive profits through the sale of goods, in contrast to the rules concerning dead usurers seen in the last chapter.

In practice, only financial punishment for price offenders is generally recorded in eyre rolls or King's Bench indictment files and rolls. An exception is the order in 1321 that poulterers guilty of withdrawing from trade rather than selling at assize prices at the London eyre should be imprisoned, though they were immediately bailed as they were deemed essential.[253] There are no signs of 'central' royal courts using corporal punishment for offenders against price regulations. At a lower level, Sutton court rolls and Wakefield tourn rolls contain no trace of corporal punishment, and show stability, or even, in the case of the Wakefield rolls, a decline in the level of amercements of offenders between 1272 and 1352. Sutton amercements were usually 2d–12d, occasionally 2s or 3s.[254] In Sutton and Wakefield records, amercement policy is generally obscure, with different people being amerced different amounts for what is recorded as the same offence.[255] This suggests that some other factor, such as the scale of the brewing, or ability to pay, was relevant but was not shown on the record.[256] The terse nature of all court records makes it

---

[248] *SR* I:309, st. 23 Edw. III, c.6; later reduced to forfeiture of the 'excess': Putnam, *Enforcement*, 82.

[249] 'grevousement puniz': *SR* II:63, 13 Ric. II, st.1 c.8.

[250] *SR* I:202.

[251] *YO*, 10–15, 18.

[252] *SR* II:19, 5 Ric. II, st.1 c.4.

[253] Cam, *London Eyre 1321*, I, 28.

[254] A different punishment can be seen in a view in 1397, common bakers, common brewers and common tipplers of ale guilty of offences against assizes not only amerced but also had their seals taken: DL 30/90/1212 m.8.

[255] Amercements ranged from 2d to 12d. Occasionally, an offence was condoned because the offender was poor.

[256] J.M. Bennett suggests that the level of amercements might be set in relation to the 'abilities of offenders to meet their expenses': Bennett, *Women*, 14.

impossible to elicit the basis on which amercements and fines were assessed. To take an example from the court of the Bishop of Ely at Littleport in 1324, a man and a woman were both found to have made halfpenny loaves which were deficient in weight. The woman's offence was making a loaf which was 5s 2d underweight, while the man's loaf was 8s 6d underweight. The fines made by these offenders were 6d and 5s respectively.[257] The relationship between offence and sum of fine is elusive. Clearly, some unrecorded factor was relevant. Whether that factor was recidivism, scale of offence in terms of how many other loaves were made at the same time, social status, or some other variable is unclear. J.M. Bennet traces the pattern of the amercements for breach of the assize of ale in one North-amptonshire manor in the first half of the fourteenth century, finding that they seem to have followed the falls and rallies of the economy, the (mode) average amercement falling to 2d, one third of its late thirteenth-century level of 6d in the 1320s, recovered slightly (to 3d) in the 1330s and fell to a new low of 1d in the 1340s.[258] She also notes that amercements in Brigstock were standardised (which goes somewhat against the idea of ability to pay as the key to amercement policy).[259] The likelihood of local variation in these practices must, of course, be borne in mind.

In contrast to a number of jurisdictions, it is clear that, although amercement was common, the pillory was used for recidivists in Oxford, obeying the provisions of the *Assisa Panis et Cervisie*.[260] The worst recidivist bakers were also compelled to abjure the trade of baking for a year and a day.[261] There are also examples of corporal punishment being used for offenders against price regulations in London. The London *Liber de Assisa Panis* shows no mention of amercements for offenders, though they would suffer financially (and the civic coffers would benefit) when their defective bread was confiscated or sold at a discount, as it often was.[262] Frequent recourse was also had to the hurdle or *claie*, and there are some examples of offenders being pilloried.[263] Occasionally, they were forced to abjure their trade in the city.[264] The *Letter Books* include other colourful examples of punishments, some of which were included in legislation, but others of which seem to have been impromptu unofficial creations.[265] There are also examples of corporal punishment

---

[257] *Court Baron*, 139.

[258] Bennett, *Women*, 14, 208.

[259] Bennett, *Women*, 208.

[260] If the pillory was used, there was not an amercement as well: Salter, *MA*, II, 142.

[261] Salter, *MA*, II, 140–1.

[262] London *Liber de Assisa Panis*, Corporation of London Record Office, MS CUST 4, contains numerous instances of forfeiture, particularly of the bread of 'foreign' bakers: see, e.g., f.20b; discounted sales of bread can be seen, e.g. at f.67a. See also LB, B, f.85 (1298, whole contents of a cart of bread, only some of which was deficient in weight, were confiscated); LB, D, f.189 (1316, deficient bread confiscated).

[263] *CLB, A*, 120–1, 208; *LA*, I, 354–5; *LC*, I, 292, 328, 329. Letter Book A has a list of twenty-five bakers condemned to the hurdle in 1282: *CLB, A*, 120, f.52b. Thrupp, however, noted correctly that 'this was a record for any one year: usual no not above 6 or 10 p. a.': Thrupp, *Short History*, 43. Later examples: *Liber de Assisa Panis* has a very large number of examples. See also, e.g., LB, D, f.190 (1316); *CLB, I*, 53, f.56 (1406). Pillory: e.g. *Liber de Assisa Panis*, f.80.

[264] *Liber de Assisa Panis*, f.9a; LB, D, f.190 (1316).

[265] See, e.g., the punishment of a man for offences in a sale of herring, which involved him being put on the pillory with herrings around his neck: *CLB, H*, 202, f.157. On the whole, such particularly humiliatory punishments tend not to be written into ordinances, though an exception is the punishment of brokers of usurious deals set out in an ordinance of 1382: LB, H, ff.155–6, involving symbolic baring of head and feet, and being made to ride on a horse backwards, without a saddle, as well as being pilloried.

for price offences in the court records for the manor of Pembrokes in Tottenham in 1377.[266] Records do, however, suggest that it was unusual to use corporal punishment for breakers of the assizes in the fourteenth century, and that punishment often seems to have been financial rather than corporal, though J.M. Bennett suggests that there may be under-recording of corporal punishment because it did not generate revenue.[267]

The *Anonimalle Chronicle* states that a large number of victuallers were imprisoned under the short lived victual statute of 1315, so many that it affected the supply of victuals to London.[268] Tuns of wine were seized by the mayor and sheriffs in London in 1354–5, for being sold at a price above the assize.[269]

Victims or accomplices? Penalising buyers

Most statutes mentioned only the punishment of the seller, not the buyer, although, arguably, the buyer at an inflated price might be held partly to blame for the adverse effects caused by such bargains. The concern with punishment of the seller rather than the buyer parallels the position with regard to usury, where only the usurer and not the borrower was penalised. The fact that, in general, only sellers were penalised suggests that, as with the borrower at usury, the buyer at an inflated price was seen as a victim of abuse rather than as an accomplice in a damaging transaction. Local rules sometimes affected purchasers as well as sellers, though the buyers in question were not really ordinary customers purchasing for their own use, but commodity speculators. London and other jurisdictions had and exercised rules against offering too high a price for corn (with a view to pushing up the price) from the second half of the fourteenth century.[270]

The statutes were not generally concerned with helping the buyer to recover compensation from the seller for an extortionate bargain. The 'injured party' was, however, given the possibility of a sort of compensation under the victual pricing provision in the Ordinance of Labourers 1349. As mentioned above, if the injured party sued the offender, the offender was to pay double the sum received to the injured party. This seems to have been based less on an idea of restitution of excessive gain than on a desire to encourage prosecution of offenders, since it was provided that, if the injured party did not pursue the matter, anyone else who would do so would be awarded the same sum.[271] In practice, there are actually a small number of presentments of buyers at excessive prices under the 1349–51 Labourers legislation.[272]

---

[266] R. Oram and F.H. Fenton (ed.), *Court Records of the Manors of Bruces, Dawbeneys, Pembrokes (Tottenham)* (Tottenham, 1961), 179, court and view 1377, manor of Pembrokes.

[267] Norwich court leet of the thirteenth and fourteenth centuries: several reports of offenders against the assizes having been amerced (though never pilloried): W. Hudson, *Leet Jurisdiction in Norwich in the Thirteenth and Fourteenth Centuries*, Selden Society vol. 5 for 1891 (London, 1892). J.M. Bennett notes that 'in late thirteenth century Tamworth, of more than 500 offences involving foodstuffs, only one resulted in corporal punishment': Bennett, *Ale*, 105. Bennett has noted a gender gap in actual use of corporal punishment, contending that corporal punishment for breach of assize of ale fell more on women than men, particularly because men could in practice pay to have it remitted: Bennett, *Ale*, 104.

[268] *Anonimalle*, 90–1.

[269] *CLB, G*, 41, f.35.

[270] Britnell, 'Price setting', 9. Examples: *CLB, G*, 170–1; *PMR*, A20 m.8r; *PMR* II *1364–81*, p. 196; Clare 1352, SC 2/203/49 m.4r.

[271] *SR* I:307, st. 23 Edw. III.

[272] See, e.g., Putnam, *Enforcement*, App., 233; JUST 1/1019 m.3.

Private actions

It seems that, in London, it may have been possible for one person to sue another in trespass for breach of price and manner of sale regulations, as can be seen from the case of *John Grene v Geoffrey de Somerceste* (1299–1300).[273] John was successful in his plea of trespass against Geoffrey. Whilst it had been ordained that two or four loaves might be sold in a fixed place, Geoffrey carried a loaf of tourte bread through the streets of London, and would not sell it for less than 3d 'to the damage of the plaintiff etc.'. Geoffrey admitted that he had done this. Price was not the only fault here, but it is some slender evidence of the possibility of a 'common plea' based on over-pricing. It also seems to have been possible in late fourteenth-century London to use over-pricing contrary to civic legislation to resist the enforcment of a bargain.[274]

Precedents which look somewhat 'trespassory' can be seen in the treatise *Court Baron*. Formulae for individual cases against those who are said to have breached the assize of bread or of ale are set out in detail, alleging the offence, requiring damages for actual damage and 'shame', and showing how to make a defence against such a case. They are, however, envisaged as being brought by a bailiff rather than a private individual who has bought over-priced bread or ale.[275]

In the common law in general, however, no private actions relating simply to the fairness of price (as opposed to warranty and deceit, trickery, minority or duress) seem to have been possible. It does not seem to have been possible to bring an individual trespass action against another person for an offence under the assizes of bread and ale. In the registers of writs examined by E. de Haas and G.D.G. Hall in the Selden Society volume on *Early Registers of Writs*, the only writs for an individual to sue another based on the assizes of bread and ale were actions concerning usurpation of jurisdiction rather than a direct action for a person who had been sold goods at too high a price.[276] Although the 1349–51 Labourers legislation envisaged private actions for price clause offences as well as wages and labour contract offences, no relevant writ appears to have been developed for breaches of the price rules.[277] No arguments as to fairness of price seem to have been raised in central courts of common law in private actions. A number of possible reasons for this apparent gap in the common law suggest themselves. Perhaps the matter was regarded as simply injusticiable, or perhaps, as with usury, arguments about terms of bargains and their fairness were unlikely to be raised if the party who wished to challenge them had any other case available. Perhaps there were problems with the common law's developing rules of evidence or its undeveloped law of restitution.

---

[273] *CEMCR*, 57–8.

[274] Case of men of the duke of Taschen against a common ostler and servant of John Pountefreit: Riley, *Memorials*, 460; LB, H, f.113.

[275] *Court Baron*, 23–5.

[276] E.g. Register CC: Cambridge University Library, MS Ee.i.I, part of a volume written for Luffield Priory in the late thirteenth century or early fourteenth century, reflecting the law at the very beginning of the reign of Edward I, in E. de Haas and G.D.G. Hall (eds), *Early Registers of Writs*, Selden Society vol. 87 for 1970 (London, 1970), 79, no.152.

[277] Putnam, *Enforcement*, 175–6.

Technical legal matters

Records concerning prosecution for price offences are usually extremely short, and, consequently, a number of questions concerning the details of the law on price offences remain somewhat obscure. Chief among these is the question of responsibility. 'Central' legislation is silent on this matter, which seems to have been left to 'local' officials, courts and juries to work out.

Different local jurisdictions punishing offenders against the assizes operated at different levels of sophistication as far as the underlying theory of responsibility for offences was concerned. The Oxford records show that people were held liable both for selling deficient bread personally and for supplying it to others who sold it for them.[278] There are examples of regraters (meaning retailers) being amerced in the Sutton rolls, but no indication that the supplier of the bread would also be amerced as an offender against the assize in such a case.[279] As might be expected, London appears to have been the most advanced jurisdiction in this respect in the thirteenth and fourteenth centuries, with rules concerning masters and servants and their responsibility for breach of pricing laws by one member of a partnership or on a sale by the servants of the master's products from at least 1316.[280] The only matter of this nature which seems to be tolerably well settled across the country as a whole is that husbands might be held responsible for their wives' breaches of the assize of ale.[281]

Other questions such as whether attempting to sell would have amounted to an offence, are obscure and probably destined to remain so.

Evaluating enforcement

It is extremely difficult to make definitive statments about enforcement of any medieval law. It is even harder in the case of price regulation because of the mass of jurisdictions involved and the fact that many records relating to the assizes of bread and ale leave doubts as to whether they are dealing with price offences, quality offences or measures offences. The general judgment of historians has, however, been negative.[282]

---

[278] An example of the latter can be seen in Salter, *MA*, II, 142: 'Panis quadr' de wastello Michaelis le Chapman de Wodestoke inventus in manibus Iohannis de Harwedone deficit in pondere – 18d.' There is some indication that this was supposed to be the case in York under the 1301 ordinances too: *YO*, 12.
[279] The term 'regraters' appears to mean 'sellers' or 'retailers'. It is discussed further in the next chapter.
[280] Riley, *Memorials*, 119, 122; LB, D, ff.188, 190 (1316); LB, E, f.221 (1392–3), *CLB, H*, 373, f.265b.
[281] Graham, 'A woman's work', 126–48.
[282] M.M. Postan assumed that price control legislation was ineffective, based on (uncited) evidence that there was evasion of the regulations: Postan, *Medieval Economy*, 255. Other work which has made judgments about the effect of the regulations based on a small amount of primary evidence includes that of the legal scholar A.I. Ogus, and the historians R. de Roover, A. Ross, and J.L. Bolton. Ogus and Ross wrote with little reference to primary sources. De Roover lumped together and dismissed as at best useless all enforcement of price controls in Europe before 1800. Bolton based his assertion that government regulation of sales of cloth was ineffective at all times between 1150 and 1500 on evidence from the fifteenth century alone: Ogus, 'Regulatory law', 1; de Roover, *JP*, 429–30; Ross, 'Assize', 332; Bolton, *MEE*, 329. There have been some exceptions to the generally negative conclusions, such as A.N. May's view that, at least in the thirteenth century, punishments for breaches of the assizes of bread and ale were quite punitive and likely to have been a deterrent against offences, and B.H. Putnam's view that the prices and wages regulations of the Labourers legislation were 'thoroughly enforced' in the 1350s: A.N. May, 'An index of thirteenth-century peasant impoverishment? Manor court fines', *EcHR* 26 (1973), 389–402; Putnam, *Enforcement*, 221.

An important line of argument on such jurisdictions is what could be called 'the licensing theory'. An early proponent was H.M. Cam, who stated that:

> The holding of the assize of bread and ale was in practice more of a fiscal than a judicial privilege. The fines imposed on brewsters for brewing contrary to the king's assize recur with such regularity on the court rolls that it is clear that the offence was winked at for the sake of the profits arising from fines: the lord was in effect taking a licensing fee . . . To pay a fine suited both parties better [than using corporal punishment for offenders].[283]

This assessment may now be described as the orthodox view, particularly with regard to the assize of ale, and sometimes in relation to other price offences, accepted by leading social and economic historians.[284] One historian has gone as far as to suggest that the assize of ale can never have been intended to be obeyed, as the standard text set out rates which were uneconomic.[285] If this is true, the whole assize of ale system must have been intended as a revenue raising device and nothing more, which seems unnecessarily 'Machiavellian'.[286]

It has been suggested that the financial penalties characteristic of lower court punishments of breakers of the assizes of bread and ale were not particularly burdensome.[287] R.H. Britnell's view is that, in local enforcement of the assize of ale at least, 'the records of law enforcement relating to the Assize of Ale reveal a more sceptical attitude to the law [than that seen in the works of moral writers and the wording of written laws]', and that 'In fact from quite early days breach of the assize of ale was commonly regarded as a technical offence whose detrimental effect upon the community was imperceptible.'[288]

The evidence upon which such conclusions are based is: (i) the repetition of names of offenders in some records and (ii) the fact that many records show only amercements, and not corporal punishment, with R.H. Hilton also mentioning (iii) 'the total lack of information about which provision of the assize was being broken'.[289] Certainly, negative things may be said, and, if one wants to find examples of poor enforcement, neglect and law breaking, then this is easily done. Whilst it would be foolish to suggest that there were no jurisdictions in which 'licensing' went on, there are a number of arguments which can be made against both the evidence and the conclusions of the 'licensing theory' and there are important positive points to be made about the system.

---

[283] H.M. Cam, *The Hundred and the Hundred Rolls: An Outline of Local Government in Medieval England* (London, 1930), 211.

[284] See, e.g., J.B. Post, 'Manorial amercements and peasant poverty', *EcHR* 28 (1975), 304–11, at 308; R.H. Hilton, *The English Peasantry in the Later Middle Ages* (Oxford, 1975), 45. See also Bennett, *Women*, 20; Britnell, *Commercialisation*, 94, describing assize of ale as 'a sort of tax on brewing rather than a serious attempt to regulate prices'; Britnell, 'Morals', 27–8. J.M. Bennett states that the assise of ale 'functioned as a *de facto* licensing system', and that 'courts more often profited from amercements of cheating brewers than they prevented the cheating itself', though elsewhere, the view is slightly modified to saying that, as actually enforced, assize fluctuated between punishing brewers and *de facto* licensing them: Bennett, *Ale*, 3, 101, 100.

[285] Post, 'Manorial amercements', 308.

[286] May, 'Index', 391.

[287] Post, 'Manorial amercements', 307; Britnell, 'Morals', 27–9; Britnell, 'Urban economic regulation', 3, citing Bennett, *Ale*, 105–6.

[288] Britnell, 'Morals', 27–9; Britnell, 'Urban economic regulation', 3, citing Bennett, *Ale*, 105–6.

[289] Hilton, *English Peasantry*, 45.

There is no doubt that jurisdiction could be seen as profitable. Both the financial rewards of jurisdiction over pricing offences and royal vigilance over unwarranted encroachment of others on this presumptively royal jurisdiction, in the time of Edward I, can be seen in an entry in the roll of the Eyre of Norfolk 1286. A jury reported that 'the king used to have custody of the correction of the assize of bread and ale in the lands of Robert de Baynard in Great Hautboys, until six years ago, when Robert de Baynard appropriated jurisdiction over the assizes, damaging the king to the amount of twelve pence per year'. Robert was amerced for appropriating jurisdiction over the offences.[290] Money was raised for the Crown.[291] Individuals also regarded jurisdiction over price offences as profitable and worth fighting over.[292] Sometimes, however, jurisdictional disputes seem to be as much about power as about money, *e.g.* that in 1317 between the abbot of St Mary's in York and the mayor of York concerning the assizes of bread and ale in Bootham, where it was alleged that the mayor had illegally pilloried offenders against the assizes.[293] It should be borne in mind that not all recorded amercements would be collected: it was, in medieval England, 'evidently one thing to levy fines, and another to collect them'.[294] It must also be emphasised that treating jurisdiction as a source of profit to be defended or fought over was by no means peculiar to pricing offences. Similar disputes occurred with relation to labour legislation, and a cursory glance at the *Quo Warranto* proceedings shows examples of disputes over the profits of other types of judicial rights.[295] It was no secret that money could be raised through fines, and the York Ordinances of 1301, and a charter to Lincoln in 1316, for example, are entirely open about the fact that certain profits are to be applied to civic coffers and, in the case of York, to cleaning the city.[296] There is also a degree of dispute (or variation) on the matter of the importance of the money raised from jurisdiction over pricing regulations.[297]

---

[290] JUST 1/573 m.64.

[291] Oxford was still paying £5 per year 'for the assizes of bread and ale' in 1382 and 1399: Salter, *MA*, vol. I, 216, 224.

[292] Dispute over jurisdiction over assizes of bread and ale, between Ebulo and Alicia Lestrange and the civic authorities of Lincoln: *CCR 1330–33*, 255 (1331). Allegedly forcible usurpation of lords' right to hold and take profits of assizes: e.g. *Abbot of Malmesbury v Men of Malmesbury* (1281–2) *Placitorum in domo capitulari Westmonasteriensi asservatorum abbreviatio* (1811), p. 202; *Prior of Canterbury v Anon* (1383): *YB 7 Ric. II (1383–4)*, ed. M.J. Holland (1969), p. 70; *Prior of Plympton v White et al.* (1383–4), *op. cit.*, p. 145, and CP 40/493 m.342. Overenthusiastic enforcement: Rochester 1376, a 'poor citizen' complained of being doubly amerced and punished for breaches of assize and other matters because both city officials and the clerk of the market were holding judicial sessions there: *RP* II:349.

[293] *CPR 1313–17*, 681.

[294] Lipson, *Economic History*, I, 296, citing W. Hudson, *Leet Jurisdiction in the City of Norwich during the Thirteenth and Fourteenth Centuries*, Selden Society vol. 5 for 1891 (London, 1892), xl: total amercements associated with various amercements at Norwich in 1289 over £72, but money actually paid into court only amounted to £17.

[295] Putnam, *Enforcement*, 158–9; Sutherland, *Quo Warranto*; *PQW*.

[296] *YO*, 11, 13, 14, 16; *CChR*, vol. III, *1300–26*, 312–13.

[297] It has been observed that revenue from offences against the assize of ale was important to borough courts: Dyer, *Standards of Living*, 209. Bennett notes that the assize of ale was 'a source of considerable income to those who held the right to its enforcement' (Bennett, *Ale*, 101) and emphasises the revenue raising aspect of such regulation (Bennett, *Ale*, 8). It has also been noted that the profits of administering price-control regulations were not, in general, great: May, 'Index', 386–7, 391. R.M. Smith, 'A periodic market and its impact upon a manorial community: Botesdale, Suffolk, and the Manor of Redgrave, 1280–1300' in Razi and Smith, *Medieval Society and the Manor Court*, 450–81, at 464, notes that the amount raised in assize of bread and ale breaches was less than the amount raised in respect of *inter vivos* property

As far as the repetition of names on lists of offenders is concerned, there is clearly a great deal of evidence that the same names recur in lists of offenders at different sessions in the same jurisdiction.[298] This is evidence that a conviction for breach of the price regulations was not necessarily a matter so shaming or so heavily punished as to deter all future breaches by the offender. A lack of social stigma attaching to breach of the assize of ale, at least in some communities, is suggested by evidence of fines imposed upon relatively prominent individuals in two different areas.[299] It also supports the argument that punishments were not an effective deterrent and were presumably regarded as being relatively light.

Related to this point is the argument that money was raised from those who had actually broken the rules and those who had not: in other words, what are presented as amercements were in fact taxes or licence fees on all producers or sellers of the regulated commodity (usually ale). J.M. Bennett states that in the manor of Brigstock, Northamptonshire, all active ale-sellers were amerced at each meeting of the court, and contends that, in general, 'all brewers, those who had brewed properly as well as those who brewed badly, usually faced amercements'.[300] In the Wakefield tourns, there are fluctuations in the numbers of offenders presented in each tourn. It is not unusual to have no presentments for offences against the assize of ale in a tourn.[301] This suggests that not all brewers – by a long way – were being amerced each time. The conclusion which seems to be most appropriate is that there was a great deal of variation. In some areas, low level courts amerced a large number of people frequently, whilst elsewhere, repetition of names on amercement lists was much less common.[302]

The regular charging of money to all active brewers, in those jurisdictions where it has been demonstrated, may, however, not be the product of perversion of the assize of ale jurisdiction, but evidence of the persistence of or confusion with the arguably separate tradition of the imposition of a tax for brewing at all. Bennett notes the existence of blanket payments or tolls (known in various places as tolcester, cannemol, alesilver) required to brew as well as amercements for doing it improperly.[303] Confusion or conflation of the two traditions may have occurred in

transactions. It is demonstrated that the amercements were of value, but were not the most important source of revenue from the manor court.

[298] See, e.g., Hilton, *English Peasantry*, 45 (a man presented for brewing at each court 1387–1400, at Shuckborough); Bennett, *Women*, 120; Britnell, 'Morals', 29; Bennett, *Ale*, 164. An examination of the names of offenders against the assizes of bread and ale in the records of the Sutton court shows that names do recur, but not with the regularity required to show that the court was engaging in systematic licensing of misconduct.

[299] Britnell, 'Morals', 29. 'In Brigstock about a third of the recorded alewives were married to men who held local offices, and who may therefore be reckoned leaders of the community': Bennett, *Women*, 122. A court of Colchester in 1377 fined the wives of three former members of Parliament: Britnell, *Colchester*, 89–90.

[300] Bennett, *Women*, 120; Bennett, *Ale*, 164.

[301] See Appendix II, graphs 1 and 2, below.

[302] For a good comparison between two neighbouring areas in late thirteenth-century Suffolk, see Smith, 'A periodic market' in Razi and Smith, *Medieval Society and the Manor Court*, 474–5. See also Graham, 'A woman's work', 126–48, at 134, 142.

[303] Bennett, *Ale*, 164–5. R.H. Britnell notes that 'In Lincoln, ale-toll is interpreted by the city's historian as "a payment made by the brewer for the right to brew"': Hill, *Lincoln*, 214–15. See also C. Dyer, *Lords and Peasants in a Changing Society* (Cambridge, 1980), 346; Britnell, 'Morals', 29. This seems to be a separate imposition from amercements under the assize of ale, rather than confirmation that everyone was penalised under the assize in a form of licensing. Britnell has also noted the existence of seigneurial taxes

some jurisdictions, but elsewhere they remained separate, as Bennett's examples show.[304] In some instances, the existence of separate traditions may be masked by inaccurate designation of impositions as connected to 'the assize'. One cannot, however, necessarily expect medieval courts and those recording their decisions to conform to the accuracy in definition of offences required in modern legal practice. Wakefield cases clearly differentiate between baking bread against the assize and breaking bread without a licence. In the tourn at Kirkburton, 12 January 1333, for example, there are two bakers amerced for baking bread against the assize, and three more for baking without licence and contrary to the assize.[305]

It must be admitted, however, that there are some fairly strong examples of what look like 'licensing', as in the case of Winchester's jurisdictions over the assizes of bread and ale in the later fourteenth century and that of Colchester over the assize of ale in the fourteenth and fifteenth centuries (where no effort to behave in a judicial manner seems to have been made).[306]

Bennett also has evidence from Brigstock that 'some brewers purchased long-term licences (*licencia braciandi*) to cover several months of brewing activity'.[307] Brewing licences, however, may well have been not licences to breach the assize, but licences to brew *at all*, akin to the quasi-taxes on baking and brewing, such as the *bacgavel* and *brewgavel* from late fourteenth-century Exeter.[308] Arguments for genuine licences 'to go on sinning' are not very powerful with regard to the thirteenth and fourteenth centuries at least. Bennett cites a licence of 1445 which does allow some misconduct (though not a complete *carte blanche*) but her fourteenth-century 'licences' seem to be permissions to brew in accordance with the assize, as licensees who offended were also amerced.[309] Licensing for the future in a more open way and permissive monopoly schemes did begin to appear in the fifteenth century and afterwards, at a similar time as what seems to have been a decline in enforcement of the assize mechanisms.[310]

If the evidence suggests licensing, it does not, in any case, show systematic licensing. Revenue was raised but this does not mean that the price regulations were treated simply as ways of raising revenue. More could have been done if that was the case. In a number of cases, amercements were clearly related to the number of brewings or offences.[311] This suggests at least some reality in the judicial nature of the process. If the punishment of offenders against the price regulations was in reality a system of regular revenue raising, one might also expect to see the same or similar sums of money being raised in each court. The Sutton and Wakefield records, however, show varying amounts being collected. The seriousness of the penalty seems to have declined in real terms over the fourteenth century, since the amercements remained similar throughout the century, despite fluctuations in

---

on tenants' sales of livestock and ale, 'inviting' concepts of the requirement of a licence for selling, or compensation for selling: Britnell, *Commercialisation*, 64.

[304] Bennett, *Ale*, 164–5.
[305] Wakefield, *F*, 139.
[306] Keene, *Survey of Winchester*, 234, 265; Britnell, *Colchester*, 89.
[307] Bennett, *Women*, 120.
[308] Bennett, *Ale*, 21, citing 1390–91 records concerning the tolls of John Littlejohn, Devon Record Office City Receivers' Accounts 1390–91.
[309] Bennett, *Ale*, 162–3.
[310] Bennett, *Ale*, 99, 106.
[311] Post, 'Manorial amercements', 308.

prices and wages, once more suggesting imposition of set judicial penalties rather than an attempt to raise revenue.[312] The fact that individual aletasters, who are named in the rolls, raised amounts which differed between the aletasters and from one year to the next also tends to go against the idea of a tax system, since it is clear that individual aletasters did not have 'revenue targets' as others entrusted with the collection of tax might have.[313]

Where corporal punishment was not administered to those breaching price control regulations, this may be portrayed as evidence that royal control over the assizes was not effective, and that jurisdiction was used as a profit-making scheme by those who exercised it. It may, however, be argued that financial penalties were seen to 'fit the crime' more than corporal punishment. The numerous other instances of financial penalties being substituted for corporal or other penalties in medieval law also needs to be borne in mind: enforcement of pricing offences would not be unique in this respect. Also, if money raised in 'licensing' was used to pay for the authorities policing the regulations, this does not necessarily mean that no one took breaches of the regulations seriously.[314] It could, rather, reflect a change of emphasis from punishment to detection or prevention. On the level of penalties imposed upon offenders against price regulations, it is not clear that amercements were less serious than with other offences. In the Littleport court in 1324–5, for example, amercements for offences against the assizes of bread and ale ranged from 6d to 2s, failures in agricultural work resulted in 2d or 3d amercements, pig damage in an amercement of 2d, gathering beans belonging to neighbours in an amercement of 2d and 'slandering sedge' in an amercement of 6d.[315]

A challenge to the licensing theory may also be made on the basis of 'not guilty verdicts'. There are examples of people being examined, and no fault being found with their product or the price at which it was for sale. J.M. Bennett notes that aletasters commonly listed in court rolls could be both ale offenders and those who had 'sold honestly' or kept the assize.[316] The fourteenth-century Norwich leet records, for example, have evidence that conviction of these offences was not a mere formality, with a number of records of those presented being acquitted because they were said not to have committed offences.[317] London evidence on the enforcement of the assize of bread also gives evidence of genuine trials of those accused of offences, who clearly believed that it was worth their while to contest guilt or liability.[318] Similarly, the Oxford records of the early fourteenth century

---

[312] Dyer, *Standards of Living*, 37, 88, 101–2, 198–9. In contrast, J.M. Bennett traces the pattern of the amercements for breach of the assize of ale in one Northamptonshire manor in the first half of the fourteenth century, finding that they seem to have followed the falls and rallies of the economy, the (mode) average amercement falling to 2d, one third of its late thirteenth-century level of 6d in the 1320s, recovering slightly (to 3d) in the 1330s and falling to a new low of 1d in the 1340s: Bennett, *Women*, 14, 208.

[313] See, e.g., Dyer, *Standards of Living*, 138, noting that 'after 1334, each village was assigned a quota of the lay subsidy and decided among themselves how to levy the money'.

[314] As is stated to have been common in Britnell, 'Urban economic regulation', 3, citing Bennett, *Ale*, 105–6.

[315] *Court Baron*, 136–40.

[316] Bennett, *Ale*, 3. See, e.g., her example of the aletasters at Preston-on-Wye (Herefordshire) who 'reported all brewers, noting how often they had brewed and whether they had sold honestly', *ibid.*

[317] e.g. Hudson, *Leet Jurisdiction*, 30. Maitland, *Select Pleas in Manorial Courts*, 89, pleas in manorial courts of the abbot of Ramsey, Hemingford, 1278: '. . . From Alice Cot, nothing for she kept the assize and only brewed once.'

[318] Examples of trials of assize of bread offences: Riley, *Memorials*, 108; LB, D, f.180 (1313, defendant pleaded

contain a number of instances of an assay being held and nobody's bread being found deficient, and of arguments being made by those accused of defects under the assize of ale that they had not, in fact, offended.[319] I have not found any records of contested cases in the eyre rolls of the period under consideration, though an interesting example of a contested claim can be seen in the roll of the Gloucestershire eyre of 1248, showing that it was possible to defend oneself against allegations of breach of price regulations, and therefore suggesting a genuine desire to identify and punish offenders rather than a method of disguised taxation on victuallers.[320] *Court Baron* also contemplates contested cases in which the correct price of bread and ale could be disputed, again suggesting that offenders could really be tried, and would have a chance to argue their innocence.[321] This certainly contradicts the picture of enforcement of the assizes as a sham used to justify indiscriminate taxation.

R.H. Hilton's point that it can be argued that the jurisdiction was not exercised seriously, because there was a total lack of information about which provision of the assize was being broken, does not hold good for all jurisdictions. In the Sutton records, the offenders against the assizes of bread and ale are carefully separated into brewers, bakers and tipplers or regraters. They do not give many details of the offending conduct, but this is true of all entries in these records. The court rolls of Wakefield for the period 1272–1352 commonly stipulate the nature of offences in terms of the price at which the bread or ale was sold, and whether this has been done occasionally, commonly, or on a particular number of occasions.[322] Furthermore, inexactness of reporting of the nature of an offence is neither unusual nor surprising in a medieval manorial court.

In favour of a more positive view of enforcement of the price regulations, it can be said that efforts were made to ensure that legislation was enforced. M. Prestwich, in discussing the enforcement of the York Ordinances of 1301, noted that complaints were made to the King's Council that the ordinances were not being kept.[323] This episode shows that there were problems, but that there was also royal concern with the enforcement of price fixing measures, since an inquiry was set up to investigate how the ordinances were being observed. Edward II issued a commission to inquire into the conduct of sheriffs in London in 1318–19, where one of the questions to be asked concerned sheriffs' neglect of enforcement of the assize of bread, amongst other delinquencies.[324] Similarly, a common petition of

that he did not make the deficient loaf for sale); Riley, *Memorials*, 119; LB, D, f.188 (1316, defendant denied making the loaf); Riley, *Memorials*, 122; LB, D, f.190 (1316, defendant attempting to excuse baking for sale at irregular prices by saying that the flour he had used had been damaged by water). Even the bakers of Stratford, whose bread was routinely forfeited, or sold at a discount for short weight, were given the benefit of the doubt when their bread was tested in the wrong way according to London law, being weighed cold: Riley, *Memorials*, 71; LB, D, f.171.

[319] Salter, *MA*, II, 156 (1311), 158 (1312), 161 (1313), 162 (1314), 192–3 (1324).
[320] 'Of wine sold contrary to the assize, they say that seven men sell wine contrary to the assize, but it is attested that this was done when the fair was in Wynchecumb. So to judgment': JUST 1/274 m.3d.
[321] *Court Baron*, 23–6.
[322] In the tourn at Wakefield, Friday after Epiphany 1331, for example, two brewers were amerced for brewing 'occasionally' at 1d: Wakefield, *E*, 167. It must, however, be admitted that it does not specifically say that this is a breach of the assize.
[323] *YO*, 6, 9.
[324] JUST 1/553.

1354 which complained that the 'Statute of Labourers and Victuallers' was not keeping prices down in London, because of the city's jurisdiction was answered by royal plans to take action – assigning justices, and providing for punishment for civic officials, leading up to seizure of the city's liberties, if the measure should not be enforced.[325] The King's Bench plea roll for the session held in 1363 at Gloucester, discussed above, seems to suggest, if not effective enforcement of victual price regulations, then at least a serious effort to enforce them, coupled with the co-operation of a section of the population in investigating and reporting offences in the later fourteenth century.[326]

Evidence for the enforcement of the assizes of bread and ale by franchise holders is plentiful. Numerous court records from manorial and borough jurisdictions show that offenders were identified and punished.[327] The creation and retention of so many sets of records is some testament to the importance of the price control regulations in local jurisdictions. The records of the tourns of Wakefield and the courts and views of frankpledge of Sutton in Lincolnshire show the continuous exercise of the jurisdiction over offences against the assizes of bread and ale from the beginning of the reign of Edward I to the middle of the fourteenth century in the first case and throughout the fourteenth century in the second case.[328] Offenders against the assizes were presented in most views of frankpledge in Sutton and in some other courts. A particularly large number of people were presented for these offences between 1327 and 1349. There seems to have been a decline in the number of offenders presented from 1349–52 onwards, but the jurisdiction was exercised actively throughout the fourteenth century. The Sutton court rolls also show serious efforts to discover and punish offenders against the assizes of bread and ale, with regular courts at which tasters gave lists of offenders. They show internal supervisory mechanisms providing for the punishment of those entrusted with the task of presenting offenders who failed to do so, and of brewers who did not send for the aletasters before selling their wares. Neither offence seems to have been common.[329] The court rolls of Wakefield for the period 1272–1352 also show serious efforts to prosecute offenders against the assizes of bread and ale, with supervisory mechanisms: regular presentments of those who did not co-operate with the aletasters, and of tasters and townships not making presentments. The Wakefield rolls in fact show a high level of co-operation with the price regulation system, in that in all of the tourn records, there are only eighteen individual presentments and two presentments of vills for concealing

---

[325] *RP* II:258b.

[326] KB 27/411.

[327] See, e.g., Bennett, *Ale*, 171; Salter, *MA*, II; Hudson, *Leet Jurisdiction in Norwich*; London, *Liber de Assisa Panis*.

[328] See Appendix II below.

[329] Examples of failures to present or to comply with the tasters do not seem to have been common. These can be seen in 1323, 1336, 1338, 1353, 1366 and 1373: DL 30/85/1163 m.9; DL 30/86/1171 m.12; DL 30/86/1172 m.8; DL 30/87/1183 m.19; DL 30/87/1190 m.12; DL 30/88/1195 m.11. Tasters in Sutton are amerced irregularly for not performing their office properly. Such presentments can be seen in courts in 1317, 1325, 1333, 1336, 1340, 1352, 1353, 1381, 1390, 1391, 1393 and 1397: DL 30/85/1162 m 2d; DL 30/85/1163 m.9; DL 30/85/1168 m.6; DL 30/86/1171 m.12; DL 30/86/1172 m.8.; DL 30/86/1174 m.6; DL 30/87/1183 m.2; DL 30/87/1183 m.9; DL 30/89/1202 m.1d; DL 30/89/1207 m.9; DL 30/89/1208 m.20; DL 30/90/1210 m.6d; DL 30/90/1212 m.9.

offenders.[330] Britnell also gives examples of apparently satisfactory reports on the enforcement of the assizes of bread and ale in Suffolk in 1315: although it seems that financial rather than corporal penalties were used, the juries examined by the clerk of the market in Haverhill and Freckenham seem to have been satisfied with local enforcement.[331] The apparently conscientious Oxford aletasters of the first half of the fourteenth century actively sought out offenders, going from house to house twice a year, to examine ale on the premises.[332] An example of jurisdiction apparently being taken seriously can be seen in a King's Bench case of Easter 1341, in which it was alleged that a man who had refused to perform the office of aletaster in Rotherham had been distrained (by seizure of his horse) to do so.[333]

Not surprisingly, the level of activity of local officials varied. Not all local officials were conscientious in enforcing price regulations. It was alleged that the London bakers had, from 1269 to 1272, ignored the assize of bread, and escaped corporal punishment by bribing the mayor and sheriffs.[334] Failures to enforce the assizes of bread and ale were reported in Bristol in 1324. A plaint in the roll of the general oyer and terminer commission sent to enquire into malpractices of mayors and officials in Bristol in 1324, states that the mayor, Richard Tilly, had not acted correctly with regard to the assizes of bread and ale. Richard Tilly was said to have administered corporal punishment to poor prisoners and to have allowed the others to make fine to be let off their corporal punishment.[335] At a lowlier level, examples of aletasters being presented and amerced for failure to do their job are quite easily found, though it has been suggested that these amercements may not have reflected a widespread problem, that they were much commoner in rural than in urban areas, and that the public nature of the job generally encouraged honesty.[336] Once again, it must be emphasised that accusations of 'concealment' of offenders on the part of those charged with reporting them is by no means peculiar to pricing offences, and so cannot be used to argue that these offences in particular were not taken seriously. Numerous similar examples could be cited in relation to weights and measures or labour offenders.[337]

The many examples which scholars have considered, and their variety, show that enforcement of the price control regulations in low level jurisdictions cannot be assumed to have been ineffectual and motivated only by a desire to raise money. Some franchise holders may have been interested only in the profits of justice, but

---

[330] The only examples of presentments for failure to send for the tasters are, in tourns: Wakefield, *A*, 189 (in 1284); *D*, 13 and 17 (1315); *E*, 112 (1327); and in courts: *E*, 159 (1330); *F*, 46 (1332); *G*, 206 (1349). Failure to send for the aletasters resulted in amercements of 2d to 12d, with no rise over more than half a century

[331] Britnell, *Commercialisation*, 96, noting the clerk of the market's inspection 30 September 1315 of Haverhill (Suffolk) (the first for for twenty years), the jury reporting 'that measures were checked annually and that bakers and brewers were duly fined for their misdemeanours', and 12 October 1315 at Freckenham (Suffolk) where the jury reported that 'no clerk of the market had visited them for eighteen years but that brewers, bakers and users of false measures were corrected once a year': BL, MS Harley 230, ff.91v, 92r.

[332] Bennett, *Ale*, 112.

[333] *Robert Rawland v Abbot of Rufford et al.*, KB 27/324 m.106d; M.S. Arnold (ed.), *Select Cases of Trespass from the King's Courts 1307–99, vol. 2*, Selden Society 103 (London, 1987), 241.

[334] T. Stapleton (ed.), *De Antiquis Legibus Liber*, Camden Society 34 (1846), 159.

[335] JUST 1/1560 m.62.

[336] Bennett, *Ale*, 163.

[337] See, e.g., Putnam, *Enforcement*, App., 152.

one cannot make sweeping comments that the assizes were badly enforced at all times and in all places, given that there is evidence of jurisdictions which seem to have functioned effectively for much of the period under consideration, with regular presentment and punishment of offenders, local officials policing sales, and internal supervisory mechanisms in operation.

Most of the evidence upon which the licensing theory is based concerns the assize of bread and ale. It cannot be assumed that, even if there was widespread 'licensing' in that area, that it affected all price regulation. Some negative views have been expressed about the level of enforcement of price controls under the Ordinance and Statute of Labourers, though there are certainly examples of presentments of both victuallers and craftsmen for over-pricing contrary to the legislation in the surviving rolls of the justices of labourers and justices of the peace with labourers jurisdiction from the 1350s onwards.[338] B.H. Putnam noted that the presentments include those for over-priced goods other than those specified in the legislation, which shows no lack of enthusiasm by justices or presenting groups for the price controls.[339] At least one man was reported to have bribed local officials to let him off prosecution for selling leather at an excessive price, again suggesting that this was not something to be taken in one's stride as a 'technical offence'.[340]

There seem to be few signs of complete disobedience or contempt of price regulations on the part of those whose conduct they regulated. Wine price regulations (or their level) could, apparently cause some hostility, as can be seen in the London case of Roger de Len, a taverner, who (eventually) confessed to having 'abused' William Leyre, 'as he was walking harmlessly along Thames Streer, and had charged him with having procured the publication of an assize of wine by the Mayor and Aldermen against the common good, in which . . . the price of better wine was fixed at 1½d per gallon'.[341] A tavern brawl in 1306 was also allegedly caused by disagreement over the assize of wine, with one man apparently offering the assize price (explicitly relating it to the assize) and the taverner and his workers taking exception to his not offering the higher price demanded for a gallon of wine.[342] Cases such as that of Juliana, wife of Richard Pykard, who, in Wakefield in 1275, 'brazenly' told the aletasters that 'she would sell ale against the will of the tasters and the bailiffs, in despite of the Earl' (though she was brought to heel, making fine with 12d) and the 1349 Wakefield case of William son of Philip Sagher, ordered to be distrained to answer the lord for threatening the aletaster in the course of carrying out his duty, are exceptional.[343] Perhaps a little more common was a refusal to sell at all if one disapproved of the prices set – as was the action of the brewsters of Exeter in 1317.[344] There was also a strike by London taverners in

---

[338] Horrox, *Black Death*, 287–9; *EEJ*, 94; Britnell, *Colchester*, 135; Putnam, *Enforcement*, 72, 75.
[339] Putnam, *Enforcement*, 75.
[340] Putnam, *Enforcement*, App., 213; KB 27/373 m.46 (1353 M.).
[341] *CEMCR*, 24 (1298–9).
[342] *CEMCR*, 252.
[343] Wakefield, *A*, 51, cited in Bennett, *Ale*, 98; Wakefield, *G*, 104, 126. A tumbrel in Sutton was the subject of an attack in 1317: DL 30/85/1162 m.2. A later example of dissent is provided by Britnell: John Badcock of Abberton's daughter, 1437, Colchester, accused of selling a pair of young pigeons at 1½d when others were asking 1d, and 'she chided and wickedly assaulted other women selling around her who did not want to sell at such a high price, against the peace' (Britnell, 'Price setting', 7; Essex Record Office, Colchester Muniments CR 1437–8, m.2d).
[344] Bennett, *Ale*, 98, citing Devon Record Office, MCR 1317–18, m.1. Other examples, Bennett, *Ale*, 101,

1331 against the price fixed for Gascon wine.[345] There are some signs of groups acting against corporal punishment of offenders, as when, in 1341, forty-eight people in Mildenhall, Suffolk, prevented the punishment of brewers in the abbot of Bury's tumbrel, saving the (probably female) brewers and assaulting the abbot's bailiff. This, however, seems to have been part of a general dispute about leet jurisdiction of the abbot, rather than a particular objection to corporal punishment for brewers.[346]

There is some evidence of contemporary resistance to the idea of kings attempting to set prices by legislation. Such resistance is implicit in the statements of the mayor of York to the King's Council in 1304, and is explicit in the *Anonimalle Chronicle*'s account of Edward II's Poultry Statute of 1315, and in the comments of the Bridlington canon on the same statute, all to the effect that such measures could not be enforced, and even that they made matters worse than they had been.[347] There was not, however, a general idea throughout the period considered that price fixing statutes were unworkable, and the examples of dissent listed above may well suggest a difference of opinion between kings and governments and some of their subjects which was confined to the early years of the fourteenth century. Petitions to kings to fix prices and to strengthen already existing price fixing legislation, which continued throughout the period under consideration, seem to show an assumption that there was some point in so legislating. Those affected by over-pricing did sometimes complain about lax enforcement of the assizes, again showing support for the laws.[348]

None of this, however, is an argument either about levels of offending and obedience or about the economic effect of the regulations, on which this book does not attempt to comment. We do not know whether 'the assizes, especially that of ale, were more honoured in the breach than in the observance'.[349] Previous commentators have been quick to assume that the medieval price control regulations were either ineffective or else damaging. R. de Roover assumed that price fixing 'usually made matters worse instead of better'.[350] In truth, the effectiveness of these measures is virtually impossible to assess. Price movements can be observed, and may be thought to indicate failure. There is, for example, some evidence in relation to wine prices in London, showing price rises despite continuous regulation by king and city in the fourteenth century.[351] We cannot, however, know what would have happened if the regulations had not been enacted.

citing *CIPM*, vol. XI, p. 92 (inquisition post mortem on Henry Duke of Lancaster 1361, noting the issues of the castle, manor and honour of Leicester, including that of the assize of ale).

[345] L.F. Salzman, *English Trade in the Middle Ages* (London, 1964), 388. There was a boycott by Gascon vintners in 1315 in connection with pricing regulations: Y. Rennuard and R. Faukner (eds), *Gascon Rolls Preserved in the Public Record Office 1307–17* (London, 1962), 425.

[346] *CPR 1340–43*, 316–17; Dyer, *Everyday Life in Medieval England*, 227, citing Cambridge University Library, Add. MS 4220, ff.133v–136v; *MLC*, 94.

[347] *YO*, 19 (mayor of York states that it is not possible to enforce the ordinances, but cannot prove this); *Anonimalle*, 90–1; W. Stubbs (ed.), *Chronicles of the Reigns of Edward I and Edward II*, Rolls Series 3 (London, 1882–3), II, 25, 47–8, cited in McKisack, *Fourteenth Century*, 50.

[348] Salter, *MC*, 29–30, cited in Bennett, *Ale*, 101.

[349] Wood, *Medieval Economic Thought*, 98.

[350] de Roover, *JP*, 429.

[351] F. Sargeant, 'The wine trade with Gascony' in G. Unwin (ed.), *Finance and Trade under Edward III* (Manchester, 1918), 257–304, at 298.

It has been suggested that, in any case, the regulations were not designed to freeze prices in general: fluctuations were to be tolerated.[352]

It should also be noted that enforcement mechanisms were (and are) extremely unlikely to function well with respect to bargains struck in private, and it has been shown that there was in medieval England a large amount of trading outside the confines of licensed markets.[353]

Rationales

Although the immediate cause of enactment of certain statutes was usually a particular emergency, such as the famine which led to the victual price statute of 1315, or the Black Death and its aftermath, that does not mean that they are totally separate legislative events, isolated and insulated from one another, with no connecting ideas.[354] The price regulations may be seen both as the product of particular emergencies, and as transcending them. They often outlasted the particular emergency and became an accepted area of government activity. In connection with wine, for example, regulation seems not to have been affected by the fluctuations in the amount of wine imported from Gascony, as regulations continued to be made and adjusted from the thirteenth century to the end of the fourteenth and beyond, despite some large-scale variations in the amount of wine reaching the country.[355] They can be seen to reflect certain underlying royal attitudes to the role of kings and governments in controlling the prices at which subjects bought and sold goods. There are signs that the price regulations were viewed as being a coherent body of law, rather than isolated, individual acts. An indication of this tendency to regard price fixing as a coherent area of action which ought to be governed by consistent rules can be seen in the wine statute of 1331, which mentions that the regime for taverners which it sets out is not in line with the regime for bread and ale (as no punishment has been fixed for offenders against the wine price regulations).[356]

Finding evidence of a degree of coherence is, however, far simpler than discovering, or constructing, the rationale for royal action in this area. One possible influence is an idea of enforcing canonical/civilian 'just price' rules. Canonists and theologians had pronounced it to be illegal and sinful to take more than a 'just price' in a sale of goods, insisting that substantially equal value should be provided by the vendor and the purchaser in such a transaction, though the exact method which was intended to be used to assess the just price was and has been a matter of some controversy, with different interpretations based on cost and demand.[357] The better, and currently orthodox, view is that just price theories did not generally expect particularly

---

[352] Britnell, *Commercialisation*, 93.
[353] Britnell, *Commercialisation*, 97–9; Dyer, *Everyday Life in Medieval England*, c.14.
[354] McKisack, *Fourteenth Century*, 40, 49; Tout, *Edward II*, 213; Gilchrist, *CEA*, 87; Dyer, *Standards of Living*, 40; Pounds, *Economic History*, 431, 435–6.
[355] Dyer, *Standards of Living*, 104.
[356] *SR* I:264, st. 4 Edw. III, c.12.
[357] J. Gordley, *The Philosophical Origins of Modern Contract Doctrine* (Oxford, 1991), 14; de Roover, *JP*, 418; Noonan, *Usury*, 86; Gilchrist, *CEA*, 58–9; Langholm, *Economics*, 55, 92–5, 179, 180, 225, 232, 257, 285–6, 304, 356, 361–3, 412, 545, 574–5; Wood, *Medieval Economic Thought*, c.6.

strict price fixing – one true, correct price.[358] There are some statements by canon lawyers and theologians to the effect that kings should take a role in ensuring just prices in their realms.[359] Some statutes refer to the achievement of a 'true' price or a 'reasonable' price, or to returning to the price as it stood at a particular time.[360] These ideas might be regarded as roughly equivalent to, or overlapping in fact with, the idea of a just price.

The wrongful nature of certain behaviour is mentioned as a factor in royal action in several statutes and ordinances, though without reference to sin and the church (in contrast, for example, to statements in thirteenth-century bread price regulations in the Low Countries).[361] The 1301 ordinances concerning prices in York mention a purpose of dealing with 'the extortions and oppressions imposed by the citizens'.[362] One account of the 1315 statute fixing prices for poultry and other victuals emphasised the wrongful behaviour of travelling merchants selling victuals at immoderately high prices as a reason for royal price fixing.[363] The text of the statute in the parliament rolls, however, concentrates not on the wrongful action of the merchants, but on its deleterious effects in terms of pushing prices up to an intolerable level.[364] Later statutes sometimes express criticism of the actions of vendors. The wine statute of 1330 mentioned with disapproval the activities of taverners, who were said to be selling corrupt wines, and selling wine at whatever price they wished.[365] Such emphasis on wrongful behaviour without reference to the rules of the church may be taken as some evidence of royal disapproval of sales at high prices which was not wholly dependent on theological or canonical principles, but which flowed from something like a 'secular commercial morality' objecting to excessive profits, and which, perhaps, saw this as either extortion or fraud, rather than a damaging but consensual bargain.[366] It is argued that moral opprobrium was a factor in urban regulation of prices, and punishment of offenders against the regulations.[367]

Where a reason for action is given in royal price fixing statutes, more stress is laid on the adverse economic consequences of the wrongdoing than on the wrongdoing in itself. A specific allegation of damage was made in the York Ordinances of

---

[358] J.W. Baldwin, 'Medieval theories of the just price: romanists, canonists and theologians in the twelfth and thirteenth centuries', *Transactions of the American Philosophical Society*, new ser., 49 part 4 (Philadelphia, 1959). J.W. Baldwin, 'The medieval merchant before the bar of canon law', *Papers of the Michigan Academy of Science, Arts and Letters* 44 (1959); Wood, *Medieval Economic Thought*, 150–1.

[359] Langholm, *Economics*, 180, 392–4.

[360] A commission dated 24 December 1307 mentions the idea of ensuring that goods be sold for their true price ('verum valorem') as they were accustomed to be sold in the reign of Edward I: F. Palgrave (ed.), *The Parliamentary Writs and Writs of Military Summons*, 2 vols (London, 1830), vol. 2, division II, 2, 8, 9; *CPR 1307–13*, 29. A statute of 1331 regulating the price of wine referred to a 'reasonable price': *SR* I:263, st. 4 Edw. III, c.8, orders that no one should dare to sell wine 'forq[e] a resonable feer'.

[361] Zylbergeld, 'Les regulations du marche du pain' in J.-M. Duvosquel and A. Dierkers (eds), *Villes et campagnes au Moyen Age* (Liège, 1991), 792, notes that the Liège measure of 1252, created by a prince-bishop of Liège, explicitly mentions the need to protect the sellers' souls.

[362] *YO*, 9.

[363] *Vita Edwardi Secundi*, 59.

[364] *RP* I:295a.

[365] *SR* I:264, st. 4 Edw. III, c.12.

[366] Britnell, *Commercialisation*, 93. Much later, Blackstone classed offences against the assize of bread and ale as 'cheating': Blackstone, *Commentaries*, Book IV, c.12, p. 159.

[367] R.H. Britnell gives examples of expressions of moral opprobrium attaching to those breaching price regulations in London in 1477, and in Coventry in 1473: Britnell, 'Urban economic regulation', 2.

1301, which were expressed to be 'for the remedy and relief of those coming to York, who could not afford to stay there and do their business because of the high prices imposed by citizens in sales of goods'.[368] As mentioned, the text of the 1315 victual price statute in the parliament rolls concentrates on the intolerably high prices of victuals, and in particular on the damage caused to the magnates by the increase in prices.[369] The 1331 wine statute said that the high price of wine was to the great hurt of the people.[370] Economic damage was also alleged in the 1363 poultry statute, expressed to have been enacted because of a dearth of poultry.[371]

Sometimes, statutes are stated to have been passed for vaguer, altruistic, reasons. The *Vita Edwardi Secundi* entry for 1315 imputes an altruistic motive to the petitioners at whose request the victual price statute of 1315 was passed, stating that the earls and barons in Parliament, 'looking to the welfare of the state' ('rei publice prospicientes') had passed a measure fixing the price of common foods.[372] The statute's text mentions the common good of all as a goal.[373]

Only one order has been found mentioning protection of the poor as a specific aim, and this clearly should be classed as an 'emergency', reactive, measure. Sheriffs were ordered in 1317 to proclaim a new assize of ale in that year, and to order its enforcement. The Close Roll entry justifies this on the grounds that grain, which is in short supply due to bad harvests, and which might have been used for bread is instead being used for ale, which brewers are selling at high prices, and if something is not done, 'a great part of the lower and poor people will shortly sufer from famine'.[374] If a more general case is to be made out for this having been an aim of the price fixing legislation, it will have to be argued that the goods, prices of which were regulated, were particularly important to the poor. This is true of bread and ale, but not at all of wine, and not particularly of small-scale craftsmen's goods.[375] There is a sense in which most of the price regulations can be seen as having been in the interest of poor people, rather than those provisioning rich households, as the latter might have rights of pre-emption including some right to keep the price down, or at least they could buy in big quantities and get favourable deals, while the less well off had to buy in small quantities, and could hardly 'shop around'.[376] The poor would also, according to 'Engel's law', spend a higher proportion of their income on (basic) food than would the better-off.[377] An interesting observation made by M. Prestwich in connection with the York Ordinances of 1301 and their enforcement shows that, whatever the intention of the legislator, pricing rules

[368] *YO*, 9.
[369] *RP* I:295a.
[370] *SR* I:264, st. 4 Edw. III, c.12.
[371] *SR* I:378, st. 37 Edw. III (1363), c.3.
[372] *Vita Edwardi Secundi*, 59. Note, however, that the *Anonimalle Chronicle* states that it was not made by the Ordainers 'nor by the wise men of the land, but by the king in his privy council' and proclaimed on the eve of Palm Sunday (15 March), as a *prive ordenance* which was enacted by the king and 'others of his privy council, without the assent of the lords of the land': *Anonimalle*, 88–91.
[373] *RP* I:295a.
[374] *CCR 1313–18*, 449.
[375] Dyer, *Standards of Living*, 55.
[376] Dyer, *Standards of Living*, 69; Bennett, *Women*, 272, citing D. and R. Attwater (eds), *The Book Concerning Piers the Plowman* (London, 1957), 21.
[377] Dyer, *Standards of Living*, 55.

could be used by 'lower orders' against an urban elite: he notes the high proportion of accusations of breach made against city freemen.[378]

It might have been in a king's financial interest to regulate the prices of various commodities in order that his own household could be supplied cheaply.[379] It might also have been to his financial benefit to enact price control statutes with financial penalties for breach of their provisions, since the amercements ought to find their way into the Exchequer. Some matters discussed in this chapter, however, can be used to argue against the primacy of financial self-interest. There is some question of the extent of royal financial gain from them once franchised out, as many of them were. There is also the fact that the price control legislation was expressed generally, dealing with sales between subjects, which did not obviously affect royal purchases. Royal purchases could, after all, be made under rights of purveyance, at a special rate.[380] There is also ample evidence of kings involving themselves in the supervision of assizes once the right to the profits of the jurisdiction had been granted away, showing a willingness to act in the sphere of price control even when doing so was not in the immediate financial interest of the king and government.

In contrast to royal action against usury, there is little sign of requests by the clergy for action against high prices, but there are several examples of kings passing or amending statutes as a response to the requests of other groups. Receipt of a petition of the magnates seems to have been one of the reasons for the enactment of the 1315 victual statute. The archbishops, bishops, earls and barons of the realm had petitioned the king, begging that he ordain a fixed price for cows, sheep, fowl, chickens, capons, doves and eggs.[381] Edward III was also prepared to alter his statutory schemes in relation to the price of wine at the instance of groups of merchants. Complaints were received from merchants in London and elsewhere, saying that the statute was impoverishing them, and at their request, inquiries were set up to adjust the prices set.[382] The Blakeney fish statute of 1357 was made 'by the advice of the merchants, wholesale buyers and ship owners'.[383] The 1363 statute including poultry prices was requested by the commons in Parliament. apparently alarmed at price inflation.[384] Richard II's government bowed to pressure from a group of petitioners when it repealed the wine statute of 1381 at the request of the commons in Parliament.[385] These examples suggest a readiness on the part of kings and governments to agree to the demands of important economic and political interest groups. Governments did not, however, always accede to requests for action against those selling at high prices, as can be seen from the fact that a petition by the commons in the Parliament at Cambridge in 1388, asking for change in the regime under the above statutes, did not receive a favourable

---

[378] *YO*, 6.

[379] J.M. Bennett speculates that the Assisa Cervisie 'was not solely an early instance of consumer protection legislation. The quasi-statute might have been designed to protect one consumer above all others: the royal household, which, because it purchased large quantities of ale as it moved about the realm, needed to be protected from inflated prices': Bennett, *Ale*, 101, citing W. Cunningham, *The Growth of English Industry and Commerce during the Early and Middle Ages* (Cambridge, 1910), 263.

[380] See further below at pp. 121–2.

[381] *RP* I:295a.

[382] *CCR 1330–33*, 545, 557–8 (1332).

[383] *SR* I:355, 31 Edw. III, st.3.

[384] *SR* II:378, 37 Edw. III, c.3; *RP* II:277; Waugh, *England in the Reign of Edward III*, 90.

[385] *SR* II:18, st. 5 Ric. II, c.4, repealed by st. 7 Ric. II, c.11, *SR* II: 34.

response.[386] This may be taken to suggest some divergence between governmental views on price regulation and the views of those represented in Parliament, in an apparent parallel with the attitude with which the commons' requests for action against usury were treated by Richard II and his government.

The problem of purveyance

As was the case with royal action against usury, royal action against high prices must be seen in the context of royal behaviour, and there is a potential difficulty in seeing a sincere or coherent royal policy against unfair returns for sales of goods when the matter of purveyance is considered. Purveyance involved compulsory sales to the king or others closely connected with him, and was seen as a (potentially) unfair process, injurious to the seller.[387] Kings and governments acknowledged that there might be problems with purveyance. Edward I stated his concern for poorer subjects who might be subject to prises.[388] Numerous statutes of the late thirteenth century and the fourteenth century deal with abuses in purveyance.[389] Some are concerned with ensuring that the price of goods is paid within a reasonable time, others with preventing unauthorised persons from purveying, or authorised purveyors from exceeding their authority or committing abuses.[390] Fairly severe penalties were stipulated, and it was envisaged that

---

[386] L.C. Hector and B.F. Harvey (eds), *The Westminster Chronicle (1381–94)* (Oxford, 1982), 356.

[387] On purveyance, see J.R. Maddicott, 'The English peasantry and the demands of the crown 1294–1342', 15, 26; C. Given-Wilson, 'Purveyance for the royal household 1362–1413', *Historical Research* 56 (1983), 145–63, no.134; Harriss, *King, Parliament and Public Finance*, 376–83; Ormrod, *Reign of Edward III*, 11, 21; W.R. Jones, 'Purveyance for war and the community of the realm', *Albion* 7 (1975), 300–16.

[388] Prestwich, *Edward I*, 582.

[389] *SR* I:27, Statute of Westminster I, 1275, c.1 (confirmed *SR* I:153–4, st. 2 Edw. II (1309)); *SR* I:175, *De Statuto p' clero inviolabiliter observand'* (1316); *SR* I:28, Statute of Westminster I, 1275, c.7.; *SR* I:116, Magna Carta (1297), c.19; *SR* I:125, *Statutum de Tallag'*, 1297 (confirmed *SR* I:262–3, st. 4 Edw. III (1330), cc.3, 4, confirmed *SR* I:265, st. 5 Edw. III (1331), c.2, confirmed *SR* I:276, 10 Edw. III (1336), st.2 c.1); *SR* I:137, *Articuli super cartas*, 1300, c.2. *EEJ*, 52: keepers of peace got power to arrest unjust purveyors, 1308: F. Palgrave (ed.), *The Parliamentary Writs and Writs of Military Summons*, 2 vols (London, 1830), vol. 2ii, app. pp. 8–9, 11–12; *SR* I:159, Ordinances, 1311, c.10; *SR* I:262–3, st. 4 Edw. III (1330), c.3 (confirmed *SR* I:265, st. 5 Edw. III (1331)); *SR* I:276, 10 Edw. III (1336), st.2 cc.2, 3; *SR* I:288, 14 Edw. III, st.1 (1340), c.19; *SR* I:319, 25 Edw. III, st.5 c.1; *SR* I:347, st. 28 Edw. III (1354), c.12; *SR* I:371, st. 36 Edw. III (1362), cc.2–6; *SR* I:321, 25 Edw. III (1351–2), st.5 cc.6, 15. General confirmation of purveyance statutes: *SR* I:301, 18 Edw. III (1344), st.2 c.7; *SR* II:30, st. 6 Ric. II (1382); *SR* II:33, st. 7 Ric. II (1383), c.8; *SR* II:37, st. 8 Ric. II (1384). Statutes concerning purveyance in Ireland: *SR* I:193 (1323–4); *SR* I:358, 31 Edw. III (1357), st.4 c.4.

[390] Payment within a reasonable time: *SR* I:27, Statute of Westminster I, 1275, c.1, provided that payment was to be made 'incontinently'; *SR* I:28, Statute of Westminster I, 1275, c.7, payment to be made within forty days generally; *SR* I:116, Magna Carta, 1297, c.19, provided that payment should be made at once to those not of the town where purveyance was made, unless there should be a voluntary respite, and within forty days to those of the town. *SR* I:262–3, st. 4 Edw. III (1330), c.3, *SR* I:265, st. 4 Edw. III (1330), c.3, provided that payment was to be made before the king left the verge. This principle was also contained in *SR* I:288, 14 Edw. III, st.1 (1340), c.19. *SR* I:347, st. 28 Edw. III (1354), c.12, introduced special rules for small-scale purchases, expressly for the benefit of poor subjects: for purchases under 20s, payment should be immediate, purchases for 20s or above should be paid for within the next quarter year, at a place convenient to the seller. *SR* I:371, st. 36 Edw. III (1362), c.2, provides that all purveyances should be paid for immediately.

Preventing unauthorised purveyance: *SR* I:137, *Articuli super cartas*, 1300, c.2; *SR* I:365, st. 34 Edw. III (1360–1), c.2; *SR* I:371, st. 36 Edw. III (1362), c.2; *SR* I:371, st. 36 Edw. III (1362), c.6; *SR* II:93, st. 20 Ric. II (1396–7), c.5.

Abuses by authorised purveyors: *SR* I:28, Statute of Westminster I, 1275, c.7; *SR* I:137, *Articuli super cartas*, 1300, c.2; *SR* I:319, 25 Edw. III (1351–2), st.5 c.1; *SR* I:371, st. 36 Edw. III (1362), cc.2, 4, 5; *SR* I:321, 25 Edw. III (1351–2), st.5 cc.6, 15.

individuals – either the aggrieved party or someone else if he chose not to proceed – would be able to sue offenders for (multiple) damages.[391] Some, puzzlingly, tried to insist that no purveyance would be made contrary to the will of the seller.[392] The 1311 Ordinances attempted to keep prises to 'ancient' precedents.[393] None, however, show any doubt of the royal right to insist on these not-wholly-voluntary sales. They cast some light on ideas of value and fair pricing. Complaint is made in a statute of 1300 that purveyors are giving much less than the value of goods.[394] A number of statutes refer to the 'true value' ('la verroie value').[395] A statute of 1330 notes abuses involving taking goods for less than their value ('a meyndre value qils ont valu', 'a meyndre pris qeles ont valu').[396] A statute of 1351–2 mentions both 'la verroie value' and the price common in the nearest markets ('come curt comunement en les proscheins marchees').[397] A 1362 statute also mentions 'le pris par quel autiels vitailles sont venduz comunement, en marchees environ'.[398]

Even more than with royal practice involving participation in usury, the apparently abusive practice of purveyance should alert us to the fact that royal ideas about fair trade were not necessarily in line with modern ideas of fair contracts, and were overlaid with privilege and status. A genuine difference could be seen between royal conduct in purveyance (where the king was the 'customer') and in setting and enforcing price regulations, for the benefit of other customers.

Conclusion

In the late thirteenth and fourteenth centuries, the basic price regulations for bread, wine and ale were maintained in force and to these were added price regulations for many more commodities. The increase in number of items covered seems to come particularly in the aftermath of the Black Death, if one confines the search to the statute roll. If the evidence of Edward I's legislation for York, the peace commissions of 1307 and 1308 and short-lived poultry and victual statute of 1315 are taken into account, however, it can be seen that the trend towards a wider scope of royal regulation was present from an earlier point. Where prices were regulated, different mechanisms were used. Private and local bodies were

---

[391] *SR* I:27, Statute of Westminster I, 1275, c.1, provided for a convicted offender to be committed to the king's prison, then make fine and be punished according to the nature of his offence and the king and his court's discretion. *SR* I:137, *Articuli super cartas*, 1300, c.2 stated that offending purveyors were to be put out of royal service for ever and imprisoned at the king's pleasure. *SR* I:159, Ordinances 1311, c.10, and *SR* I:265, st.,5 Edw. III (1331), c.2, confirmed *SR* I:319, 25 Edw. III (1351–2), st.5 c.1 provided that the taker of unauthorised and involuntary prises was to be treated as a robber or thief. *SR* I:371, st. 36 Edw. III (1362), c.2 confirms this, stipulating punishment of life and member. *SR* II:93, st. 20 Ric. II (1396–7), c.5 specified imprisonment until the offender should make fine. Multiple damages were prescribed in the *SR* I:27. Statute of Westminster I, 1275, c.1.

[392] *SR* I:125, *Statutum de Tallag'*, 1297 (no purveyance 'sine voluntate & assensu'); *SR* I:288, 14 Edw. III (1340), st.1 c.19 (purveyance to be made 'pur foer fait entre les acatours & les vendours & p' le bon gree des vendours'); *SR* I:371, st. 36 Edw. III (1362), c.2 (purveyance, changed in this statute to 'buying', because of the bad reputation of purveyors, to be made in a convenient and easy manner – 'covenable & ease manere' – without duress, compulsions, menace or other villainy).

[393] *SR* I:159, Ordinances, 1311, c.10.

[394] *SR* I:137, *Articuli super cartas*, 1300, c.2, 'bien meins q' la value'.

[395] *SR* I:159, Ordinances, 1311, c.10; *SR* I:319, 25 Edw. III (1351–2), st.5 c.1.

[396] *SR* I:262–3, st. 4 Edw. III (1330), c.3.

[397] *SR* I:321, 25 Edw. III (1351–2), st.5 cc.6, 15.

[398] *SR* I:371, st. 36 Edw. III (1362), c.2.

frequently allowed or instructed to carry out the basic enforcement, but they were often to be accountable to the king for their conduct, a fact which was made more specific as the fourteenth century progressed. Variation was also found in the punishment specified for offenders. Punishments ranged from amercements to corporal punishment, with forfeiture of goods, imprisonment and abjuration of one's craft also prescribed in some measures. The trend in statutes of the fourteenth century, however, was towards financial punishment of price control offences other than the assizes of bread and ale. A common thread running through the statutes was that it was only the seller of goods at inflated prices who was ordered to be punished. Punishment or compensation of the buyer was not usually mentioned. In this sense, there is a similarity between royal price regulations and royal measures against usury: neither sought, in general, to penalise or compensate the 'customer'.

There is no sign of a general desire to ensure absolute equality in exchange. The idea which emerges is of an intention to ensure that sellers were not charging wildly excessive prices for certain key products. There were some signs of aspirations to extend the scope of royal price regulation in the early fourteenth century, but not of centralised fixing of exact prices for all goods. There is no evidence of a settled policy of intervention in all sales to ensure that a fair price was charged: royal action was limited in scope to sales of certain commodities. The implicit policy is one of becoming involved in price regulation when there was evidence or danger of particular sellers abusing their position, either, in the case of the assizes of bread and ale, because they were selling staple goods needed by the whole population, or in other cases because there was, or was liable to be, a scarcity of a particular commodity and sellers were able to ask whatever price they wished. Kings and governments could not and did not hope to protect every consumer in his or her bargains, to make sure that he or she was charged a fair price for every purchase, but they could and did act to prevent abusive pricing in particular fields, which would give unjustified and shocking profits to sellers of particular items. Once an item came to be covered by price regulation, however, it did not usually leave the fold, despite variations in its price, or the disappearance of the emergency which had caused its price to be regulated. In this way, the scope of royal price control was increased over the thirteenth and fourteenth centuries. There was a burst of activity in terms of legislation and efforts to enforce price controls after the Black Death, in conjunction with the legislation on labourers, but a general tendency to increase the scope of royal price control can be seen throughout the period. This expansion was in some cases inspired by 'local' examples, and often required local 'input' in the form of refinement and specification of standards, as well as 'local' enforcement.

As far as enforcement is concerned, the evidence is harder to interpret, but it can be argued that the system was taken seriously. There is ample evidence of direct enforcement by kings and governments of their regulations, and, where the right to exercise jurisdiction was granted out, it was not forgotten about. Kings retained rights of supervision over franchise holders, and it is very clear that these were exercised. The evidence provided by franchise holders themselves in the shape of manorial and borough records shows that, there were at least some jurisdictions where the price control regulations were enforced in an adequate manner, and these should be considered alongside the examples of abuse which can be found in royal records.

Evidence of the fact that price control was seen as an area in which kings and governments thought it their duty to make serious efforts can be found in an examination of the history of government action after statutes were enacted. If it seemed that there were problems with the working of the statutes, they were revised, as can be seen in Edward I's revision of the procedure for punishing offenders against the assize of wine, and the efforts of Edward II and Richard II to combat malpractice or suspicion of malpractice by those who administered the assizes of bread and ale, or they were withdrawn, as was the case with the poultry statute of 1315.[399] As mentioned, the modern assumption that the laws were at best ineffective, at worst damaging, does not seem to have been made by a large number of people in medieval England. Medieval opinion certainly did not assume that price fixing measures must fail.[400]

Finally, some comparisons with the material on usury may be made. Royal intervention in subjects' bargains to control the price of sales of goods differed from royal action against usury in a number of ways. First, the 'stranger angle' is virtually absent: there is no trace of action on prices having been directed against particular minority groups such as Jews and Italians, whereas action against usury was partly, though not wholly, directed against such groups.[401] Secondly, the Church does not seem to have sought to exercise any jurisdiction over sales at excessive prices. Thirdly, whilst the greatest efforts against usury seem to have been made in the reign of Edward I, the scope of royal action on prices increased throughout the fourteenth century.

The broad assertion that an increasing level of royal attention was focussed on price control in the fourteenth century must be further refined. In particular, it is necessary to consider the different emphases within the field of price control itself. This chapter has considered direct controls, setting prices or setting up mechanisms to fix them. Some royal action, however, attempted to control prices more indirectly, by concentrating on the question of whether a bargain or series of bargains was being made with the intention or result of inflating prices, and it is this action which will be considered in the next chapter.

---

[399] The Statute of York of 1318 provided that they were not to be involved in selling controlled items whilst in charge of administering the assizes: *SR* I:178. The principle was re-iterated in a statute of 1382: *SR* II:28, 6 Ric. II, st.1 c.9.

[400] There is even earlier evidence that some measures may have been regarded as having worked too well, as is alleged of King John's wine price decree, which caused the price of wine to fall so that 'the land was filled with drink and drinkers': Hudson, *Formation*, 135.

[401] On occasion, however, urban rules might operate different price levels for 'insiders' and 'outsiders': see, e.g., the London *Liber de Assisa Panis* and its different prices for bakers from London and those from Stratford.

4

Laws against Forestalling,
Regrating and Related Conduct

The following appears in the King's Bench Indictment File for the session at Chelmsford in Michaelmas 1352.

> *Item dicunt quod William de Hereford (FF) de Wodeham Ferers pultarius est communis forstallere de pulteria ad grave dampnum patrie & vendit ad triplum ultra quod em[i]t.*[1]
> (They say that William de Hereford (who has made fine) of Woodham Ferrers, poulterer, is a common forestaller of poultry, to the great damage of the county, and sells for three times the price at which he bought.)

William's offence brings us to the last area of royal intervention which will be examined: action taken against certain retailing practices variously described as forestalling, regrating, engrossing and a range of related but less defined practices. In modern terms, this intervention would fall under the heading of action against 'abusive monopoly practices', or 'anti-competitive practices', though such terms are nowhere to be found in medieval royal sources, making it necessary to use more cumbersome expressions.

'Forestalling', the offence of William of Hereford, involved contracting sales of goods outside legally approved markets There was a shift in the meaning of 'forestalling' over the course of the late medieval period. As has been demonstrated, this term was originally used to describe a violent offence – an offence called *'forstal'* appears in the laws of Cnut, meaning an ambush on the king's highway – but, during the late thirteenth and fourteenth centuries, it came to be used to indicate a (more or less) consensual but illegitimate bargain, a sale contracted outside a licensed market.[2] The old sense of the term was, however, slow to disappear, and had not fully disappeared by the end of the fourteenth century. There are occasional indications that the old idea of violent interception remained, as will be seen later in this chapter. It is with the consensual, rather than the forcible, offence which I am concerned, since the forcible offence is a matter of royal intervention to prevent violence rather than an example of royal intervention in bargains, but it is necessary to note that these two concepts of forestalling can be detected in the thirteenth and fourteenth centuries. 'Regrating' will be used here to mean the practice of buying goods in a licensed market and selling them on to a third party at a higher price. 'Engrossing', is sometimes used by modern

---

[1] JUST 1/267 m.18.
[2] Warren, *Governance*, 48; Cam, *London Eyre 1321*, lxxvii; Britnell, 'Forstall'.

commentators, and was occasionally used in the fourteenth century. It originally meant wholesale dealing but came to cover conduct similar to the definition of regrating given above, particularly the practice of buying goods and obtaining such a proportion of available supplies of a commodity that one could dictate the price to potential buyers, or 'buying up supplies in advance, . . . and withholding them from market until the price had risen'.[3] 'Related conduct' will be used to cover other practices outside these core meanings which nevertheless involve making bargains intended to or deemed likely to raise the price at which certain goods could be sold. In particular, agreements between sellers of a particular item to sell it only at a certain price would be covered by this phrase. As will become apparent, there was little consistency in the way in which the terms were employed even within the area of consensual bargains. The fact that terminology was not settled should alert us to the possibility that ideas were in the process of change in this area in the thirteenth and fourteenth centuries.

Royal action: the scope and nature of legal intervention

As was the case with some price fixing laws, it has been demonstrated that important elements of the laws under consideration originated with 'local' models and 'royal private' models before being adopted 'centrally' and 'nationally'. It has been noted that rules in charters of the 1250s and 1260s making brokerage illegal, and forbidding merchants from going to meet goods destined for the town or city, 'came together' in 1274–5 in rules issued by the marshalsea to prohibit 'forestalling', at first only around the king's court'. The marshalsea rules were applied in some local courts in the 1290s, and in 1307 commissioners were ordered by Edward II to enforce them nationally, from which time, 'forestalling was penalised by local authorities as a statutory offence'.[4] This account is of great importance, and must be borne in mind, but from the point of view of this book, it is not the end of the story. The rules in charters are not entirely 'local' or 'non-royal' – they were, after all, approved by the king. Their proliferation into a number of different areas suggests some conscious copying, perhaps the growth of a rule which was more than 'local' though less than 'national'. The rules did not 'come together' accidentally in the marshalsea: active intervention was required, and there would seem to have been a decision that they should be used nationally – a decision which is no less interesting for there being antecedents in 'local' or 'private' measures.[5]

Consensual forestalling and regrating seem to have been penalised by royal measures from at least the reign of Henry III. Under the *Judicium Pillorie*, the same tribunal which was to inquire into breaches of the assizes of bread, ale, and wine was also to ask about forestallers who bought anything before the 'due and accustomed hour' ('ante horam debitam . . . statutam') or who went out of the town, to meet goods on their way to market, intending to sell them in the town to

---

[3] Wood, *Medieval Economic Thought*, 139; Gilchrist, *CEA*, 61. See, e.g., Putnam, *PJP*, 68, no.104, for a medieval example of the use of this term.

[4] Britnell, *Commercialisation*, 93, and 'Forstall', 90–2, 97–9, 100–2.

[5] D.L. Farmer, 'Marketing the produce of the countryside' in E. Miller (ed.), *Agrarian History of England and Wales, vol. III, 1348–1500* (Cambridge, 1991), 324, 426.

regraters who would sell them on at a higher price than that at which they would have been sold if the original vendors had come to town and sold them.[6] It is not absolutely clear whether the second offence, going out of town to meet sellers of goods, indicates coerced or consensual transactions, but the first offence involves buying, and indicates a consensual bargain.[7]

Statutes and orders against forestalling were enacted at a number of points throughout the period under consideration. The *Statutum Mareschaucie*, which, it has been demonstrated, originated for the instruction of officials of the king's marshalsea, came to be regarded as a full statute in later years, certainly from the early part of Edward II's reign, and possibly from the latter part of his father's reign (another example of this period being important in the development of royal intervention in relation to the terms of subjects' bargains to set alongside apparent changes in the focus of usury cases and the beginning of an increase in the scope of royal ambition with regard to price fixing seen in previous chapters).[8] This order or piece of legislation clearly understood 'forestalling' to be a consensual transaction.[9] The *Composicio* contains a definition of consensual forestalling.[10] The York Ordinances of 1301 prohibits (apparently consensual) forestalling of fish and other goods.[11] Commissions of 1307 provided for investigation of consensual forestalling.[12] Forestalling was prohibited during the course of the eyre by the proclamations at the beginning of the eyre, at least in the eyre of Northamptonshire 1329–30.[13] There was legislation against consensual forestalling in 1351 when an ordinance prohibited forestalling of wines, victuals and all other goods and merchandise coming to towns by land or water.[14] A statute of 1353 provided that no one was to go by land or water to forestall goods before they were brought into towns or ports.[15] In 1362 and 1378, it was ordered that existing legislation against forestalling should be enforced.[16]

As well as these general measures, forestalling was prohibited in particular trades at points throughout the fourteenth century. A statute of 1315 referring to the Gascon wine trade ordered that Englishmen should not cross the sea to forestall wine.[17] A similar provision was made in 1353, also covering 'engrossing' of Gascon

---

[6] *SR* I:201–2.

[7] It should, of course, be borne in mind that the distinction between the forced and the consensual is not always easy to draw, as is demonstrated in the jurisprudence on the tort of battery and criminal offences against the person. One cannot, however, hope to reconstruct the nuances of the medieval conception of consent from the terse materials available in this context, so the forcible/consensual dichotomy must be used.

[8] Britnell, 'Forstall', 100; Britnell, *Commercialisation*, 93.

[9] Britnell, 'Forstall', 94–5.

[10] *SR* I:202–4; Britnell, 'Forstall', 94.

[11] *YO*, 13–14.

[12] *CPR 1307–13*, 29–31, 53–5, 361–2.

[13] W. Sutherland (ed.), *The Eyre of Northamptonshire 3–4 Edw. III 1329–30*, Selden Society vol. 97 for 1981 and vol. 98 for 1982 (London, 1983), I, 9.

[14] *RP* II:232a; *SR* I:315. This statute presumed that payment was made, and so seems to indicate consensual forestalling. The *Little Red Book of Bristol* contains a fourteenth-century copy of the royal 'statute' against forestalling: *LRB*, II, p. 220, f.192.

[15] *SR* I:337–8, 27 Edw. III, st.2 c.11. This clause concerns those who meet merchants to 'forestall or buy' their goods before they reach a market, and therefore concerns consensual forestalling alone, or else both consensual and coerced transactions.

[16] *RP* II:270b; *RP* III:48a; *SR* II:7, 2 Ric. II, st.1.

[17] Entry for 1315 in *Vita Edwardi Secundi*, 59.

wine.[18] There was legislation against forestalling in the herring trade in 1357.[19] In a statute of 1382, hosts in coastal towns were prohibited from forestalling fish or other victuals.[20]

With the exception of the *Judicium Pillorie*, and the York Ordinances of 1301, the term 'regrating' or 'regrater' is not seen in legislation until considerably later than 'forestalling'.[21] A statute of 1353 provided that justices were to be appointed to enquire into and punish the deeds and outrages of hostelers, regraters, labourers and others.[22] Conduct which fits the definition of regrating (or engrossing) given above was banned in an ordinance of 1357 regulating the trade in salt fish at Blakeney, which provided that fish bought there was not to be kept in houses to be sold at a later date at retail.[23] 'Regrating' of wool and other 'merchandise of the staple' was prohibited in a statute of 1390.[24] The fact that neither the word 'regrating' nor conduct clearly involving purchases within a licensed market appear much in statutes until the 1350s does not necessarily show a 'progression' from regarding only forestalling outside markets as an offence to regarding profiteering within the same market as an offence too. It is probable that both ideas were present from the late thirteenth century onwards, but were not consistently described using separate terms.

'Related conduct', in the shape of concerted action by a group to increase prices, can be seen to have been the target of the provision concerning the behaviour of hosts in coastal towns in the statute of 1357 mentioned above, and was also the subject of a prohibition in the statute of 1362 concerning those who made a bargain or confederacy (*coveigne*) to set high prices for victuals, to increase their own profit.[25] The *Composicio* includes an 'information' offence. Forestallers are portrayed and condemned for telling merchants that they could sell more dearly than they had thought. Such provisions are not uncommon in 'local' rules and practice, but this is the only possibly 'national' measure in which such a rule appears.[26]

Although this book is concerned with consensual bargains and the ways in which kings and governments intervened to regulate their substance, it should be noted that the rules against consensual forestalling, regrating and similar conduct existed against a background of royal regulation of coercive practices which sometimes seems to have been intertwined with regulation of the consensual practices under consideration here. In 1315, for example, Edward II issued orders to the sheriffs of London to deal both with consensual forestalling and with forcible forestalling of victuals coming to London.[27] The coercion of those with merchandise to sell, so that they would sell to regraters rather than to consumers, may have been a concern of the 1335 Statute of York, which gave all people the right to buy and sell goods in

[18] *SR* I:331, 27 Edw. III, st.1 c.5.
[19] *SR* I:353, 31 Edw. III, st.2.
[20] *SR* II:28–9. This statute concerned both coercive conduct on the part of hosts and also consensual forestalling and regrating on the part of London fishmongers.
[21] *YO*, 11–12.
[22] *SR* I:330, 27 Edw. III, st.1 c.3.
[23] *SR* I:356, 31 Edw. III, st.3 c.2.
[24] *SR* II:76, 14 Ric. II, c.4.
[25] *SR* I:353, 31 Edw. III, st.2.; *RP* II:270b.
[26] *SR* I:202–4. For similar local rules in Colchester, see Britnell, 'Price setting', 8, and *Colchester*, 36.
[27] *LC*, f.134a, pp. 678–9; f.134b, pp. 680–2. Both seem to have elements of coercive and consensual forestalling.

markets and towns without hindrance, though this was certainly also concerned with overcoming restrictive rules in certain urban areas against 'foreigners' selling at retail.[28] Freedom for all to come and sell wine and other goods in the staple, cities, boroughs, towns and ports in the realm, in gross or at retail, or by parcels, at their will, to anyone they wished, was guaranteed in 1351.[29] A statute of 1378 confirmed these statutes for aliens who wished to come and trade at retail and in gross in victuals and small wares, though there was some immunity from these regulations for London at points in the reigns of Edward III and Richard II.[30] A more specialised application of such rules can be seen in the Great Yarmouth Herring Statute of 1357, which provided that fishermen should be free to sell their herring to all at the fair of Great Yarmouth without hindrance.[31] Even more restrictive conduct relating to sales of goods was proscribed by royal legislation in a statute of 1354 which provided that no ship was to be compelled to come to any port of England or to stay there against the will of the masters, mariners or merchants whose goods were on board. They were to be allowed to sell their goods as and when they wished.[32] In 1382, hosts were also ordered not to stop fishermen or victuallers selling where and to whom they wished.[33] It can be deduced that a link was perceived between the rules against forestalling, regrating and related consensual conduct and the rules against coercive and restrictive trade practices.

As well as making rules at national level against forestalling and regrating, kings and governments were also involved to some extent in the rules made on a local level. London was particularly closely regulated in this as in other commercial matters. Pronouncements had already been made on the subject of forestalling in London in the reign of Henry III. His charter of 1268 to the city had provided that no one should meet merchants coming to the city with their merchandise, to buy their goods in order to sell them on in the city.[34] This provision reappeared in charters to London by Henry's successors.[35] Edward I was involved in the creation of London ordinances on the regraters or 'hucksters' of fish and poultry. In 1276, he ordered the civic authorities to make statutes regulating them.[36] Such ordinances were made, banning forestalling outside the city, and restricting hucksters as to when they might make their purchases in the city so that they would be unable to buy until after the king, barons and citizens of London had purchased their goods, and ordinances were made concerning forestalling and similar practices in particular trades.[37] Further measures concerning forestalling and regrating in

---

[28] *SR* I:269, 9 Edw. III, st.1 c.1.

[29] *RP* II:249a.

[30] *SR* II:7, 2 Ric. II, st.1, confirming 9 Edw. III, st.1 c.12, and 25 Edw. III, st.2 c.5; Ormrod, *Reign of Edward III*, 133.

[31] *SR* I:353, 31 Edw. III, st.2. The ordinance was to apply not only in Great Yarmouth but in all towns where herring was taken and dried.

[32] *SR* I:348, 28 Edw. III, c.13.

[33] *SR* II:28, st. 5 Ric. II, c.4.

[34] *LC*, II, i, 251–5; *CChR 1257–1300*, 98; W. de Gray Birch, *The Historical Charter and Constitutional Documents of the City of London* (rev. edn, London, 1887), 38; *LA*, 138.

[35] e.g. *CChR 1257–1300*, 447 (1299).

[36] Walford, 'Early laws and customs', 71; *CLB, A*, 215–19; CLRO, Liber Ordinacionem, ff.190b–202b.

[37] Walford, 'Early laws and customs', 71; *CLB, A*, 215–19; LB, A, f.129b; Liber Ordinacionum, f.135r; *LC*, ff.66r and v, 68r, 198r; Liber Memorandum, pp. 42–3, cited in Britnell, 'Forstall', 97–8; *LA*, 229, 231, 243, 308, 310.

London were enacted during the period in which London was in Edward I's hands.[38] Provisions concerning forestalling and regrating were repeated and expanded on numerous occasions in the reigns of Edward III and Richard II, both by civic authorities and by the king.[39]

London was not the only area in which forestalling, regrating and related conduct received attention. The charters of several towns (and the universities of Oxford and Cambridge) include prohibitions of forestalling and similar conduct.[40] Towns also made their own regulations. This must have been essential in terms of defining the exact scope of the offence, since it was necessary to specify the time and location of the local licensed market.[41]

Subject matter

'National' statutes against forestalling, regrating and engrossing often concentrated on victuals, especially fish and wine, though they also often left the class of items covered rather indefinite. A parallel can be drawn here with the price fixing laws, which generally concentrated on specific categories of goods, usually victuals, but which occasionally showed a conception of a more general principle which should apply to all sales of goods. Thirteenth-century 'national' legislation against forestalling was expressed in general terms, but fourteenth-century legislation concentrated more on particular commodities. This change may relate to the evolution of the definition of forestalling from forcible seizure to consensual sale, since whilst all forcible forestalling could be argued to be disruptive and worthy of prosecution, once the word 'forestalling' came to be used for a consensual offence, only those instances which caused severely adverse economic effects might seem worthy of attention. It is clear that universal coverage was not a prime concern for fourteenth-century legislators, as can be seen in the exclusion of common fish from the ban on forestalling fish in the statute of 1382.[42] The concentration on victuals suggests a desire to ensure a reasonably-priced food supply for everyone. There is evidence of a growing focus on the forestalling of fish in the fourteenth-century legislation, which may be explained by the fact that the danger posed by forestalling was particularly acute with regard to the supply of fish, especially sea fish, as the supply and the price could be controlled by a limited number of people. There was

---

[38] London was in Edward I's hand from June 1285 and was put under a warden for thirteen years: *Thirteenth Century*, 626–30; Liber Ordinacionem, ff.195r ff.

[39] See, e.g., LB, E, f.313 (1335); *CLB, F*, 100–1, f.81b (1344); Riley, *Memorials*, 220 (1345); *CLB, F*, 141, f.119 (1357); *CLB, G*, 138, 146, ff.99b, 100, 107 (1362–3); *CLB, G*, 271, f.259b (1370); *CLB, G*, 278, f.235 (1371); Riley, *Memorials*, 347; *LA*, 396 (1382–3); LB, H, f.172 (1383).

[40] Oxford 1255, Great Yarmouth 1256, 1306, Canterbury 1256, Grimsby 1258, Bakewell 1286, Chesterfield 1294: A. Ballard and J. Tait (eds), *British Borough Charters 1216–1307* (Cambridge, 1923), 294–8; *Foedera* I, 323; *RP* V:426; JUST 1/705 m.26d (Oxford, charter temp. Henry III, proffered at eyre, 1285); *CPR 1292–1301*, 18 (1293) (Cambridge: Edward I, Edward II, Edward III and Richard II all confirmed Henry III's grant concerning regraters); *CPR 1307–13*, 119 (1309); *CChR*, vol. III, *1300–1326*, 332 (1317); *CPR 1327–1330*, 60 (1327); *CChR*, vol. V, *1341–1417*, 247 (1378). Other similar examples can be seen in Edward I's charter to Melcombe: *CChR*, vol. II, *1257–1300*, 224 (1280); in Edward III's charter to Clifton, Dartmouth and Hardenesse: *CChR*, vol. V, *1341–1417*, 3 (1341); in Richard II's charter to Bedford: *CChR*, vol. V, *1341–1417*, 357 (1396). F.W. Maitland (ed.), *Records of the Parliament holden at Westminster on the Twenty-Eighth Day of February in the 33rd Year of the Reign of King Edward the First AD 1305* (London, 1893), 45 (Oxford, 1305, Edward I approves agreement between the university and town authorities concerning regraters).

[41] See, e.g., W. Hudson and J.C. Tingey, *Records of the City of Norwich*, 2 vols (Norwich, 1906, 1910), I, 183.

[42] *SR* II:28, st. 5 Ric. II, c.4.

also a public health concern about (fresh) fish being bought up and kept for a long time, in an attempt to sell it at a high price despite it being unwholesome.[43]

In practice, almost all cases brought before the King's Bench and Justices of the Peace as forestalling, regrating or similar conduct concerned victuals, particularly fish, though salt, meat, grain, poultry, wine, iron and victuals in general are also mentioned in presentments.[44] Examples of non-victuals being forestalled appear in a Close Roll record of 1309 relating to a Warwickshire man found to be a common forestaller of timber and in a peace roll of 1361 from Yorkshire, where a man was prosecuted for forestalling iron.[45] Items mentioned as having been forestalled in the Wakefield tourns were: poultry, eggs, butter, cheese and other victuals, oats, meat and fish. In the Sutton manor court rolls, where the subject matter of the bargain is mentioned in forestalling cases, it is always fish. Similarly in other local courts, most charges related to dealings with victuals. The records of courts in Colchester between 1310 and 1352 show examples of forestallers of poultry, cheese, eggs, corn, fish, oysters, apples and pears.[46] The Tamworth borough court rolls from 1289 to 1358 contain presentments of forestallers of ox hides as well as forestallers of fish and salt; wood and coal were reported to have been forestalled in a case before London civic courts in 1300, and fruit was the subject of forestalling accusations in London in 1303–4 and 1305–6.[47]

Substance of the rules

Because definitions of forestalling and related offences and royal attitudes towards them were in the process of changing during the fourteenth century, 'the rules' cannot be stated in a simple, definitive fashion which applies throughout the late thirteenth and fourteenth centuries. Pinpointing 'the rules' at any particular point also has its difficulties. Sometimes, entries in court rolls do not show anything more than the fact that people were reported, prosecuted or convicted for breach of the laws proscribing forestalling and/or regrating. The roll of the Northumberland eyre 1293, for example, contains a long list of 'forestallers' from Newcastle in the amercements section, but gives no details beyond the fact that the offence was 'forestalling', and the level of amercement imposed.[48] Fourteenth-century records such as those of the King's Bench and Justices of the Peace, are slightly fuller, making it possible to offer some description of the sorts of offences being brought to the attention of courts.

Changing scope, definitions, terminology
R.H. Britnell has suggested that some of the confusion concerning the definition of forestalling offences in local courts is connected with the overlap with already

---

[43] See, e.g., *Court Baron*, 26.
[44] JUST 1/267 m.18 (poultry); KB 9/38 m.25 (victuals); JUST 1/268 m.4, KB 9/144 m.21 (grain); KB 9/141 m.59 (fish); KB 9/102 m.6 (iron); Putnam, *PJP*, 81 no.290, JUST 1/193 m.8d (meat, fish, grain, various victuals); Putnam, *PJP*, 64 no.29, JUST 1/195 m.2 (salt).
[45] *CCR 1307–13*, 92; JUST 1/1135 m.5.
[46] I.H. Jeayes (ed.), *Court Rolls of the Borough of Colchester 1310–79*, 3 vols (Colchester, 1921).
[47] M.K. Dale (ed.), *Court Rolls of Tamworth* (Tamworth, 1959), 50, 52, 66, 68, 72, 96, 99, 107, 114, 115, 117; LB, C, f.49; *CEMCR*, 158, 238.
[48] JUST 1/651 m.35.

existing marketing regulations in the urban context.[49] In royal courts, this may also be part of the explanation, but the genesis of forestalling as a coercive offence is probably also a factor. In some early judicial commissions, there is doubt as to whether forcible or consensual forestalling is to be understood. In the Norwich commission of 1304, for example, the complaint upon which it was founded contains elements of (allegedly) coercive and consensual conduct. The 'poor men of the commonalty of the town of Norwich' had complained that 'certain rich men and forestallers' of Norwich, 'by collusion amoiongst themselves buy from merchants of those parts bringing victuals and other goods to the city for sale such goods without and within the city before they are exposed for sale, and afterwards expose them at higher prices, and prevent victuals and other goods from being brought for sale to the town by the hands of the sellers or others but only by the hands of their own servants'.[50] In the proceedings before 'keepers of the peace' in Tendring Hundred under a commission of 1308 including forestalling, it is common form in allegations of forestalling to note that forestallers' activities mean that those who want to come and sell in person are prevented from so doing, which sounds as if it is either a matter of coercion, or, perhaps, a vestigial verbal formula deriving from the formerly coercive nature of the offence.[51]

Coercive or semi-coercive conduct in the nature of forestalling and regrating was sometimes reported in King's Bench indictments. The indictment file for the session at St Albans in 1354 contains a presentment by Berkhamsted town of a man not allowing strangers to sell as they pleased. It was claimed that Henry Mathe, a fisherman of Berkhamsted, had stopped a stranger fisherman in the town, and made him sell herrings at two for a penny in future, whereas the stranger had wanted to sell three herrings for a penny. Henry was held to be a forestaller of victuals coming to the town.[52] More widespread, concerted, coercion was alleged in an indictment before the King's Bench at Shrewsbury in 1374. Here, it was presented that four men would not allow any stranger to sell cloth from Wales in the vill of Shrewsbury, unless they sold the whole bale. The four bought 'by oppression, by regrating', all such bales coming to the vill from Wales and sold them in shorter lengths at their pleasure by regrating for a much higher price than that at which the strangers wanted to sell them.[53] Coercive 'regrating' involving not allowing others to sell fish in a particular place can be seen in an indictment in the file for the King's Bench session of 1392 in York.[54]

The complexity caused by the development of consensual forestalling from the ancient offence of *forstal* can be seen even at the end of the fourteenth century. Traces of the old offence of *forstal* can be seen in the 1390s, as a presentment from a Yorkshire King's Bench indictment file shows. The vill of Hedon presented that William de Coton of Wyton was a common forestaller of grain in various market vills in Yorkshire and on market days 'lay in wait' in roads leading to the markets, buying each bushel for 12d less than it could be sold in the market to which it was

[49] Britnell, 'Forstall', 101.
[50] *CPR 1301–7*, 294.
[51] H. Cam, *Liberties and Communities in Medieval England* (London, 1963), 165, 170–2.
[52] KB 9/38 m.25 (1354).
[53] KB 9/102 m.6.
[54] KB 9/144 m.2d.

going.[55] This has the appearance of a hybrid between a non-consensual offence (hence the lying in wait) and a consensual offence (hence the description of buying the grain at a low price rather than taking it by force).

Court rolls show some evidence of the lack of a strict boundary between the concepts of forestalling and regrating, as can be seen in one presentment from a 1362 indictment file from the King's Bench session in York, which stated that three men had been forestalling meat and fish in a market.[56] At times, 'hoarding' cases were presented as forestalling. In a case from 1351 from the peace roll of Devon, it was presented that, although grain and other merchandise coming to Barnstaple, Toryton and Bideford on market and fair days should have been exposed for sale and sold for a reasonable price, Henry Hoxhull of Toryton bought the grain and merchandise, detained it and refused to sell it, 'in oppression and impoverishment of the people'.[57] In one similar case, the term 'engrossing' was used as well as 'forestalling'.[58] Both buying outside a market and selling on goods so bought might be described as 'forestalling', as in a case on the peace roll for Devon from 1351–3, where nine men were presented as common forestallers of meat, fish, grain and various other victuals, buying these things outside Barnstaple, Toryton and elsewhere at a small price and selling in these vills for a higher price at their will to the damage of the country.[59] At a 'local' level, those offering to pay too much were also sometimes described as forestallers.[60] 'Forestalling' and 'engrossing' were even, at times, used with respect to practices in the labour market.[61]

The Norwich leet rolls show the development of the classification of the offences under consideration in this chapter in one 'local' jurisdiction. In the 1277–8 record mentioned, the offence of buying goods outside the market is not called forestalling. In the roll for 1288–9, the terms 'forestalment and forbarrment' are used to describe offences committed in the market, and 'forestalling' is also mentioned alone, though without details. In the roll for 1295–6, some light is cast on the offence of 'forbarrment', which seems to accord with the definition of forestalling given at the start of this chapter, in that a man was presented as a 'forbarrer' for 'privily leading merchants by signs to his house and buying hides from them'. The roll of 1299–1300 has the first use of the word 'regrating', though without details of the offence. In the roll of 1312–13, the term 'regrating' is used to denote the activity of buying (oats, cheese and poultry) outside markets. There is a large gap in the rolls from this point until 1374–5. In 1374–5, activity which fits the description of forestalling given at the start of this chapter is described as 'forestalling'.[62]

Understanding of what was, in fact, prohibited may be fleshed out by

[55] KB 9/144 m.21 (1392 M.).

[56] JUST 1/1144 m.56.

[57] Putnam, *PJP*, 64 no.30, JUST 1/195 m.2d, Devon 1351. Similar cases can be seen in Putnam, *PJP*, 64 no.29, 67 no.103 (m.4d from the same roll), from 1351 and 1352 respectively.

[58] Putnam, *PJP*, 68 no.104, JUST 1/193 m.4d, Devon 1352.

[59] Putnam, *PJP*, 81 no.290, JUST 1/193 m.8d, Devon, 1353.

[60] Britnell, 'Price setting', 10 (fifteenth-century examples from Colchester).

[61] 'In 1381, Henry Maddy of Lincolnshire was described as a "common forestaller of labourers and servants so that no one in the neighbourhood is able to hire any servant without his approval" and a painter was described as the "chief engrosser of craftsmen in the city"': C. Dyer, *Everyday Life in Medieval England* (London, 1994), 178.

[62] Hudson, *Leet Jurisdiction*, 26, 48, 51, 59, 63–4.

considering common law sources. R.H. Britnell deduced from the words of Herle J and an anonymous commentator in the 1321 eyre of London that forestalling was regarded as 'an offence peculiar to middlemen', and that it was a 'collusive activity between a buyer and seller and not a violent seizure of goods'.[63] It is certainly clear that forestalling under this definition involved a person acting as a 'middleman', though there is no implication that he would have to be a habitual or 'professional' middleman. Court roll entries sometimes describe a person as a 'common forestaller' or note that s/he has been forestalling for a length of time, but this is by no means invariable.[64] It is also true that forestalling was understood here as a non-violent activity, though it is probably better to describe it as consensual rather than necessarily collusive.

All profit or only excessive profit?

The 1321 common law definitions show that forestalling laws are understood to be connected with elimination of profit, though they actually suggest that *any* profit, not just an excessive one, is illegitimate. A definition of forestalling in another source (the earlier *Composicio*), however, suggests that forestalling involves selling goods on *much more dearly* rather than simply *more* dearly than the original merchants intended, thus, presumably implying an 'excessive' profit rather than just any profit.[65] The York Ordinances 1301 suggest that taking any profit by regraters is an offence.[66]

A large 'mark up' is mentioned in a 1308 forestalling allegation in proceedings before the keepers of the peace in Tendring, Essex. Walter le Cogger and another twenty-one men are said to be forestallers of various goods, including fish, which they sell for five times what they paid, or more.[67] A number of King's Bench entries mention that the goods forestalled were sold at an excessive price, or that there was a large difference between the price at which goods were bought and the price at which they were sold. In the 1352 case of William de Hereford of Woodham Ferers mentioned at the beginning of the chapter, William was stated to be a common forestaller of poultry who sold for three times the price at which he bought.[68] An indictment from Pickering in Yorkshire from 1362 states that sixteen men had forestalled fish, herring and salt at Scarborough and sold it for twice its value, 'in great extortion and oppression of the people coming to Scarborough'.[69] In a case from the file for the King's Bench session at York in Trinity term 1362, three common forestallers were said to sell fish for double the price they should.[70] A number of peace roll entries make a point of the difference between the price at which an item was bought and the price at which it was sold.[71] Some show presentments for buying and

[63] Britnell, 'Forstall', 89, citing Cam, *London Eyre 1321*, 310–11, 357–8.
[64] See, e.g., an indictment from the King's Bench session at York in 1362 which states that three common forestallers of meat and fish had been operating for ten years: JUST 1/1144 m.56.
[65] *SR* I:202–4.
[66] *YO*, 12: regraters not to sell merchandise for more than the tradesman who produced it.
[67] Cam, *Liberties and Communities*, 170.
[68] JUST 1/267 m.18.
[69] KB 9/141 m.59.
[70] JUST 1/1144 m.62.
[71] Putnam, *PJP*, 214 no.8, 218 no.24, 223 no.46, 361 no.359, 363 no.463.

selling at an 'excessive' profit, as can be seen in this presentment from the peace roll of Suffolk 1361–4:

> *Thomas le Smyth' de Combis emit vj barella tarpice quodlibet barellum pro iv.s vi.d et vendidit quodlibet barellum pro vi.s, et sic lucratus est excessive anno xxxvi et xxxvii.*[72]

(Thomas the Smith of Combs bought six barrels of tar, paying 4s 6d per barrel, and sold each barrel for 6s, and so he made an excessive profit in 1362 and 1363.)

A focus on intention or on harm?

The 1321 judicial definition of forestalling by Herle J that 'It is only forestalling if you buy to sell again', confirmed in the later note that 'it is not forestalling when I see a man coming to a fair or market and I buy from him meat or wheat or anything else for my own use and I do not resell the same thing in order to make a profit, but if I do, that is forestalling', suggests that it is not enough simply to show that somebody has bought outside the licensed market: some attention must also be paid to the intention with which the sale was transacted – at least that of the buyer – and perhaps to the conduct following the sale, since proving that the 'forestaller' had in fact sold at a profit would be the best way to demonstrate his intention in the original bargain.[73]

Often, some reference was made to the damage caused by forestalling or regrating. This might be in general terms, as can be seen in indictments in the King's Bench file for the session at Chelmsford in 1352, where nine men were alleged to be common forestallers of fish 'to the great oppression and impoverishment of the people', and Sir John Chapleyn the parson of Goldhanger was indicted as a common forestaller of victuals 'to the great oppression and damage of the people'.[74] It was frequently alleged that forestalling had caused a rise in prices in the goods forestalled. An indictment from the King's Bench session at Chelmsford in 1351 noted that the price of grain had increased 'a great deal' because of the activities of three forestallers.[75] In an indictment in the King's Bench at Shrewsbury in 1374, it was presented that William atte Waterhous and William Meke's forestalling and subsequent regrating of iron had caused iron to triple in price in the county.[76] On occasion, the damage allegedly caused by forestalling was quantified, as can be seen in an indictment in the same roll which stated that the forestalling of iron by the accused had caused £20 worth of damage to the whole county of Shropshire.[77] The cases do not, however, always discuss whether harm was in fact inflicted by forestalling and similar practices: it seems that it was not formally necessary to do so. Intention is virtually never mentioned, though some cases suggest that it was relevant, in the sense that one could be punished simply for preparing to make a profit by 'cornering a market' The later fourteenth-century working definition of forestalling could encompass keeping a scarce commodity and refusing to sell it even without actually making a profit, or selling it, as can be seen in this case from the peace roll of Devon 1351–3:

---

[72] Putnam, *PJP*, 365 no.463.
[73] Cam, *London Eyre 1321*, 310–11, 357–8.
[74] 'a grant oppression & empoverisement du poeple'. See App. I below.
[75] JUST 1/267 m.32.
[76] KB 9/102 m.6, KB 9/144 m.21, KBIF 1392 M. York, have a similar statement.
[77] KB 9/102 m.6. How this figure representing damage was produced is obscure.

Item dicunt quod Adam Ganne de Teignemouth cariauit per mare ad portum de Apeldore iiii quarteria salis et ea voluit vendidisse hominibus de patria per bussellum et quarterium, et decessit, et predictum sal in testamento suo reliquit Iohanne uxori eius que cepit in virum quemdam Iohannem Garlaund', qui modo predicto illud voluit vendidisse, et Mauricius Ganne idem sal emebat in grossum et illud forstallauit et sub arta custodia detinuit et illud vendicioni exponere recusauit, in oppressionem et depauperacionem populi. [Margin: *transgressio mauricius Ganne*][78]

(Adam Ganne of Teignmouth brought four quarters of salt to Appledore by sea, intending to sell it to the men of the county by bushels and quarters. He died, leaving the salt in his will to Joanna, his wife, who married John Garland, who wished to sell the salt as above, and Maurice Ganne bought the salt in gross and forestalled it and kept it, refusing to sell it, in oppression and impoverishment of the populace. [Margin: trespass, Maurice Ganne])

The situation in the King's Bench indictments of the second half of the fourteenth century shows that although there is no investigation as to whether a monopoly has in fact been created or the exact intention of the alleged forestaller in this regard, descriptive comments, such as those mentioning conspiracy, excessive profit or a long period of offending, are concerned with the offender's culpability, whilst others concentrate on consequences, mentioning the deleterious effects of the offence. Both elements were clearly important to those framing these indictments in the mid- and late fourteenth century, whether or not they were legally required.[79]

Aiding and abetting, attempts and intended actions

As with the royal rules against usury and the price fixing regulations, all the action in bargains tainted by forestalling, regrating or similar conduct seems to have been directed against one party to the bargain, in this case penalising only the buyers and retailers, not the original sellers and not the eventual buyers. On occasions when forestalling was clearly seen as a consensual activity, as in the *Composicio*, in which the forestaller is shown persuading merchant-strangers that it is to their advantage to sell their goods to him outside the town at a higher price than they would or could charge if they sold them themselves in the town, one might expect to see both seller and buyer being punished, but no penalty seems to have been applied to the sellers. This document did, however, provide that the same punishments would apply to the forestaller and to 'those giving counsel, aid or favour', which might, at a stretch, be taken to include those selling goods to forestallers.[80]

Almost all those reports of presentments or trials of 'forestallers' or 'regraters' which give any details indicate that those presented or indicted were the buyers and 'middlemen', not the original sellers, even where the latter were mentioned. In a King's Bench indictment of 1387, for example, an allegation of regrating fish was

---

[78] Putnam, *PJP*, 64 no.29; JUST 1/195 m.2.

[79] R.H. Britnell has noted (in relation to 'local' jurisdictions) that 'In practice juries were rarely interested in establishing whether a forestaller was aiming to create a monopoly or whether any degree of monopoly had in fact been created': Britnell, 'Price setting', 13, citing Nottingham 1395, nineteen people amerced simultaneously as common 'forestallers and gatherers of coal, selling it excessively high': W.H. Stevenson (ed.), *Records of the Borough of Nottingham*, 5 vols (London, 1882–1900), I, 272–3. He doubts whether monopolies were often created by forestallers: Britnell, 'Price setting', 13–14.

[80] *SR* I:202–4.

made against William Serle of Bristol. He had been selling at an unacceptably great profit ('pro excessivo lucro') but, although it was noted that this was with the agreement of the fishermen ('per assensum'), they do not seem to have been accused of an offence.[81] In contrast, there are exceptional presentments for selling to forestallers in the Sutton court rolls. In 1351, twenty-four men were stated to have been fishermen in the habit of selling fish before they came to the place where they ought to sell according to custom, and so were amerced, and at a view of frankpledge in 1391, fifteen men were presented, convicted and amerced for fishing at sea and selling to forestallers rather than bringing the fish to shore to sell them.[82]

An offence of 'maintaining forestallers' is glimpsed in a Close Roll entry of 1309, relating to earlier sessions before keepers of the peace in Warwickshire. Henry de Hatton was in the king's prison at Warwick for maintaining forestallers Nicholas en le Hurne of Stratford (allegedly a common forestaller of timber) and John le Prest (allegedly a common forestaller of all manner of fish) and others, 'and for taking ransoms from them and other trespassers'.[83] No similar examples have been found and it is not clear whether the principal forestalling offence was coercive or consensual in this case. 'Local' rules in a Grimsby charter of 1258 set out a punishment for those helping forestallers by transporting them to ships waiting off the coast, in order to buy goods before they reached land, and another for those reserving wares as well as actually buying them.[84] Norwich rules of the early fourteenth century suggest that those helping or encouraging forestallers might be guilty of an offence.[85] A pardon on the Patent Roll for 1364, of a forestaller on a large scale, Thomas Harding of Manningtree, shows that he was indicted for offences including 'consenting to and maintaining the forestalling' of others.[86]

It is not clear why those selling to forestallers should not be punished, if the contract was truly consensual. It seems likely that the idea of forestalling as a non-consensual activity retained some influence on attitudes towards and treatment of forestalling, even after it had come to be seen as a consensual offence

No cases of attempted forestalling or regrating appear in national/royal records, but a London roll of 1298 contains a case where a man was accused of buying geese in order to sell them to regraters.[87] Legislation against forestalling in 1350–1 set out a penalty where there had been agreement but the purchase price had not been paid over.[88] A Yorkshire Peace Roll case of 1361–4 describes as forestalling the purchase of salmon by Thomas de Ingilby (a common forestaller) from fishermen, before they had caught the fish.[89] It would therefore seem that it was not necessary for delivery of the goods or full payment to be made before one could be guilty of forestalling.

---

[81] KB 9/32 m.8.

[82] DL 30/86/1182, Court Wednesday after St Ambrose, 1351; DL 30/89/1208 m.10d.

[83] *CCR 1307–13*, 92.

[84] Ballard and Tait, *British Borough Charters*, 295–6.

[85] Hudson and Tingey, *Records of the City of Norwich*, I, 183, Custumal c.37. This provision is also interesting in showing the closing of a potential 'legal loophole' by stipulating that giving earnest, as opposed to transacting a complete sale, outside the market was an offence.

[86] *CPR 1364–7*, 40 (1364).

[87] *CEMCR*, 18.

[88] *RP* II:232a. On sales of goods, see Baker, *Introduction*, 384–6.

[89] B.H. Putnam (ed.), *Yorkshire Sessions of the Peace 1361–4*, Yorkshire Archaeological Society 6 (1939), 110; JUST 1/1135 m.4.

Collusion and conspiracy

There may have been some idea that concerted action to raise prices was an offence in itself, even when the prices of the goods in question were not previously regulated. This is suggested by an entry in the London Mayor's Court Rolls of 1298, in which a number of coopers were found guilty of making an ordinance raising the price of their wares, backed up by oaths. They were imprisoned, then released after paying a fine for their trespasses against the king.[90]

Some reports relating to forestalling and regrating in King's Bench indictment files mention the fact that the action was done by conspiracy with others. A confederacy to fix the price of wool was presented before the King's Bench in York in 1348, where it was stated that eight men agreed by confederacy that none of them would buy wool except at a certain price agreed between them.[91] In a case from King's Bench indictment file for the session in Sherborne in 1358, it was alleged that William Russel and five other fishmongers and victuallers of the borough of Shaftesbury, had entered into an 'evil conspiracy and agreement' to the effect that they would set the price of fish coming to the market by common consent, rather than unilaterally, and that by this means had taken excessive and extortionate profit for two years, contrary to the statute.[92] A confederation was mentioned in a case in the file for the session in York in 1362, where three men were presented as common forestallers of fish and it was noted that when they bought fish at sea they sold it for double the price they should 'in deceit of the people, by confederation made between them'.[93]

A peace roll for 1361 includes a presentment from the North Riding of Yorkshire of a 'fraudulent' confederacy between three fishermen and eight fish merchants which seems to have involved the merchants buying fish in gross so that they were able to dictate terms to consumers, who were forced to pay a high price for fish, rather than being able to buy their fish at a reasonable price.[94] The mischief alleged was that the lords and free tenants of the county could not have their necessary victuals at a reasonable price.[95] In 1392, the hundred of Pickering presented that three tanners had combined over the prices at which they would buy cow hide in the market or elsewhere.[96] An explicit conspiracy was also alleged among buyers of grain in Yorkshire in the same year. It was presented that John Shakell and nine other burgesses of Hedon, buyers of grain in various markets in Yorkshire, had confederated and bound themselves not to buy grain there except at a price agreed amongst themselves, to the great impoverishment of the king's people. Details of some of their deals were given, showing that they traded outside the market and sold at a large profit.[97] Local records have more examples of 'combination' offences.[98]

---

[90] *CEMCR*, 1–2.
[91] KB 9/156 m.124.
[92] KB 9/19 m.10.
[93] JUST 1/1144 m.68.
[94] 'ad racionabile precium'.
[95] JUST 1/1135 m.4d. It was noted that the merchants were common forestallers, though it is not clear whether this is a description of their confederacy, or whether this is a separate accusation.
[96] KB 9/144 m.48.
[97] KB 9/144 m.42.
[98] See, e.g., the fine of Norwich chandlers in 1300 for fixing an extortionate price for candles: Hudson, *Leet Jurisdiction*, 52, cited in Wood, *Medieval Economic Thought*, 142. There is also an interesting 'cartel' offence

'Local' and 'national' rules

Despite what appears to have been a dispute over powers to legislate in this area in the reign of Edward II, between the king and the London civic authorities, with particular regard to London ordinances banning the sale of fish by retail at the Fish Wharf, urban centres were generally allowed, and expected, to make their own rules here.[99]

Urban authorities acted in a noticeably different manner with respect to 'monopolistic practices' than did 'the centre'. This is hardly surprising as they acted in part with a view to the self-interest of the dominant citizen traders, at the expense of outsiders.[100] The practical result was that urban centres had more and further-reaching laws against monopolistic practices. London and Bristol, for example, made laws against the engrossing of grain, storing it from one market to the next to sell at a high price, on pain of losing the goods so engrossed.[101] There were no explicit comparable national regulations.

The difference in 'local' and 'national' concerns should not be pushed too far. 'Local' though not 'national' laws also emphasise out of hours trading.and a particular geographical limit – a belt around the licensed market in which the forestalling prohibition applied. The regime in London included regulation of the times and places at which victuals should be bought and sold. Numerous other areas also had extensive regulation.[102] This is, however, less a matter of differing outlooks between 'local' and 'national' authorities and more the product of the greater specificity relating to local customs and geography possible in a 'local' as opposed to 'national' measure It should be borne in mind that there was considerable royal input into the creation of the detailed laws for London in particular. Urban rules going beyond national rules were certainly approved or adopted in royal charters. In the eyre at Oxford in 1285, a charter of Henry III was proffered, showing the rule that no regrater was to buy victuals in or coming to Oxford before a certain time.[103] A similar rule was set out for Cambridge. Edward I, Edward II, Edward III and Richard II all confirmed Henry III's grant that 'regraters' were banned from buying goods coming into Cambridge before 'the third hour'.[104]

---

from the tourn at Kirkburton on 14 May 1349: William Magotson and Ralph Salter made a confederacy between themselves and sold salt dearly to divers strangers and neighbours. They were amerced 12d each: Wakefield, *G*, 113.

[99] *P&M*, I, 645; *LC*, i, 385–407. According to the king's counsel, 'The city of London is the city of our Lord the king, and of his demesne, and it is not lawful for the mayor and commonalty, nor for any other, to make any ordinances in the said city without consulting the king.'

[100] A.B. Hibbert, 'The economic policies of towns' in *CEH III*, c.4; Dyer, *Standards of Living*, 195, 199; Britnell, 'Price setting', especially 11–14; Britnell, 'Morals'; L.C. Hector and B.F. Harvey (eds), *The Westminster Chronicle (1381–94)* (Oxford, 1982), 58–63. See also n.98 in c.1 above.

[101] Wood, *Medieval Economic Thought*, citing Lipson, *Economic History*, 301.

[102] See, e.g., Bristol's rules from the 1320s with regard to timing of corn purchases, and a case involving the purchase of fish before the appointed hour, where the offender was convicted as a forestaller in the Colchester borough court in 1334: *LRB*, II, p. 221, f.192b, De Pistoribus (Of bakers); I.H. Jeayes (ed.), *Court Rolls of the Borough of Colchester 1310–79*, 3 vols (Colchester, 1921), I, 135; Britnell, 'Forstall', 89–90.

[103] JUST 1/705 m.26d.

[104] *CPR 1292–1301*, 18 (1293); *CPR 1307–13*, 119 (1309); *CChR*, vol. III, *1300–26*, 332 (1317); *CPR 1327–30*, 60 (1327); *CChR*, vol. V, *1341–1417*, 247 (1378). Other similar examples can be seen in Edward I's charter to Melcombe: *CChR*, vol. II, *1257–1300*, 224 (1280); Edward III's charter to

Jurisdiction

The next matter to consider is by whom offenders against the laws under consideration were to be tried. The statutes are often silent on how offences were to be investigated and punished. The *Judicium Pillorie* provided for a presentment process.[105] The 1351 statute against forestalling envisaged suits being brought against offenders either on behalf of the king or by a private individual, as well as mentioning that offences of forestalling could be tried before the mayor and bailiffs, or by the justices assigned for this purpose, or else in the king's court.[106]

A variety of courts and officials were instructed to hear cases of forestalling, regrating and related conduct. There seems to have been no idea that any particular tribunal was the solely appropriate venue for trying such offences. R.H. Britnell has stated that enforcement of matters such as the laws against forestalling was generally left to local courts, but that the justices in eyre and the clerk of the market might also punish offenders or check that local policing was being carried out.[107] This is not necessarily to suggest a lack of royal interest, however, as central royal officials had an important role throughout the fourteenth century in investigating forestalling and sometimes other related conduct, and, from the 1360s, the local royal appointees, justices of the peace, came to the fore in this respect.

At the highest level of royal courts, the eyre was, in the early part of the period under consideration, one of the possible tribunals which might hear cases of forestalling, regrating and similar conduct. In the standard lists of eyre articles, there is no article on forestalling and regrating, but there are signs that forestalling, in one of its senses, was a matter which should be drawn to the attention of the eyre.[108] The late thirteenth-century law text *Britton* noted that one of the eyre articles is 'of forestallers'.[109] A set of articles from the Channel Islands eyre of 1331 also included an article on 'forestallers'.[110] Although not mentioned in the eyre's articles, forestallers and those raising prices because of the eyre's presence in the town are condemned in the preliminary matters at the beginning of the eyre of Northamptonshire 1329–30.[111] The fact that earlier sets of eyre articles do not include forestalling and regrating as one of the matters to be looked into is not surprising as the standard sets of eyre articles were issued long before kings and governments showed any signs of interest in (consensual) forestalling, regrating and similar offences. It is less obvious why later sets of articles do not mention the matter. It can, perhaps, be seen as an indication that forestalling was not seen as a priority for national jurisdiction in the last quarter of the thirteenth century.

Clifton, Dartmouth and Hardenesse: *CChR*, vol. V, *1341–1417*, 3 (1341); Richard II's charter to Bedford: *CChR*, vol. V, *1341–1417*, 357 (1396).

[105] *SR* I:202.

[106] *RP* II:232a.; *SR* I:315.

[107] Britnell, *Commercialisation*, 96. Britnell presumably includes the jurisdiction of justices of the peace amongst local courts.

[108] See eyre of Surrey 1293 veredicta, JUST 1/895–906; W. Sutherland (ed.), *The Eyre of Northamptonshire 3–4 Edw. III 1329–30*, Selden Society vol. 97 for 1981 and vol. 98 for 1982 (London, 1983), 775.

[109] *Britton*, I, 84, Book I, c.21.

[110] JUST 1/1166 m.1: 'De forstallatoribus quibuscumque tam inter terris qu[am] in aqua . . .'.

[111] Sutherland, *Eyre of Northamptonshire*, I, 9; Britnell, 'Forstall', 97.

The 'pleas of the marshalsea' of 1274–5 and thereafter include forestalling.[112] It is possible that (consensual) forestalling was understood to come under the heading of 'pleas of the market' inquired into in special commissions from 1273 onwards, and perhaps even earlier commissions under Henry III.[113] According to *Britton*, clerks of the market (or the royal 'officer of measures' and his jury) had jurisdiction over 'forestallers who raise the market price of victuals by their dealings outside the market'.[114] They kept this jurisdiction until the end of the period under discussion and beyond, and seem to have exercised it, since, in 1394, Richard II made a grant to the cathedral chapter of Hereford that it, rather than the clerk of the market, should have jurisdiction over forestalling.[115]

As well as making general provisions for, or tolerating the exercise of, continuing jurisdiction over forestalling, regrating and related offences, temporary or *ad hoc* action was also ordered. An early example of a presentmen of 'forestalling and regrating' can be seen in the 1305–6 roll of a commission of oyer and terminer in Hereford.[116] It demonstrates that a proclamation was made when royal justices came to a town, forbidding forestalling:

> *Nich[ola]s de Warham, Joh[anne]s Cachepol & Rogerus le Yongehosband convicti sunt per xii jur[atores] civitatis Herford quod sunt regratores et forestallatores carn[is] et piscium ad grave dampnum totius com[itatus] & maxime post adventum predictorum Justic[ariorum] hic & post proclamacionem defensionem eorundem justic[ariorum] in contemptum dom[ini] reg[is] & predictorum justic[ariorum]. Ideo commitantur gaole. Et postea predictis fecerunt finem ut pat[et] in rotulo de finibus.*

> (Nicholas de Warham, John Cachepol and Roger le Yongehosband were convicted by the twelve jurors of the city of Hereford of being regrators and forestallers of meat and fish, to the grave damage of the whole county and especially after the advent of the . . . justices here, and after the prohibitory proclamation of these justices, in contempt of the lord king and of the aforesaid justices. Therefore let them be imprisoned. And afterwards they made fine, as appears in the fine roll.)

Kings made a number of individual commissions to hear and determine cases, from the reign of Edward I to the 1360s.[117] In 1315, sheriffs of London were

---

[112] Britnell, 'Forstall', 95–6, citing BL, MS Stowe 386, ff.50r–51r, and BL, MS Harley 645, ff.147r–148v; *LC*, ff.60r–61v; *Fleta II*, c.12.

[113] *CPR 1272–81*, 16, 31, 73, 136; Britnell, 'Forstall', 95; *CPR 1247–58*, 427, 488, 502, 569; *CPR 1258–72*, 454.

[114] *Britton*, 193, f.76b.

[115] *CChR*, vol. V, *1341–1417* (1916), 349 (1394).

[116] JUST 1/306 m.4. No specific mention on list of fines m.11.

[117] 1288 (mentioned in a commission of 1309: *CPR 1307–13*, 130, 241, probably *CPR 1281–92*, 304: commission to three justices to hear and determine offences of forestalling in London). 1304 (*CPR 1301–7*, 284: commissions of oyer and terminer to examine complaints about forestallers intercepting goods and victuals, so raising prices, in Norwich, Great Yarmouth and Ipswich). 1305, 1308 (*CPR 1307–13*, 42: renewal of commission of 1304 to inquire into forestalling in Norwich). 1307–8 (appointment of commissioners to enforce matters including forestalling laws, renewed and updated 1308. Not completed 1311 *CPR 1307–13*, 29–31, 53–5, 361–2. *EEJ*, 91, special commissions to keepers of the peace including jurisdiction over forestalling proceedings of 1308 commission in Tendring, Essex, can be seen in H. Cam, *Liberties and Communities in Medieval England* (London, 1963), 165, 170–2). 1309 (*CPR 1307–13*, 130, 241; LB, C, f.92. Britnell, 'Forstall', 94, London, commission into offences committed against the Statute of Forestallers since 1288). 1318 (*CPR 1313–17*, 282: commissions to investigate forestalling in Linconshire). 1322 (*CPR 1321–24*, 151: commission to investigate forestalling in the city of York). 1342 (*CPR 1343–5*, 398, 426: commission to investigate forestallers in Yorkshire). 1342

ordered to arrest and attach forestallers to appear before the king and council. on a certain date.[118] Forestalling and regrating were also regularly to be found in the commissions of the justices of the peace from 1364 onwards.[119] Justices of the peace had, however, tried forestalling even when it was not specifically included in their commission, possibly under the jurisdiction over 'all trespasses whatsoever'.[120]

The right and duty to punish forestallers and regraters was sometimes delegated to municipal authorities. Such grants might be made generally, as in the 1351 forestalling statute, which provided that one of the ways in which cases of forestalling could be tried was by mayors and bailiffs, or in the 1382 herring forestalling ordinance which delegated jurisdiction over offences of forestalling to all 'chief officers' of towns corporate.[121] Sometimes, however, specific grants were made, as, for example, when Edward I decided that forestalling and regrating in Oxford and Cambridge should be tried by town and university authorities, or in 1355, when Edward III granted sole jurisdiction over forestallers and regraters of meat and fish to the university authorities in Oxford, or in 1385, 1391 and 1394, when Richard II granted the right to try cases of forestalling to the borough of Northampton, to the prior and canons of Bridlington, and to the bishop, dean and chapter of Hereford respectively.[122]

Jurisdiction over forestalling, regrating and related conduct was not, however, delegated as often as was jurisdiction over the assizes of bread and ale, and, in particular, it was not often granted to individuals in connection with a grant of land or a grant of a market or fair. This is partly a result of the late development of consensual forestalling type offences, in relation to jurisdiction over the assizes.

(*CPR 1345–8*, 320, 453; *CPR 1345–8*, 387: commissions to investigate forestalling of the markets of Exeter and unlawful confederacies to forestall in Nottinghamshire). 1350 (*CPR 1348–50*, 527: commission to investigate forestalling in Yorkshire). 1351 (*CPR 1350–4*, 94; *CPR 1350–4*, 157: commissions to investigate forestalling in the East and North Ridings of Yorkshire and in Lincolnshire). 1352 (*CPR 1350–4*, 275, 334: commission to investigate forestalling in Yorkshire, Kent, Essex, Surrey and Sussex). 1353 (*CPR 1350–4*, 509: commission to investigate forestalling in Colchester). 1354 (*CPR 1354–8*, 65, 125, 129, 162, 165; JUST 1/191 m.12: commission to investigate forestalling in Lincolnshire, Kent, Surrey, Sussex, Essex, Great Yarmouth, Scarborough and Devon). 1356 (*CPR 1354–8*, 399, 458: commission to investigate forestalling in Scarborough). 1357 (JUST 1/609, JUST 1/610A: commission to investigate forestalling in Great Yarmouth). 1358 (*CPR 1358–61*, 76: commission to investigate forestalling in Cumberland). 1359 (*CPR 1358–61*, 220, 223, 323: commissions to investigate forestalling in the city of York, the West Riding, Yorkshire, Nottinghamshire and Derbyshire, Westmorland, Cumberland and Northumberland). 1364 (*CPR 1364–7*, 73: commission to investigate forestalling in Lindsey). 1365 (*CPR 1364–7*, 144: commission concerning forestalling and regrating in Lancashire). 1367 (*CPR 1364–67*, 444: similar commission for Cornwall).

[118] *LC*, f.134, pp. 678–9.

[119] Putnam, *PJP*, xxiii. For other examples of commissions to justices of the peace containing the instruction to try and punish forestallers and regraters, see JUST 1/293 peace roll 1378; R. Sillem, 'Commissions of the Peace', *BIHR* 6 (1932–3), 98. The commission of 1380 to various justices of the peace, for example, included an instruction to investigate forestalling and regrating: commission 3 Ric. II 26 May 1380, patent roll 3, part 3, m.13d; *RP* III:84; *EEJ*, 94.

[120] B.H. Putnam (ed.), *Yorkshire Sessions of the Peace 1361–4*, Yorkshire Archaeological Society Record Series vol. C for 1939 (Wakefield, 1939), xvi.

[121] *RP* II:232a; *SR* I:315; *SR* II:28, st. 5 Ric. II, c.4.

[122] Salter, *MA*, 88ff, m.50. Inspeximus by Edward II of terms of peace between town and university drawn up in 1290 by Edward I, 1315. *CPR 1292–1301*, 18 (1293); *CPR 1307–13*, 119 (1309); *CChR*, vol. III, *1300–26*, 26 (1317); *CPR 1327–30*, 60 (1327); *CChR*, vol. V, *1341–1417*, 143–6; C.A. Markham, *Records of the Borough of Northampton*, vol. I (Northampton, 1898), 68, from Liber Custumarum Villae Northamptoniae, c.1460, f.105a, charter of Richard II, 1385, confirming previous charters of Henry III and Edward I and granting that the mayor and bailiffs of Northampton should take cognizance of forestallers and regraters. *CChR*, vol. V, *1341–1417*, 332; *CChR*, vol. V, *1341–1417*, 349 (1394).

Whilst it could be argued that jurisdiction over the assizes had been acquired long ago in conjunction with a grant of a market or fair, or a view of frankpledge, jurisdiction over forestalling and related offences was not seen as essentially bound up with these rights.

There seems to have been no specific article on forestalling and regrating in the articles of the court leet and court baron.[123] The *Mirror of Justices* says that the view of frankpledge articles included 'Of every forestalment done on the public highway'.[124] This suggests that the offence to be inquired of was old-style *forstal* rather than the later idea of consensual forestalling.

Unlike usury, but in common with price fixing, there seems to have been no quarrel with the church over jurisdiction, even though there were canonical and theological pronouncements against certain 'monopolistic' practices, and 'according to canon law, monopoly profits were *turpe lucrum*, which, like usury, was subject to restitution'.[125] As with selling at an excessive price, it is unclear whether English church courts actually did take action against monopoly abusers.[126] Jurisdiction over these offences is never raised as a probem in the lists of clerical *gravamina*.[127]

As with the usury prohibition and the price control laws, there is evidence that offenders against royal laws were investigated, tried and punished. Relevant entries appear in the rolls of various different courts and special commissions. At the highest level, there are very occasional examples of cases involving forestalling being dealt with in Parliament. A case of 'forestalling' can be seen in the rolls for 1290.[128] There are also reports of presentments and actions for 'forestalling' before the royal justices: in the records of the eyres and before the court of King's Bench.[129] Most eyres examined do not contain forestalling presentments, but they are present in the eyres of Cumberland and Northumberland 1293 and the 1331 Channel Islands eyre.[130] There are examples of presentments and convictions for forestalling in the surviving records of various judicial commissions. The Hundred Rolls investigations did not contain an article on forestalling, but one borough did present a 'forestaller'.[131] There are records or evidence of presentments for forestalling made in sessions under commissions relating to Hereford 1305–6, Tendring Hundred in Essex, 1308, Warwickshire for 1307x1309, Devon and

---

[123] J.S. Beckerman, 'The articles of presentment of a court leet and court baron, in English, c.1400', *BIHR* 47 (1974), 230. (BL MS Lansdowne 474); *Court Baron.*

[124] *Mirror*, Book 1, c.12.

[125] de Roover, *JP*, 429.

[126] J. Brundage says that church courts were 'prepared to penalize' such offenders, but provides no examples: J.A. Brundage, *Medieval Canon Law* (London, 1995), 76. He cites J.W. Baldwin, 'The medieval merchant before the bar of canon law', *Papers of the Michigan Academy of Science, Arts and Letters* 44 (1959), 287–99, but this gives no relevant examples of prosecution, and, in any case, deals mainly with the twelfth century. L.R. Poos (ed.), *Lower Level Jurisdiction in Late Medieval England: The Courts of the Dean and Chapter of Lincoln 1336–49 and Deanery of Wisbech 1458–1484* (Oxford, 2001), has no relevant cases.

[127] Jones, 'Bishops, politics and the two laws: gravamina'.

[128] *RP* I:26. Petition relating to this matter: C.M. Fraser (ed.), *Ancient Petitions Relating to Northumberland*, Surtees Society 176 (Durham, 1966), 232–4, no.207.

[129] e.g. JUST 1/651 m.35, JUST 1/306 m.4.

[130] Because of lack of detail, it is not clear whether these refer to forestalling during the course of the eyre or before it. Forestalling was prohibited during the course of the eyre by the proclamations at the beginning of the eyre, at least in the eyre of Northamptonshire 1329–30: Sutherland, *Eyre of Northamptonshire 1329–30*, I, 9.

[131] *Hundred Rolls*, 182. It is not clear whether this presentment relates to consensual or coerced transactions.

Cornwall in the 1350s. and Great Yarmouth in 1357.[132] The commissions for the 1341–3 inquiries dealt with in chapter 2 do not make specific mention of forestalling, but there are some presentments in the rolls of these enquiries of 'forestallers'.[133] Eyre records of the late thirteenth century and early fourteenth century contain presentments of 'forestallers' but no presentments using the word 'regrating'. King's Bench files also contain presentments for 'regrating'.[134] Cases of 'forestalling' were commonly brought before the justices of the peace from the 1360s onwards.[135] Cases of 'forestalling' can be found in the London civic courts from at least 1298 and Chester civic courts from 1296, the court leet at Norwich from 1287 onwards, the fair courts of St Ives from the time of Edward I and Edward II, Tamworth borough court from the 1290s until at least the 1360s, Colchester borough courts between 1310 and 1352, tourns at Wakefield, where 'forestalling' was presented and punished from 1316 onwards, and the view of frankpledge at Sutton, where 'forestallers', at least some of whom were guilty of consensual forestalling, were amerced from 1308 onwards.[136]

Presentments for 'regrating' are also seen in lower courts, but it is difficult to be sure that those presented as 'regraters' were being charged with conduct fitting the definition of regrating used in this chapter. The word 'regrater' is commonly encountered in presentments in manor court records, such as those of Sutton, and those of Tottenham, but it seems likely that 'regrater' is understood in those records simply to mean 'seller', without any necessary implication of monopolistic behaviour.[137] None of them would seem to have acquired such a stranglehold on supplies that they could dictate the price of bread or ale to consumers. In contrast to the frequent use of the term 'regrater' in the Sutton and Tottenham rolls, the Wakefield tourn rolls contain only one report using the term 'regrating': in a 1349 entry, a man was alleged to have been forestalling and regrating.[138]

---

[132] JUST 1/306 m.4; Cam, *Liberties and Communities*, 170–2; *CCR 1307–13*, 130; JUST 1/191, Devon general oyer and terminer 1354–5; KB 9/9, Cornwall general oyer and terminer 1358–9; JUST 1/609; JUST 1/610A.

[133] e.g. JUST 1/521 m.5d and m.16 (Lincolnshire); JUST 1/337 m.3 (Hertfordshire).

[134] It is seen relatively frequently in the records of the King's Bench from the 1350s onwards. See, e.g., KB 9/19 m.11 (1358 T.); KB 9/144 m.2d (1392).

[135] e.g. Putnam, *PJP*, 64, 67.

[136] London: *CEMCR*, 7; Riley, *Memorials*, 83 (1310); LB, D, f.123; LB, H, f.22 (1375); LB, E, f.102b (1320); LB, F, f.177; LB, C, f.40 (1299–1300); LB, E, f.120; *LA*, f.186a, Bk III, part I, p. 172; LB, H, f.88 (1378); LB, H, f.107 (1382–3). Chester: R. Stewart Brown (ed.), *Calendar of County Court, City Court and Eyre Rolls of Chester*, Chetham Society 84 (Aberdeen, 1925), 204–5; Hudson, *Leet Jurisdiction*, 62, the case of Roger Calf in 1374–5, which is a consensual forestalling case; SC 2/178/100 m.2d (1300); SC 2/178/103 m.5d (1311). M.K. Dale (ed.), *Court Rolls of the Borough of Tamworth* (Tamworth, 1959), 50, 52, 66, 68, 72, 96, 99, 107, 114, 115, 117. The first note of forestalling is from 1294. I.H. Jeayes (ed.), *Court Rolls of the Borough of Colchester 1310–1379*, vol. 1, *1310–52* (Colchester, 1921), e.g. 2, 159. R.H. Britnell notes the peak of forestalling cases in Colchester came between 1310 and 1312: Britnell, *Colchester*, 40. Wakefield, Sutton: see Appendix II graph 6 below; DL 30/85/1159 m.6d.

[137] Sutton: the record of a view of frankpledge held in 1306, for example, lists several men and women as regraters of ale, bread or both: DL 30/85/1157 m.7; R. Oram and F.H. Fenton (eds), *Tottenham Manorial Rolls 1377–99: Court Rolls of the Manors of Bruces, Dawbeneys, Pembrokes (Tottenham) 1 Ric. II – 1 Hen. IV, 1377–1399* (Tottenham, 1961). In the Tottenham Manorial Rolls for 1377–99, there are many examples of the type 'X is a regrater' with an amercement marked. There are also reports of the type 'X is a regrater and sells contrary to the assize'.

[138] Wakefield, *G*, 113.

Private actions

It seems that individuals could bring an 'action on the Statute of Forestallers': a trespass action against an individual for forestalling, as can be seen in an apparently unsuccessful case of 1309 brought by the mayor and community of London against a man, stating that 'he was a common forestaller etc., of oats and salt etc., in that when he bought them, he sold them for twice as much etc.'[139] A royal response to a petition in Parliament, of an uncertain date in the reign of Edward III, though certainly after 1351, orders that writs to sheriffs and bailiffs should be made for all wishing to sue concerning forestalling and regrating.[140] An apparent 'private trespass' action can be seen in the London jurisdiction in 1305–6, when Nicholas le Keu was sued by the pepperers of Sopernslane for allegedly forestalling figs and raisins at Sandwich.[141]

Treatment of offenders

Roman law and some medieval 'scholastics' apparently suggested very harsh penalties for monopoly, with the death penalty, confiscation of all goods, banishment, perpetual exile and excommunication all featuring.[142] The only comparably severe punishment laid down for forestallers and engrossers in medieval English sources was that in a 1353 statute against forestalling and engrossing Gascon wine, which provided penalty of life and member, plus forfeiture of all goods and chattels to the king, and lands to their feudal superior.[143] This is, however, exceptional.

Other punishments laid down by the statutes for forestallers, regraters and those convicted of similar conduct varied. The *Statutum Mareschaucie* and *Composicio* provided that forestallers were not to be allowed to live in any town, though they also stated that forestallers would only be forced to abjure the town on their fourth conviction.[144] Later statutes did not mention banishment as a possible punishment. Some 'local' rules did emphasise exclusion. A number of charters attempted completely to ban forestallers from cities or towns.[145] London's civic rules also made attempts to exclude hucksters or middlemen from sales of certain victuals.[146] Exile from the city was provided for a third forestalling offence in the

---

[139] R. Tottell (printed), A. Fitzherbert, *La Graunde Abridgement* (London, 1577), f.9, no.26, Accion sur le statut. 3 Edw. II M. (1309). The case failed because the allegation that the man was a 'common forestaller' was deemed insufficiently specific outside the eyre.

[140] *RP* II:404a.

[141] *CEMCR*, 238. The case was compromised with the permission of the court.

[142] Langholm, *Economics*, 131, 408, 516; Wood, *Medieval Economic Thought*, 139, citing the Emperor Diocletian's imposition of the death penalty in 301, Zeno's confiscation of all the goods of monopolists and dispatch of them into perpetual exile, and Alexander of Hales' statement that monopolists were 'abominable' and should be thrown out of the church. An early fourteenth-century Oxford philosopher found the activites of regraters, defined as those buying and selling to profit, without adding value, harmful, and suggested their banishment: John Duns Scotus (d.1308) discussed in Langholm, *Economics*, 408, and Wood, *Medieval Economic Thought*, 140.

[143] 27 Edw. III, st.1 c.5, *SR* I:331.

[144] *SR* I:202–4; Anstey, *MA*, I, 184.

[145] See, e.g., Edward III's 1341 charter to Clifton, Dertemuth and Hardenesse that no forestaller should be permitted there: *CChR*, vol. V, *1341–1417*, 3.

[146] *CLB, G*, 139, f.100 (1361, fish); *CLB, G*, 255, f.206b (1368, ale); *CLB, H*, 121, f.107b (1379, fish); *CLB, H*, 214, f.164 (1383, ale); *CLB, H*, 337, f.236 (1388, ale); *CLB, H*, 373, f.265b (1391–2, fish).

York Ordinances of 1301.[147] In 1305, Edward I approved an agreement between the university and town authorities in Oxford to the effect that only thirty-two regraters would be allowed in the town.[148] This is the only example which has been seen of such a compromise, though it could be seen as similar to the fourteenth-century London rules restricting and controlling brokers.[149]

Forfeiture of the forestalled goods was commonly prescribed, as in the ninth charter of Henry III to London, and subsequent charters granted to London by Henry's successors.[150] Forfeiture was prescribed for forestalled goods in the *Composicio*, in Edward I's ordinances for London, in the York Ordinances of 1301 in relation to forestalled fish and in legislation against forestalling in 1351 (in the last case, only if the purchase price had actually been paid).[151] When private prosecutions were envisaged, as in the forestalling legislation of 1351, it was provided that the successful prosecutor would be awarded a share of the forfeited goods, the remainder going to the king.[152] Forfeiture of the goods forestalled was a fairly severe punishment which went beyond the damage which the forestaller would inflict on the community, since he was not merely ordered to restore or pay over the profit which he made on the whole transaction, but was to be obliged to give up the goods for which he had paid. The nature of this penalty may have been a relic of forestalling's forcible past, since forfeiture of goods seized would be an obviously just penalty if no money at all had been paid for them.

Imprisonment was also prescribed in several enactments, such as the 1268 charter of Henry III to London.[153] The *Composicio* prescribed imprisonment for a third forestalling conviction.[154] The York Ordinances provided 40 days' imprisonment for a third offence.[155] In the forestalling legislation of 1351, imprisonment was to be used as an alternative to forfeiture of goods in cases where the sale had not been completed and the offender did not have sufficient assets to pay this penalty.[156] The 1357 ordinance regulating the trade in salt fish at Blakeney provided that fish not sold reasonably within the bounds of the fair would be forfeited and the seller imprisoned.[157]

Corporal punishment can be seen as one of the punishments contemplated in the *Composicio*, in which a second forestalling offence was ordered to be punished by a period in the pillory.[158] 'Heavy chastisement' for forestallers was mentioned in an ordinance of Edward I for London.[159] The York Ordinances of 1301 prescribe the pillory for a first forestalling offence, and the hurdle for a second offence.[160]

---

[147] *YO*, 14.

[148] F.W. Maitland (ed.), *Records of the Parliament holden at Westminster on the Twenty-Eighth Day of February in the 33rd Year of the Reign of King Edward the First AD 1305* (London, 1893), 45.

[149] See Seabourne, 'Controlling commercial morality'; LB, G, ff.118b, 127b, 308; LB, H, f.247b.

[150] *LA*, 123, 126, 138; *LC*, II, i, 251–5; *CChR 1257–1300*, 98, 447; W. de Gray Birch, *The Historical Charters and Constitutional Documents of the City of London*, rev. edn (London, 1887), 38.

[151] *SR* I:202–4; *LA*, f.198b, temp. Edw. I; *YO*, 13; *RP* II:232a; *SR* I:315.

[152] *RP* II:232a.; *SR* I:315.

[153] *LA*, 123, 126, 138; *LC*, II, i, 251–5; *CChR 1257–1300*, 98, 447; Birch, *Historical Charters of London*, 38.

[154] *SR* I:202–4.

[155] *YO*, 14.

[156] *SR* I:315.

[157] *SR* I:355, 31 Edw. III, st.3.

[158] *SR* I:202–4.

[159] *LA*, 229, Book 3, part II, f.198b, temp. Edw. I.

[160] Britnell, 'Forstall', 96; *YO*, 14.

In practice, the almost invariable result of a conviction before the royal justices or justices of the peace for forestalling or regrating was a money payment to the king.[161] I have found only a few examples of offenders being punished other than by financial penalty, and none post-dates the reign of Edward II. *Abbreviato Placitorum* has a 'forestalling and regrating' case from 1296 from Roxburgh which ended with the defendants being imprisoned until they made fine.[162] A Hereford general commission of oyer and terminer of 1305–6 gives an example of three men being convicted of forestalling meat and fish, and being imprisoned, at least until they made fine.[163] Three men were in prison in Warwick in 1309 after being found to be forestallers (or in one case, a 'maintainer of forestallers') in a session before the keepers of the peace.[164] In these cases, imprisonment may have been less of a punishment in its own right than a way of coercing offenders to make fine with the king. There are no examples of banishment. Evidence of punishment by local courts shows some variation from that by royal courts. Records of London courts show some examples of offenders losing the freedom of the city for forestalling, and some examples of offenders being sent to the pillory and prison.[165] In London's Letter Book F, for example, there is a record of the pleas held before the mayor and sheriffs of London on 23 April 1350, when twenty-three poulterers were indicted as forestallers of poultry. Twenty-two were found guilty by a jury. One man who had been formerly convicted of the same offence before the mayor and sheriffs was condemned to the pillory. The other twenty-one were sent to prison, as it was their first offence.[166] The records of the fair courts of St Ives show that forestallers were sometimes obliged to swear not to forestall again, as can be seen in an example from 1300, when two men and a woman who had been found to be forestallers were distrained to make fine for their offence and to swear never to do it again, though amercement was often the only penalty employed for offenders.[167] In the Colchester borough court, the pillory was one of the contemplated penalties, as can be seen from a case in 1334 in which a man and a woman confessed to forestalling of fish and were amerced, but were warned that if it happened again, they would be condemned to the pillory.[168] Not all local courts used non-pecuniary punishments, however. There is no sign of punishments other than amercements being imposed on forestallers or regraters in the Sutton or Wakefield court rolls.[169]

Evaluating enforcement

The next question to examine is that of enforcement of the laws against forestalling and similar conduct. The currently orthodox view is that, like price laws, they were

---

[161] e.g. KB 27/356 m.6, m.57.
[162] *Abbreviato Placitorum*, 301, 24 Edw. I, r.5.
[163] JUST 1/306 m.4.
[164] *CCR 1307–13*, 92.
[165] Loss of freedom: LB, C, f.40 (February 1299–1300) and f.49 (1300).
[166] LB, F, f.177.
[167] SC2/178/100 m.2d; SC2/178/103 m.5d.
[168] I.H. Jeayes (ed.), *Court Rolls of the Borough of Colchester 1310–79*, 3 vols (Colchester, 1921), 135.
[169] The Wakefield rolls have no forestalling presentments before 1316. Thereafter, there are presentments of

often enforced as a form of taxation rather than as a serious attempt to influence behaviour or punish offenders, and that (at the 'local' level)

[L]ack of understanding was one obstacle to implementation of the law, another was limited goodwill. The penalties required by the law were universally considered inappropriate . . . Occasionally authorities got as far as condemning persistent forestallers to the pillory, but even this was plainly a waste of a good opportunity for collecting cash . . . Forestallers were allowed to remain in town, and contributed to the common chest out of their vicious profit.[170]

There are examples of jurisdiction over forestalling being used as a method of raising money. A commission sent to investigate and punish the malpractices of mayors and officials of Bristol, for example, heard a complaint from John Rondel, merchant of Amiens, that Richard Tilly, former mayor of Bristol, and five ministers of the king in Bristol had had him attached on false charges of forestalling in 1321–2, and took a fine from him of goods worth £300.[171] More corruption, in the shape of officials taking a bribe not to enforce penalties against forestalling, can be seen in an inquisition of 1367, concerning herring forestalling off Scarborough.[172] Instances of alleged corruption by officials are hardly, however, confined to abuses of the jurisdiction over forestalling and related offences.

It is certainly true to say that the usual penalty was financial. Some variation from the prescribed corporal penalties should not, however, be a surprise when we consider the general nature of medieval law enforcement, and the particular contorted evolution of forestalling offences from forcible crimes to prohibited consensual transactions. Corporal penalties may have been regarded as more appropriate to the former than to the latter. The use of financial penalties does not show that enforcement of the laws under consideration was simply a matter of licensing and revenue raising. A case which seems to cast doubt on the view of this regulation as a matter of revenue-raising can be seen in the Colchester borough court rolls for 1334, where two confessed forestallers' financial penalty was reduced below the level stipulated in legislation, 'on the prayer of two mounted king's messengers present in court', though the offenders were warned that if they forestalled again, they would be condemned to the pillory. They had forestalled eight mullet, the price of which was 21d, so 21d should have been forfeit, but this was reduced to 10d.[173] The records which show that cases concerning these offences were actually tried, rather than guilt being presumed, few as they are, can also be used to argue against the idea of jurisdiction over forestalling and regrating having been used as a mode of indirect taxation.[174]

---

forestallers of eggs and poultry, salt, meat, fish, oats, butter, eggs and cheese and other victuals. The outcome, where recorded, was always an amercement, of 6d to 2s.

[170] Quotation from Britnell, 'Forstall', 102. Britnell takes a dim view of the enforcement of forestalling legislation, seeing at as a 'legitimation for local taxes on trade' in line with his views on the assizes of bread and ale and other statutes 'concerning prices and profits': Britnell, *Commercialisation*, 173. D.L. Farmer suggested that, sometimes, punishment of offenders was minimal, amounting to 'in effect, licences to go on sinning': D.L. Farmer, 'Marketing the produce of the countryside' in E. Miller (ed.), *The Agrarian History of England and Wales*, vol. 3 (Cambridge, 1991), 324, 427. See also Holdsworth, *HEL*, IV, 36.

[171] JUST 1/1560 m.38.

[172] *CIM*, vol. III, *1348–77*, 659.

[173] Jeayes, *Court Rolls of Colchester*, 135.

[174] See, e.g., JUST 1/191 m.5, Devon GOT 1354–5, Walter Kok tried for forestalling and regrating of

There is clear evidence that efforts were made to enforce the rules against forestalling and regrating. Various mechanisms of presentment and determination were used. There is evidence of serious and continued effort to prosecute forestallers and regraters of victuals even at the 'local' level. Sutton courts have forestalling presentments from 1314 until 1396, though they are by no means regular.[175] Serious efforts were made to pursue offenders, e.g. in a court in 1327, Robert Noy – presumably a pledge – was in mercy for failing to have William Pew in court for forestalling, and three others were distrained to come and answer for their forestalling.[176] There is evidence in the Sutton rolls that the prosecution of forestallers and regraters was considered important enough to be the subject of special inquiries in 1313 and 1355.[177] Although the records do not give details about the task given to these inquisitions, apart from the fact that the later inquisition was looking at forestalling of fish, and although their findings are not reported, the fact that the unusual step of ordering a special inquiry was taken shows that the lords of Sutton were attempting to take an active role in pursuing offenders, and were not merely taking the profits of justice when forestalling or similar conduct came to their attention.

Legislation was created and updated. Action against a sophisticated form of forestalling also seems to be suggested by the provision in a 1382 statute that hosts in coastal towns were not to buy fresh sea fish on behalf of fishmongers of London.[178] It appears that the London fishmongers had been attempting to extend their capacity to forestall by using agents to make purchases for them in or off coastal towns. It can be argued that such attention to changing tactics on the part of offenders shows that forestalling was a real concern of fourteenth-century kings and governments.

As to the effectiveness of the laws in terms of keeping down prices, if we assume that to have been their aim, this is considerably more questionable, though it is outside the scope of this book and the competence of its author to comment.[179] There is an argument that the laws on forestalling as actually enforced hit the wrong target. R.H. Britnell has noted that they were liable to catch only minor offenders, since, because they '[theoretically at least] gave free rein to buying up of produce that was not on its way to market', 'in the grain trade, they tended to catch minor dealers rather than major ones with large capitals, who dealt directly with producers, bought in bulk and were more likely to be able to engineer monopolistic opportunities'.[180]

---

victuals; B.H. Putnam (ed.), *Yorkshire Sessions of the Peace 1361–4*, Yorkshire Archaeological Society 6 (1939), 14, 99 (preparations for a trial made in two forestalling cases, but the accused eventually confesses and makes fine before there is a trial).

[175] Appendix II graph 6 below. Examples: DL 30/85/1161 m.3d; DL 30/85/1161 m.8; DL 30/85/1163 m.9; DL 30/85/1164 m.1; DL 30/85/1165 m.3; DL 30/88/1199 m.15d; DL 30/89/1208 m.20. Note that there were some forestalling presentments in a view in 1391, but the exact number is unclear, as the manuscript is illegible: DL 30/89/1208 m.20.

[176] DL 30/85/1164 m.1.

[177] DL 30/85/1160 m.6d; DL 30/87/1184 m.1d.

[178] *SR* II:28–9. This statute concerned both coercive conduct on the part of hosts and also consensual forestalling and regrating on the part of London fishmongers.

[179] R.H. Britnell has stated that urban regulations were ineffective in '[regulating] sources of supply or the context in which prices were formed': Britnell, 'Urban economic regulation', 3.

[180] Britnell, 'Urban economic regulation', 3. Following Britnell, S.H. Rigby notes that 'In Colchester,

Rationale

It would be a mistake to see royal regulation in this area as being prompted by a policy of promoting freedom of contract as a general principle.[181] This would be an anachronism for two reasons. First of all, statements extolling the virtues of free competition do not occur in sources relating to English secular law, canon law or theology from the period under consideration, and it has been doubted that medieval governments had free market objectives, or that the encouragement of free markets in the modern sense would have been a priority where this objective clashed with other royal duties or objectives.[182] Even when kings did enact measures which seemed to promote 'free trade', such as the provision in the *Magna Carta* of 1297, or the 1383 proclamation in the king's name allowing all to sell fish freely in the city of London, royal pronouncements were made in terms of grants of privileges to certain groups, rather than endorsing a general policy of free trade for the whole realm. Petitioners asking the king to enforce their rights to trade freely based their requests on a particular traditional right or on a specific charter right, not an argument that there was a general principle or policy of free trade, again suggesting that there was no such policy to which they might appeal.[183] Parliamentary petitions of 1305 and 1335 illustrate this point. A petition before Parliament in 1305 from the 'poor burgesses of Newcastle' asked the king to enforce their right to trade freely, which was contained in charters of Edward I and his predecessors. A petition of 1335 from the 'good people' of Ely and elsewhere in Cambridgeshire asked for action to enforce the rights which they and their ancestors from time immemorial had had to sell victuals as they pleased.[184] In neither case was a wider principle of free trade invoked.

The second reason for arguing that there was no royal policy of encouraging free competition in thirteenth- and fourteenth-century England is the existence of many examples of statutes and orders which would seem to be contradictory to a general policy of upholding 'market freedom'. *Pollock and Maitland* notes the lack of a consistent policy as early as Magna Carta, which allowed foreign merchants freely to come and go, to dwell in England, and to buy and sell, but also guaranteed the ancient freedoms of cities and boroughs.[185] In the 1272–1399 period, the prime example of a measure which seems to fit into the model of royal action based on a policy of encouraging free trade is the Statute of York 1335, which 'allowed all merchants, native and foreign, to trade freely throughout

---

forestalling was more a strategy for survival adopted by the wives of stallholders, some of whom were too impoverished to pay their court fines, than a monopolistic conspiracy to defraud the pooe as contemporary moralists so often portrayed it', and 'At Coventry of 139 regraters and forestallers presented in the years 1377–80, 45% were women dealing in commodities such as fish, poultry, ale, butter, charcoal, eggs, cheese and fruit.' See also Rigby, *English Society*, 273, citing C.M. Barron, 'The golden age of women in medieval London', *Reading Medieval Studies* 15 (1989), 40; R.H. Hilton, *Class Conflict and the Crisis of Feudalism* (London, 1985), 213; Britnell, *Colchester*, 40.

[181] Pirenne, *Economic and Social History of Medieval Europe*, 175.
[182] de Roover, *JP*, 425; Bridbury, 'Markets and freedom', 233.
[183] *SR* 1:117. See also E. Miller in *CEH III*, c.6; *SR* 1:259 (Statute of Northampton 1328, all merchants to be free to trade in the realm), 270 (9 Edw. III, st.1 c.1, 1335, all merchants to be free to sell goods as they wish). Riley *Memorials*, 481; LB, H, f.172.
[184] F.W. Maitland (ed.), *Records of the Parliament holden at Westminster on the Twenty-Eighth Day of February in the Thirty-Third Year of the Reign of King Edward the First A.D. 1305* (London, 1893), 95; *RP* II:93.
[185] *P&M*, I, 172, citing Magna Carta, 1215, c.41 and c.13.

England'.[186] Soon after its enactment, however, exceptions were made in favour of the citizens of London. In 1337, Edward III exempted London from the statute, though he went back on this in 1351.[187] In 1376, the London authorities were given a power to control trade by aliens in the city.[188] These exceptions and modifications suggest that, if there was a 'free trade' policy, it was not a priority for kings and governments. Moreover, if there was such a policy, it clearly did not extend to all subjects, as can be seen by the fact that one of the demands of the peasant rebels of 1381 was that they should have the full liberty of buying and selling, like other men, in all fairs and markets.[189]

Action which seems to deny the existence of a free trade policy includes royal sanctioning of the foundation of guilds, institutions which put controls on sales of goods in certain areas for the benefit of their members. G. Unwin went as far as to write that 'Edward III's natural tendency' was to allow monopoly, because it made it easier for him to borrow money.[190] There are other examples of kings and governments acting against 'free trade' principles, such as the long-standing staple policy in the fourteenth century, or the special monopoly trading privileges granted in charters to towns.[191] The royal policy of concentrating trade in licensed markets could also be seen as 'anti-competitive' intervention, obliging people to trade at certain places and times.[192]

More generally, it is clear that there was no governmental or other consensus that monopoly was necessarily wrong. Status based monopolies were certainly accepted – e.g. the 'various legally enforceable monopolies claimed by manorial lords' such as tenants' obligations to perform 'suit of mill', and the profusion of rules promoting the trading rights of burgesses, citizens or freemen at the expense of 'foreigners'.[193] Monopoly was unexceptionable unless it caused actual problems: particularly price rises.[194]

Clearly, governments had an interest in gaining the support both of urban oligarchies and, at times, outsiders and alien traders. This was unlikely to make for an extreme or consistent position, and gave them a rather different perspective to that of urban or 'local' authorities. This was most obvious in the case of London, and the fluctuations in royal policy in this area show the different interests which kings had to balance in deciding whether to allow towns to follow their monopolistic urges or to curb these in favour of aliens.[195]

---

[186] Ormrod, *Reign of Edward III*, 133.
[187] Ormrod, *Reign of Edward III*, 173, citing *CPR 1334–8*, 460; *SR* I:314–15.
[188] Ormrod, *Reign of Edward III*, 247, citing *CLB, H*, 53.
[189] Prof. de Vericour, 'Wat Tyler', *TRHS*, new ser., 2 (1873), 77, 87.
[190] Unwin, *Finance and Trade under Edward III*, xviii. See also A.R. Bridbury, 'Markets and freedom in the Middle Ages', 233. Similar views are expressed in Britnell, *Commercialisation*, xv.
[191] McKisack, *Fourteenth Century*, 350ff. See, e.g., *CChR*, vol. II *1257–1300*, 414 (1292, Overton); *CChR*, vol. II *1257–1300*, 474 (1298, charter to the burgesses of Newcastle in respect of Pandon); *CChR*, vol. III, *1300–1326*, 27 (1302, Berwick on Tweed); *CChR*, vol. V, *1341–1417*, 237 (1377, London); *CChR*, vol. V, *1341–1417*, 358 (1396, Bedford).
[192] R.H. Britnell, 'The proliferation of markets in England 1200–1349', *EHR* 96 (1981), 209–21; Britnell, *Commercialisation*, 16. The policy of restricting trade to licensed markets may, however, be seen as a way of enabling rules on fair trading to be enforced: Bolton, *MEE*, 119.
[193] Rigby, *English Society*, 33; Britnell, 'Urban economic regulation', 2.
[194] Waugh, *England in the Reign of Edward III*, 90.
[195] Ormrod, *Reign of Edward III*, 173.

Were the laws meant to enforce religious and moral condemnation of these practices as vicious or wrongful? Canon lawyers and theologians had stated that forestalling, regrating and similar conduct was sinful and abusive long before the late thirteenth century, and continued to advance this view.[196] Their objections to these practices were linked to the doctrine of the just price. Some formulations of the just price doctrine give it in terms of 'the price determined without trickery, without . . . artificially cornering the market'.[197] Forestalling, regrating and similar conduct would, therefore, fall foul of the rule that goods should be sold at just prices (or should not be sold at unjust prices). As well as this theoretical objection, there was also a suggestion by theologians that princes ought to take action against those who engaged in the abusive practices considered in this chapter, either by banishing offenders, or by intervening and setting a just price where collusion forced up prices.[198] As with the price fixing regulations considered in the last chapter, however, royal documents banning forestalling, regrating and similar conduct show little sign of the influence of theological and canonical condemnation of these practices. In the *Statutum Mareschaucie* and ithe *Composicio*, objections to forestalling based on moral condemnation of forestallers can be seen.[199] Forestallers are described as 'thirsting for evil profit', 'open oppressors of poor people and all the commonalty', and '[enemies] of the whole shire and county' who '[act] from a desire for vicious profit, oppressing the poor and deceiving those who are richer'.[200] These objections bear some resemblance to canon law texts on usury.[201] In a statute of 1382 concerning forestalling and other damaging practices in the fishing trade, forestalling was associated with 'wickedness', though it is not clear whether forestalling itself was described as 'wicked'.[202] These, however, are the only examples of morally condemnatory language which I have found in legislation relating to forestalling, regrating and similar conduct, and nothing similar occurs in entries relating to enforcement of the laws. It would therefore seem that there are few signs of theological concepts, or the rules of canon law, or of moral ideas not wholly dependent on canon law or theology, being drawn upon or being referred to as justifications of the royal role in intervening in the areas considered here. This may be in contrast to the position in certain urban areas. R.H. Britnell notes instances of moral condemnation of forestalling, from the 'local' sphere.[203]

The damage which 'monopolistic practices' could cause is the discovery neither of great insight, nor of modern economics. Chaucer put the kernel of the matter

---

[196] de Roover, *JP*, 425; W. Ullmann, 'The medieval theory of legal and illegal organisations' in G. Garnett (ed.), *Law and Jurisdiction in the Middle Ages* (London, 1988), 289; *Gratian* C.14 q.4 c.9, cited by Gilchrist, *CEA*, 61. Langholm, *Economics*, 131–2, 136, 171, 385, 592.

[197] R.N. Swanson, *Church and Society in Late Medieval England* (Oxford, 1989), 194. See also Gilchrist, *CEA*, 61, Langholm, *Economics*, 131–2, 136, 171, 385, 592.

[198] Langholm, *Economics*, 408; de Roover, *JP*, 420.

[199] Britnell, 'Forstall', 94–6; BL, MS Stowe 386, ff.50r–51r; *SR* I:202–4.

[200] *SR* I:202–4.

[201] Britnell, 'Forstall', 94–5, notes the connection of language in the *Composicio* (SR I:202–4) with the idea of usurers as manifest oppressors of the poor in the work of the Lyons Council 1274. The idea of not allowing forestallers to remain in the jurisdiction also echoes the same source.

[202] *SR* II:28, st. 5 Ric. II, c.4. Hosts (*hospites*) in coastal towns were prohibited from forestalling fish or other victuals, and were ordered to 'cease their noyance and wicked deeds and forestallings'.

[203] Britnell, 'Urban economic regulation', 2; Britnell, *Colchester*, 134; W.H. Stevenson (ed.), *Records of the Borough of Nottingham*, 5 vols (London, 1882–1900), III no.37, p. 54.

into the mouth of a woman of no particular education (indeed something of a hostility to book-learning). Alisoun, the Wife of Bath, who noted that 'Grete prees at market maketh deere ware.'[204] Some concern with economic damage is manifested in the laws considered in this chapter. Concern that the action of forestallers, regraters and those engaged in similar conduct caused a shortage of certain goods can be seen in a number of statutes and royal orders. A 1315 mandate of Edward II concerning forestalling in London stated that the forestallers were affecting the supply of victuals in the city by their insistence on buying from those on their way to market.[205] Similar points were made in a petition of the commons in Parliament of 1363 made the point that the activities of those who made an agreement to keep goods back until the price rose caused shortages and price rises.[206] The concern that forestalling, regrating and similar conduct raised the price of goods was also commonly expressed in royal sources. The preamble to the York Ordinances of 1301 mentions the high prices caused by agreement between the citizens of York.[207] The preamble to the Statute of York of 1335 notes that the coercion of travelling sellers of goods to sell to citizens of towns as middlemen, rather than selling the goods directly to consumers, caused prices to be higher than they would have been if sellers had been allowed to sell them as they pleased.[208] A statute of 1353 described the great and outrageous expense of victuals throughout the realm caused by hostelers and other regraters of victuals.[209] In 1362, it was noted in a common petition that a price-setting agreement which had been made had raised the price of wine and other victuals in London, York, Bristol, Hull, Boston and elsewhere in the realm but the response was that existing legislation should be enforced, rather than suggesting anything new.[210] These problems were also raised in parliamentary petitions in 1314, 1322, 1358, 1363 and 1376–7. In 1314, the community of the city of Lincoln complained that the collusive action of some merchants of Lincoln resulted in prices of goods being twice or three times the value of the goods, causing sellers of fish and meat to stay away from Lincoln.[211] A petition from 'the magnates' in 1322 suggested that the price of victuals in York was raised before the king's visit because of the activities of forestallers of York and London.[212] A commons petition in Parliament after Easter 1358 complained that forestalling and regrating of fish at Great Yarmouth caused price rises and deterred the fishermen from coming to the area.[213] A petition of 1363 mentioned price rises as a consequence of engrossing. The complaint was that merchants, hostelers, regraters, forestallers and others were engrossing merchandise and victuals, and selling them at any price they wished to charge. Things bought for 12d were being sold for 3s or half a mark, and, in hostelries, a bushel of oats would be sold for 8d, when it had been bought for 3d. This was said to be to

---

[204] Wife of Bath's prologue, line 522 (a great crowd of buyers in the market makes things dear): A.C. Cawley (ed.), *Canterbury Tales* (London, 1992), 172.
[205] *LC*, 678–9.
[206] *RP* II:277b.
[207] *YO*, 9.
[208] *SR* I:269, 9 Edw. III, st.1 c.1.
[209] *SR* I:330, 27 Edw III, st.1 c.3.
[210] *RP* II:270b.
[211] *RP* I:290b.
[212] *CPR 1321–24*, 151. A commission of oyer and terminer was issued with respect to this petition.
[213] *SR* I:353, 31 Edw. III, st.2.

the great damage of the king, magnates, nobles and commons, and to be a contravention of the ordinances made on this point.[214] The commons complained in 1376–7 that the price of herring had increased and it had become scarcer because of the activities of forestallers.[215] Concerns about the adverse economic effects of forestalling, regrating and related conduct were therefore commonly stated both by petitioners and in royal measures. As mentioned, they also appear in some court records.

A strategy of intervening only where necessary to prevent deleterious economic consequences is suggested by a statute of 1382, in which hosts in coastal towns were generally prohibited from forestalling fish or other victuals, but, although fishmongers and citizens of London were ordered not to forestall fish, exceptions were made for eels, fresh luces and pike, because they were common.[216] The existence of such an exception suggests a concern by the legislator with the adverse economic effects of forestalling in cases of scarcity, and not with the punishment of forestalling *per se* as an immoral act.

Although forestallers were called by the church 'manifest oppressors of the poor', and this is echoed in the *Composicio* and Statute of the Marshalsea, few royal pronouncements mention the sectional interests of the poor as a particular concern.[217] Even the two documents mentioned do not concentrate on the poor, also mentioning that forestallers deceive those who are richer. Some petitions did ask that action should be taken against forestalling because of its adverse effects on the poor, as in an appeal of 1304 from the 'poor men of Norwich' complaining about the activities of 'certain rich men and forestallers' of the same city.[218] A petition of unknown date in the reign of Edward III also mentioned the plight of the poor as a consequence of forestalling. The complaint was that poor people could not live because of the price rise caused by the activities of forestallers. The petition received a mildly positive response – anyone who asked for the existing laws to be enforced should have their request granted.[219] On one occasion, the 'poor and infirm' were the beneficiaries of the forestalling laws in a different sense, when Edward I ordered that items confiscated after being forestalled in Oxford were to be given to them.[220]

Whilst urban rules in this area were made by and for local elites, and often directed against outsiders, the focus and use of royal laws and jurisdiction was naturally not so biased. Comparatively prominent people, who might not be challenged by local forestalling laws, could find themselves accused under royal justice, as in a presentment to the King's Bench at Chelmsford, 1352 concerning Sir John Chapleyn, parson of the church of Goldhanger.

> *Item ils pres[entent] q[e] Sir John Chapleyn la Parson de la Esglise de Goldhangr' est un comm[un] forstaller dez Auenes brans & altres vitailles issint qe p[er cause de] sa Richess ne li ose contreder en grant oppression & arerisement du poeple.*[221]

---

214 *RP* II:276b.
215 *RP* II:370.
216 *SR* II:28–9.
217 Harding, *England in the Thirteenth Century*, 135; Langholm, *Economics*, 427; *Composicio*, *SR* I:202–4.
218 *CPR 1301–7*, 284, which also mentions Yarmouth and Ipswich.
219 *RP* II:404a, no.143.
220 A. Ballard and J. Tait (eds), *British Borough Charters 1216–1307* (Cambridge, 1923), 297 (1284).
221 JUST 1/268 m.4.

(They present that Sir John Chapleyn, parson of the church of Goldhanger, is a common forestaller of oats, malt and other victuals, and that, on account of his wealth, no one dares to act against him, in great oppression and damage of the people.)

Although this does not demonstrate that royal action was intended to benefit the poor, it does show that it was seen as having some hope of helping the comparatively disadvantaged against more powerful neighbours.

Self-interested motives for royal action might include the wish to ensure that kings' own purchases, and those of their close associates, were not affected by excessive prices. The 1371 proclamation as to the sale of victuals in London made by the mayor and aldermen of London on their own behalf and that of the peers of the realm and others attending Parliament, stated that action was being taken because the high prices were causing hardship to those summoned to Parliament.[222] Forestalling might diminish royal income from tolls in royal markets and customs in royal ports, and the amercements and fines which would be paid by offenders against royal measures concerning forestalling, regrating and similar conduct might also have been a factor encouraging kings and governments to act in this area. A petition of 1308–9 suggested that action against forestallers would give the king considerable financial benefit. The petition, in the name of John of Ely, suggested that action against those who broke the Statute of Forestallers and Regraters would raise substantial sums of ten thousand marks or more for the king. Royal justices were already investigating the matter.[223] Royal interest of a financial nature is mentioned as a reason for intervention in some legislation concerning forestalling, regrating and related conduct. The preamble to a statute of 1363 refers to the 'great mischiefs which have happened to the king as well as to the great men and commons' through forestalling, regrating and related conduct.[224] There are also signs of royal concern to combat forestalling in order to preserve the level of customs and tolls coming to the exchequer from markets and ports. In 1347–8 the burgesses of Scarborough petitioned Parliament, complaining that some merchants and mariners were involved in a forestalling arrangement which evaded customs owed to the king's castle of Scarborough, 'to the great damage of the king as well as to the damage of the vill'. The royal response directed action: the bailiffs were to attach and punish offenders, and anyone who wished to sue them would have an action of trespass.[225] The avoidance of customs on goods, particularly wines brought into the realm, was noted in a statute or ordinance of 1351 which provided that no one was to forestall goods on their way to the realm.[226]

Furthermore, royal self-interest in terms of acting to win the support of important groups of subjects can, arguably, be seen in the positive responses to petitions which led to some of the legislation in this area. Petitions made to the king in Parliament to act against forestallers, regraters or those engaged in similar

[222] LB, G, f.235; Riley, *Memorials*, 347.
[223] *RP* I:275b. On John of Ely, see *CEMCR*, pp. 228–9, 233, and G.A. Williams, *Medieval London: From Commune to Capital* (London, 1963), 265. M. Weinbaum, *London under Edward I and Edward II* (Stuttgart, 1933), II, 176: 'In 1305, a fishmonger, John de Ely, prosecuted some of his colleagues on behalf of the king. A few years later they killed him.'
[224] *SR* I:379; st. 37 Edw. III.
[225] *RP* II:221a.
[226] *RP* II:249a.

conduct are recorded for 1308–9,[227] 1314, 1320, 1347–8, ?1358, 1363 (2), 1376–7 (2), an unknown date in the reign of Edward III, 1389 and 1394.[228] Judicial commissions were sometimes issued in response to petitions. Commissions were also issued in response to collective petitions, as was the case in 1347, when a commission of oyer and terminer was issued to investigate complaints by the men of Exeter and its environs of the forestalling of the markets of Exeter.[229] A.R. Bridbury portrayed royal intervention in this area as undertaken for the benefit of market franchisees, whose income from market dues would be affected by the activities of forestallers and regraters, and this may have been one factor.[230] Not all intervention can be seen as 'reactive', however: it has been noted that the important 1351 statute on forestalling was 'left almost completely to the council'.[231] It is also worth noting that there is no sign of pressure from the clergy to act against forestallers, regraters and those who engaged in similar conduct. This is in contrast to the activity and complaints of the clergy noted in the chapter on usury, but in line with the lack of clerical requests for royal price fixing.

A significant component in royal perception of the necessity for action against forestalling, regrating and similar conduct is the concern that these practices interfered with the efficacy of price fixing legislation. This idea can be seen in a mandate of Edward II of March 1315, prescribing action against forestallers of victuals in London. The forestallers were said to be acting fraudulently, in contravention of the king's price setting statute of just over a week before.[232] A connection between price fixing and the prohibition of forestalling can also be seen in the treatment by a non-governmental source of the 1315 price regulations and a forestalling statute. The *Vita Edwardi Secundi*, a chronicle written in about 1325, mentions together the 1315 price fixing laws and a statute of 1315 referring to the Gascon wine trade, which ordered that Englishmen should not in future cross the sea as forestallers seeking wine.[233]

The statements in statutes and related material express four major objections to forestalling and regrating. Firstly, there were objections to the profits so made. Secondly, there was concern for the effect which the conduct had on the price and supply of goods. Thirdly, there was concern that forestalling and regrating undermined other royal policies and legislation, in particular the laws fixing the price of certain victuals. Finally, there were some statements to the effect that forestalling and regrating adversely affected the king's interests. The most striking

---

[227] Though this was an individual concerned with the king's interest.
[228] *RP* I:275b (petition by John of Ely); *RP* I:290–291, 330a (petition by commons of Lincoln); *RP* I:370b (petition by one group of fishmongers of London, complaining of the activities of another group of fishmongers); *RP* II:221a (petition by burgesses of Scarborough). A common petition in Parliament is mentioned as the spur for 31 Edw. III, st.2; *SR* I:353. *RP* II:276b, 277b (common petition); *RP* II:370 (common petition); *RP* II:404a (common petition); *RP* III:271 (common petition); *SR* II:65, 13 Ric. II, st.1.
[229] *CPR 1345–8*, 320; *CPR 1348–50*, 453, m.20d (1349).
[230] A.R. Bridbury, 'Markets and freedom in the Middle Ages', 233.
[231] B.H. Putnam, 'Chief Justice Shareshull and the economic and legal codes of 1351–1352', *University of Toronto Law Journal* [1943–4], 251–81, at 255.
[232] 'ordinationem illam fraudulenter et malitiose enervare et adnullare machinantes': *LC*, II, 678–9. A further order was issued on this matter within another month: *LC*, II, 679–81.
[233] *Vita Edwardi Secundi*, 59.

fact is that the main concern which was expressed was with the observed negative effects of these practices, rather than with the immorality or illegality of the profits made. Governments explained their actions in terms of preserving the supply of goods and keeping prices from becoming too high.

Many urban rules were different in emphasis to royal rules, being overtly concerned with the self-interest of urban oligarchies or the like against outside traders.[234] Even in the case of urban action, however, motives were probably mixed, and there is some suggestion of change over the late thirteenth and fourteenth centuries. In an entry in the earliest surviving roll of the Norwich court leet, from 1287–8, where the offence of buying goods outside the market is mentioned, associated with this conduct is the loss of customs and tolls rather than adverse effects on the price of goods in the market.[235] Another entry on the same roll mentions what seems to be a similar offence, again not calling it forestalling, but cites different mischief, stating that '[A]ll the fishermen and poulterers buy meat and fish in order to heighten the Norwich market.'[236] In subsequent rolls, the idea of 'heightening the market' comes to the fore in descriptions of such offences, though the loss of tolls is mentioned as the mischief caused by forestalling as late as 1374.[237] There would therefore seem to have been two bases for action: forestallers were to be punished because of the effect which their action had on prices in the market in Norwich, and also because of the effect which it had on the tolls and customs of the market. The effect on prices came to be regarded as more important, with increasingly detailed descriptions of the effects. Whereas in 1287 the representatives of the parishes of St Laurence and St Gregory merely asserted that the activity of buying oysters at sea 'heightened the market' in Norwich, in 1374–5 more details were provided about the effects of the activities of Roger Calf, who 'bought by forestalment four boats full of oysters at divers times whereby the price of a hundred rose by one and a half pence for a day'.[238]

Conclusion

Variations over time can again be seen in the scope and subject matter of the laws. The definitions of the offences considered in this chapter were developing during the late thirteenth and fourteenth centuries, from an idea of an individual committing a wrong to the idea of two people entering into a consensual bargain with damaging consequences for others. There was increasing prescription of conduct, with regulations becoming ever more detailed over the fourteenth century. After a series of investigations in the 1270s, and until the last years of Edward I, it is plausible to argue that the king and governments had the limited and self-interested ambition of regulating forestalling and regrating in the verge.[239] There was much greater interest in the fourteenth century. The period of closest

---

[234] See, e.g., Britnell, *Commercialisation*, 177; M. Kowaleski, 'The commercial dominance of a medieval provincial oligarchy: Exeter in the late fourteenth century', *Medieval Studies* 46 (1984), 355–84, at 359. See above, n.98 in c.1.

[235] Hudson, *Leet Jurisdiction*, 2.

[236] Hudson, *Leet Jurisdiction*, 3.

[237] Hudson, *Leet Jurisdiction*, 64.

[238] Hudson, *Leet Jurisdiction*, 9, 64.

[239] Britnell, 'Forstall', 99.

involvement of central government in inquiring into offences seems to have been the period from the 1350s onwards, when *ad hoc* judicial commissions were common, and cases seem to have been heard frequently in the King's Bench and in the shires by the new justices of the peace. Concerted action following the Black Death must also be assumed to have a link to the policies underlying the labour legislation. It did not, however, come 'out of the blue': the first half of the fourteenth century saw increasing levels of government and 'central' action in the area of forestalling and related conduct. In contrast to R.C. Palmer's theory on the effect of the Black Death and consequent economic problems on royal intervention in subjects' lives, the material considered in this chapter does not show a radical change in prescription or enforcement in the immediate aftermath of the Black Death. It is clear that there was an increase in royal concern and activity in this area in the latter half of the fourteenth century, but it seems to have been the product of a gradual transformation of ideas over a longer period, rather than a sudden expansion of royal control. Once again, the last years of Edward I and the first years of Edward II seem to mark an increase in government intervention, and, once again, there seems to be a slow-down in intervention, or at least in innovation, during the reign of Richard II. The granting of commissions mentioned above shows an active interest in enforcing the laws against forestalling, regrating and related conduct. It can be contrasted with the apparent decrease of active royal involvement in searching out and punishing usury over the fourteenth century.

The material considered in this chapter shows another area of serious and increasing royal intervention in prescribing the substance of the bargains of subjects over the years 1272–1399, with a move from the regulation of forcible or coercive conduct alone to the inclusion of consensual but damaging conduct in the list of areas in which royal action was appropriate. This move was not complete by the end of the fourteenth century.

Considering the evidence of enforcement, there has, perhaps, been an underestimation of the activity of governments in this area. There are definite signs of action by kings, governments and courts in prescribing rules and in enforcing them against offenders. The existence of presentments of offenders in many rolls at many different levels of jurisdiction over much of the period shows that these laws were not a dead letter as far as the government or various local communities (who presented offenders) or local officials were concerned, and, although there were occasional statements of unhappiness with the way in which the laws were being enforced, petitions continued to ask for royal action in this area throughout the fourteenth century, suggesting that there was no general conception that royal enforcement mechanisms did not work. Subjects requested royal action in this area on a number of occasions, and sometimes complained if royal measures were not being properly enforced, suggesting a degree of support for royal policy from at least some quarters.

The discussion of why governments acted in this area shows several motives for action, from that of self-interest, to condemnation of the unearned profit of the middleman, to concerns for the supply of goods to subjects at prices which were not inflated. It is certainly the last which is to the fore in official sources such as statutes and also in the petitions put to successive kings. It is perhaps arguable that a change in attitude occurred from the condemnation of the evil profit of the forestaller in the 1275 Marshalsea regulations on forestalling, to the fourteenth-century focus on the economic effects of forestalling and similar practices. It should be stressed, however, that at no time in the period under consideration did governments move beyond simple, tangible, economic ideas, such as supply of goods and prices, to embrace a policy of free trade or *laissez faire*. Forestalling and regrating were clearly considered to be connected to the price fixing mechanisms of the assizes of bread and ale, often being included in the same legislation, and being prosecuted together. Overall, the evidence on the scope of royal legislation on forestalling and related conduct points to an increasing interest by kings and governments in proscribing certain particularly damaging bargains between subjects, but not an intention to regulate sales of all commodities.

Conclusion

What conclusions may be drawn on the laws which ensnared the allegedly-offending characters used to introduce the chapters above? Were they foolish and ultimately doomed interventions, a dead letter in practice and a dead-end in terms of legal theory: 'monkish superstition and civil tyranny'? This book concludes that they were not. Despite all the mistakes, faults and inconsistencies, there is evidence that they were taken seriously within the context of medieval law, and that it was considered worthwhile and necessary for kings and governments, and other authorities, to take action to regulate the substance of loans and sales between private individuals.

The general pattern shows increased 'central' intervention in terms of making rules. In 1272, there existed a royal prohibition of usury, and there was regulation of the price of bread, ale and wine at national level. By 1399, laws against forestalling in the sense of an illicit contractual practice rather than a criminal seizing of goods en route for market had emerged, and goods other than bread, ale and wine had been brought under statutory price fixing regimes, whilst the older laws also remained in force. There was particular activity against usury in the first part of the reign of Edward I, and, though usury was prosecuted by royal tribunals or by other tribunals with royal blessing or tolerance in the fourteenth century, and though others were clearly concerned by the effects of usury, the concern of the king and government to act against usury never subsequently seems to have reached the same level. A large increase in the number of items covered by royal price regulation came in the aftermath of the Black Death, though a tendency towards bringing more items within the scope of royal and 'national' price fixing laws can be seen from at least 1307–8, when commissions to royal justices mentioned a jurisdiction over the price of all goods, and 1315, when Edward II attempted to legislate for the prices of poultry and other victuals. National legislation in the 1350s and 1360s covered new classes of sales. After the early 1360s, the expansion of royal legislation in this area slowed down. Such statutes as were passed in the latter part of Edward III's reign and in the reign of Richard II generally adjusted the rules in areas already covered by royal legislation, rather than bringing new areas under its sway. A broadly similar pattern can be detected in the related area of forestalling and similar conduct. Consensual forestalling began to be brought within the fold of royal justice in limited respects in the reign of Henry III, in Edward I's reign there was development towards a greater royal interest in the area and this continued under Edward II. Like direct price control, it was brought together with the labour legislation in 1349–51, with consolidation and minor adjustments in the law and regular 'central' enforcement thereafter.

A firm conclusion of the book is that it is necessary to modify the idea that there was a sudden, unprecedented, degree of royal intervention in subjects' economic affairs after the Black Death. In contrast to the thesis of R.C. Palmer, the pattern suggested is not one of a simple change, 'transformation' or 'revolution' immediately after the Black Death.[1] There was a particular burst of activity after the Black Death, but this represented a change in the degree rather than the nature of activity. If a 'watershed' is desired, it should be sought earlier, at the end of the reign of Edward I and in that of Edward II. An important change in conception of the royal role in this area seems to have occurred in the early years of the fourteenth century. Several key alterations can be seen to have occurred at this time: the change in the justifications given for royal action, the move away from taking action against dead usurers, the advent of forestalling as an important area of royal activity and the beginning of attempts to broaden the scope of price control legislation all seem to have occurred from 1299 to 1315, years taking in the troubled later period of Edward I's reign and part of the reign of Edward II. The idea of Edward II's reign as a period of change in the spheres of administration and constitutional and economic theory was highlighted by T.F. Tout in the early twentieth century, and has not been the subject of serious doubt since then.[2] G.L. Harriss also described the reign of Edward II as 'one of the most formative periods of English history'.[3] This book suggests another area in which the reign, and the few years before it, was pivotal. This period was hardly a high point of royal power, political or financial, so that the apparent expansion of jurisdiction cannot be put down to royal expansionism in opposition to any particular element of society: expansion must have been a matter of a reasonable degree of consensus and co-operation.[4] The regulation of subjects' loans and sales which was later to appear 'tyrannical' seems to have become part of royal justice with little objection, with the exception of the negative views taken of the 1315 victual statute, the history of which suggests a disagreement as to the advisability of royal fixing of prices. Any such disagreement on this issue would seem to have been resolved by the late 1340s and 1350s, when interventionist legislation was passed with the compliance and support of Parliament. There are signs of a new divergence of opinion as to the way in which the king and government ought to intervene in this area in last quarter of the fourteenth century, perhaps particularly in 1388–90, when, as has been seen in the chapters on usury and price regulation, there were disagreements between the government and the commons in Parliament as to reform of the law on investigation and punishment of usury and price offences. In the final quarter of the fourteenth century, political troubles may have encouraged less concern and a less interventionist government line on the substance of subjects' bargains.[5]

---

[1] Palmer, *Black Death*, 1 and generally; *EEJ*, 4.
[2] Tout, *Edward II*, vii, 31, 32, 217, 235.
[3] Harriss, *King, Parliament and Public Finance*, 187.
[4] See, e.g., Prestwich, *The Three Edwards*, 82–3; Harding, *England in the Thirteenth Century*, 309–21.
[5] McKisack, *Fourteenth Century*, cc.13–15; C. Given-Wilson, *Chronicles of the Revolution 1397–1400: The Reign of Richard II* (Manchester, 1993), introduction. Richard II certainly 'innovated' – in ways which might be considered illegitimate – in the areas of constitutional law and his relations with subjects: see, e.g., N. Saul, *Richard II* (New Haven, 1997); C.M. Barron, 'The quarrel of Richard II with London, 1392–7' in F.R.H. Du Boulay and C.M. Barron (eds), *The Reign of Richard II* (London, 1971), 173–201; Barron, 'Tyranny of Richard II', *BIHR* 41 (1968), 10–14. On the economic situation, Bolton, *MEE*, 62, describes an improved standard of living for many as prices fell and wages rose.

Despite his increasing perception of his own majesty, Richard II did not seek increased intervention and power on this everyday level.[6]

Certain periods seem, therefore, to have been particularly important in accelerating the rate of change or altering its direction, but the picture which has emerged is evolutionary rather than revolutionary very much in line with the model of evolutionary change outlined by Musson and Ormrod for English law in general in the late thirteenth and fourteenth centuries.[7] This 'gradualist' view also serves somewhat to undermine the assertion that 'economic' laws are tied to the self-interested pressure of Parliament, as it grew in power in the fourteenth century.[8] If there was already a well-established pattern of royal intervention which merely intensified after the Black Death, that gives an independent basis for the increased legislative and other intervention apart from reaction to self-interested requests.

Given that the period covered is longer than a century, and that, during that period, there were several changes in the mechanisms available for law enforcement, with the early fourteenth century in particular being 'a period of much judicial experimentation and improvisation', it is not surprising that various different courts and tribunals were used for the trial of offences against the laws under consideration.[9] The general comments which can be made are that, in the case of usury and forestalling and regrating, there was less delegation of jurisdiction to low-level tribunals than there was in the case of the early price regulations, and, in the case of the price regulations, there was a move to enforce these by royal appointees rather than franchising them out in the fourteenth century, particularly after the Black Death.

As well as variation in the tribunals used, there was also variation in the ways in which the laws themselves were set out. It has been seen that on some occasions when kings and governments set out rules, they used a comprehensive statute, setting out in full the rules which were to govern a particular area. In other cases, a degree of discretion in deciding the rules was left to a specified or unspecified authority. An important role was left for 'local' jurisdictions, both in enforcement and in varying or setting rules.

The evidence examined suggests that there were serious attempts to enforce the rules and to punish offenders against them. There do seem to have been fluctuations over time in the intensity of enforcement activity, but this is neither surprising nor out of line with other aspects of medieval law enforcement. The rolls

---

[6] McKisack, *Fourteenth Century*, 427–78; N. Saul, 'Richard II and the vocabulary of kingship', *EHR* 110 (1993), 854–77; R.H. Jones, *The Royal Policy of Richard II: Absolutism in the Middle Ages* (Oxford, 1968). There was a perceptible slowing down of innovation in the area of central economic regulation. Such measures as were passed were consolidating, or extending in minor ways, the developments of the past century, rather than doing much that was new. Central involvement may have decreased in the next reign, as the 1399 'revolution' has been seen to herald important changes in royal policy towards changing and making law, with an avowedly undynamic policy emerging. Barraclough, 'Law and legislation', 91, notes Henry IV's non-interventionist attitude to the law, citing his statement 'Le Roy ne vorroit ascunement chaunger les bones Custumes et Usages faitz et usez d'auncien temps' (The King does not wish to change in any way the good customs and usages made and used from olden times. 1401: *RP* III:458), and contrasting it with statements from the time of Richard II

[7] *EEJ*, 4–5, 92, 112. A 'gradualist' view of royal intervention in 'matters economic' is also evident in Bolton, *MEE*, 327.

[8] Bolton, *MEE*, 329.

[9] *EEJ*, 53.

of various courts show efforts being made to enforce the laws. Court rolls sometimes show surprising detail in accusations, which suggests that mechanisms of detection worked reasonably well, with a degree of co-operation from enforcement agencies and 'the public'.[10] It is true that financial penalties were often imposed where the law prescribed another method of punishment, but this was not unusual in medieval legal practice. Petitions in Parliament asking for royal action against certain bargains show that influential elements in the realm did not think that royal action in this area was useless.

The study of court rolls has revealed particular aspects of enforcement which could not have been predicted from examination of the laws alone. It has been seen, for example, that, after the reign of Edward I, there is no trace in the rolls of reports of dead usurers, but there are cases against living usurers, despite the model of exclusive competence for the church over the living and the king over the dead which has been assumed to have held sway. In terms of timing of the change, once again, the end of the thirteenth century and the beginning of the fourteenth seems to be the crucial time – with the last dead usurer found in royal rolls appearing in 1299. The (re)statement of exclusive jurisdictions in 1341 is likely to represent an unsuccessful attempt to turn back the clock after a change had occurred.

A particular fascination of examining these particular laws in this particular time is that they are clearly floating on top of turbulent conceptual seas, struggling with ideas of coercion and consent. Ideas of voluntariness and consent were in the process of development in a number of areas of law.[11] The rules on purveyance, which attempted to ensure that the sale is not wholly involuntary whilst doing nothing to alter its basic nature as a forced sale, show something of the conceptual uncertainty in this area. A similar disagreement about voluntariness can be seen in the labour legislation from 1349 onwards, with a number of changes of policy as to whether the employer 'forced' to pay high wages should be punished or not.[12] The slow and incomplete change in understanding of forestalling – from a forcible act to a consensual but damaging arangement – can also be fitted into this pattern of conceptual ferment. Tensions and change between punishment by corporal means and fining, and perhaps between punishment and 'licensing', may be seen in a similar light. The century and a quarter examined saw a general movement to financial penalties from corporal ones, but the move was not complete by the end of the fourteenth century, with some elements of society still wishing to bring back corporal punishment which was seen as inappropriate by others. Some of the disagreement may spring from the genealogy of pricing laws, with their origins in local and then national regulations which did not always separate 'cheating' offences – adulteration, selling goods of an unhealthy nature, deceit and use of

---

[10] Compare the conclusion of Poos that there was a fair degree of co-operation from different levels of society in connection with the enforcement of the labour laws: Poos, 'Social context', 36, 52; Given-Wilson, 'The problem of labour', 98.

[11] This was an issue, for example, in suicide (in the case of those with mental illness): see G. and A. Seabourne, 'The law on suicide in medieval England', *Journal of Legal History* 21 (2000), 21–48. It was also an issue in other matters: for instance, the 'consent' of a woman in a case in the bishop of Ely's court at Littleport in 1324, consent (*assensu*) being obtained of the wife of Walter Albin to the removal of some goods by William Fowler 'by frequently kicking her' (seen in *Court Baron*, 138), would not have been acceptable in other contexts. On duress in the law of obligations, see Ibbetson, *Obligations*, 71–4.

[12] Given-Wilson, 'The problem of labour', 87.

unfair measures – from over-pricing. More generally, we should not treat the laws examined as derogations from a free contract model of relations: so many matters legal and social were still dominated by status not contract, despite the fact that some of the more extreme ramifications of feudal relations were on the decline.[13] Society and law were far from being organised around a principle of consent.[14] The prime example of this is the fact that the king or the 'crown' simply did not act according to the same rules as others. Consent was not necessarily required for loans or sales to the crown by subjects.[15]

Royal involvement in the substance of subjects' sales and loans *inter se* may be explained in a number of ways. There is certainly evidence that financial self-interest was one factor motivating kings and governments. The action of Edward I in connection with Jewish and Italian usurers, for example, suggests a major concern for financial self-interest. Royal action in these areas was not, however, based solely on self-interest. The evidence examined allows several arguments to be made. First, it is clear that kings and governments did not use their jurisdiction as extensively as they might have done. There does not, for example, seem to have been widespread confiscation of the assets of deceased usurers, though this was accepted as being a royal right. This lack of action can be contrasted with the mechanisms used to confiscate the goods of deceased felons and suicides, records of which can be seen in the eyre rolls and coroners' rolls throughout the period under consideration.[16] A second argument against financial self-interest as the sole spur for royal action is the fact that kings and governments intervened even when it was not in their immediate financial interest to do so. In particular, they continued to supervise the enforcement of the assizes of bread and ale even when they had franchised out the jurisdiction and the right to the profits, in a way which does not look particularly 'money-grabbing'. The nature of the laws passed also shows that governments went beyond their own financial self-interest, since they not only regulated deals which affected themselves, but created rules for the whole realm. They did make some money from amercement of offenders, but this was a normal feature of medieval law enforcement, rather than something peculiar to the enforcement of these laws.

Some of the action taken to regulate subjects' bargains was taken in response to the request of powerful interest groups. Not all royal action, however, seems to fit this pattern. There is often little information about the way in which thirteenth-century statutes developed. Sometimes, once better parliamentary records are available, however, royal intervention or non-intervention can be seen not to have

---

[13] Harding, *England in the Thirteenth Century*, 321. E. Miller and J. Hatcher, *Medieval England, Rural Society and Economic Change 1086–1348* (London, 1978), xii–xiv, 112–17.

[14] Note that Professor Ibbetson observes the move, in a wider medieval period, towards viewing a sale as 'a bilateral rather than a simply unilateral transaction', though warns against too early an assumption of a 'transition to a "consensual" theory of sale': D. Ibbetson, 'From property to contract: the transformation of sale in the middle ages', *Journal of Legal History* 13 (1992), 1–22, at 1, 2, 13.

[15] See, e.g., the forced loans of wool to the crown of 1337–8: Ormrod, *Reign of Edward III*, 135; Schofield, 'Introduction', 8–9 and the material on purveyance in c.3. The same applies to wages, Edward III offering excess wages to building workers on some building projects in order to ensure sufficient labour: Ormrod, *Reign of Edward III*, 90.

[16] See, e.g., R.F. Hunnisett, *The Medieval Coroner* (Cambridge, 1961), especially at 4–6, 21, 29–34, 80–1, 116, 198.

accorded with the requests of petitioners, as in the response to the 1388 petition for action against those who breached the assizes of bread and ale, and the response to the 1390 request for civic authorities to be given power to investigate and try usury. Some measures even seem to have been enacted in the face of opposition from powerful groups, as can be seen from the descriptions in the *Rotuli Parliamentorum* and in chronicles of the enactment of the 1315 victual price statute.

Official documents provided a variety of different reasons for royal intervention. A trend can, however, be detected in the type of justification which was offered. In the reign of Edward I, the emphasis in official documents was on the inherent evil or immoral nature of certain deeds. In the remainder of the fourteenth century, more weight was placed upon the adverse practical consequences of certain bargains. Material on usury and forestalling from the reign of Edward I has overtones of religious or moral condemnation which all but disappear in later statutes, statements and ordinances concerning all of the areas under consideration, even though all of the areas continued to be the subject of theological and canon law investigation and condemnation throughout the fourteenth century. This change may suggest a mere change in formula, or it may be that there was a genuine change in royal outlook from the reign of Edward II onwards, with a degree of 'secularisation' of the justification for royal intervention in the substance of subjects' bargains: a move from concern with the sin and guilt of those engaging in particular behaviour to concern with the detrimental consequences to others of particular bargains. This cannot, however, be seen as a complete shift from a desire to punish the guilty to a desire to avoid adverse consequences of particular behaviour: both elements were present in royal action throughout the period under consideration.

That medieval English monarchs did see fit to make serious – even if patchy – efforts in this area is a matter of interest when considering their role in general. The argument of this book is that there is something more than simply a collection of individual instances of royal intervention. There was, rather, a genuine royal view that it was appropriate to intervene in subjects' private bargains, for the benefit of those subjects who were suffering, or were likely to suffer at the hands of others, in a way so serious that it transcended, or spread beyond the parties to any particular bargain, and affected the community of the realm. Ideas as to which bargains could do this might vary somewhat from time to time, but it is clear that subjects' loans and sales were 'in the frame' throughout the thirteenth and fourteenth centuries.

Evidence from court rolls and royal pronouncements suggests that kings were not particularly interested in the individuals who suffered, except as a cipher to bring prosecutions or be part of the accusation. Restitution was not a primary consideration. Royal justice could not hope even to discover all offenders, never mind restore or bring about complete fairness or justice in all exchanges. Importantly, it also made few claims to exclusivity, existing against a background of and interacting reasonably harmoniously with other jurisdictions and authorities also involved in regulation of subjects' sales and loans. There were many rule-making and rule-enforcing bodies as well as 'the centre'. Variation was generally tolerated, or expected. We should not take it as evidence of necessary 'opposition'.[17] If we see the whole legal system as organic, in line with the most sophisticated views, and in parallel with common images of society as a body, or a set of orders, separate in function and yet linked,[18] we will see something like modern principles of 'subsidiarity' at work, rather than a failure of royal government to set universal rules and ensure that they were enforced identically in all jurisdictions.[19] It is probably better not to see 'the law of the land degenerat[ing] into local custom interpreted by local people', but to see that local enforcement and interpretation (within fairly broad parameters) was tolerated and expected.[20] That there should be variation in local laws is hardly surprising: this was accepted in thirteenth-century treatises.[21] Where rules had come from was not always crucial, and the writer of the *Court Baron* saw no problem in describing a breach of the assize of bread as being against 'the general constitution of the realm, . . . the statutes of the lord and his franchise'.[22] For 'the centre', the existence of other jurisdictions was necessary. The 'centre' relied on local enforcement because it had not the resources to ensure obedience to its laws. Bodies other than 'central legislature and executive' were also relied upon to flesh out the bare bones of royal laws. The royal law assumes the existence of ecclesiastical rules on usury even if it does sometimes show a conflict or lack of complete agreement, royal laws on forestalling, for example, assume local rules on details of the bounds and timing of markets. Price regulations involving assessments of quality assumed local standards.

The matter of centralisation or devolution of enforcement jurisdiction cannot be described in simple terms. Jurisdiction over the assizes of bread and ale, for example, was often franchised out to manorial authorities in the early thirteenth century. In the case of usury, different jurisdictions handled the same matter at the same time. Judicial responsibility had been delegated to other authorities for centuries – or had been exercised by other authorities without royal interest, and this continued to be the case, though the available delegates were different. A frequent pattern was for the basic rules to be made centrally, with an obligation on some other authority either to interpret loose rules or to adjust the rules as appropriate.[23]

An 'organic' or 'interdependent' view of the nature of medieval institutions is also helpful in considering the emergence of laws. The origin of rules is often emphasised as local or private rather than royal, but this does not necessarily mean

---

[17]   See, e.g., Musson, *Public Order and Law Enforcement*, 225.

[18]   See, e.g., Rigby, *English Society*, 182–6 and c.5.

[19]   This inelegant word describes a concept of law used in the European Union system: 'In areas which do not fall within its exclusive competence, the Community shall take action, in accordance with the principle of subsidiarity, only if and insofar as the objectives of the proposed action cannot be sufficiently achieved by the Member States and can therefore by reason of the scale or effects of the proposed action, be better achieved by the Community'; 'The broad idea underlying the principle of subsidiarity is a simple one: that public powers should normally be located at the lowest tier of government where they can be exercised effectively': Art. 5 EC: A.M. Arnull, A. Dashwood, M.G. Ross and D.A. Wyatt, *European Union Law*, 4th edn (London, 2000), 132, 156. In a related sphere, W.M. Ormrod notes that 'Local assemblies existed not in isolation but as part of a hierarchy of representation and governance culminating in parliament and the crown': Ormrod, *Political Life*, 50.

[20]   Britnell, 'Morals', 29.

[21]   Doe, *Fundamental Authority*, 43; *Bracton*, Introduction, 19; *Mirror*, 5.

[22]   *Court Baron*, 25.

[23]   See *EEJ*, 113.

that 'local' or 'private' laws were adopted without thought by 'central' authorities, or that there is something wrong or lazy in such adoptions. 'There was', after all, 'no concept of plagiarism in the Middle Ages.'[24] The subject matter or content of legislation could originate from 'top' or 'bottom', or at least from 'higher' or 'lower' authorities, or, perhaps, it might arise independently in different authorities. Even where it has been shown that there were 'local' or 'private' precursors of royal or 'national' rules, one cannot simply say that the origin of economic laws was 'local' or 'central'. On occasion, influences may be traced, but the overall picture is one of interplay, overlap and cross-fertilisation.[25] From a variety of sources, ecclesiastical law, local and urban custom and the rules pertaining in the verge, a body of royal 'national' rules was being created, regulating the substance of subjects' sales and loans to an unprecedented level and influencing law and society for centuries to come.

---

[24] Wood, *Medieval Economic Thought*, 6.

[25] See, e.g., the work of Anthony Musson (*MLC*, 208), who notes that 'central' legislation may have encouraged local communities in making and recording their own laws, and that 'local' legislation and practices could also 'provide the inspiration and example for national legislation'.

Appendix I: Cases and Reports from Central Royal Courts

Table 1: Information about usurious conduct from eyre presentments

Eyre	Article	Allegation	Dead or living?	Outcome
Worcestershire 1275[1]	Of Christian usurers	Milo of Evesham was accustomed to sell his grain at a higher price than it was worth on the day of the sale, on account of the loan.	Dead	Milo was reported to have had goods in the vill of Evesham, so inquiries were to be made as to the goods (or the matter) there.
Devon 1281[2]	Of Christian usurers	William the beadle lent 20s on one occasion, and received 22d in profit (de lucro), and so for a loan of a quarter of grain, he sometimes took a bushel and sometimes two bushels, depending on the length of the loan.	Living	Ordered to be arrested.
Lincolnshire 1281–4[3]	Of Christian usurers etc.	Maugeruss de Manthorp and William son of Walter of the same place are usurers.	Living	Ordered to be arrested. Afterwards, they came and were acquitted.
Lincolnshire 1281–4[4]	Of usurers etc.	Thomas Hert of Willingham, Robert of Angulo in Stowe and Alice, his sister, and Gillota Crake of Stowe are in mercy for the trespass of usury.	Living	In mercy.
Gloucestershire 1287[5]	Of Christian usurers etc.	William Goatchild of Broad Campden lent Ranulph Lefoy of Quenton and Helewys his wife 8s and the said William took for the aforesaid loan a quarter of wheat in profit (de incremento).	Living	In mercy.
Gloucestershire 1287[6]	Of usurers etc.	Thomas son of William Kenemerford lent (mutuavit) Walter Malicorn of Kenemerford four quarters of wheat and took in profit (de incremento) eight quarters.	Living	The sheriff was ordered to make Thomas come to court. He did come and denied everything, and put himself on the country. He was acquitted. The jurors were to be judged for 'concealing' this presentment.

Table 1: (*cont.*)

Eyre	Article	Allegation	Dead or living?	Outcome
Westmorland 1292[7]	Of usurers etc.	Roger de Burton is a manifest and common usurer, lending money and selling or selling on credit goods of all kinds, such as wool, cattle, sheep and other goods and chattels, which he sells on credit for future payment, taking on account of the term[8] more than the proper value, sometimes doubling the sale price. And he did this after the Jews had left England, to the damage of all those making contracts with him on all sorts of goods etc.	Living	Sheriff ordered to have him at Carlisle a fortnight after St Martin's day. On that day, Roger came and found security to be at Newcastle on the octaves of St Hillary. He was given a day at Carlisle on the quinzaine of St Martin.[9]
Westmorland 1292[10]	Of usurers etc.	William de Goldington is a manifest usurer, lending money and selling wool, cloth and other merchandise [on credit], taking as usury, on account of credit from each person contracting with him, profit above the amount owed. And he did this [in his dealings with] William de Stirkland, knight, from whom he once took 10½ marks for 40s, and on another occasion, 22 marks for 40s.	Living	Sheriff ordered to make him come. Afterwards he came and denied everything and put himself on the country.
Westmorland 1292[11]	Of usurers etc.	John de Goldington bought from Thomas son of Master William de Goldington three sacks of wool for 10½ marks paid immediately, the wool to be delivered at a certain date, i.e. Pentecost. When the date came, Thomas gave him a sack worth 9 marks and for the remaining two sacks, paid 17 marks. And the said John commonly did this.	Living	To be discussed. A day was set to hear judgment at Carlisle a fortnight after St Martin's day.[12]
Cambridgeshire 1299[13]	Of dead Christian usurers	The late Master William de Luda, bishop of Ely, made loans to various men of this hundred, through William Boreward and Ralph of Littlebury, his bailiffs of this hundred; that is to say at Lyndon, he lent forty quarters of wheat, sixty quarters of barley, twenty quarters of beans and peas, and, at Wilberton, twenty quarters of rye, fifty quarters of barley and fifteen quarters of peas, and, at	Dead	To be discussed.

Stretham, thirty quarters of wheat, fifty quarters of barley and twenty quarters of dredge, and, at Dodyngton, twenty quarters of wheat and forty quarters of dredge, fourteen quarters of peas, taking for each quarter of the aforesaid grain eight pence above the sum for which it could have been sold in the said island at the time when it was lent, until new harvest. [It was done in such a way that] all of the profit came into the hands of this bishop, who knew of it and ordered it.

To be discussed.

Cambridgeshire 1299[14]

Of dead Christian usurers

Dead

The late Master William de Luda, bishop of Ely, was a usurer, through [the agency of] Hugh the chaplain, formerly bailiff of Wisbech, for this Hugh, by the order of this bishop lent the bishop's grain in this hundred, that is to say in the twenty-second year of the present king's reign, he lent three hundred quarters of wheat to various men of the county, taking for each quarter 2s above the common sale price of wheat in the region of Ely, on account of the respite of repayment until the new harvest. And similarly in the twenty-third, twenty-fourth and twenty-fifth years of the present king's reign, in each year, he lent three hundred quarters of wheat, taking [profit] on them in the aforesaid manner. And similarly in the twenty-second year, and in the twenty-third year, and in the twenty-fifth year, he lent forty quarters of maslin, taking for each quarter 2s above the price at which it could have been sold according to its true value at the aforesaid time of the year. And similarly with oats in the twenty-fourth and twenty-fifth years, each year he sold fifty quarters of oats, taking for each quarter twelve pence above the price at which it could have been sold between the feast of St John the Baptist and the feast of the Exaltation of Holy Cross. [And this was done in such a way that] all of the profits of the aforesaid sale and loan came into the hands of this bishop, with his knowledge and by his order.

Table 1: (*cont.*)

Eyre	Article	Allegation	Dead or living?	Outcome
Channel Islands 1331[15]	Of usurers etc.	Jominus son of Elias de Submonte lent 20s to John Renward until a fixed date, so that at the said date he was to pay him 25s as usury.	Living	In mercy. Amercement assessed at 15s sterling.[16]

[1] JUST 1/1025 m.4; JUST 1/1026 m.35; JUST 1/1028 m.16.

[2] JUST 1/181 m.38d.

[3] JUST 1/497 m.3; JUST 1/491 m.2d. Another version of the accusation can be found in JUST 1/486 m.2d.

[4] JUST 1/497 m.38; JUST 1/486 m.28d. This presentment is not mentioned at all in another version of the eyre of Lincoln: JUST 1/491, Mettingham's roll of crown pleas, even though some presentments from Well Wappentake are recorded.

[5] JUST 1/278 m.41; another version: JUST 1/284 m.15.

[6] JUST 1/278 m.51d.

[7] JUST 1/986 m.7. Also in JUST 1/988 m.7d. I am grateful to Dr P. Brand for the latter reference.

[8] i.e. the granting of credit.

[9] It is not recorded whether or not Roger was convicted, either here or on the rolls of the eyres in Cumbria or Northumberland.

[10] JUST 1/986 m.7d. Also in JUST 1/988 m.8d. I am grateful to Dr P. Brand for the latter reference and part of the translation.

[11] JUST 1/986 m.9.

[12] JUST 1/135, eyre of Cumberland, 1292–3. There is no sign of any of these alleged usurers in the eyre at Carlisle.

[13] JUST 1/96 m.73, also in JUST 1/95 m.65.

[14] JUST 1/96 m.75r, also in JUST 1/95 m.70r. The version of these presentments from JUST 1/95 is mentioned in E. Miller, *The Abbey and Archbishopric of Ely* (Cambridge, 1951), 265 n.3.

[15] JUST 1/1166 m.8.

[16] The amount of the amercement is a little unclear. In the text, it is stated 'Et affer' ad xv.s sterling' but in the margin, the record shows 'misericordia xl.s', struck through. The amount in the margin suggests that the defendant was to pay over both the amount set as usury and the amercement of 15s.

Table 2: Information about usurious conduct from other presentments (all accused persons living)

Source	Allegation	Outcome
KBIF Chelmsford, 1352 H[17]	Thomas Judde of Bradewell is a common usurer, lending his money to various people for a great profit to the impoverishment of the people, that is to say that he lent to one Elys Chunther 20s at [the rate of] 4s in profit per year. He lent Thomas Adam 30s for 6s in profit per year and did the same to many others in the same way, contrary to the king's peace.	Unknown.
Somerset inquiry 1341[18]	Richard of Keynsham, vicar of the church of Dunster, through wicked usury loaned 48s of his money to William Reneshulle, for which loan he took 2s as well as the money loaned, in the fourteenth year of the present king, and he is a common usurer etc.	Richard was attached and did not deny the allegations, but made fine with the king for the usury with 40d.
Essex inquiry 1341[19]	John Sawyere on Thursday after the feast of St John the Baptist in the thirteenth year of the present king [1339] lent Simon Mantel 10s and afterwards took from this Simon 3s in usurious profit, and he is a common usurer. John Hereward of Little Badewe on Thursday next after All Saints in the tenth year of the present king [1336] lent Thomas de Appelfeld 40s and afterwards took 10s in usurious profit from this Thomas. And he is a common usurer. John Sale of Colchester on Tuesday after the feast of St Edward in the twelfth year of the present king [1338] took from Richard atte Welle of Leyre half a quarter of wheat, by way of usury, for a loan of 13s 4d for four weeks. In the eleventh year of the reign of the present king [1337–8], John de Botyngham of Colchester lent Thomas Oryvngton 60s for a term of [the next] three years, rendering annually 20s usury, and at the end of the aforesaid three years, Thomas was to pay John the 60s principal. And because the aforesaid Thomas did not pay the aforesaid John the aforesaid 60s at the end of the aforesaid term, the aforesaid John, using his official position, imprisoned the aforesaid Thomas until he satisfied him in full for the aforesaid 60s.	John Hereward ordered to be mainprised. John Sawe [sic], John de Botyngham and John Sawyer said that they were not guilty, and put themselves on the country. A jury was summoned and the jurors found John Sawe and the others not guilty of these charges. They therefore went free.
Hertfordshire inquiry 1341[20]	Robert le Poleter makes the market more expensive by selling his own grain,[21] and what is more, he is a common usurer, so it is said.	Unknown.

Table 2: (*cont.*)

Source	Allegation	Outcome
Lancashire inquiry 1343[22]	Henry de Rudyng senior lent a certain John Whitsyde 20s for a week, for which loan the said Henry took from the said John 2s by way of usury. And the same Henry was attached to appear before the justices on this matter, he came and was asked how he wished to acquit himself of the usury, and he said that he could not deny that he had taken from John the 2s as set out above. Adam son of Robert de Blakeborye of Berston, bastard, loaned Roger son of Adam de Hulle of Berston 4 marks, for which loan Adam took from the aforesaid Roger 2 marks in usury. And Adam is a common usurer.	Henry was committed to prison, and afterwards made fine with the king for the usury by half a mark by pledge of William de Pakynton and Robert de Souky. Henry was therefore released from prison and went quit. Adam was attached and came before the justices, and was unable to deny the accusations. He was imprisoned, and afterwards made fine with the king for one mark, by pledges of Robert de Radecroft and John de Grelle. and was therefore released from prison and went quit.
Norfolk peace roll for 1378[23]	John Hagezerd of Hakford lent Thomas Waleys of Boton' twelve pounds of gold and silver, at the feast of the Exaltation of the Holy Cross in the first year of Richard II, and on account of the loan from that feast until the next feast of the Lord's Epiphany, John took from Thomas 40s in usury, and in this way he made unjust extortions, contrary to Christian law and the law of England, of 43s 4d from Thomas and from various other men in one year, against law as mentioned etc. [Margin: trespass]	It was noted that this matter did not come under the commission of the peace.

17 JUST 1/268 m.7.
18 JUST 1/770 m.12d.
19 JUST 1/258 m.7; JUST 1/258 m.12d.
20 JUST 1/337 m.3. It is not clear whether he was found guilty and punished. He does not seem to have been amerced, since there is no sign of him on the copious amercement roll.
21 The sense of this is presumably that the way in which he sold his grain was causing a rise in prices.
22 JUST 1/430 m.25.
23 Putnam, *PJP*, 111 no.40; KB 9/80 m.4, 1378.

Texts

(i) Eyre of Worcestershire 1275

De usurar[iis] christianis dicunt quod Milo de Evesham carius solebat vendere blad[um] suu[m]causa mutui quam valebat die quo vendidit et est mortuus. Et habuit bona in villa de Evesham. I[de]o ibi inquir[atu]r.[24]

Another version

De usur[ariis] christianis dicunt quod Milo de Evesham carius vendere solebat bladum suum causa mutui quam valebat die quo vendidit. Et est mortuus.[25]

(ii) Eyre of Devon 1281

De christianis usurar[iis] dicunt quod Willelmus le Bedel accomodavit aliqu[ando] xx.s & recepit de lucro xxii. den[arios] & sic de uno quarter[io] bladi aliqu[ando] unu[m] busell[um] aliqu[ando] duo secundum minus et maius. Ideo ipse cap[iatur]. [Margin: *cap[iatur]*][26]

(iii) Eyre of Lincolnshire 1281–4

De usur[ariis] christianis etc. Dicunt quod Maugerus de Manthorp' et Willelmus fil[ius] Walteri de ead[e]m sunt usur[arii]. Ideo ipsi capiantur. Postea ven[iunt] et quieti sunt p[er] patriam. [Margin: *capiantur*, struck through][27]

De usur[ariis] etc. dicunt quod Thomas Hert de Wivelingham, Robertus in Angulo in Stowe, Alice soror eius et Gillota Crake de Stowe in mi[sericordi]a pro trans[gressione] usur[ae]. [Margin: *mi[sericordi]a*, struck through][28]

(iv) Eyre of Gloucestershire 1287

De usurariis christianis etc. dicunt quod Willelmus Goatchild de brode campedene mutuavit Ranulpho Lefoy de Quenton et Helewys ux[ore] eius viii solidos. Et predictus Willelmus cepit pro predicto mutuo unum quarterium frumentum de incremento. Ideo ipse in misericordia.[29]

De usurar[iis] etc. dicunt quod Thomas filius Will[elmi] Kenemerford mutuavit Waltero Malicorn de Kenemerford iv quart[eria] frumemt[i] et recepit de incremento octo q[uarteria]. Ideo prec[eptum] est vic[ecomes] quod venire fac[iat] predictum Thom[am]. Postea ven[it] predict[us] Thom[as] et defend[it] tot[um] etc. Et de bono et malo ponit se super patriam. Et jur[atores] dicunt super sacramentum suum quod non est culp[abilis].
Ideo ipse inde quietus. Et quia jur[atores] co[ncelaverunt]presenta[cionem], ideo adiud[icium] de eis. [Margin: *ad iud[icium]*].[30]

---

[24] JUST 1/1028 m.16, Hundred of Oswoldeslawe. This is also to be found in JUST 1/1026 m.35, Saham's roll for the eyre of Worcestershire 1275, in virtually identical terms, though there it is also noted that Milo had goods in Evesham, of which inquiry should be made. In the margin is 'inquir[atur]'.

[25] JUST 1/1025 m.4.

[26] JUST 1/181 m.38d.

[27] JUST 1/497 m.3; JUST 1/491 m.2d. Another version of the accusation can be found in JUST 1/486 m.2d.

[28] JUST 1/497 m.38; JUST 1/486 m.28d. This presentment is not mentioned at all in another version of the eyre of Lincoln (JUST 1/491, Mettingham's roll of crown pleas), even though some presentments from Well Wappentake are recorded.

[29] JUST 1/278 m.41; another version: JUST 1/284, m.15.

[30] JUST 1/278 m.51d.

(v) Eyre of Westmorland 1292

De usur[ariis] etc. dicunt quod Rogerus de Burton est manifestus usurarius et communis in pecunia numerata mutuand[a] et in al[iis] singulis mercibus vendend[is] et dimittend[is] ut de lan[is], bobus, bidentibus et aliis bonis et catal[is] que dimittit ad certum terminum cap[iendo]pro respectu term[ini] ultra verum valorem rei vend[ite] vel dimisse aliquid certum et aliquand[o] duplum, et hoc fecit post recessum Judeorum ab Angl[ia] ad nocumentum omnium secum contraencium de quocumque mercimonio etc. Ideo pre[ceptum] est vic[ecomiti] quod fac[iat] eum venire ad resp[ondendum] etc. Et quod habeat corp[us] eius apud Karliolum in com[itatu] Cumbr[ie] a die sancti Martini in xv dies etc. Postea ad diem illum venit predictus Rogerus et invenit securitatem essendi apud Nov[um] Castr[um] in com[itatu] Northumberl' in octab[is] sancti hillarii. Et sunt pleg[ii] eius Rogerus de Coquina et Willelmus de Dageworth etc. Ideo n[ichil] de exitibus. Datus est ei dies in xv sancti martini apud Karliolum in comitatu Cumbr[ie].[31,32]

De usur[ariis] etc. dicunt quod Willelmus de Goldington est manifestus usurarius in den[ariis] mutuand[is] et lana pannis et aliis mercimoniis quibuscumque vendend[is] et cap[iendo] nomine usure pro respectu de quolibet contrahenti cum ip[so] increment[um] ultra debitum quod debetur. Et hoc fecit de Willelmo de Stirkelande milite de quo cep[it] una vice pro xl. s[olidis] dece[m] m[arcas] et di[midiam] et de eodem per aliam vice[m] p[ro] xl. s, xxii m[arcas]. Ideo pre[ceptum] est vic[ecomiti] quod fac[iat] eum venire post ven[it] et defend[it] tot[um] et ponit se super patriam.[33]

Villa de Appleby. De usurar[ariis] etc. dicunt quod Johannes de Goldington emit premanibus de Thom[a] fil[io] Mag[istri]Will[elmi] de Goldington" tres saccos lane pro decem mar[cis] et dim[idia] quos ad certum terminum videlicet ad pent[ecostem] debuit recepisse quo termino adveniente idem Thom[as] soluit ei unum saccum de precio nonem mar[carum] et pro residuis duobus saccis soluit sibi xvii mar[cas] etc. Et sic facit communiter predict[u]s Johannes. Ideo inde loq[uendum]. Et datus est ei dies de audiendo jud[icium] su[um] apud Karliolum a die sancti Martini in xv dies etc.[34,35]

(vi) Eyre of Cambridgeshire 1299

De Christianis usurariis mortuis dicunt quod Magister Willelmus de Luda episcopus Elyensis qui obiit per Willelmum Boreward et Radulphum de Littlebir' ballivos suos istius hundr[edi] mutuavit diversis hominibus istius hundr[edi] videlicet apud Lyndon quadraginta quarteria fr[umenti], sexaginta quarteria ordei, viginti quarteria fab[arum]et pis[arum] et apud Wilbertone viginti quart[eria] siliginis, quinquaginta quarteria ordei et quindecim quarteria pisar[um], et apud Straham triginta quarteria fr[umenti], l quarteria ordei et viginti quarteria pisarum, *et apud Dodyngton xx quarteria fr[umenti] et quadraginta quarteria drageti, quatuordecim quarteria pisarum,* capiendo pro quolibet quarterio predicti bladi octo den[arios] ultra summam quam vendi potuit in insula predicta a tempore quo predictum blad[um] mut[uatum]

---

[31] JUST 1/986 m.7. Also in JUST 1/988 m.7d. I am grateful to Dr P. Brand for the latter reference.

[32] It is not recorded whether or not Roger was convicted, either here or on the rolls of the eyres in Cumberland or Northumberland.

[33] JUST 1/986 m.7d. Also in JUST 1/988 m.8d. I am grateful to Dr P. Brand for the latter reference and part of the translation.

[34] JUST 1/986 m.9.

[35] JUST 1/135, eyre of Cumberland 1292–3. There is no sign of any of these alleged usurers in the eyre at Carlisle.

fuit, usque ad novum granum. Ita quod totum profitum pervenit ad manus ipsius episcopi ipso sciente et precipienti. Ideo inde loq[uendum] [Margin: *loq[uendum]*].[36]

De usurariis Christianis mortuis dicunt quod magister Willelmus de Luda episcopus Elyensis qui obiit fuit usurarius per Hugonem capellanum quondam ballivum de Wysebeche qui quidem Hugo per preceptum ipsius episcopi mutuavit bladum ipsius episcopi in hundredo isto videlicet anno domini regis nunc xxij. diversis hominibus patrie trecenta quarteria fr[umenti] capiendo pro q[uo]libet quarter[io] duos solidos ultra commun[em] prec[ium] vendicionis blad[i] in partibus Elyensis pro respectu habendo medio tempore mutuacionis usque ad nouum granum. Et similiter anno r. Regis nunc xxiij.o et anno xxiiij.o et anno xxv mutuavit q[uo]libet anno tricenta quarteria fr[umenti] capiendo pro eisdem in forma predicta. Et similiter anno xxij.o quatergenta quarteria mixtil[ionis]. Et anno xxiij. Et anno xxiiij, et anno xxv totidem quarteria mix[tilionis] capiendo pro q[uo]libet quarteri[o] ij.s ultra quam vendi potuit secundum verum valorem aliquo tempore anni ut predict[u]m est. Et similiter de auenis anno xxiiij et xxv.o quolibet anno quingenta quarteria auenarum capiendo pro quolibet quarter[io] xij.d ultra quam vendi potuit a festo sancti Johannis baptiste usque ad festum Exaltacionis sancte crucis. Ita quod totum profitum predicte vendicionis et prestiti pervenit ad manus ipsius episcopi, ipso sciente et precipiente. Ideo inde loq[uendum].[37]

(vii) Channel Islands Eyre 1331

De usurariis etc. dicunt quod Jominus filius Elie de Submonte mutuo tradidit viginti solid[os] Johanni Renward usque ad certum diem per sic quod ipse ad diem predict[u]m solueret ei xxv s. per usuram. Ideo ipse in misericordia. Et affer[atum est] ad xv.s sterling[orum]. [Margin – *xl s*, struck through][38]

(viii) KBIF for the session at Chelmsford, 1352 H.

Item ils pres[entent] q[e] Thomas Judde de Brodewell est un commun usurer apprestant seon argent a diverces gentz p[ur] graunt encres en empoverysements de puple ceo est a savoir a un Elys Chunther xx.s p[ur] iv.s de encres par aan, a Thomas Adam xxx.s p[ur] vi.s de encres par aan & a plusours altres en mesme la manere encountr[e] la pes nostr[e] seign[ur] le Roy.[39]

(ix) Usury indictments in *ad hoc* inquiries of 1341–3

Somerset 1341
[Margin: *Dunstre Wachet*]
Juratores presentant quod Ricardus de Keynesham, vicar ecclesie de Dunstere, usuraria pravitate acommodavit pecuniam suam videlicet: Willelmo Ranneshulle xlviij.s pro quo mutuo habuit de eodem ii.s cum summa mutuata etc. anno regis nunc xiv.o, et est communis usurarius etc, qui quidem Ricardus attachiatus est & inde allocutus, hoc non dedicit, scilicet finem fecit domino Rege

---

36 JUST 1/96 m.73, Hundred of Wicheford, also in JUST 1/95 m.65. The section between asterisks does not appear in the latter.
37 JUST 1/96 m.75r, Hundred of Wisbech, also in JUST 1/95 m.70r. The version of these presentments from JUST 1/95 is mentioned in Miller, *The Abbey and Archbishopric of Ely*, 265 n.3.
38 JUST 1/1166 m.8. The amount of the amercement in the text is stated as 'xv.s sterling' but in the margin the record shows 'misericordia xl.s', struck through. The amount in the margin suggests that the defendant was to pay over both the amount set as usury and the amercement of 15s.
39 JUST 1/268 m.7.

pro dicta usura pro xl.d per plegios Thom[e] de Auele et Ade Brekesper. [Margin: *finis xl.d* struck through][40]

Essex 1341

Item presen[tant] quod Johannes Sawyere die Jovis prox[ima] post festum sancti Johannis Baptist[e] anno reg[is] nunc terciodecimo accomodavit Simon Mantel x.s et postea cepit de eodem Simone de incremento in usura iij.s, et est communis usurarius.

Item present[ant] quod Johannees Hereward de Parva Badewe die Jovis proxima post festum Omnium Sanctorum anno regis nunc decimo accomodavit Thome de Appelfeld xl.s et postea cepit de eodem Thoma de incremento in usura x.s. Et est communis usurarius. [Margin: *manuc[apiatur/-captus est]*][41]

Item present[ant] quod Johannes Sale de Colecestr' die Martis proxima post festum sancti Edwardi anno regni Regis nunc duodecimo cepit de Ricardo atte Welle de Leyre del Hay dimid[ium] quarter[ium] fr[umenti] usurario pro mutuacione xiij.s iiij.d per quatuorum [sic] septimanas.[42]

Item present[ant] quod Johannes de Botyngham de Colecestr anno regis nunc undecimo accomodavit Thome Orvyngton lx.s ad finem trium annorum prox[imorum] sequent[ium] reddend[o] annuatim pro eisde[m] usura xx.s et in finem predictorum trium annorum solvend[o] eidem Johanni predictos lx.s. Et quia predictus Thom[as] non soluit predicti Johanni predictos lx.s in finem terminum predicti predicus Johannes colore officii sui predictum Thomam imprisonavit quousque de eisdem lx.s ei plene fuit satisfactum.[43]

*John Sawe, John de Botyngham, John Sawyer . . . ques[itis] qualiter se velint de premissis acquietare separatim dicunt quod in nullo sunt inde culpabiles. Et de hoc ponunt se super patriam. Ideo fac' inde jur' unde jur' ad hoc cla[morem]et jur[atores] dicunt super sacr[*amentum] suum quod predict[us] Johannis Sawe et alii de premissis in nullo sunt culpabiles. Ideo eant inde quieti.*[44]

Hertfordshire 1341

Jur[atores] diversorum hundredorum . . . Item present[ant] quod Robert le Poleter redd[it]mercat[um]carius per mercandisat[ionem] sui proprij bladi et ultra hoc est communis usurator ut dicitur.[45]

Lancashire 1343

Lanc'. Presentat[um] est per xii Jur[atores] secund[e] Inquis[itionis] Wapent[acii] de Derbyshire quod Henr[icus] de Rudyng senior accommodavit cuidam Joh[anni] Whitsyde viginti solidos tenend[os] p[er]unam septimanam pro qua quidem accomodacione predic[tus] Henr[icus] cepit de predicto Johanne duos solidos in usura. Et super hoc idem Henr[icus] ea occasione attachiatus ven[it] coram Justic[ariis] et allocutus qualiter se velit de usura predicta acquietare dicit quod ipse

---

[40] JUST 1/770 m.12d. The amount of money which was given as a fine seems very small. We are not told the length of the loan period, but the amount of money taken as usury seems quite small in comparison with the principal debt. Attention was particularly directed towards the relationship between the amount of the principal and the usury.

[41] Or 'he is to be mainprised': *ibid.*

[42] JUST 1/258 m.7.

[43] *ibid.*

[44] JUST 1/258 m.12d.

[45] JUST 1/337 m.3. It is not clear whether he was found guilty and punished. He does not seem to have been amerced, since there is no sign of him on the copious amercement roll.

non potest dedicere quin ipse cepit de predicto Johanne predictos duos solidoss in forma superius presentata. Ideo idem Henr[icus] committ[itur] gaole etc. Postea idem Henr[icus] fecit finem domino Reg[i] pro usura predicta per dim[idiam] marc[am] per pleg[ium] Willelmi de Pakynton et Roberti de Souky de eodem com[itatu]. Ideo idem Henr[icus] deliberetur a gaola predicta et sic inde quietus etc. [Margin: *gaola* and *di.' mar'*, both struck through].[46]

[Presentatum est per xij juratores secunde inquisicionis wapentacii de Derbyshire quod] Adam fil[ius] Roberti de Blakeborne de Berstan bastard[us] accomodavit Rogero fil[io] Ade de Hulle de Berstan quatuor marcas pro qua quidem accommodacione idem Adam cepit de predict[o] Roger[o] duas marcas in usura. Et quod idem Adam est communis usurarius. Et super hoc idem Adam hiis occasionibus attachiatus venit coram justicariis et allocutus qualiter se velit de articulis predictis acquietare dicit quod non potest dedicere articulos predictos prout super ipsum superius presentantur. Ideo idem Ad[am] committ[itur] gaole etc. Postea predictus Adam fecit finem domino Reg[i] pro articulis predictis per i. marc[am] per pl[egiu]m Roberti de Radecroft & Johannis de Grelle de eodem com[itatu]. Ideo idem Adam deliberetur a gaola predicta et sic inde quietus etc.[47,48]

(x) Norfolk peace roll for 1378

[Twelve jurors] *dicunt [. . .] quod Iohannes Hagezerd de Hakford' (quia non tangit commissionem) mutuavit Thome Waleys de Boton' duodecim libras auri et argenti, videlicet ad festum Exaltacionis Sancte Crucis anno regni regis Ricardi secundi post conquestum primo, et causa mutui a dicto festo usque ad festum*

Epiphanie Domini proximo sequens idem Iohannes cepit de dicto Thoma (in Boton') ex usura xl.s, et sic extorquebat iniuste et contra legem Christianam et contra legem Anglie de prefato Thoma et de aliis diversis hominibus per unum annum xl.s iv.d, contra legem ut supra etc. [Margin: *transgressio*][49]

(xi) A usury impeachment in 1393

Memorandum quod quinto decimo die martij anno presenti Radulphus ffitz Richard de com[itatu] Bed', Ricardus Broke de London', Johanes Yedele & Stephanis Ovenden' de com[itatu] Kanc' coram domino rege in cancellar[ia] sua personaliter constituti manuceperunt videlicet quilibet eorum sub pena duorum mil[iu]m librarum pro Walter Dautre coram dicto domino rege & consilio suo super usura impetito de habendo ipsum Walterum promptum et paratum de die in diem coram eodem domino Rege et dicto consilio suo in cancellar[iam] predicta[m] ad respondendum super premissis ac aliis que sibi ex parte dicti domini regis obiecient[u]r tunc ibidem & ad faciend[um] ___[50] & recipiend[um] quod de eo contigit ordinari quam quidem [?summam] quilibet manucaptorum predictorum concessit de terris et catallis suis ad opus dicti domini Regis levari si prefatum Walterum coram eodem domino Rege & dicto consilio suo in forma predicta non habuerunt super premissis responsurus.'[51]

---

[46] JUST 1/430 m.25.
[47] JUST 1/430 m.25.
[48] JUST 1/430 m.25.
[49] Putnam, *PJP*, 111 no.40; KB 9/80 m.4, 7 June 1378.
[50] Word obscured.
[51] C 54/234 m.12d. The entry is crossed through to indicate cancellation. There is a marginal note to the effect that the entry was cancelled with the assent of the court and the justices, since the court was assured that Walter was dead. Material mentioning a Walter Dautre can be seen in C 1 7/7 (a Chancery petition concerning debts), in *CPR 1391–6*, 234 (a commission to the king's serjeant at arms, Robert Behenon, to arrest and bring before the King and Council Walter Dautry), and in *CPR 1391–6*, 590 (a commission of 30 March 1395 to Nicholas Carreu, Thomas de Feriby, clerk, William Cressewyk and the sheriff of Surrey

Let it be remembered that on the fifteenth of March in the present year, Ralph fitz Richard of the county of Bedford, Richard Broke of London, John Yedele and Stephen Ovenden of the county of Kent, before the lord King in the chancery gave personal security, on pain of two thousand pounds each, for Walter Dautre, impeached before the King and Council on a charge of usury, guaranteeing that they would produce Walter Dautre before the said lord King and his council in the said Chancery, ready to answer the things mentioned before or other matters which might be laid against him then, and to accept what might be ordered there concerning these things. They agreed that if they failed to have the said Walter before the lord king and his said council as mentioned, to answer the aforesaid matters, that the sums put up as security could be raised for the benefit of the lord King from their lands and chattels.[52]

to enquire by jury of that county whether Walter Dautre, who lately lived in the priory of Bermondseye, died there, as the king is informed, and on what day and how). There is, however, no trace of Walter Dautre in the *Calendars of Inquisitions*.

[52] A description of this entry can be found in *CCR 1392–6*, 131.

Appendix II: Cases from other courts

Table 3: Usury in Wakefield courts and tourns

Court or tourn	Details of offence and punishment
Wakefield, *A*, 1: court at Halifax, 16 October 1274	Usury mentioned tangentially in a slander case: 'John de Miggeley brought a suit against John son of Robert of Sourby, and said that John called him a usurer (*usuarius*). John son of Robert denied this and successfully waged his law. John son of Robert was acquitted and John de Miggeley was in mercy. He made fine with 12d.'
Wakefield, *A*, 90: court at Wakefield, 22 November 1274	Usury mentioned in a debt case: 'John de Querneby comes and acknowledges that he owes Raymond de Doncaster 20s, and all that has come about in usury (*judeismus*) through his default. He has a day for payment, namely Sunday, the morrow of St Clement.'
Wakefield, *A*, 172: tourn at Halifax Tuesday after the Translation of St Thomas Martyr 1274	Presentment of usury: 'Felicia de Bothemley sells contrary to the assize, has a false measure, and is a usurer.'
Wakefield, *A*, 281: court at Rastrick Monday after the Feast of St John of Beverley 1297	Usury mentioned in a debt or slander case: 'William del Bothes complains of William de Hiperum and says that he owes £20 for a certain tithe sold to him, and that he called him a usurer. The defendant denies the debt and must wage his law. As to calling him a usurer, the defendant says that he gave the plaintiff 12d to have respite of a debt of 10s which he owed for a certain tithe. The plaintiff admits the payment of the 12d, but says that he allowed it as the first payment for the said tithe. He must therefore wage his law.'[1]
Wakefield, *D*, 156: tourn at Wakefield 16 November 1316	A man is mentioned as having been amerced for usury: 'William, son of Richard of the Haghe, is amerced 40d because he lent 20s to Alice the Stinter, taking 10d in usury every week.'
Wakefield, *D*, 159: court at Wakefield 26 November 1316	A man made fine for usury: 'Henry Wade, indicted at Byrton tourn of usury, gives 13s 4d for the said trespass.'
Wakefield, *E*, 160: sheriff's tourn at Birton Tuesday after the Feast of St Andrew 1330	A usury indictment: 'Adam Strekeyse, indicted at this present tourn by twelve jurors for usury, comes and fines with the lord for this trespass and for all the other counts of trespass in any wise to be charged against him up to this moment by the lord – £10 in silver, to be paid in equal parts at the next feasts of the Purification, Whitsuntide and Michaelmas, with the stipulation that if the said Adam should be convicted again of committing the crime of usury against any specified person for any specified sum, from the day of this present fine, then Adam confesses and allows that he shall be bound to the earl in another sum of £10, in silver, payable at the lord's pleasure sine die.'
Wakefield, *G*, 115: tourn of Wakefield 27 May 1349	A usury presentment: 'The vill of Normanton presents that Henry Attecrosse is a common usurer of grain – 2s.'

[1] No conclusion to this suit is reported.

Graph 1: Offences against assize of ale in individual tourns in Halifax[2]

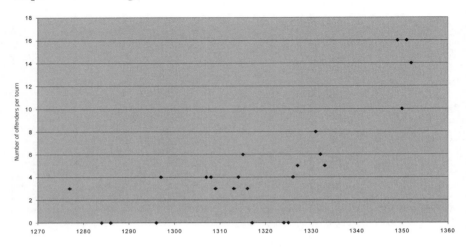

Graph 2: Offences against assize of ale in individual tourns: Wakefield[3]

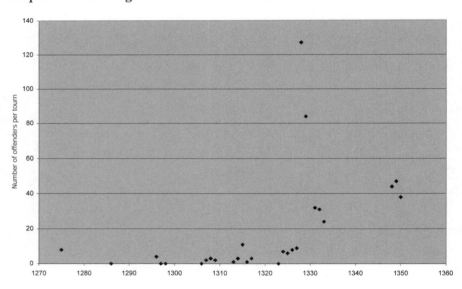

[2] Not including non-co-operation with the aletasters. Where there is a record of more than one tourn per year, an average has been taken: Wakefield, *A* 38, 172, 188, 246, 285; *B* 9, 88, 124, 157, 186, 207; *C* 8, 45, 73, 116, 159; *D* 13, 81, 146; *E* 37, 52, 66, 83, 108, 164, 183; *F* 20, 69, 132, 186; *G* 55, 114, 210, 245; *H* 4, 42, 71, 91. Trend lines are used on graphs when the nature of the data makes it appropriate. Where there are large gaps in the data, scatter graphs are used.

[3] Not including non-co-operation with the aletasters. Where there is a record of more than one tourn per year, an average has been taken: Wakefield, *A* 49, 166, 247, 287; *B* 44, 56, 92, 128, 162, 190, 212; *C* 3, 51, 85, 124; *D* 21, 95, 153, 184; *E* 8, 12, 41, 55, 66, 89, 112, 135, 145, 152, 167, 186; *F* 6, 79, 127, 183; *G* 31, 115, 177.

Sutton: breaches of the assizes of bread and ale[4]

Graph 3: Sutton: offenders brewing against the assize of ale

[Graph 1]

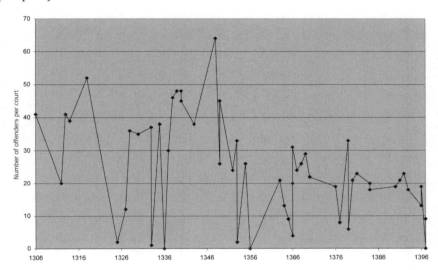

Graph 4: Sutton: offenders baking against the assize

[Graph 2]

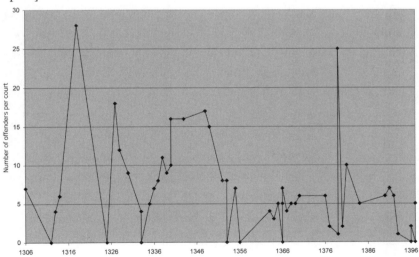

[4] DL 30/85/1157 m.7; DL 30/85/1160 m.2, m.6d, m.13; DL 30/85/1161 m.3; DL 30/85/1162 m.16d, m.8, m.24; DL 30/85/1165 m.4; DL 30/85/1166 m.3d; DL 30/85/1168 m.6, m.8d; DL 30/86/1170 m.8; DL 30/86/1171 m.12; DL 30/86/1172 m.2d, m.14; DL 30/86/1173 m.4; DL 30/86/1174 m.6, m.9d; DL 30/86/1176 m.3; DL 30/86/1179 m.3d; DL 30/86/1180 m.8, m.12; DL 30/87/1183 m.2, m.9, m.19; DL

Graph 5: Sutton: offenders regrating bread and/or ale

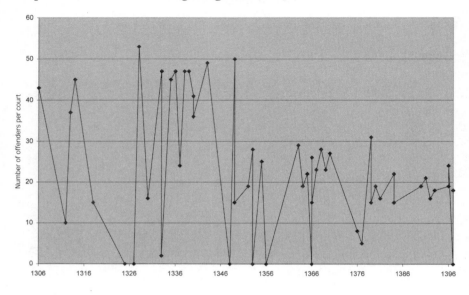

Graph 6: Sutton: forestalling

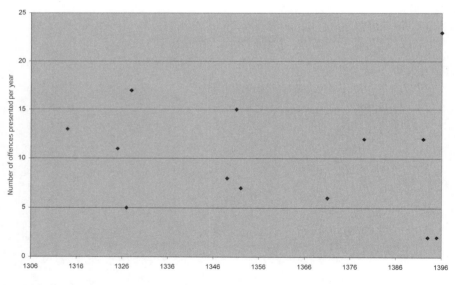

The invariable penalty for forestallers was amercement, most amercements were in the 2d – 12d range, with one large amercement of 16s 2d in 1351.[5]

30/87/1184 m.1d; DL 30/87/1184 m.21d; DL 30/87/1188 m.4, m.10; DL 30/87/1190 m.1d, m.5, m.12; DL 30/87/1191 m.3, m.15; DL 30/87/1192 m.4, m.20; DL 30/88/1194 m.1d; DL 30/88/1196 m.11; DL 30/88/1199 m.4d, m.15d; DL 30/88/1200 m.15d; DL 30/89/1202 m.1d, m.11d; DL 30/89/1203 m.11d; DL 30/89/1204 m.1d; DL 30/89/1208 m.10d, m.20; DL 30/89/1209 m.12d, m.13; DL 30/90/1210 m.6; DL 30/90/1211 m.6d, m.7, m.24d; DL 30/90/1212 m.8.
[5] DL 30/86/1182 m.7.

Appendix III: Usury and Common Pleas in the Central Royal Courts

As mentioned in Chapter 2, only a limited amount of work on common pleas has been undertaken. Anything which can be said about common pleas and usury must, therefore, be tentative. It is, however, worth presenting the findings here, so that those interested in this area may take it further, without 'reinventing the wheel'.

It is clear that usury could be raised as an issue in common pleas (individual actions between subjects) in royal courts or before royal justices.

A writ on the statute of Jewry against a Jew charging usury to a Christian was available.[1] An undated case based on this writ alleged a demand of two sacks of wool worth twenty pounds for a loan of either twenty shillings or twenty marks. The writ was directed to the justices of the Jews, and, in one version, to a sheriff. It is undated. A case of 1286 in the King's Bench suggests the possibility of an action based on an unidentified royal usury statute or provision.[2]

Usury could also be pleaded under the rules of common law (as opposed to statute). An important debt case concerning usury was *Alan de Sutton v Peter, prior of Berden and Robert le Walkelyn* from Michaelmas 1299, in which royal judges ruled that a creditor could not enforce a usurious arrangement in a royal court.[3] The case shows that lawyers were aware that it was possible to argue on the basis of usury in debt cases. Usury could be used as an exception in a debt action, disqualifying the plaintiff from recovering the debt claimed. The possibility of arguing that the plaintiff was claiming a usurious debt which should not be enforced by a royal court was confirmed in a Year Book case of 1346, and the rule also held sway in some manor courts.[4]

[1] Brand, 'Jews and the law', 1155, refers to three manuscripts which contain a writ for Thomas of London (or 'de B') against Haketin Polet, a Jew: BL, MS Harley 748, ff.30r–v; Library of Congress, MS 131, ff.27r–v; Philadelphia Free Library, MS LC 14.18, f.174r.

[2] *SR* I:53. G.O. Sayles (ed.), *Select Cases in King's Bench Edward I, vol. 1*, Selden Society vol. 55 for 1936 (London, 1939), xiii, 163, *Thomas de Berevile v Master Nicholas of Ellerker*, Coram Rege Roll no.101, m.4, 1286 M. Although the report stresses the usury, in terms reminiscent of the 1275 commission to Lovetot to investigate this offence, the case seems to have placed greater emphasis on the fact that the lender imprisoned the debtor 'maliciously', to make him sign up to the usurious deal.

[3] BL, MS Add. 31826, f.102b, also in BL, MS Harley 572. The record of the case is in CP 40/130 m.204d, mentioned in Palmer, *County Courts*, 201; Palmer, *Black Death*, 79n; P. Brand, 'Inside the courtroom: lawyers, litigants and justices in England in the later middle ages', in P. Coss (ed.), *The Moral World of the Law* (Cambridge, 2000), 91–112, 102. The case only concerns recovery of the usury, not the principal.

[4] *YB (RS)*, 20 Edw. III, Part 1, 321. See the case from Witcham Rectory in Cambridgeshire, from October 1282, in which usury was raised as an exception to a debt case, and in which the plaintiff was amerced by the court for his claim, although the plaintiff was an executor of the estate of the original usurer: L.R. Poos and C. Bonfield, *Select Cases in Manorial Courts 1250–1550: Property and Family Law*, Selden Society vol. 114 for 1997 (London, 1998), no.207.

It is interesting to note what appears to be a reluctance amongst common lawyers to base their cases on usury. Even though the *Alan de Sutton* case seems to have involved an obviously usurious arrangement, and even though at least one of the judges thought that this was enough to allow the defendants to win, the choice of the defendants' pleader was a plea based on a 'legal technicality' – a 'variance' or discrepancy between the deed evidencing the debt and the count which was narrated in court – rather than usury. The 1346 Year Book case also confirms the idea that usury was a somewhat risky plea, since the defendant's lawyer preferred to rely on a technical argument based on the fact that the deed in question was in favour of the plaintiff and another person, and not just the plaintiff.[5] The preference for 'technical' pleas, rather than raising usury is probably a result of rules of pleading in medieval royal courts which involved just one issue being pleaded. Lawyers, whose main concern was to win the case for a client rather than to contribute to the principled development of the common law, would naturally choose the safest plea, preferably one, such as a plea of variance, which could be demonstrated by looking at documents, rather than arguing a more difficult issue such as usury, which would involve admitting the plaintiff's case as to the existence of the debt.[6] Contemporary legal treatises also contained an accepted order in which one would plead different matters or 'exceptions' in a common law case, which put 'technicalities' ahead of issues of substance and circumstance on the list.[7] Finally, it should be noted that Maitland claims that it was common practice in loan contracts to renounce future objections on grounds of usury.[8] This could mean that a defendant in debt would be barred from pleading usury in litigation.

Usury, then, could be brought up in a common plea of debt. Royal courts sometimes, however, helped to recover usury, as in a case of of debt and detinue of chattels from 1306 (though referring to arrangements going back to 1288) *Executors of Laurence of Bootham v John Sampson of York*.[9] In this case, executors of Laurence, a surety for John's debt, successfully sued the debtor for recovery of a loan which Laurence had arranged and had to pay off, plus chattels forfeited as a penalty for non-payment and usury, plus damages. There is no record of any objection to the usury either by John, the debtor, or by the court or jury. John may have been handicapped by the fact that he had consented to Laurence's arrangement, and by the fact that it was a surety who had demonstrably lost out, having actually forfeited the chattels.

On the more detailed question of whether the whole of a usurious debt was unenforceable, or merely the usury, sources are less helpful. J.H. Baker states that '[t]he common law . . . did not invalidate usurious agreements', but it is hard to see whether the common law courts were operating a rule that debts tainted by usury were irrecoverable *in toto* or whether it was simply the usurious portion of the alleged debt which could not be recovered.[10] The only way in which this question

---

[5] YB, 20 Edw. III, Part 1, 321.
[6] On rules of pleading, see Milsom, *HFCL*, 42–8.
[7] J.S. Beckerman, 'Law writing and law teaching: treatise evidence of the formal teaching of English law in the late thirteenth century', in Bush and Wijffels (eds), *Learning the Law*, 33–50, at 44.
[8] *P&M* I, 122.
[9] Brand, 'Aspects', citing CP 40/151 m.199, 1288.
[10] Baker, *Introduction*, 353.

could arise for discussion in the common law courts would have been a case in which a creditor in a usurious loan, waiving any claim to the usury, claimed only the principal sum from the debtor, and the debtor raised the question of usury. No such case has been found. Medieval rules of pleading would, in any case, make it unlikely that a litigant would rest his case on an attempt to sever the licit and illicit parts of the bargain so that the creditor could recover the principal only. A case from 1260 seems to show the parties assuming that the principal sum could still be recovered even if the creditor was found to have claimed usury from the debtor and was imprisoned for so doing.[11] In a 1282 manorial court case from Witcham Rectory in Cambridgeshire, the debtor admitted that he owed the principal sum, and objected only to the usury, and the court's statement seems to support the idea that the principal could still be claimed in such a case, but it is not decisive.[12]

Some cases dealt with the scope and definition of usury at common law.[13] There was a particular debate as to whether or not it was usurious to stipulate a penalty in advance for breach of an obligation.[14] R.C. Palmer has argued that there was a change in the law on this point in 1352 in the case of *Executors of Moigne v Haunsard*.[15] He described a sudden change or liberalisation of the common law in this area such that, whereas previously penalties had not been allowed, after 1352, they were allowed.[16] Less of a *volte face* is seen in the view of D. Ibbetson, who believes that, although matters were settled in favour of penalties at that time, the previous situation had been one of uncertainty rather than there having been a definite rule against penalties.[17] A 1244 prohibition of usury by merchants covered penalties.[18] There are some references to a general rule against penalties in cases from the later part of the reign of Edward I: *David or Adam Crok v Master of Hospital of St Mark at Billeswick by Bristol* (1287), a case in the 1286 Suffolk eyre, *Thomas s. Edmund Pecche v Aumary Pecche et al.*; *Agnes widow of John Gour v Hugh of Risbury, parson of Old Radnor* (1299).[19] The Year Book report of the last-mentioned case shows Tilton, the defendant's serjeant, claiming that Edward I had made a rule that penalties could only be levied where the king was a party to the contract (though the defendant did not rely on this argument). The pre-1350s position does seem to

---

[11] H.G. Richardson and G.O. Sayles, *Select Cases of Procedure without Writ under Henry III*, Selden Society vol. 60 for 1941 (London, 1941), 104 no.95, citing JUST 1/456, *William, parson of Glen v Lawrence Oliver*.

[12] Poos and Bonfield, *Select Cases in Manorial Courts*, no.207.

[13] There is evidence, albeit not from a royal court, that usury could not be claimed by executors of a usurer, which seems logical. In one manor case of 1282, an executor sued for a usurious debt owed by the defendant to the dead usurer. The court amerced the plaintiff (the executor) for a false claim: Poos and Bonfield, *Select Cases in Manorial Courts*, no.207.

[14] *Scott v Beracre* in Maitland, *Eyre of Kent 1313–1314*, 23ff, discussed in Palmer, *Black Death*, 79. *Executors of Morgan v Haunsard* (1352), CP40/369 m.62: *YB*, M. 26 Edw. III, f.17, pl.9; discussed in Palmer, *Black Death*, 81. See also Ibbetson, *Obligations*, 29–30. In 1290, William de Clervaus petitioned the king in Parliament for a remedy against the usurious conduct of Peter de Appleby, bailiff of York: *RP* I:46b. The original petition is in the PRO: SC 8/263 no.13138 (reference from Dr P. Brand) and suggests that this was a case of a penalty for late payment being fixed in advance.

[15] CP 40/369 m.62; *YB*, M. 26 Edw. III, f.17, pl.9 (1352).

[16] Palmer, *Black Death*, 79–81.

[17] Ibbetson, *Obligations*, 29. Ibbetson cites *YB*, 21 Edw. III, f.29, pl.9, which seems to be wrong.

[18] *CCR 1242–7*, 242. I am grateful to Dr P. Brand for this reference. It is ordered that 'nullus mercator decetero mutuo det pecuniam pro aliquo lucro vel super penam . . .'

[19] CP 40/89 m.97; JUST 1/828 m.12; CP 40/127 m.8 and BL, MS Stowe 388, f.149v. I am grateful to Dr P. Brand for these references.

have been uncertain. The case of *Roger la Zuche v William de Rokeny* (1297), seems to contradict Palmer's picture of a simple rule that penalties on debt were illicit before 1352.[20] In this case, the defendant argued that penalties could not be claimed at common law, since they were odious in themselves and equivalent to usury.[21] This argument did not win the case, and seems to have been disallowed by the judge, though Bereford J did not say this in so many words. He criticised the conduct of the defendant's lawyer in raising a new argument rather than replying to the deed which he had made. Bereford expressed doubts about the enforceability of penalties in a case of 1308–9.[22] There is evidence that common lawyers were not particularly keen to avoid enforcing penalties before the 1350s. This can be seen in *Scott v Beracre* (1313–14), in which a penalty was allowed,[23] and in *Anon v Prior of Trinity.* (1321).[24] Here, a ten pound penalty was claimed in a debt case. It was admitted by the judge, Hervy de Stanton, that if the money was claimed as a penalty, that claim 'sounded in usury', i.e. that it would be an inadmissible claim because it amounted to usury, but in the end the plaintiff was awarded damages of ten pounds; thus the usurious penalty was effectively enforced by the justices in eyre. This seems to contradict the idea of a very strict rule against penalties prior to the 1350s.[25]

Although penalties seem to have been enforced without demur in the latter fourteenth century, some lingering doubt may have existed: a reading in Gray's Inn from 1437 shows disagreement as to whether penalties were usurious or not.[26] The position seems to be that the rules were in the process of being formed during the period from the late thirteenth century to the mid fourteenth century, and were almost entirely settled thereafter. The matter is further complicated by the fact that objections to penalties might be on other grounds than that of their usury.[27] Given the fact that many rules concerning the enforceability of debts had not been settled by the later fourteenth-century common lawyers, it cannot be contended that rules concerning the enforceability of possibly usurious debts were particularly slow to be fixed.[28] The relationship between damages, penalities, usury and interest is complex. Brand has noted that '[d]amages were . . . English law's version of lawful interest'.[29]

---

[20] CP 40/118 m.114; BL, MS Add. 35116, f.240r; BL, MS Harley 25, ff.180v, 182r, and Bodleian MS Holkham Misc. 30, f.35v. I am grateful to Dr P. Brand for this reference and text.

[21] 'Hunt': '. . . cele manere de peines e usures sont de une condicion'.

[22] *YB*, 2 and 3 Edw. II, 58 *Umfraville v Lonstede*, Ibbetson, *Obligations*, 29.

[23] 27 SS 23 25, 27; Ibbetson, *Obligations*, 29. The slight qualification is that the 'penalty' seems to have been agreed at arbitration. The report contains a dictum of Staunton J that 'penalty and usury are . . . irrecoverable when they grow out of the sum in which the obligee is primarily bound' (in contrast to 'a debt arising out of a covenant' as here). The strong statement that penalties are irrecoverable usury is by Passeley, the defendant's counsel.

[24] Cam, *London Eyre 1321*, vol. 85, cix, and vol. 86, 345.

[25] A local London case seems to forbid penalties: Ibbetson, *Obligations*, 29, citing *LA*, 186–7.

[26] Simpson, *Contract*, 113; Ibbetson, *Obligations*, 29; S.E. Thorne (ed.), *Readings and Moots at the Inns of Court, vol. 1*, Selden Society vol. 71 for 1952 (London, 1954), cxliv.

[27] True penalties are unenforceable in modern contract law 'because courts are reluctant to allow a party to recover a sum which is obviously and considerably greater than his loss': G. Treitel, *The Law of Contract*, 10th edn (London, 1999), 929. This is less a question of usury than of abuse of the function of courts and damages.

[28] See Simpson, *Contract*, 98, 133, 537.

[29] Brand, 'Aspects', 33.

Other matters of interest which could be further investigated concern common pleas involving land. Questions of usury in terns of acquisition of lands held as security in a usurious arrangement, or of the lands of deceased usurers, might be raised in a variety of different common pleas concerning land. The daunting task of trawling through more than a century of land actions from the voluminous common pleas rolls has not, however, been attempted. One sign that lands mortgaged and lost could be recovered at common law on payment of the principal sum due, can be seen in a case from Norfolk in the King's Bench rolls for 1290.[30] Alan son of Richard sued Hamo de la Grene concerning land in Wygenhal and South Clenchewarten, currently held by Hamo, but owned by Alan. Alan's case was that the lands in question had been gaged to John Lambert and Simon Barun, and had been lost to them 'through Jewish collusion and seduction'. Hamo had come into possession of the land by paying the principal sum due on the first loan to John and Simon on Alan's behalf, on condition that when Alan paid Hamo back, Hamo would transfer the land back to him. Although Alan had often offered Hamo the money due, however, Hamo refused to return the land to Alan. At Alan's request, the king had recently assigned John de Lovetot as his justice to enquire into Christian usurers in the county of Norfolk, and in the *curia regis* at Lynn before John and others, Alan had been awarded recovery of his land. Hamo apparently had not returned it. The case is mentioned again in the next two King's Bench Rolls. In KB 27/124, it is in virtually identical terms. In KB 27/125 m.7r, Hamo turned up to court but Alan did not. Hamo went without day and Alan and his pledges were in mercy.

---

[30] KB 27/123 m.27; KB 27/124 m.10d; KB 27/125 m.7r. I am grateful to Dr P. Brand for the first reference and text.

Appendix IV: Other Documents Relating to Usury

(i) Commons legislative programme provision on usury 1322x1326

Fet a remembrer qe le peple dEngleterre se seit souvent oppresse grevt entut autres choses de cestes suthescriptes[1]

[. . .]

Item de ceo q[ui] cristens sont usurers en diverses maneres aucunes covertes & aucunes ouvertes de grant suff[rance] du poeple q' . . . soit fate. Prefati vocatis [magnatibus &] justic' delibarent.

Let it be recorded that the people of England are often oppressed in many ways, as is described below:

[. . .]

Concerning those Christians who are usurers in various ways, some secret and some open, causing great suffering to the people, [inquiry?] is to be made. They are to be delivered to the [previously named] magnates and judges.

(ii) Commission to justices, 1340 (abbreviated)[2]

Edwardus dei gratia rex Angl[ie][. . .]dil[ect]is & fidelibus suis Thome de Berkele, Joh[annis] de Beauchamp, Henr[ico] Power & Willelmo de Chiltenam salutem.

Quia datum est nob[is] intellig[i] quod diversa oppressiones, extorsiones, dampna, gravamina & excessus per Justic[arios], escaetores, subescaetores, coronatores, vicecom[ites], subvicecomites & eorum clericos & ministros, taxatores, subtaxatores & eorum clericos, admirallos flotarum naviu[m] & eorum deputatos, venditores, assessores & receptores . . . ., Barones de Scaccar[io], clericos de Cancellar[ia] & de scaccario ac de recepta et de aliis placeis n[ostris] & eorum [clericos], custodes, forestarios, viridarios, clericos et alios ministros chacearum & parcorum, collectores custumarum nostrarum, contrarotulatores, tronatores pincernas nostros et eorum substitutos, receptores den[ariorum]nostrorum in patria, custodes equorum nostrorum & eorum garciones, senescallos & marescallos hospicij nostr[i] tam tempore quo extra dictum regnum nostrum Angl[ie] quam in eodem regno fuerimus, clericos mercati provisores victualiam, provisores hospicij nostr[i] ac hospiciorum consortis nostr[ae] & Edwardi Ducis Cornub[ie] & Comitis Cestr[ie] filii n[ostri] carissimi, custodes gaolarum, electores., ballivos itinerantes & alios ballivos & ministros nostros ac aliorum populo regni nostri multipliciter sunt illata . . . & diversa alia mala & facinora nob[is] & dicto populo nostro fecerunt tam in nostr[i] quam dicti populi nostr[i] grave dampnum & status eiusd[em] regn[i] depressionem & depauperacionem manifestam;

Nos tam indempnit[ati] nostre quam tranquillitati & quieti dicti populi nostr[i] providere & remedium super premissis apponere cupientes prout decet; assignavimus vos [. . .] ad inquirend[um] per sacramentum proborum & leg[alium] hom[inum] in com[itatibus] Somers'

---

[1] The text up to this point can be found in W.M. Ormrod, 'Agenda for legislation 1322–c.1340', *EHR* 105 (1990), 1, 31. As Ormrod notes, the document is extremely difficult to read.

[2] JUST 1/770 m.1: roll of pleas before Thomas de Berkele and his fellow justices, at Wells, Monday next after Octaves of the Purification of the Blessed Virgin Mary, 15 Edw. III.

& Dors' tam infra libertates quam extra per quos rei veritas melius scir[i] poterit de oppressionibus, extorsionibus, dampnis, gravaminibus & excessibus predictis, [. . .] et de pecuniarum summis & aliis muneribus que a dicto populo nostr[o] colore officiorum suorum . . . et eciam de pecuniarum summis quas ad opus nostrum ceperunt & [. . .] fraudulenter extra regnum nostrum duxerunt, [. . .], & eciam de nominibus om[nium] & singulorum qui per mutuacionem pecunie seu aliarum rem vel quocumque colore quesito usi fuerunt usuraria pravitate, . . . & alia oppressiones extorsiones & dampna tam per conspiratores iuratores usurarios confederatores, [. . .], audiend[um] & terminand[um] secundum legem & consuetudinem regni nostr[i] Angl[ie][. . .].

Et ideo vobis mandamus quia ad certos dies & loca [. . .] diligenter super premisse faciatis inquisiciones & transgressiones, oppressiones, extorsiones, dampna, gravamina & excessus pred[icta] audiatis & terminetis & omnia alia & singula premissis fac[iatis]& expleatis . . . inde quod ad iustic[iam] pertinet secundum legem & consuetudinem regn[i] nostr[i] Ang[lie] saluis nob[is] amerciamentis & aliis ad nos inde spectantibus.[. . .] In cuius res testimonium hac litteras nostras fier[i] fecimus patentes. Test[e] me ipso apud Turrim London' x. die Decembr' anno regni [nostri] quartodecimo [. . .].

Edward, by the grace of God King of England . . . to his dear and faithful Thomas de Berkeley, John de Beauchamp, Henry Power and William de Chiltenham, greetings.

Whereas we have been informed that various oppressions, extortions, damage, grievances and excesses have been occasioned by justices, escheators, sub-escheators, coroners, sheriffs, under-sheriffs, their clerks and ministers, assessors, sub-assessors, their clerks, admirals and their deputies, sellers, assessors and receivers, clerks of Chancery and the Exchequer and others of our departments, their clerks, keepers, foresters, verderers, collectors of our customs, comptrollers, officials involved in weighing goods, our butlers and their deputies, receivers of taxes in the counties, keepers of our horses, their lads, stewards and marshals of our household, both when we were abroad and when we were in our realm of England, clerks of the market, purveyors of victuals, purveyors for our household and that of our consort, and that of Edward, duke of Cornwall and earl of Chester, our dear son, gaolers, scrutineers, itinerant bailiffs and other bailiffs and ministers of ours and of others, [that they have committed offences concerning avoidance of customs on wool] and they have done various other sorts of evil to us and to our said people, to the grave damage of both ourself and our people, and in obvious depression and impoverishment of the realm.

We, desiring to provide an appropriate remedy for these matters which will bring both recompense for ourself and also peace and tranquility for our aforesaid people, have assigned you to inquire by the oath of good and loyal men in the counties of Somerset and Devon, both within liberties and without, in which manner the truth of the matter can best be known, of the aforesaid oppressions, extortions, damage, grievances and excesses, [of the conduct of officials during the King's absence abroad], and of the sums of money and amounts of other goods which they took from the people, on the pretext of doing their duty, [. . .], and also of the sums of money which they took to our use and fraudulently took out of our realm, [and offences involving fraud in assessing wool customs], and also of the names of all who, either by lending money or by lending other things, or in any other way, have been accustomed to take wicked usury on the pretext of [honest] gain, [and of those who have impeded officials involved in collecting and assessing subsidies, and of other oppressions, extortions, damage, grievances and excesses against us and our people, as mentioned], and other oppressions, extortions and damage both by conspirators, jurors, usurers, those involved in [illicit] confederations, [and those interfering with justice, violent offenders, those demanding money with menaces and those harbouring them, and of any others about anybody wishes to complain].

You are to hear and determine these matters according to the law and customs of our realm of England [and to make certain inquiries concerning wool in these counties], and therefore, we order you that on a certain day, at a certain place, you [...] are to inquire diligently into the aforesaid matters and trespasses, oppressions, extortions, damage, grievances and excesses, hear and determine these matters and do justice, according to the law and customs of our realm of England, saving to us the amercements and other things belonging to us in this matter. [...] In evidence of which things, we have caused these, our letters patent, to be made. Witnessed by myself at the Tower of London, 10th December in the fourteenth year of our reign over England. [...]

Bibliography

Primary Sources

All manuscripts are at the Public Record Office, Kew, unless otherwise stated. Printed primary sources are listed chronologically where appropriate, i.e. where a series of similar documents are available in printed form. Where this is not the case, printed primary sources are listed alphabetically by editor.

I: Statutes, Ordinances, Commissions, Charters and Associated Documents

Manuscripts

C 49/5   Legislative proposal 1322x1326.
C 66/199 m.2d   Commission 1340.
C 66/345 m.14d   Commission 1396–7

Printed

B. Thorpe (ed.), *Ancient Laws and Institutes of England*, 2 vols (London, 1840).
Record Commissioners, *Statutes of the Realm*, 11 vols (London, 1810–28).
J. Topham, P. Morant and T. Astle (eds), *Rotuli Parliamentorum, ut et petitiones et placita in Parliamento*, 6 vols (London, 1783).
F.W. Maitland (ed.) *Records of the Parliament holden at Westminster on the Twenty-Eighth Day of February in the 33rd Year of the Reign of King Edward the First AD 1305* (London, 1893).
H.G. Richardson and G.O. Sayles (ed.), *Rotuli Parliamentorum Hactenus Inediti 1279–1373*, Camden Society, third series, vol. 51 (London, 1935).
F. Palgrave (ed.), *The Parliamentary Writs and Writs of Military Summons*, 2 vols (London, 1830).
M. Prestwich, *York Civic Ordinances 1301*, Borthwick Papers no.49 (York, 1976).
T. Rymer, *Foedera, convenciones, litterae et cujuscunque generis acta publica, inter reges Angliae et alios quosvis imperatores, reges, pontifices, principes, vel communitates, ab ingressu Gulielmi I in Angliam, A.D. 1066, ad nostra usque tempora*, 4 vols in 7 parts (London, 1816–69).
HMSO, *Calendars of the Patent Rolls (1232–1509)*, 52 vols (London, 1895–68).
HMSO, *Calendars of the Close Rolls (1272–1485)*, 45 vols (London, 1892–1963).
HMSO, *Calendars of Inquisitions Post Mortem* vols 2–17 (London, 1906–1988).
HMSO, *Calendars of Inquisitions Miscellaneous (Chancery)* (London, 1916–68).
HMSO, *Calendars of Charter Rolls*, vols 2–5 (1257–1417) (London, 1906–1918).
Y. Rennuard and R. Faukner (eds), *Gascon Rolls Preserved in the Public Record Office 1307–17* (London. 1962)

Local and foreign regulations and charters

Manuscript

Little Red Book of Bristol   Bristol Record Office.
Liber de Assisa Panis   Corporation of London Record Office.

Printed

Anstey, H., *Munimenta Academica or Documents Illustrative of Academical Life and Studies at Oxford*, Rolls Series 50.1 and 50.2 (London, 1868).

Ballard, A. (ed.), *British Borough Charters 1042–1216* (Cambridge, 1913).

Ballard, A., and J. Tait (eds), *British Borough Charters 1216–1307* (Cambridge, 1923).

Bateson, M. (ed.), *Borough Customs*, 2 vols, Selden Society vol. 18 for 1904 and vol. 21 for 1906 (London, 1904 and 1906).

Bickley, F.B. (ed.), *The Little Red Book of Bristol* (London, 1900).

Birch, W. de Gray, *The Historical Charters and Constitutional Documents of the City of London*, rev. edn (London, 1887).

Coss, P. (ed.), *The Early Records of Medieval Coventry*, British Academy Records of Social and Economic History, new ser., 11 (Oxford, 1986).

Cronne, H.A. (ed.), *Bristol Charters 1378–1499*, Bristol Record Society 11 (Bristol, 1946).

Dermot Harding, N. (ed.), *Bristol Charters 1155–1373*, Bristol Record Society 1 (Bristol, 1930).

Gidden, H.W. (ed.), *The Charters of the Borough of Southampton, vol. I: 1199–1480*, Southampton Record Society (Southampton, 1909).

Hudson W., and J.C. Tingey, *Records of the City of Norwich*, 2 vols (Norwich, 1906, 1910).

Markham, C.A. (ed.), *Records of the Borough of Northampton*, vol. 1 (Northampton, 1898).

Riley, H.T. (ed.), *Munimenta Gildhallae Londoniensis, vol. I: Liber Albus, compiled A.D. 1419*, Rolls Series 12.1 (London, 1859).

Riley, H.T. (ed.), *Munimenta Gildhallae Londoniensis, vol. II part i: Liber Custumarum*, Rolls Series 12.2.i (London, 1860).

Riley, H.T. (ed.), *Munimenta Gildhallae Londoniensis, vol. II part ii: Liber Custumarum*, Rolls Series 12.2.ii (London, 1860).

Riley, H.T. (ed.), *Munimenta Gildhallae Londoniensis, vol. III: Liber Albus*, Rolls Series 12.3 (London, 1862).

Riley, H.T. (ed.), *Memorials of London and London Life in the Thirteenth, Fourteenth and Fifteenth Centuries* (London, 1868).

Salter, H.E., *Medieval Archives of the University of Oxford*, 2 vols, Oxford Historical Society vol. 70 for 1917 and vol. 73 for 1919 (Oxford, 1920 and 1921).

Salter, H.E. (ed.), *Munimenta Civitatis Oxonie*, Oxford Historical Society vol. 71 for 1917 (Devizes, 1920).

Sharpe, R.R. (ed.) *Calendars of Letter Books Preserved among the Archives of the Corporation of the City of London: Calendars of Letter Books A-I* (London, 1885–1909).

Stevenson, W.H. (ed.), *Records of the Borough of Nottingham*, 5 vols (London, 1882–1900).

Studer, P. (ed.), *The Oak Book of Southampton, vol. I: The Anglo-French Ordinances of the Ancient Guild Merchant of Southampton* (Southampton, 1910).

Thomson, T., and C. Innes (eds), *The Acts of the Parliaments of Scotalnd 1124–1707*, 12 vols (London, 1814–75).

II: Parliamentary and Court Records

Parliament

J. Topham, P. Morant and T. Astle (eds), *Rotuli Parliamentorum, ut et petitiones et placita in Parliamento*, 6 vols (London, 1783).

Eyres

Manuscripts

PRO class JUST 1
JUST 1/8, 12, 24, 25, 37, 40, 44, 55, 56, 60, 62, 82, 85, 86, 95, 96, 111, 117A, 133, 135, 148,
  166, 175, 176, 181, 184, 204, 213, 242, 272, 274, 278, 279, 300C, 302, 325, 345, 351B,
  369, 374, 377, 383, 384, 389, 455, 457, 486, 491, 497, 536, 538, 543, 544, 562, 568, 569A,
  572, 573, 621, 632, 651, 664, 683, 700, 701, 703, 705, 722, 736, 739, 759, 775, 776, 778,
  780, 784, 803, 806, 818, 827, 829, 867, 872, 874, 876, 883, 915, 916, 956, 982, 986, 998A,
  1006, 1025, 1026, 1028, 1051, 1078, 1098, 1013, 1043, 1109, 1158, 1165, 1166, 1603.

Printed

D.M. Stenton (ed.), *Pleas before the King or his Justices 1198–1202*, vols II and III, Selden
  Society vol. 68 for 1949 and vol. 83 for 1966 (London, 1952 and 1967).
F.W. Maitland (ed.), *Select Pleas of the Crown 1200–1225*, Selden Society vol. 1 for 1887
  (London, 1888).
D.M. Stenton (ed.), *Rolls of the Justices in Eyre in Yorkshire 1218–19*, Selden Society vol. 56 for
  1937 (London, 1937).
D.M. Stenton (ed.), *Rolls of the Justices in Eyre for Lincolnshire (1218–19) and Worcestershire 1221*,
  Selden Society vol. 53 for 1934 (London, 1934).
D.M. Stenton (ed.), *Rolls of the Justices in Eyre for Gloucestershire, Warwickshire and Shropshire
  1221–22*, Selden Society vol. 59 for 1940 (London, 1940).
H. Chew and M. Weinbaum (eds), *The London Eyre of 1244*, London Record Society
  Publications 6 (London, 1970).
C.A.F. Meekings and D. Crook (eds), *1235 Surrey Eyre*, Surrey Record Society vols 31 and 32
  (Guildford, 1982 and 1983).
M.T. Clanchy (ed.), *The Roll and Writ File of the Berkshire Eyre 1248*, Selden Society vol. 90 for
  1972–3 (London, 1973).
A. Harding (ed.), *The Roll of the Shropshire Eyre 1256*, Selden Society vol. 96 for 1980 (London,
  1981).
W. Page (ed.), *Three Early Assize Rolls for the County of Northumberland*, Surtees Society 88
  (Durham, 1890).
M. Weinbaum (ed.), *The London Eyre of 1276*, London Record Society Publications 12
  (London, 1976).
F.W. Maitland, W.V. Harcourt and W.C. Bolland (eds), *Year Book of the Eyre of Kent 6 & 7
  Edw. II 1313–14*, Selden Society vol. 24 for 1909, vol. 27 for 1912 and vol. 29 for 1913
  (London, 1910, 1912 and 1913).
H.M. Cam (ed.), *The Eyre of London, 14 Edw. II 1321*, Selden Society vol. 85 for 1968 and vol.
  86 for 1969 (London, 1968 and 1969).
W. Sutherland (ed.), *The Eyre of Northamptonshire 3–4 Edw. III 1329–30*, Selden Society vol.
  97 for 1981 and vol. 98 for 1982 (London, 1983).

Eyre Veredicta

Manuscripts

PRO class JUST 1
JUST 1/36, 895–906, 1567, 1568, 1569, 1571, 1572, 1573, 1575, 1576, 1577, 1578, 1591,
  1593, 1598, 1599.

Common Pleas Rolls

Manuscripts

PRO class CP 40
CP 40/30, 76, 126, 177, 228, 279, 320, 358, 398, 436, 474, 513, 541.

King's Bench Rolls

Manuscripts

PRO class KB 27
KB 27/11, 12, 15, 124, 125, 134, 247, 255, 265, 266, 267, 270, 411, 471, 525, 526, 527, 528, 539, 540, 544, 545, 546, 548, 549.

Printed

Phillimore, W.P.W. (ed.), *Pleas of King's Bench in Trinity Term 25 Edward I (1297)*, British Record Society (London, 1898).
Sayles, G.O. (ed.), *Select Cases in the Court of King's Bench under Edward I*, Selden Society vol. 55 for 1936, vol. 57 for 1938 and vol. 58 for 1939 (London, 1936, 1938 and 1939).
Tupling, G.H., *South Lancashire in the Reign of Edward II as Illustrated by the Pleas at Wigan Recorded in Coram Rege Roll no.254*, Chetham Society, new series, 1 (Manchester, 1949).

King's Bench Indictment Files and Presentment Rolls

Manuscripts

PRO classes KB 9, JUST 1, JUST 2
KB 9/19, 25, 31, 32; 38, 66, 67, 97, 102, 139, 141, 154, 155, 156, 167, 168, 169, 170, 171, 172, 173, 174, 175; JUST 1/106, 267, 401/1, 528, 533, 1144; JUST 2/36/3.

Other Sessions of Royal Justices

Manuscripts

PRO classes JUST 1 and KB 9
JUST 1/ 31, 74, 94/2, 119, 188, 191, 226, 254, 255, 286, 287, 290, 291, 299/7, 306, 337, 353, 396, 399, 421, 422, 430, 439, 452, 453, 521, 525, 548, 553, 609, 610A, 638, 715, 770, 858, 945, 971, 1133, 1151, 1256, 1451, 1560, 1565; KB 9/1, 2, 9.

Printed

Boatwright, L. (ed.), *Inquests and Indictments from Late Fourteenth Century Buckinghamshire: The Superior Eyre of Michaelmas 1389 at High Wycombe*, Buckinghamshire Record Society 29 (Aylesbury, 1994).
Harding, A. (ed.), 'Early trailbaston proceedings from the Lincoln roll of 1305' in R.F. Hunnisett and J.B. Post (eds), *Medieval Legal Records* (London, 1978), 144–69.
Illingworth, W. (ed.), *Rotuli Hundredorum temp. Henr. III & Edw. I in Turr' Lond' et in curia receptae scaccarii Westm. asservata*, 2 vols (London, 1812–18).
Illingworth, W. (ed.), *Placita de Quo Warranto temporibus Edw. I, II & III in curia receptae scaccarii westm. asservata* (London, 1818).

Wrottesley, G., 'The Staffordshire Hundred Rolls', *William Salt Archaeological Society* 5 (London, 1884), 105–22.

Wrottesley, G., 'Staffordshire Pleas from B.Mus. Add. MS 12269', *William Salt Archaeological Society* 6 (London, 1885), 29–36.

Wrottesley, G. (ed.), 'Extracts from Assize Rolls and De Banco Rolls 1307–1327', *William Salt Society* 9 (London, 1888), 1–120.

Wrottesley, G. (ed.), 'Extracts from the Coram Rege Rolls and Pleas of the Crown 1307–1327', *William Salt Society* 10 (London, 1889), 1–78.

Wrottesley, G. (ed.), 'Extracts from Plea Rolls of Edward III', *William Salt Society* 11 (London, 1890), 1–123.

Wrottesley, G. (ed.), 'Extracts from Plea Rolls 16–33 Edw. III', *William Salt Society* 12 (London, 1891), 1–65.

Wrottesley, G. (ed.), 'Extracts from Plea Rolls of Edward III and Richard II', *William Salt Society* 13 (London, 1892), 1–176.

Pipe Rolls

Manuscripts

PRO class E 372
E 372/119, 120, 121, 122, 125, 126, 153, 154, 155A, 156, 157, 158, 186.

Peace Sessions

Manuscripts

PRO class JUST 1
JUST 1/107, 266, 293, 297, 298.

Printed

Kimball, E.G. (ed.), *Some Sessions of the Peace in Lincolnshire 1381–1396*, Publications of the Lincolnshire Record Society vol. 49 for 1955 and vol. 56 for 1961 (Hereford, 1955 and 1962).

Kimball, E.G. (ed.), *Sessions of the Peace in the City of Lincoln 1351–4 and the Borough of Stamford 1351*, Publications of the Lincolnshire Record Society vol. 65 for 1971 (Lincoln, 1971).

Kimball, E.G. (ed.), *Sessions of the Peace for Bedfordshire 1355–9; 1363–4*, Bedfordshire Historical Record Society 48 (Bedford, 1969).

Kimball, E.G. (ed.), *Oxfordshire Sessions of the Peace in the Reign of Richard II*, Oxfordshire Record Society vol. 53 for 1979 and 1980 (Banbury, 1983).

Kimball, E.G. (ed.), *Rolls of the Gloucestershire Sessions of the Peace 1361–1378*, Transactions of the Bristol and Gloucestershire Archaeological Society vol. 62 for 1940 (Kendal, 1942).

Kimball, E.G. (ed.), *Rolls of the Warwickshire and Coventry Sessions of the Peace 1377–97*, Dugdale Society 16 (London, 1939).

Putnam, B.H., *Proceedings before the Justices of the Peace in the Fourteenth and Fifteenth Centuries* (London, 1938).

Putnam, B.H. (ed.), *Yorkshire Sessions of the Peace*, Yorkshire Archaeological Society 100 (Wakefield, 1939).

Sillem, R. (ed.), *Some Sessions of the Peace in Lincolnshire 1360–1375*, Publications of the Lincolnshire Record Society vol. 30 for 1937 (Hereford, 1936).

Tourns

Manuscripts

PRO classes JUST 1 and SC 2
JUST 1/221, 451, SC 2/161/75.

Printed

Baildon, W. Paley (ed.), *Court Rolls of the Manor of Wakefield, vol. I: 1274–1297*, Yorkshire
    Archaeological Society Record Series vol. 29 for 1900 (Leeds, 1901).
Baildon, W. Paley (ed.), *Court Rolls of the Manor of Wakefield, vol. II: 1297–1309*, Yorkshire
    Archaeological Society Record Series vol. 36 for 1906 (Leeds, 1906).
Lister, J. (ed.), *Court Rolls of the Manor of Wakefield, vol. III: 1313–1316 and 1286*, Yorkshire
    Archaeological Society Record Series vol. 57 for 1917 (Leeds, 1917).
Lister, J. (ed.), *Court Rolls of the Manor of Wakefield, vol. IV: 1316–1317*, Yorkshire
    Archaeological Society Record Series vol. 78 for 1930 (Leeds, 1930).
Walker, J. (ed.), *Court Rolls of the Manor of Wakefield, vol. V: 1322–1331*, Yorkshire
    Archaeological Society Record Series vol. 109 for 1944 (Wakefield, 1945).
Walker, S.S. (ed.), *Court Rolls of the Manor of Wakefield from October 1331 to September 1333*,
    Wakefield Court Rolls Series of the Yorkshire Archaeological Society vol. 3 for 1982
    (Leeds, 1983).
Jewell, H.M. (ed.), *Court Rolls of the Manor of Wakefield from September 1348 to September 1350*,
    Yorkshire Archaeological Society, Wakefield Court Rolls second series vol. 2 (Leeds,
    1981).
Habberjam, M., O'Regan, M., and Hale, B. (eds), *Court Rolls of the Manor of Wakefield from
    October 1350 to September 1352*, Yorkshire Archaeological Society, Wakefield Court Rolls
    Series vol. 6 for 1985 (Leeds, 1987).

Sheriffs' Account Rolls

Manuscripts

PRO class E 389
E 389/88, 90, 96, 104, 149.

City and Town Court Rolls

Manuscripts

PRO SC 2/178/47–54, Stevenage court rolls 1298–1395.

Printed

Dale, M.K. (ed.), *Court Rolls of Tamworth* (Tamworth, 1959).
Hopkins, A., *Selected Rolls of the Chester City Courts, Late Thirteenth Century and Early Fourteenth
    Century*, Chetham Society, new series, vol 2 (Manchester, 1950).
Jeayes, I.H. (ed.), *Court Rolls of the Borough of Colchester 1310–79*, 3 vols (Colchester, 1921).
Jones, G.P., and H. Owen, *Caernarvon Court Rolls 1361–1402*, Caernarvonshire Historical
    Society Record Series no.1 (Caernarvon, 1951).
Stewart-Brown, R. (ed.), *Calendar of County Court, City Court and Eyre Rolls of Chester, 1259–97*,
    Chetham Society 84 (Aberdeen, 1925).

Thomas, A.H. (ed.), *Calendar of Early Mayor's Court Rolls Preserved among the Archives of the Corporation of the City of London at the Guildhall A.D. 1298–1307* (Cambridge, 1924).

Thomas, A.H. (ed.), *Calendars of Plea Rolls and Memoranda Rolls of the City of London Preserved among the Archives of the Corporation of the City of London at the Guildhall A.D. 1323–1402* (Cambridge, 1926–61)..

Manor Court Rolls

Manuscripts (including)

Sutton, Lincolnshire
DL 30/85/1157 – DL 30/90/1212 (1305–1398).
Rickling, Essex
SC2/173/52–56 (1315 to 1395, incomplete).

Printed

Dale, M.K. (ed.), *The Court Rolls of Chalgrave Manor 1278–1313*, Bedfordshire Historical Record Society 28 (Luton, 1949).

Farr, B., *Highworth Hundred Rolls 1275–87*, Wiltshire Record Society 21 and 22 (Devizes, 1967 and 1968).

Hall, G.D.G. (ed.), 'Three courts of the hundred of Penwith, 1333' in R.F. Hunnisett and J.B. Post (eds), *Medieval Legal Records* (London, 1978), 170.

Hassall, W., and J. Beauray, *Lordship and Landscape in Norfolk 1250–1350*, British Academy Records of Social and Economic History, new series, vol. 20 (Oxford, 1993).

Maitland, F.W., and W. Paley Baildon (eds), *The Court Baron, being precedents for use in seignorial and other local courts, together with select pleas from the Bishop of Ely's Court of Littleport*, Selden Society vol. 4 for 1890 (London, 1891).

Massingberd, W.J. (ed.), *Court Rolls of the Manor of Ingoldmells in the County of Lincolnshire* (London, 1902).

Oram, R., and F.H. Fenton (eds), *Tottenham Manorial Rolls 1377–99: Court Rolls of the Manors of Bruces, Dawbeneys, Pembrokes (Tottenham), 1 Ric. II – 1 Hen. IV, 1377–1399* (Tottenham, 1961).

Poos, L.R., and A.L. Bonfield (eds), *Select Cases in Manorial Courts 1250–1550, Property and Family Law*, Selden Society vol. 114 for 1997 (London, 1998).

Pugh, R.B. (ed.), *Court Rolls of the Wiltshire Manor of Adam de Stratton*, Wiltshire Record Society 24 (Devizes, 1970).

Raspin, G.E.A., 'Transcript and Descriptive List of the Medieval Court Rolls of the Marcher Lordship of Clun deposited in the Salop R.O. by the Earl of Powis' (unpublished, 1963).

Courts Leet and Fair Courts

Manuscripts

SC2/178/93–106:   Rolls of fair court of St Ives, Huntingdonshire 1297–1396 (incomplete series).

Printed

W. Hudson, *Leet Jurisdiction in the City of Norwich during the Thirteenth and Fourteenth Centuries*, Selden Society vol. 5 for 1891 (London, 1892).

III: Law Reports

Manuscripts

British Library

Add. 31826	Year Book for 1276, 1299–1306 and other unspecified years.
Add. 38821	Register of Writs, assorted cases.
Egerton 2811	Year Books temp. Edw. I and Edw. II.
Harley MS 811	Year Book temp. Edw. III.
Harley MS 739	Year Book 1334–7.
Add. 5926	Cases in eyre in Nottinghamshire, Bedfordshire and Derbyshire 1330.
Harley 572	Year Book temp. Edw. I.
Add. 34783	Various Year Books.
Add. 32087	Digest of cases from the reigns of Edward II and Richard II.

Printed

Edward I

A.J. Horwood (ed.), *Year Books of the Reign of King Edward the First, Year XX and Year XXI*, Rolls Series 31.1 (London, 1866).

A.J. Horwood (ed.), *Year Books of the Reign of King Edward the First, Year XXI and Year XXII*, Rolls Series 31.2 (London, 1875).

A.J. Horwood (ed.), *Year Books of the Reign of King Edward the First, Michaelmas Term Year XXXIII and Years XXXIV and XXXV*, Rolls Series 31.5 (London, 1879).

Edward II

R. de Winchedon (compiled), *Les Reports des cases argue & ajudge in le temps del Roy Edward le Second, et auxy memoranda del Exchequer en temps le Roy Edward le Primer. Solonque les ancient manuscripts ore remanent en les maines de Sir Jehan' Maynard chevaler, serjeant de la ley* (London, 1678).

F.W. Maitland (ed.), *Year Books of Edward II, vol. I, 1 & 2 Edw. II, A.D. 1307–1309*, Selden Society vol. 17 for 1903 (London, 1903).

F.W. Maitland (ed.), *Year Books of Edward II, 2 & 3 Edw. II, 1308–9 and 1309–10*, Selden Society vol. 19 for 1904, Year Books Series 2 (London, 1904).

F.W. Maitland (ed.), *Year Books of Edward II, 3 Edw. II, 1309–10*, Selden Society vol. 20 for 1905, Year Books Series 3 (London, 1905).

F.W. Maitland and G.J. Turner (eds), *Year Books of Edward II, 3 & 4 Edw. II, 1309–11*, Selden Society vol. 22 for 1907, Year Books Series 4 (London, 1907).

G.J. Turner (ed.), *Year Books of Edward II, 4 Edw. II, 1310–11*, Selden Society vol. 26 for 1911, Year Books Series 6 (London, 1914).

G.J. Turner (ed.), *Year Books of Edward II, 4 Edw. II, 1311*, Selden Society vol. 42 for 1925, Year Books Series 9 (London, 1926).

G.J. Turner and T.F.T. Plucknett (eds), *Year Books of Edward II, 5 Edw. II, 1311*, Selden Society vol. 63 for 1944, Year Books Series 10 (London, 1947).

W.C. Bolland (ed.), *Year Books of Edward II, 5 Edw. II, 1311–12*, Selden Society vol. 31 for 1915, Year Books Series 11 (London, 1915).

W.C. Bolland (ed.), *Year Books of Edward II, 5 Edw. II, 1312*, Selden Society vol. 33 for 1916, Year Books Series 12 (London, 1916).

P. Vinogradoff and L. Ehrlich (eds), *Year Books of Edward II, 6 Edw. II, 1312–13*, Selden Society vol. 34 for 1917, Year Books Series 13 (London, 1918).

P. Vinogradoff and L. Ehrlich (eds), *Year Books of Edward II, 6 Edw. II, 1312–13*, Selden Society vol. 38 for 1921, Year Books Series 14 part 1 (London, 1921).

W.C. Bolland (ed.), *Year Books of Edward II, 6 Edw. II, 1313*, Selden Society vol. 43 for 1926, Year Books Series 14 part 2 (London, 1927).

W.C. Bolland (ed.), *Year Books of Edward II, 6 & 7 Edw. II, 1313*, Selden Society vol. 36 for 1918, Year Books Series 15 (London, 1918).

W.C. Bolland, F.W. Maitland and L.W.V. Harcourt (eds), *Eyre of Kent 6 & 7 Edw. II, 1313–14*, vol. 1, Selden Society vol. 24 for 1909, Year Books Series 5 (London, 1910).

W.C. Bolland, F.W. Maitland and L.W.V. Harcourt (eds), *Eyre of Kent 6 & 7 Edw. II, 1313–14*, vol. 2, Selden Society vol. 27 for 1912, Year Books Series 7 (London, 1912).

W.C. Bolland (ed.), *Eyre of Kent 6 & 7 Edw. II, 1313–14*, vol. 3, Selden Society vol. 29 for 1913, Year Books Series 8 (London, 1913).

W.C. Bolland (ed.), *Year Books of Edward II, 7 Edw. II, 1313–14*, Selden Society vol. 39 for 1922, Year Books Series 16 (London, 1922).

W.C. Bolland (ed.), *Year Books of Edward II, 8 Edw. II, 1314–15*, Selden Society vol. 41 for 1924, Year Books Series 17 (London, 1925).

W.C. Bolland (ed.), *Year Books of Edward II, 8 Edw. II, 1315*, Selden Society vol. 37 for 1920, Year Books Series 18 (London, 1920).

G.J. Turner and W.C. Bolland (eds), *Year Books of Edward II, 9 Edw. II, 1315–16*, Selden Society vol. 45 for 1928, Year Books Series 19 (London, 1929).

M.D. Legge and W. Holdsworth (eds), *Year Books of Edward II, 10 Edw. II, 1316–17*, Selden Society vol. 52 for 1934, Year Books Series 20 (London, 1934).

M.D. Legge and W. Holdsworth (eds), *Year Books of Edward II, 10 Edw. II, 1316–17*, Selden Society vol. 54 for 1935, Year Books Series 21 (London, 1935).

J.P. Collas and W. Holdsworth (eds), *Year Books of Edward II, 11 Edw. II, 1317–18*, Selden Society vol. 61 for 1942, Year Books Series 22 (London, 1942).

J.P. Collas and T.F.T. Plucknett (eds), *Year Books of Edward II, 12 Edw. II, 1318*, Selden Society vol. 63 for 1946, Year Books Series 23 (London, 1950).

J.P. Collas and T.F.T. Plucknett (eds), *Year Books of Edward II, 12 Edw. II, 1319*, Selden Society vol. 70 for 1951, Year Books Series 24 (London, 1953).

J.P. Collas (ed.), *Year Books of Edward II, 12 Edw. II, 1319*, Selden Society vol. 81 for 1964, Year Books Series 25 (London, 1964).

H.M. Cam (ed.), *Eyre of London 14 Edw. II, 1321*, 2 vols, Selden Society vol. 85 for 1968 and vol. 86 for 1969, Year Books Series 26 parts 1 and 2 (London, 1968 and 1969).

S.J. Stoljar and L.J. Downer (eds), *Year Books of Edward II, 14 Edw. II, 1320*, Selden Society vol. 104 for 1988, Year Books Series 27 (London, 1988).

Edward III

Year Books of Edward III, *Anni decem priores regis Edwardi tertii* (London, 1596).

G. Sawbridge, W. Rawlins and S. Roycroft (printed), *Le livre des Assizes et Pleas del Corone moves et dependants devant les Justices si bien en lour circuits come aylours, en temps du Roy Edward le Tiers* (London, 1679).

G. Sawbridge, W. Rawlins and S. Roycroft (printed), *Les Reports del Cases en ley que furent argues a Quadragesimo ad Quinquagesimum annum de tres haut et Puissant Prince Roy Edward le Tierce* (London, 1679).

G. Sawbridge, W. Rawlins and S. Roycroft (printed), *Le Premier Part de les reports del Cases en Ley que furent argues en le temps de le tres Haut & Puissant Prince Roy Edward le Tierce* (London, 1679).

D.W. Sutherland (ed.), *Eyre of Northamptonshire 3–4 Edw. III, 1329–1330*, 2 vols, Selden Society vol. 97 for 1981 and vol. 98 for 1982 (London, 1983).

A.J. Horwood (ed.), *Year Books of the Reign of King Edward III Years XI and XII*, Rolls Series 31.6 (London, 1883).

L.O. Pike (ed.), *Year Books of the Reign of King Edward III Years XII and XIII*, Rolls Series 31.7 (London, 1885).

L.O. Pike (ed.), *Year Books of the Reign of King Edward III Years XIII and XIV*, Rolls Series 31.8 (London, 1886).

L.O. Pike (ed.), *Year Books of the Reign of King Edward III Year XIV*, Rolls Series 31.9 (London, 1888).

L.O. Pike (ed.), *Year Books of the Reign of King Edward III Years XIV and XV*, Rolls Series 31.10 (London, 1889).

L.O. Pike (ed.), *Year Books of the Reign of King Edward III Year XV*, Rolls Series 31.11 (London, 1891).

L.O. Pike (ed.), *Year Books of the Reign of King Edward III Year XVI*, Rolls Series 31.12 (London, 1896–1900).

L.O. Pike (ed.), *Year Books of the Reign of King Edward III Year XVII*, Rolls Series 31.13 (London, 1901).

L.O. Pike (ed.), *Year Books of the Reign of King Edward III Years XVII and XVIII*, Rolls Series 31.14 (London, 1903).

L.O. Pike (ed.), *Year Books of the Reign of King Edward III Year XVIII*, Rolls Series 31.15 (London, 1904).

L.O. Pike (ed.), *Year Books of the Reign of King Edward III Years XVIII and XIX*, Rolls Series 31.16 (London, 1905).

L.O. Pike (ed.), *Year Books of the Reign of King Edward III Year XIX*, Rolls Series 31.17 (London, 1906).

L.O. Pike (ed.), *Year Books of the Reign of King Edward III Year XX*, Rolls Series 31.18 (London, 1908).

Richard II

M.S. Arnold (ed.), *Year Books of Richard II: 2 Ric. II, 1378–9* (London, 1975).

S.E. Thorne (ed.), *Year Books of Richard II: 6 Ric. II, 1382–3* (Cambridge, MA, 1996).

M.J. Holland (ed.), *Year Books of Richard II: 7 Ric. II, 1383–4* (Cambridge, MA, 1989).

L.C. Hector and M.J. Hager (eds), *Year Books of Richard II: 8–10 Ric. II, 1385–7* (London, 1987).

I.D. Thornley (ed.), *Year Books of Richard II: 11 Ric. II, 1387–8* (London, 1977).

G.F. Deiser (ed.), *Year Books of Richard II: 12 Ric. II, 1388–9* (Cambridge, MA, 1914).

T.F.T. Plucknett (ed.), *Year Books of Richard II: 13 Ric. II, 1389–90* (London, 1929).

Others

Brook, Sir R. R. Tottell (ed.), *La Graunde Abridgement* (London, 1576).

Illingworth, W. (ed.), *Placitorum in domo capitulari Westmonasteriensi asservatorum abbreviatio temporibus regum Ric. I, Johann., Henr. III, Edw. I, Edw. II* (London, 1811).

Collected court records

Baildon, W.P., *Select Cases in Chancery 1364–1471*, Selden Society vol. 10 for 1896 (London, 1896).

Brand, P.A. (ed.), *The Earliest English Law Reports*, Selden Society vol. 111 for 1995 and vol. 112 for 1996 (London, 1996).

Rigg, J.M., *Select Pleas, Starrs and Other Records from the Rolls of the Exchequer of the Jews A.D. 1220–1284*, Selden Society vol. 15 for 1901 (London, 1902).

Rigg, J.M., *Calendar of the Plea Rolls of the Exchequer of the Jews*, vol. I, *1218–1272* and vol. II, *1273–1275*, Jewish Historical Society of England (London, 1905 and 1910).

Jenkinson, H. (ed.), *Calendar of the Plea Rolls of the Exchequer of the Jews*, vol. III, *1275–1277* (London, 1929).

Richardson, H.G. (ed.), *Calendar of the Plea Rolls of the Exchequer of the Jews*, vol. IV, *1272, 1275–1277* (London, 1972).

Cohen, S. (ed.), rev. P. Brand, *Plea Rolls of the Exchequer of the Jews*, vol. V, *1277–1299* (London, 1992).

IV: Treatises

Genet, J.P. (ed.), *Four English Political Tracts of the Later Middle Ages*, Camden Society, fourth series, 18 (London, 1977).

Hall, G.D.G. (ed.), *The Treatise on the Laws and Customs of England Commonly Called Glanvill* (London, 1965).

Johnson, C. (ed.), *Dialogus de Scaccario* (London, 1950).

Maitland, F.W. (ed.), *Court Baron*, Selden Society vol. 4 for 1890 (London, 1891).

Nicholls, F.M. (ed.), *Britton* (Oxford, 1865).

Richardson, H.G., and G.O. Sayles (eds), *Fleta*, vol. II, Selden Society vol. 72 for 1953 (London, 1955).

Whittaker, W.J. (ed.), *The Mirror of Justices*, Selden Society vol. 7 for 1895 (London, 1895).

Woodbine, G.E., and S.E. Thorne (eds), *Bracton 'On the Laws and Customs of England'*, 4 vols (Cambridge, MA, 1968–77).

V: Miscellaneous

English ecclesiastical records

Bannister, A.T. (ed.), *Registrum Ade de Orleton* (London, 1908).

Brown, W. (ed.), *The Register of John le Romeyn, Lord Archbishop of York 1286–1296, part I*, Surtees Society 123 (Durham, 1913).

Brown, W. (ed.), *The Register of Thomas of Corbridge, Lord Archbishop of York 1300–1304, part I*, Surtees Society 138 (Durham, 1925).

Brown, W., and A.H. Thompson (eds), *The Register of William Greenfield, Archbishop of York 1306–1315*, Surtees Society 152 (Durham, 1938).

Hill, R.M.T. (ed.), *The Rolls and Register of Bishop Oliver Sutton, 1286–1299, vol. IV*, Publications of the Lincolnshire Record Society 52 for 1957 (Hereford, 1958).

Johnson, C. (ed.), *Registrum Hamonis Hethe* (Canterbury, 1915–48).

Poos, L.R. (ed.), *Lower Level Jurisdiction in Late Medieval England: The Courts of the Dean and Chapter of Lincoln 1336–49 and Deanery of Wisbech 1458–1484* (Oxford, 2001).

Willis Bund, J.W., *Worcester Registrum Sede Vacante 1301–1435* (Oxford, 1897).

Papal

Bliss, W.H. (ed.), *Calendar of Entries in the Papal Registers Relating to Great Britain and Ireland, vol. I: 1198–1304* (London, 1893).

Bliss, W.H., and C. Johnson (eds), *Calendar of Entries in the Papal Registers Relating to Great Britain and Ireland, vol. II: 1305–1342* (London, 1895).

Bliss, W.H., and C. Johnson (eds), *Calendar of Entries in the Papal Registers Relating to Great Britain and Ireland, vol. III: 1342–62* (London, 1897).

Bliss, W.H., and J.A. Twemlow (eds), *Calendar of Entries in the Papal Registers Relating to Great Britain and Ireland, vol. IV: 1362–1404* (London, 1902).

Bliss, W.H., and J.A. Twemlow (eds), *Calendar of Entries in the Papal Registers Relating to Great Britain and Ireland, vol. V: 1396–1404* (London, 1904).
Zutshi, P.N.R., *Original Papal Letters in England 1305–1415* (Vatican, 1990).

Common law

de Haas, E., and G.D.G. Hall (eds), *Early Registers of Writs*, Selden Society vol. 87 for 1970 (London, 1970).
Shanks, E. and S.F.C. Milsom (eds), *Novae Narrationes*, Selden Society vol. 80 for 1963 (London, 1963).
Turner, G.J. and T.F.T. Plucknett (eds), *Brevia Placitata*, Selden Society vol. 66 for 1947 (London, 1951).

Canon law

Friedberg, E. (ed.), *Corpus Iuris Canonici*, 2 vols (Leipzig, 1879–81; reprinted Graz, 1959).
Mansi, J.D. (ed.), *Sacrorum Conciliorum nova et amplissimus collectio*, 53 vols (Graz, 1960–62).

Selected documents of various types

Baker, J.H., and S.F.C. Milsom, *Sources of English Legal History: Private Law to 1750* (London, 1986).
Bland, A.E., P.A. Brown and R.H. Tawney (eds), *English Economic History: Selected Documents* (London, 1914).
Dobson, R.B. (ed.), *The Peasants' Revolt of 1381*, 2nd edn (London, 1983).
HMSO, *The Register of Edward, the Black Prince* (London, 1932).
Myers, A.R. (ed.), *English Historical Documents, vol. IV: 1327–1485* (London, 1969).
Powicke, M., and C.R. Cheney, *Councils and Synods with Other Documents Relating to the English Church*, 2 vols (Oxford, 1964).
Rigg, J.M. (ed.), *Select Pleas, Starrs and Records of the Jewish Exchequer*, Selden Society vol. 15 for 1901 (London, 1902).
Rothwell, H. (ed.), *English Historical Documents, vol. III: 1189–1327* (London, 1975).
Thorne, S.E. (ed.), *Readings and Moots at the Inns of Court, vol. I*, Selden Society vol. 71 for 1952 (London, 1954).
Treharne, R.F., and I.J. Sanders, *Documents of the Baronial Movement of Reform* (Oxford, 1973).
Whitelock, D., M. Brett and C.N.L. Brooke (eds), *Councils and Synods with other Documents Relating to the English Church 1066–1204*, 2 vols (Oxford, 1981).

Chronicles

Childs, W.R., and J. Taylor (eds), *The Anonimalle Chronicle 1307 to 1334 from Brotherton Collection MS 29* (Leeds, 1991).
Denholm-Young, N. (ed.), *The Life of Edward the Second by the so-called Monk of Malmesbury* (London, 1957).
Hector, L.C., and B.F. Harvey (eds), *The Westminster Chronicle (1381–94)* (Oxford, 1982).

Secondary Works

Abrahams, I., *Jewish Life in the Middle Ages* (New York, 1896).
Anderson, B.L., and A.J.H. Latham (eds), *The Market in History* (London, 1986).

Arnold, M.S., 'Fourteenth century promises', *Cambridge Law Journal* 55 (1976), 321–34.

Arnold, M.S., 'Statutes as judgments: the natural law theory of parliamentary activity in medieval England', *University of Pennsylvania Law Review* 126 (1977), 329–43.

Arnold, T. (ed.), *Select English Works of John Wyclif* (Oxford, 1871).

Ashley, W., *An Introduction to English Economic History and Theory* (New York, 1966).

Atiyah, P.S., *The Rise and Fall of Freedom of Contract* (Oxford, 1979).

Bailey, M., 'The commercialisation of the English economy 1086–1500', *Journal of Medieval History* 24 (1998), 297–311.

Baker, J.H. (ed.), *Legal Records and the Historian* (London, 1978).

Baker, J.H., 'Why the history of English law has not been finished' *Cambridge Law Journal* 59 (2000), 62–84.

Baker, J.H., *An Introduction to English Legal History*, 4th edn (London, 2002).

Baldwin, J.W., *Masters, Princes and Merchants: The Social Views of Peter the Chanter and his Circle* (Princeton, 1970).

Bannister, A.T., 'Visitation returns of the Diocese of Hereford in 1397', *EHR* 44 (1929), 279, 444.

Barraclough, G., 'Law and legislation in medieval England', *Law Quarterly Review* 56 (1940), 75–92.

Barron, C.M., 'Tyranny of Richard II', *BIHR* 41 (1968) 1–18.

Bennett, J.M., *Women in the Medieval English Countryside: Gender and Household in Brigstock before the Plague* (New York and Oxford, 1987).

Bennett, J.M., *Ale, Beer and Brewsters in England: Women's Work in a Changing World 1300–1600* (New York and Oxford, 1996).

Black, A., *Political Thought in Europe 1250–1450* (Cambridge, 1992).

Blackstone, Sir W., *Commentaries on the Laws of England* (London, 1765–9).

Bolton, J.L., *The Medieval English Economy* (London, 1980).

Bolton, J.L., 'Inflation, economics and politics in thirteenth century England' in P.R. Coss and S.D. Lloyd (eds), *Thirteenth Century England IV: Proceedings of the Newcastle upon Tyne Conference 1991* (Woodbridge, 1992), 1–14.

Bothwell, J., PJP Goldberg and W.M. Ormrod (eds), *The Problem of Labour in Fourteenth Century England* (York, 2000).

Bowers, R.H., 'A Middle English mnemonic poem on usury', *Medieval Studies* 17 (1955), 226–32.

Brand, P.A., 'The control of mortmain alienation in England 1200–1300' in J.H. Baker (ed.), *Legal Records and the Historian* (Cambridge, 1978), 29–40.

Brand, P., 'Edward I and the judges: the state trials of 1289–93' in P.R. Coss and S.A. Lloyd (eds), *Thirteenth Century England I: Proceedings of the Newcastle upon Tyne Conference* (Woodbridge, 1986), 31–40.

Brand, P., *Origins of the English Legal Profession* (Oxford, 1992).

Brand, P., 'Aspects of the law of debt 1189–1307' in P.R. Schofield and N.J. Mayhew (eds), *Credit and Debt in Medieval England c.1180–c.1350* (Oxford, 2002), 1–41.

Bridbury, A.R., *The English Economy from Bede to the Reformation* (Woodbridge, 1992).

Britnell, R.H., *Growth and Decline in Colchester 1300–1525* (Cambridge, 1986).

Britnell, R.H., 'Forstall, forestalling and the Statute of Forestallers', *EHR* 102 (1987), 89–102.

Britnell, R.H., 'Morals, laws and ale in medieval England' in U. Mueller, F. Hundsnurcher and C. Sommer (eds), *Le droit et sa perception dans la littérature et les mentalités médiévales* (Göppingen, 1993), 21–9.

Britnell, R.H., *The Commercialisation of English Society 1000–1500*, 2nd edn (Manchester, 1996).

Britnell, R.H., 'Price setting in English borough markets 1349–1500', *Canadian Journal of History* 31 (1996), 1–15.

Britnell, R.H., 'Urban economic regulation and economic morality in medieval England', http://www.dur.ac.uk/r.h.britnell/articles/Morality.html (paper at Economic History Society Conference April 2001).

Britnell, R.H., and M.S. Campbell (eds), *A Commercialising Economy: England 1086–c.1300* (Manchester, 1995).

Britnell, R.H., and J. Hatcher, *Progress and Problems in Medieval England: Essays in honour of Edward Miller* (Cambridge, 1996).

Brown, A.L., *The Governance of Late Medieval England 1272–1461* (London, 1989).

Brundage, J.A., *Medieval Canon Law* (London, 1995).

Buck, M., *Politics, Finance and the Church in the Reign of Edward II: Walter Stapeldon, Treasurer of England* (Cambridge, 1983).

Burns, J.H. (ed.), *The Cambridge History of Medieval Political Thought c.350–c.1450* (Cambridge, 1988).

Bush, J.A., and A. Wijffels (eds), *Learning the Law: Teaching and the Transmission of English Law, 1150–1900* (London, 1999).

Cam, H.M., 'Studies in the Hundred Rolls: some aspects of thirteenth century administration' in P. Vinogradoff (ed.), *Oxford Studies in Legal History*, vol. VI (Oxford, 1921), 5–198.

Cam, H.M., 'On the material available in the eyre rolls', *BIHR* 3 (1925–6), 152–9.

Cam, H.M., *The Hundred and the Hundred Rolls: an outline of Local Government in Medieval England* (London, 1930).

Cam, H., *Liberties and Communities in Medieval England* (London, 1963).

Campbell, B.S. (ed.), *Before the Black Death: Studies in the 'Crisis' of the Early Fourteenth Century* (Manchester, 1991).

Cheney, C.R., *The English Church and its Laws, Twelfth to Fourteenth Centuries* (London, 1982).

Chrimes, S.B., *An Introduction to the Administrative History of Medieval England* (Oxford, 1965).

Clanchy, M.T., *From Memory to Written Record*, 2nd edn (Oxford, 1993).

Clark, E., 'Medieval labour law in English local courts', *American Journal of Legal History* 27 (1983), 330–3.

Coke, Sir E., *Institutes of the Lawes of England*, 4 vols, 4th edn (London, 1644).

Coleman, D.C., *What has Happened to Economic History?* (Cambridge, 1972).

Coleman, D.C., and A.H. John (eds), *Trade, Government and Economy in Pre-Industrial Europe* (London, 1978).

Coss, P. (ed.), *The Moral World of the Law* (Cambridge, 2000).

Coulton, G.G., *Social Life in Britain from the Conquest to the Reformation* (Cambridge, 1918).

Cripps, J., R. Hilton and J. Williamson, 'A survey of medieval manorial court rolls in England' in Z. Razi and M. Smith (eds), *Medieval Society and the Manor Court* (Oxford, 1996), 569–637.

Crook, D., *Records of the General Eyre* (London, 1982).

Cunningham, W., 'The commercial policy of Edward III', *TRHS*, new ser., 4 (1889), 197–220.

Davis, H.W.C. (ed.), *Medieval England* (Oxford, 1924).

Davis, J., 'The Representation, Regulation and Behaviour of Petty Traders in Late Medieval England' (Ph.D. thesis, Cambridge, 2001).

d'Avray, D.L., *The Preaching of the Friars* (Oxford, 1985).

Day, J., *The Medieval Market Economy* (Oxford, 1987).

de Roover, R., *Money, Banking and Credit in Medieval Bruges* (Cambridge, MA, 1948).

de Roover, R., 'The concept of the just price: theory and economic policy', *Journal of Economic History* 18 (1958), 418–38.

de Roover, R. (ed.), *Business, Banking and Economic Thought in Late Medieval and Early Modern Europe* (Chicago, 1974).

de Zulueta, F., and P. Stein, *The Teaching of Roman Law in England*, Selden Society Supplementary Series 8 (London, 1990).

Dietz, F.C., *An Economic History of England* (New York, 1942).

Dodd, G., 'The hidden presence: parliament and the private petition in the fourteenth century' in A. Musson (ed.), *Expectations of Law in the Middle Ages* (Woodbridge, 2001), 135–49.

Doe, N., *Fundamental Authority in Late Medieval England* (Cambridge, 1990).

Du Boulay, F.R.H., *An Age of Ambition: England in the Late Middle Ages* (London, 1970).

Du Boulay, F.R.H., and C.M. Barron (eds), *The Reign of Richard II* (London, 1971).

Dubnov, S., *History of the Jews, vol. III: From the Later Middle Ages to the Renaissance*, 4th edn (South Brunswick, 1969).

Dyer, C., *Standards of Living in the Later Middle Ages* (Cambridge, 1989).

Dyer, C., *Everyday Life in Medieval England* (London, 1994).

Epstein, S.A., 'The theory and practice of the just wage', *Journal of Medieval History* 17 (1991), 53–70.

Epstein, S.A., *Wage Labour and Guilds in Medieval Europe* (Chapel Hill and London, 1991).

Evans, G.R., *Law and Theology in the Middle Ages* (London and New York 2002).

Farmer, D.L., 'Prices and wages' in H.E. Hallam (ed.), *The Agrarian History of England and Wales, vol. II: 1042–1350* (Cambridge, 1988), 716–827.

Farmer, D.L., 'Prices and wages 1350–1500' in E. Miller (ed.), *The Agrarian History of England and Wales, vol. III: 1348–1500* (Cambridge, 1991), 431–525.

Farmer, D.L., 'Marketing the produce of the countryside' in E. Miller (ed.), *The Agrarian History of England and Wales, vol. III: 1348–1500* (Cambridge, 1991), 324–430.

Frame, R., *The Political Development of the British Isles 1100–1400* (Oxford, 1995).

Fryde, N.M., 'Edward III's removal of his ministers and judges 1340–1', *BIHR* 48 (1975), 149–61.

Galenson, D.W. (ed.), *Markets in History: Economic Studies of the Past* (Cambridge, 1989).

Garnett, G. (ed.), *Law and Jurisdiction in the Middle Ages* (London, 1988).

Gilchrist, J., *The Church and Economic Activity in the Middle Ages* (London, 1969).

Given-Wilson, C., 'Purveyance for the royal household 1362–1413', *Historical Research* 56 (1983), 145–63.

Given-Wilson, C., 'Wealth and credit, public and private: the Earls of Arundel 1306–97', *EHR* 106 (1991), 1–26.

Given-Wilson, C., 'The problem of labour in the context of English government c.1350–1450' in J. Bothwell, PJP Goldberg and W.M. Ormrod (eds), *The Problem of Labour in Fourteenth Century England* (York, 2000), 85–101.

Glaeser, E.L., and J. Scheinkman, 'Neither a borrower nor a lender be: an economic analysis of interest restrictions and usury laws', *Journal of Law and Economics* 61 (1998), 1–36.

Gordley, J., *The Philosophical Origins of Modern Contract Doctrine* (Oxford, 1991).

Graham, H., 'A woman's work . . . : labour and gender in the late medieval countryside' in PJP Goldberg (ed.), *Women in Medieval English Society* (Stroud, 1997), 126–48.

Graves, E.B., 'Circumspecte Agatis', *EHR* 43 (1928), 1–20.

Gross, C., *The Gild Merchant*, 2 vols (Oxford, 1890).

Gross, J., *Shylock: A Legend and its Legacy* (New York, 1992).

Hanawalt, B.A., *Crime and Conflict in English Communities, 1300–1348* (Harvard, 1979).

Harding, A., *Law Courts in Medieval England* (London, 1973).

Harding, A., *England in the Thirteenth Century* (Cambridge, 1993).

Harriss, G.L., 'Cardinal Beaufort: patriot or usurer?' *TRHS* 5th ser., 20 (1970), 129–48.

Harriss, G.L., *King, Parliament and Public Finance in Medieval England to 1369* (Oxford, 1975).

Harriss, G.L., 'Political society and the growth of government in late medieval England', *Past and Present* 138 (1993), 46–56.

Haverkamp, A., and H. Vollrath (eds), *England and Germany in the High Middle Ages* (Oxford, 1996).

Hay, D., *Europe in the Fourteenth and Fifteenth Centuries*, 2nd edn (Harlow, 1989).

Hearnshaw, F.J.C., *Leet Jurisdiction in England* (Southampton, 1908).

Heath, P., *Church and Realm 1272–1461: Conflict and Collaboration in an Age of Crises* (London, 1988).

Helmholz, R.H., 'Usury and the medieval English church courts', *Speculum* 61 (1986), 364–80.

Helmholz, R.H., *Canon Law and the Law of England* (London, 1987).

Henneman, J.B., 'Enquêteurs-réformateurs and fiscal officers in fourteenth century France', *Traditio* 24 (1968), 309–49.

Hettinger, M.J., 'Defining the servant: legal and extra-legal terms of employment in fifteenth century England' in A.J. Frantzen and D. Moffat (eds), *The Work of Work: Servitude, Slavery and Labor in Medieval England* (Glasgow, 1994), 206–28.

Hilton, R.H., *The English Peasantry in the Later Middle Ages* (Oxford, 1975).

Hilton, R.H., *Bond Men Made Free: medieval peasant movements and the English rising of 1381* (London, 1977).

Hilton, R.H., 'Lords, burgesses and hucksters', *Past and Present* 97 (1982), 3–15.

Holdsworth, W.S., *History of English Law*, 16 vols (London, 1922–66).

Horrox, R., 'Local and national politics in fifteenth century England', *Journal of Medieval History* 18 (1992), 391–403.

Hoyt, R.S., 'The coronation oath of 1308', *Traditio* 11 (1955), 235–57.

Hudson, J., *The Formation of the English Common Law: Law and Society in England from the Norman Conquest to Magna Carta* (Harlow, 1996).

Huizinga, J., trans. F. Hopman, *The Waning of the Middle Ages* (London, 1924; reprinted 2001).

Hunt, E.S., and J.M. Murray, *A History of Business in Medieval Europe 1200–1550* (Cambridge, 1999).

Hyams, P., 'The origins of a peasant land market in England', *EcHR* 23 (1970), 18–31.

Hyams, P.R., 'The charter as a source for the early common law', *Journal of Legal History* 12 (1991), 173–89.

Ibbetson, D.J., 'Words and deeds: the action of covenant in the reign of Edward I', *Law and History Review* 4 (1986), 71–94.

Ibbetson, D.J., *A Historical Introduction to the Law of Obligations* (Oxford, 1999).

Jolliffe, J.E.A., *Angevin Kingship* (London, 1955).

Jones, W.R., 'Bishops, politics and the two laws: the gravamina of the English clergy 1237–1399', *Speculum* 41 (1966), 209–45.

Jordan, W.C., *The Great Famine* (Princeton, 1996).

Kaeuper, R.W., *War, Justice and Public Order: England and France in the Later Middle Ages* (Oxford, 1988).

Kaye, J., *Economy and Nature in the Fourteenth Century: Money, Market Exchange and the Emergence of Scientific Thought* (Cambridge, 1998).

Keen, M.H., *England in the Later Middle Ages: A Political History* (London, 1973).

Keen, M., *English Society in the Later Middle Ages 1348–1500* (St Ives, 1990).

Keene, D., *Survey of Medieval Winchester*, 2 vols (Oxford, 1985).

Keene, D., 'Shops and shopping in medieval London' in L. Grant (ed.), *Medieval Art Architecture and Archaeology in London* (London, 1990), 29–46.

Kennedy, D., 'Form and substance in private law adjudications', *Harvard Law Review* 89 (1976), 1685–778.

Ker, N.R., *Medieval Manuscripts in British Libraries, vol. I: London* (Oxford, 1969), 27–34.

Kern, F. (trans. and ed. S.B. Chrimes), *Kingship and Law in the Middle Ages* (Oxford, 1939).

Kershaw, I., 'The Great Famine and agrarian crisis in England 1315–22' in R.H. Hilton (ed.), *Peasants, Knights and Heretics* (Cambridge, 1976), 85–132.

Keynes, J.M., 'Saving and usury', *Economic Journal* 42 (1932), 415–23.

Knappen, M.M., *Constitutional and Legal History of England* (Hamden, Connecticut, 1960).

Kowaleski, M., *Local Markets and Regional Trade in Medieval Exeter* (Cambridge, 1995).

Langholm, O., *The Aristotelian Analysis of Usury* (Bergen, 1984).

Langholm, O., *Economics in the Medieval Schools: Wealth, Exchange, Value, Money and Usury according to the Paris Theological Tradition 1200–1350* (Leiden, 1992).

Lapsley, G., 'Archbishop Stratford and the Parliamentary Crisis of 1341', *EHR* 36 (1915), 6–18.

Lapsley, G.T. (ed. H.M. Cam and G. Barraclough), *Crown, Community and Parliament in the Later Middle Ages* (Oxford, 1951).

Lander, J.R., *The Limitations of English Monarchy in the Later Middle Ages* (Toronto, 1989).

Le Bras, G., 'Conceptions of economy and society' in M.M. Postan, E.E. Rich and E. Miller (eds), *Cambridge Economic History of Europe*, vol. III (Cambridge, 1965), 554–75.

Le Goff, J., trans. A. Goldhammer, *Time, Work and Culture in the Middle Ages* (Chicago, 1980).

Le Goff, J., trans. P. Ranum, *Your Money or Your Life: Economy and Religion in the Middle Ages* (New York, 1988).

Le Goff, J. (ed.), *L'Homme médiéval* (Paris, 1989).

Le Goff, J., 'Le roi dans l'occident médiéval: caractères originaux' in A.J. Duggan (ed.), *Kings and Kingship in Medieval Europe*, King's College London Centre for Late Antique and Medieval Studies (London, 1993).

Lee, R.W., *The Elements of Roman Law*, 4th edn (London, 1956).

Leonard, G.H., 'The expulsion of the Jews by Edward I: an essay in explanation of the exodus, A.D. 1290', *TRHS*, new ser., 5 (1891), 103–22.

Lindley, P.G., 'The tomb of Bishop William de Luda: an architectural model at Ely Cathedral', *Proceedings of the Cambridge Antiquarian Society* 70 (Cambridge, 1984), 227–32.

Lipson, E., *Economic History of England*, vol. I, 9th edn (London, 1947).

Little, L.K., 'Pride goes before avarice: social change and the vices in Latin Christendom', *American Historical Review*, 76 (1971), 16–49.

Lloyd, T.H., *Alien Merchants in the High Middle Ages* (Brighton, 1982).

Loewe, H., 'On usury' in H. Loewe (ed.), *Starrs and Charters Preserved in the British Museum, vol. II* (London, 1932), xcv–cviii.

Logan, F.D., *Excommunication and the Secular Arm in Medieval England* (Toronto, 1968).

Maddicott, J.R., 'The English peasantry and the demands of the crown 1294–1341', *Past and Present* supplement I (Oxford, 1975).

Maddicott, J.R., 'Poems of social protest in early fourteenth century England' in W.M. Ormrod (ed.), *England in the Fourteenth Century: Proceedings of the Harlaxton Symposium* (Woodbridge, 1986), 130–44.

Maddicott, J.R., 'Edward I and the lessons of baronial reform: local government 1258–80' in P.R. Coss and S.A. Lloyd (eds), *Thirteenth Century England I: Proceedings of the Newcastle upon Tyne Conference* (Woodbridge, 1986), 1–30.

Madox, T., *History and Antiquities of the Exchequer* (London, 1769).

Mahoney, M.S., 'Mathematics' in D.C. Lindberg (ed.), *Science in the Middle Ages* (Chicago, 1978), 145–67.

Maine, H., *Ancient Law* (first published 1861; reprinted London, 1954).

Maitland, F.W., *The Forms of Action at Common Law* (Cambridge, 1909).

Maitland, F.W., *The Constitutional History of England* (Cambridge, 1961).

May, A.N., 'An index of thirteenth century peasant impoverishment? Manor court fines', *EcHR*, 2nd ser., 26 (1973), 389–402.

McGovern, J.F., 'The rise of new economic attitudes during the later middle ages and renaissance', *Traditio* 26 (1970), 217–54.

McIntosh, M.K., *Controlling Misbehaviour in England 1370–1600* (Cambridge, 1998).

McKisack, M., *The Fourteenth Century* (Oxford, 1959).

McLaughlin, T.P., 'The teaching of the canonists on usury (XII, XIII and XIV centuries)', *Medieval Studies* 1 (1939), 82–107, and *Medieval Studies* 2 (1940), 1–22.

McNall, C., 'The Recognition and Enforcement of Debts under the Statutes of Acton Burnel (1283) and Merchants (1285) 1283–1307' (D. Phil. thesis, Oxford, 2000).

McNall, C., 'The business of statutory debt registries 1283–1307' in P.R. Schofield and N.J. Mayhew (eds), *Credit and Debt in Medieval England c.1180–c.1350* (Oxford, 2002), 68–88.

McNeill, J.T., and H.M. Garner, *Medieval Handbooks of Penance* (New York, 1938, 1990).

Meekings, C.A.F., 'King's Bench files' in J.H. Baker (ed.), *Legal Records and the Historian* (London, 1978), 97–139.

Menache, S., 'The king, the church and the Jews: some considerations on the expulsions from England and France', *Journal of Medieval History* 13 (1987), 223–36.

Miller, E., 'The economic policies of governments: France and England' in M.M. Postan, E.E. Rich and E. Miller (eds), *Cambridge Economic History of Europe*, vol. III (Cambridge, 1965), 281–339.

Miller, E., and J. Hatcher, *Medieval England: Rural Society and Economic Change 1086–1348* (5th impression, London, 1992).

Miller, E., and J. Hatcher, *Medieval England: Towns, Commerce and Crafts 1086–1348* (London, 1995).

Millon, D., 'Common Law and Canon Law during the Reign of Edward I' (Ph.D. thesis, Cornell, 1982).

Milsom, S.F.C., 'Sale of goods in the fifteenth century', *Law Quarterly Review* 77 (1961), 257–84.

Milsom, S.F.C., *The Legal Framework of English Feudalism* (Cambridge, 1976).

Milsom, S.F.C., *Historical Foundations of the Common Law*, 2nd edn (Toronto, 1981).

Mollat, M., trans. A. Goldhammer, *The Poor in the Middle Ages: An Essay in Social History* (Yale, 1986).

Mundill, R.R., *England's Jewish Solution: Experiment and Expulsion, 1262–1290* (Cambridge, 1998).

Munro, J.H., 'Wage-stickiness, monetary changes and real incomes in late medieval England and the Low Countries 1300–1450: Did money really matter?' *Research in Economic History* (forthcoming).

Musson, A., *Public Order and Law Enforcement: The Local Administration of Criminal Justice, 1294–1350* (Woodbridge, 1996).

Musson, A., 'New labour laws, new remedies? Legal reaction to the Black Death "crisis" ' in N. Saul, *Fourteenth Century England I* (Woodbridge, 2000), 73–88.

Musson, A., *Medieval Law in Context: The Growth of Legal Consciousness from Magna Carta to the Peasants' Revolt* (Manchester, 2001).

Musson, A. (ed.), *Expectations of Law in the Middle Ages* (Woodbridge, 2001).

Musson, A., and W.M. Ormrod, *The Evolution of English Justice: Law, Politics and Society in the Fourteenth Century* (Basingstoke, 1999).

Neale, W.C., 'The market in theory and history' in K. Polanyi, C.M. Arensberg and H.W. Pearson, *Trade and Markets in the Early Empires: Economics in History and Theory* (Glencoe, 1957), 357–72.

Nelson, B., *The Idea of Usury: From Tribal Brotherhood to Universal Otherhood* (Chicago, 1969).

Nicholas, F., 'The assize of bread in London during the sixteenth century', *Economic History* 2 (1932), 323–47.

Nightingale, P., *A Medieval Mercantile Community: The Grocers' Company and the Politics and Trade of London 1000–1485* (Yale, 1995).

Noonan, J.T., *The Scholastic Analysis of Usury* (Cambridge, MA, 1957).

O'Brien, B.R., *God's Peace and King's Peace: The Laws of Edward the Confessor* (Philadelphia, 1999).

Ogus, A.I., 'Regulatory law: some lessons from the past', *Legal Studies* 12 (1992), 1–19.

Olivier-Martin, Fr., *Histoire de droit français*, 2nd edn (Paris, 1995).

Ormrod, W.M. (ed.), *England in the Fourteenth Century* (Woodbridge, 1986).

Ormrod, W.M., *The Reign of Edward III: Crown and Political Society in England 1327–77* (Yale, 1990).

Ormrod, W.M., 'Agenda for legislation 1322–c.1340', *EHR* 105 (1990), 1–33.

Ormrod, W.M., 'The crown and the English economy 1290–1348' in B.S. Campbell (ed.) *Before the Black Death: Studies in the 'Crisis' of the Early Fourteenth Century* (Manchester, 1991), 149–72.

Ormrod, W.M., *Political Life in Medieval England 1300–1450* (Basingstoke, 1995).

Owst, G.R., *Literature and Pulpit in Medieval England* (Oxford, 1961).

Packe, M., *King Edward III* (London, 1983–5).

Palliser, D.M., 'Towns and the English State 1066–1500' in J.R. Maddicott and D.M. Palliser (eds), *The Medieval State: Essays presented to James Campbell* (London, 2000), 127–146.

Palmer, R.C., *The County Courts of Medieval England* (Princeton, 1982).

Palmer, R.C., 'Covenant, *justicies* writs and reasonable showings', *American Journal of Legal History* 31 (1987), 97–117.

Palmer, R.C., *English Law in the Age of the Black Death 1348–1381: A Transformation of Governance and Law* (Chapel Hill, NC, 1993).

Pantin, W.A., *The English Church in the Fourteenth Century* (Notre Dame, 1962).

Parsons, J. Carmi, *Eleanor of Castille: Queen and Society in Thirteenth Century England* (Basingstoke, 1995).

Penn, S.A.C., and C. Dyer, 'Wages and earnings in late medieval England: evidence from the enforcement of the labour laws', *EcHR*, 2nd ser., 43 (1990), 356–76.

Pirenne, H., trans. E. Clegg, *Economic and Social History of Medieval Europe* (6th impression, London, 1958).

Plucknett, T.F.T., *Statutes and their Interpretation in the First Half of the Fourteenth Century* (Cambridge, 1922).

Plucknett, T.F.T., *The Legislation of Edward I* (Oxford, 1949).

Plucknett, T.F.T., *A Concise History of the Common Law*, 5th edn (London, 1956).

Plucknett, T.F.T., *Early English Legal Literature* (Cambridge, 1958).

Pollock, F., and F.W. Maitland, *The History of English Law before the Time of Edward I*, rev. 2nd edn (Cambridge, 1968).

Poos, L.R., 'The social context of Statute of Labourers enforcement', *Law and History Review* 1 (1983), 27–53.

Post, G., *Studies in Medieval Legal Thought* (Princeton, 1964).

Post, J.B, 'Manorial Amercements and Peasant Poverty', *EcHR* 28 (1975), 304–11.

Postan, M.M., E. Rich and E. Miller (eds), *Cambridge Economic History of Europe*, vol. III, *Economic Organisation and Policies in the Middle Ages* (Cambridge, 1963).

Postan, M.M., *The Medieval Economy and Society* (London, 1972).

Pounds, N.J.G., *An Economic History of Medieval Europe* (London, 1974).

Powell, E., 'Social research and the use of medieval criminal records', *Michigan Law Review* 79 (1981), 967–78.

Powell, E., *Kingship, Law and Society: Criminal Justice in the Reign of Henry V* (Oxford, 1989).

Powicke, M., *The Thirteenth Century 1216–1307* (Oxford, 1962).

Powicke, F.M., and C.R. Cheney, *Councils and Synods and Other Documents Relating to the English Church*, 2 vols (Oxford, 1964).

Prestwich, M., *The Three Edwards: War and State in England 1272–1377* (London, 1980).

Prestwich, M. *Edward I* (London, 1988).

Prestwich, M., *English Politics in the Thirteenth Century* (Basingstoke, 1990).

Pugh, R.B., *Imprisonment in Medieval England* (Cambridge, 1970).

Purvis, J.H., *A Medieval Act Book with Some Account of Ecclesiastical Jurisdiction at York* (York, 1943).

Putnam, B.H., *The Enforcement of the Statute of Labourers during the First Decade after the Black Death* (New York, 1908).

Putnam, B.H., 'Maximum wage laws for priests after the Black Death', *American Historical Review* 21 (1915–16), 12–32.

Putnam, B.H., 'Chief Justice Shareshull and the economic and legal codes of 1351–1352', *University of Toronto Law Journal* [1943–4], 251–81.

Razi, Z. and R. Smith, *Medieval Society and the Manor Court* (Oxford, 1996).

Reid, K., and R. Zimmermann (eds), *A History of Private Law in Scotland*, 2 vols (Oxford, 2000).

Reynolds, S., *Kingdoms and Communities in Western Europe 900–1300*, 2nd edn (Oxford, 1997).

Richards, J., *Sex, Dissidence and Damnation: Minority Groups in the Middle Ages* (London, 1991).

Richardson, H.G., 'Richard Fitzneal and the *Dialogus de Scaccario*', *EHR* 43 (1928), 161–71.

Richardson, H.G., 'The English coronation oath', *Speculum* 24 (1949), 44–75.

Richardson, H.G., *The English Jewry under Angevin Kings* (London, 1960).

Richardson, H.G., and G.O. Sayles, *The Governance of Medieval England from the Conquest to Magna Carta* (Edinburgh, 1963).

Richardson, H.G., and G.O. Sayles, *Law and Legislation from Aethelberht to Magna Carta* (Edinburgh, 1966).

Riesenberg, P., 'Roman law, renunciations and business in the twelfth and thirteenth centuries' in J.H. Mundy, R.W. Emery and B.N. Nelson (eds), *Essays in Medieval Life and Thought presented in honor of Austin Patterson Evans* (New York, 1955).

Rigby, S.H., *English Society in the Later Middle Ages: Class, Status and Gender* (Basingstoke, 1995).

Ross, A., 'The assize of bread', *EcHR*, 2nd ser., 9 (1956–7), 332–42.

Roth, C., 'The European age in Jewish history (to 1648)' in L. Finkelstein (ed.), *The Jews: Their History, Culture and Religion, vol. I* (Philadelphia, 1949), 216–42.

Rubin, M., *Charity and Community in Medieval Cambridge* (Cambridge, 1987).

Russell, E., 'The societies of the Bardi and the Peruzzi and their dealings with Edward III 1327–1345' in G. Unwin (ed.), *Finance and Trade under Edward III* (Manchester, 1918), 93–135.

Sainty, J., *The Judges of England 1272–1990*, Selden Society Supplementary Series 10 (London, 1993).

Salzman, L.F., *English Trade in the Middle Ages* (London, 1964).

Sargeant, F., 'The wine trade with Gascony' in G. Unwin (ed.), *Finance and Trade under Edward III* (Manchester, 1918), 257–311.

Saul, N. (ed.), *The Oxford Illustrated History of Medieval England* (Oxford, 1997).

Saul, N., *Richard II* (New Haven, 1997).

Sawyer, P.H., 'Kings and merchants' in P.H. Sawyer and I.N. Wood (eds), *Early Medieval Kingship* (Leeds, 1977), 54–71.

Schofield, P.R., and N.J. Mayhew (eds), *Credit and Debt in Medieval England c.1180–c.1350* (Oxford, 2002).

Seabourne, G., 'Controlling commercial morality: the London usury trials of 1421', *Journal of Legal History* 19 (1998), 116–42.

Seipp, D.J., 'Crime in the Year Books' in C. Stebbings (ed.), *Law Reporting in Britain* (London, 1995), 15–34.

Seipp, D.J., 'The Mirror of Justices' in Bush and Wijffels (eds), *Learning the Law*, 85–112.

Simpson, A.W.B., *History of the Common Law of Contract: The Rise of the Action of Assumpsit* (Oxford, 1975).

Simpson, A.W.B., *A History of the Land Law*, 2nd edn (Oxford, 1986).

Skyrme, T., *History of the Justices of the Peace* (Chichester, 1994).

Snooks, G.D., 'The dynamic role of the market in the Anglo-Norman economy and beyond, 1086–1300' in R.H. Britnell and M.S. Campbell (eds), *A Commercialising Economy: England 1086–c.1300* (Manchester, 1995), 27–54.

Spufford, P., *Money and its Use in Medieval Europe* (Cambridge, 1988).

Stacey, R.C., 'Parliamentary negotiations and the expulsion of the Jews from England' in M. Prestwich, R.H. Britnell and R. Frame (eds), *Thirteenth Century England VI: Proceedings of the Durham Conference 1995* (Woodbridge, 1997), 77–102.

Stoljar, S.J., *A History of Contract at Common Law* (Canberra, 1975).

Strohm, P., *England's Empty Throne: Usurpation and the Language of Legitimation 1399–1422* (New Haven, 1998).

Stubbs, W., *The Constitutional History of England in its Origin and Development*, 3 vols (Oxford, 1880).

Summerson, H.R.T., 'The structure of law enforcement in thirteenth century England', *American Journal of Legal History* 23 (1979), 313–27.

Summerson, H., *Medieval Carlisle*, 2 vols (Kendal, 1993).

Swanson, R.N., *Church and Society in Late Medieval England* (Oxford, 1989).

Sweeney, T.R., and S. Chodorow (eds), *Popes, Teachers and Canon Law in the Middle Ages* (Cornell, 1989).

Tawney, R.H., *Religion and the Rise of Capitalism* (London, 1926; reprinted 1972).

Thomson, J.A.F., *The Transformation of Medieval England 1370–1529* (London, 1983).

Thorold Rogers, J.E., *A History of Agriculture and Prices in England*, 7 vols (Oxford, 1866–1902).

Thrupp, S.L., *A Short History of the Worshipful Company of Bakers* (London, 1933).

Tout, T.F., *The Place of the Reign of Edward II in English History*, 2nd edn (Manchester, 1936).

Tuck, A., *Crown and Nobility 1272–1461* (London, 1985).

Ullmann, W., *The Medieval Idea of Law as Represented by Lucas de Penna: A Study in Fourteenth Century Legal Scholarship* (London, 1946).

Unwin, G. (ed.), *Finance and Trade under Edward III* (Manchester, 1918).

Walford, C., 'Early laws and customs in Great Britain regarding food', *TRHS*, new ser., 8 (1880), 70–88.

Walker, S., 'Richard II's views on kingship' in R.E. Archer and S. Walker (eds), *Rulers and Ruled in Late Medieval England: Essays presented to Gerald Harriss* (London, 1995), 49–64.

Warren, W.L., *The Governance of Norman and Angevin England 1086–1272* (London, 1987).

Waugh, S.L., *England in the Reign of Edward III* (Cambridge, 1992).

Wilkinson, B., *The Chancery under Edward III* (Manchester, 1929).

Wilkinson, B., *Constitutional History of Medieval England 1216–1399 with Select Documents*, 3 vols (London, 1948–1958).

Wilkinson, B., *Studies in the Constitutional History of the Thirteenth and Fourteenth Centuries* (Manchester, 1957).

Wilkinson, B., *The Later Middle Ages in England, 1216–1485* (London, 1969).

Williams, G.A., *Medieval London: From Commune to Capital* (London, 1963).

Wood, D., *Medieval Economic Thought* (Cambridge, 2002).

Wormald, P., *The Making of English Law: King Alfred to the Twelfth Century, vol. I: Legislation and its Limits* (Oxford, 1999).

Wright, T. (ed.), *The Political Songs of England* (London, 1839).

Zimmerman, R., *The Law of Obligations: Roman Foundations of the Civilian Tradition* (Cape Town, 1990).

Index